Capability Building for Organizational Transformation

Management Cases from Multiple Disciplines

Capability Building for Organizational Transformation

Management Cases from Multiple Disciplines

Editors

G.D. SARDANA
TOJO THATCHENKERY

BLOOMSBURY

LONDON • NEW DELHI • NEW YORK • SYDNEY

© BIMTECH, 2013

First published, 2013

BLOOMSBURY PUBLISHING INDIA PVT. LTD.
London New Delhi New York Sydney

ISBN: 978-93-82563-41-9

Published by Bloomsbury Publishing India Pvt. Ltd.
VISHRUT Building, DDA Complex, Building No. 3, Pocket C-6 & 7
Vasant Kunj, New Delhi 110 070

Typeset by FORTUNE GRAPHICS
WZ-911/2, Shankarlal Street, Ring Road, Naraina, New Delhi

Printed at ANVI COMPOSERS
1 DDA Market, Block A-1B, Pachim Vihar, New Delhi 110 063

Contents

Acknowledgements

The papers included in this volume represent selected manuscripts received from across the globe for presentation at the International Conference on Management Cases, ICMC 2012, organised by Birla Institute of Management Technology, Greater Noida, and the School of Public Policy, George Mason University, Arlington, VA, USA, at the BIMTECH Campus on November 29-30, 2012.

Every paper has undergone a double blind review. We are grateful to reviewers who took great pains to go through the manuscripts and provide critical comments in many cases to improve the papers. In some of the cases, the papers underwent revisions necessitating re-reviews by the same reviewer. It is a time consuming job, needs patience and a passion to carry out the responsibilities. We wish to acknowledge the very valuable help we received from our peers, former colleagues, research scholars, our past -students who came forward to extend their support. The reviewers include: Tojo Thatchenkery, Kenneth Wall, Harjit Singh, Nikunj Aggarwal, Alok Goel, Archana Shrivastav, Ruchi Tyagi, Raveesh Agarwal, Smriti Pande, Sriparna Basu, John Walsh, Abha Rishi, Mayur Dande, Pratigya Kwatra, Krishna Akalamkam, Ken Long, Bob Palk, Angela Parish, Wallace Edson, Jackie Bsharah, Kevin LeGrand, Keith Hosea, Julie Huffaker, Keli Yen, Kerry Mitchel, Bob Lucius, Aaron Finney, Andrea McCormick, Eric Matheny, Warren Vaughan and G.D. Sardana.

Prior to the blind review, all the papers were subjected for Originality report and Similarity index, using Turnitin Soft ware installed at Bimtech Library. We wish to thank Subhash Sharma, Priyanshi Rastogi and Naqi Murtaza all office bearers at the library for taking up the task often at short and urgent notice.

Proof reading and language corrections of such a large volume of papers in a such a short time of four weeks is literally a neck-breaking job. This became possible because of full understanding and support from our respective family members, who often shared the load of proof reading.

We also express our thanks to Mr. Suresh Gopal, Publisher-Special Projects and Ms. Jyoti Mehrotra, Development Editor, Bloomsbury Publishing India Pvt. Limited for their support, cooperation and attention to details for timely publication of this book.

G.D. Sardana
Tojo Thatchenkery

Introduction

GD Sardana and Tojo Thatchenkery

The title of this volume comprises of two concepts which describe in totality about the contents of the cases included: *Capability building*, and *Organizational transformation*. Seen in isolation to each other the concepts convey management process to bring excellence to the organization. Together they contain a lot many more about the outcome of running a business and these include creation of wealth, competencies, working for sustainability, survival in competition and dynamic economic environment , social concern and more. It is imperative to understand these two concepts to reach a rational of decision to have included the listed management cases.

We take up first 'capability building' and go to the roots of two prominent approaches on developing strategy. Management literature refers to these as the 'market-based approach' and the 'resource based approach'. Venugopal (1999) points out that resource-based approach occupies centre-stage in strategic management theory and practice. In essence this approach seeks to direct attention inward to understand the strengths and weaknesses of an organization as contrasted to the approach enunciated by Porter which laid stress on market-based view or 'positioning' of the organization, also popularly referred as the 'five forces' framework. The resource based approach is presumed to be first mentioned by Birger Wernerfelt (1984). It found a powerful support from Prahlad and Hammel (1990) in the approach referred to as 'core competencies'. In many respects Business Process Reengineering also carries affinities with this approach. Richard Lynch (2000) defines it as, 'the approach stresses the importance of the individual resources of the organization in delivering the competitive advantage of the organization This approach basically conceptualizes an organization as a store house of resources. The essence of the resource based approach is explained by Lynch (2000) in terms of 'its focus on the *individual* resources of the organization rather than the strategies that are common to all companies in an industry'. Lynch (2000) further stresses the importance of development of resource-based view with objectives to identify its elements that help to reach particular strengths. That leads us to understand next what constitute as resources.

Resource has been variously defined. Venugopal (1999) refers to some of these: Collis and Montgomerry (1998) define it as the stock of assets, skills and capabilities of a firm; Grant (1991) refers to it as factor inputs into the production process. Then there are diversity of views if the resource be as considered only as possessed or should the term also include such resources to which it has access. Venugopal (1999) offers a more broader definition as, 'those entities that actually belong to an organization-entities that are *"semi-permanently" tied to the firm, and also other potential entities that the firm is in a position to acquire'*. Hall (1992) classifies resources as 'assets' and 'skills'. Hill clarifies that while assets are related to 'having', skills are related to 'doing'. Venugopal (1999) goes on to explain further that assets are passive entities and are not capable of acting on their own; skills on the other hand are individual abilities of human beings, capable to perform an action; and skills can be employed to build assets. The assets can be classified as tangibles and intangibles. Tangibles have a physical existence. Intangible assets on the other hand are invisible, as financial assets, informational assets, organisational attributes.

With these fundamental notes, we can now take up understanding the concept of capability. Venugopal (1999) points out that resources do not exist as isolated entities but in close relationship with other resources. These are referred to exist as 'bundles', implying these exist in packs of 'many' bound together. Venugopal (1999) conceptualizes capability *as 'ability or capacity of a bundle of resources to perform an activity'*. Thus capability can be seen as a resultant function of resources which in turn comprises of tangible assets, intangible assets, and skills. The capabilities can be categorised for a relevant strategic analysis, understanding their strengths or weaknesses or for a planning exercise for enhancing their capacity to perform. Venugopal (1999) has proposed capabilities as functional capability, value chain capability, organising capability, strategic management capability, and networking capability.

Capability building refers to enhancing the ability or capacity of resources as present in each of the capabilities mentioned to perform an activity better with a view to get a better return in terms of performance criteria. This performance criteria in terms of resources is generally implied in terms of cost, quality, delivery, flexibility, customer service, new product development, innovation, organization development, continuous improvement and more. More of the customised performance criteria aligned with the vision of the organization are often developed.

This leads us to understand the second concept that appears in the title. 'Organizational transformation' is a much broader term and has many issues to be answered to understand the same. There is hardly a consensus on issues as the meaning of transformation, the goals of transformation, areas in an organization needing transformation, what is successful transformation, the time frame of a transformation, types of transformation and more. It is not a well developed science(or art). There is hardly any serious literature dedicated and devoted to this subject, even though it is a buzz word from any economist, behavioural scientist, corporate executive and policy makers from the state. There is always an appeal to each and everyone to work for transformation. The concept appears in literature devoted to studies on 'Strategy' where its gets a mention in a few randomly placed sections spread over the publication, implying that transformation has a strategic dimension.

The term occupies comparatively a larger space in publications covering Business Process Reengineering. We take recourse to such readings in understanding some of the issues raised.

Barbara Blumenthal and Philipe Haspeslagh (1998) refer to a universal truth, ' The first step is to recognize that the firm *is* or will become uncompetitive'. To become uncompetitive means loss of market share. This in turn gets reflected in stocks getting built-up pushing up the costs. The corrective steps are invariably to reduce production, pushing up further the costs of production and more uncompetitiveness. The organization is thus caught up in a vicious circle, leading to a slow death unless there are some corrective measures initiated. The uncompetitiveness is a result of several variables, some of them may not be related to each other. There are several reasons cited for the same. A dynamic state of economy throws up new players both from domestic ground or from outside the national boundaries. The new players can carry advantage of zeal, energy and a higher degree of commitment to carve up a share. Customer preferences change throwing away the old concepts, models and the products. Technology brings in new innovations, products, services with accompanying low cost, better quality, faster delivery, and customization. Then of course there is a common factor of remaining complacent to changes. This usually happens in large organizations where there are always many explanations available explaining the slow down of business. These explanations cover a large domain losing the focus in analysis. Often this is related to the lack of knowledge or refusing to take note of the long term impact of changes initiated by the competitor or the regulator. The larger organizations often wake up when it has become too late to recognize the impact of the change. It is only a rare few of the CEO's who sense the threat and take a plunge to what is called 'transformation' – a recovery process to become once again competitive.

Thus 'transformation' can be easily related to as the process to result in improvement aligned with the aims of the organization. Barbara Blumenthal and Philipe Haspeslagh (1998) expand this basic need to a broader concept: 'to qualify as a corporate transformation, a majority of individuals in an organization must change their 'behaviour'. Explained further, it implies that if an organization seeks to acquire or develop new capabilities, such as global quality, networking or a high customer satisfaction, its employees must be also be transformed in behaviour to think globally, make friends with customers, and be sensitive to the needs of the customers.

Barbara Blumenthal and Philipe Haspeslagh (1998) refer to three types of transformations. Improving Operations refers to change process to improve operations generally with a view to reduce costs, improve quality, better customer service, and reduce development time. The outcomes are achieved normally by creating teamwork, coordination across functional areas, or organizational boundaries, identification and resolving problems and learning new skills. These type of transformations are largely incremental, take longer time to achieve and initiatives can come from the employees at junior/middle levels

Strategic Transformation has aims to get a sustainable competitive advantage. The organization needs to initiate bold and major initiatives. The process involves redefining of business objectives in changed business environment, creation of new competencies, capabilities and skills, bringing in new technology. The steps of initiatives involve identification of core competencies, choice of strategic intent and creation of a framework of general direction for the middle and senior level managers to get commitment of execution. Strategic transformation calls for investment, and is more time consuming to execute and reach the results. There is no surety that the results of transformation will come through and hence is counted riskier.

Corporate self-renewal makes the organization capable to anticipate and cope with change so that there are no operational or strategic gaps developed. It is an 'always ready and vigilant' organization to sense the changes as an ongoing structured process. It calls for a creation of a learning organization, elimination of bureaucracy and fastness in decision making. The organization has a major need of gathering information on various fronts. The new management imperatives call for staying ahead of the competition. There would always be organizations that will sooner than expected copy a product or service. 'Corporate Self-renewal' organization will be ready to meet the challenge through an innovation, a new model of the product. The approach in such organizations is to create team of employees , eliminating unwieldy structures, and give them a free hand. Such type of employees need to be retained and this is a challenging job.

This volume includes cases which deal with capacity building in various functional areas involving various capacities and skills. The objectives are to aim at transforming the organization. Some of the papers have taken a route to demonstrate as to how the capabilities could be built up in presence of challenges. Other papers illustrate the process of transformation achieved through built up capabilities. The papers contained in this volume have left out papers covering 'Corporate Self-Renewal' transformation. These are covered in *'Reframing human capital for organizational excellence'* a sister volume of this conference, also published by the same publishers.

The selection of the cases has gone through a tough process of selection. After the initial editorial review to check that the case developed falls within the ambit of themes selected, all the cases so approved were subjected to check on plagiarism through a standard software. In some of the doubtful cases the authors were requested to clarify or carry out modifications. Otherwise, in general , clearance in plagiarism became the acid test to process the case further. The papers were blinded and sent for double blind review. The borderline cases were referred to the authors for revisions.

Only such of the cases were selected to be presented at the conference and eventually included in the volume when one of the authors agreed to be physical present to present his case. The conference does not accept virtual presentation or presentation in absentia as its USP.

The compilation of the cases in this volume showcases competitive strategies adopted and highlights the capabilities which have gone into building up the competencies. The cases cover experiences of both the private sector and the public sector. Both the manufacturing and services find place. The volume has both the research and the teaching cases. All the cases are based on actual situations and present live occurrences. In many cases the authors have used primary source of information. In all such cases care has been taken of ethical considerations. The authors have obtained permissions from the organizations case studied and these find expressions in acknowledgements appearing at the end of the papers. The research cases have taken two streams. A section of cases are dealt as projects to supplement proven concepts through re-evaluation or assessment of such domains as customer preferences, customer satisfaction, gap analysis, quality and service efficacy in new environment through use of such tools as SPSS, factor analysis , financial ratios, productivity ratios, etc. The other stream of research cases demonstrates the use of existing concepts in new applications. These cases use management science concepts (Lapin and Whisler, 1996).The reader is called upon to debate the application, question the desirability of innovation or take up the interpretation of the outcome.

This volume is structured in six Parts and comprises of 36 cases. The Parts are titled and organized to present cases on a common theme at one place. However, the borderlines between the functional management areas is fast getting blurred. There are overlaps. In other instances, the same concepts can be found to have application in various functional areas. It is therefore possible that some of our readers may not find positioning of a case in one particular Part as appropriate. In such instances we have been guided more by holistic impact of decision making process as presented in the case.

PART 1: FOCUS ON FINANCIAL MANAGEMENT

First Bank of Nigeria Plc (FBN), established in 1894, has over the decades maintained its position as the No. 1 bank in Nigeria. However in the last couple of years, a number of new-generation banks have posed a threat to FBN's jealously guarded position. Chapter 1 from Ifedapo Adeleye is designed to showcase the benefits of initiatives undertaken by First Bank of Nigeria and provide a platform for solutions to possible challenges or problems that could arise in implementing them. Research input was gathered through company reports, published articles, and interviews with company staff.

Anju Arora in Chapter 2 explores the art of implementing benchmark practices relating to Credit Risk Management (CRM) operations and systems at portfolio level in commercial banks. The study also offers an empirical analysis based on current practices. The study concludes that Credit portfolio risk management practices in Indian banking system has not yet reached benchmark level in terms of both the methodology and the implementation (in terms of tools & targets). The paper brings out that the various implementation challenges in designing and implementing credit portfolio risk operations and systems center on four issues: data availability, standardization of information, in-house staff training and system integration.

Rajeeva Sinha et al. in Chapter 3 discuss that effective financial literacy and education is a requirement for inclusive financial growth. In this paper, the authors use a framework from the service innovation literature to evaluate program effectiveness of Sanchayan, a non-governmental organization, in India. The analysis based on insights from the service innovation literature and the case method shows that Sanchayan's success in providing financial literacy and services to these population segments and create a new market for services draws largely from its ability to take the context and the needs of its clients into account and deliver the services to its clients.

Poverty in India remains to be one of the biggest policy concerns. Though the countrys' policy makers claim that the economy is growing around 9 percent and there is a consistent promise that it will continue to do so, the growth is not inclusive with the economic condition of the people in rural areas and city slums is worsening further. One of the typical reasons for poverty is being financially excluded. This research case in Chapter 4 by HMM Jha Bidyarthi et al. is based on a study of four sample villages drawn from two districts of Vidarbha region of India and a survey of 650 villagers regarding their financial needs, access to financial institutions, availability of needed finance connecting them to multinational bank through UID-enabled 24-hour door-step banking using business correspondence model.

Chapter 5 by Anna Heikkinen et al. presents a situation where a Finnish forest industry company, Metsä-Botnia Ltd., was caught in the cross fire of a heated debate between two countries, Uruguay and Argentina. Botnia decided to build a major pulp mill in the city of Fray Bentos by the Rio Uruguay River. The Argentine government and local people on the Argentinian side of the Rio Uruguay River voiced environmental concerns related to the pollution of the river and to the negative effect on revenues from tourism. The authors focus on the use of stakeholder dialogue in a situation where a multinational company's foreign green field investment raises both opposing and supporting views among the local interest groups.

PART II: INNOVATIONS AND TECHNOLOGY

Geographical Information Systems (GIS) has emerged as a very useful tool for analyzing public health data. Uma Kelekar and Xiang Liu in Chapter 6 review the use of visualization techniques and spatial analysis generated in GIS for decision support in the field of public health by some of the developing countries. It extends the study by examining the potential uses of GIS applications for public health decision-making, specifically disease surveillance in the Philippines. It particularly explores the spatial aspects of diarrhoea incidence among provinces in the Philippines – its spatial distribution and dependence with neighbouring provinces.

Crowdsourcing has been the core model behind many Internet success stories. Mini War Gaming uses this model for raising funds through many small donations from its eager supporters. The next case study in Chapter 7 by Daniel Roy explores and examines the successful use of a new and innovative approach for financing NPD projects by a Canadian small business. The authors analyse the necessary steps taken to formulate a successful crowd funding campaign and deliver a model which can be applied to other businesses wishing to raise capital from supporters of a small business in exchange for perks or rewards.

Enterprise Resource Planning is an enterprise solution software system that allows a company to automate and integrate the majority of its business processes, and share common data and practices across the enterprise through integration of various functions in the organization. The share of implementation of ERP software in corporate world is increasing day by day and to compete with them, government agencies and organizations are also on the path of implementing them. The usage of ERP system in public offices can definitely provide better results. This case developed by Resmi et al. in Chapter 8, as an application at Food Corporation of India makes a comparison of ERP software with bespoke software from a public policy perspective.

Marketing of software firm is a challenging task. This requires constant analysis of customer needs and technology up gradation. Surabhi Singh in the next paper in Chapter 9, identifies the marketing challenges small software firms face during the growth process. Marketing strategy is more important for software companies now than it has ever been. The strategy of a software firm determines the phases it will undergo. In such a competitive scenario where every software company is competing with each other, strong strategy enables them to have a competitive advantage over others. This case illustrates the determinants of successful marketing strategy for the software firm and how it impacts the future of the firm.

P&G has a long history of envisioning sustainability as a responsibility to do the right things for the environment and for human safety. Innovation is the fundamental driver to develop brands as leading brands in the global market. P&G strives to ensure that consumers need not make a choice between sustainability, performance, and value. At the same time, sustainability could be more than just responsibility, it could also be an opportunity to build the business. To understand how a company such as P&G can make products more environmentally sustainable, Raveesh Agarwal and Monica Thiel in Chapter 10, present a study on approach called Life Cycle Assessment (LCA) adopted by P&G to deliver sustainable innovations without tradeoffs in performance or value of the products.

PART III: FOCUS ON OPERATIONAL COMPETENCIES

In a dynamic economic environment an organization has not only to seek better performance against competition but has to be alert to changing needs of its stakeholders to sustain its' value in their eyes. That determines the logic of remaining in the business. The business and the logic behind it change accordingly. Hanna Lehtimäki et al. in Chapter 11, entitled co-creation of value in stakeholder relationships discuss these issues through a case study. The authors present a case study on a medium-sized company providing industrial services. Stakeholder relationships are studied in a process where the company transformed from a division of a large industrial corporation into an independent service company.

In Japan, automobiles with very small engines are called light cars, or 'K-cars', and they sell very well. Two major K-car companies are 'Daihatsu' and 'Suzuki'. These small cars were developed in Japan to meet local requirements of narrow roads. Over the decades, however, these have followed different routes and have found new homes for different reasons. In some of the new homes these occupy a place of pride both in terms of volume and customer acceptance. Iijima Masaki and Itoh in Chapter 12, aim to discuss the difference in foreign business development of these companies for their success and failure as part of the story of the company's history.

Networks of informal entrepreneurs or rag-pickers operate within large cities of the developing world. These rag-pickers collect, sort, process, and dispose of solid waste. Rag-pickers' networks and waste streams hold not only economic, but also environmental and social value. In this research case in Chapter 13, Sameer Prasad et al. use qualitative methodology and archival data to develop a model connecting supply chain linkages to the three value streams within this informal solid waste network. The authors find that the tight supply chain links between the rag-pickers and their upstream and downstream network agents yield superior economic, social, and environmental returns.

All India Warehousing Private Limited, has been in business for over 25 years. The company has provided a complete range of services related to warehousing, handling and storage services, to manufacturers, exporters, clearing agents, transporters and distributors. Saroj Koul and Ankush Guha in Chapter 14 trace the growth and the tribulations the company met on its journey to occupy its present status. This case study may prove useful to practicing managers and management students on understanding the working of a family run private warehouse, business environment in the warehousing sector, use of technology and organizational capability to manage multi-product, multi-location warehouses.

Controlled and well-monitored materials flow will allow robust and accurate understanding of the usage and waste of materials within a process, the cost to run the process, etc. Improper material flow can result in increase in overhead costs , increased waste, increased expenses, loss of potential profit, inaccuracies in monitoring and documenting materials flow . The case in Chapter 15 from Shettiger and Sudhamsavalli seeks to analyze the material flow in medium duty vehicle assembly line of Ashok Leyland located in Hosur. The purpose of the paper is to find the reason behind the accumulated stocks of parts and improper flow of materials and to provide suggestions to address these issues.

The cargo mix of major ports of India suggests that one to two types of cargo constitute the major share. Natural resources are depleting in nature and hence may not be viable for the port in long run. The case by Ashutosh Kar and Deepankar Sinha in Chapter 16 identifies the constraints in deciding on the cargo mix that a port would support and plausible course of action in this regard. Two ports, namely New Mangalore port and Haldia Dock Complex are studied to identify their cargo mix, the shift in such mix and future course of action to offset the loss arising out of stoppage of flow of cargo for which the port was originally designed to handle.

Collaboration between Subcontractors and RERI (University-affiliated Regional Economic Research Institutions) in the technological field has produced satisfactory synergistic results. On the other hand, successful collaboration on the strategic management level is still unprecedented. Long term business experience, as well as manufacturing high quality products, used to be very important elements for SMEs to establish sustainability. Hiro Mitsuyama in Chapter 17 presents a research case that aims how important it is for SMEs' managers to improve their theoretical management capabilities and verify what comprises successful collaboration on a strategic management level.

Standardization of quality in services is not an easy task, especially in a multi-service organization. If there are too many service variants, like in an eatery, the services can be highly customized. On the other side, some sort of standardization in quality of services needs to be provided to keep customers happy, leading to repeat buys and develop loyalty. This case attempts to study the working of an Indian restaurant in Lithuania. The restaurant suffers from substantial variability in service quality. Arvind Chaturvedi et al. in case in Chapter 18 analyze the process of providing service to the customer in detail. A project management approach (PERT) has been used for this analysis.

PART IV: MARKETING MANAGEMENT

Poonam Sharma et al. in Chapter 19 present a case study on Aakash Android-based tablet computer that opens up a world of new technology to millions of individuals in India and other emerging markets around the world. With a low price product, many at the bottom of the pyramid gain the potential to purchase a tablet. The tablet provides an outlet for young professionals to experience the excitement of interacting with a broader community. .A business model that delivers self-sustaining products, such as the Aakash tablet, establishes the first step towards economic sustainability. The objective of the this case is to outline ways in which organizations can develop strategic partnerships, expand strategy to consider a market that has largely been untouched.

International trade occupies a significant place in Indian economy. About one third of all goods and services which are produced are exchanged internationally. Anuj Sharma and Sudeep Mehrotra in Chapter 20 focus on international trade operations of HHEC North for its major client FABTECH a German apparel retail brand. The case traces the entire process of international trade operations beginning from receiving of export order to the final shipment. The case aims at finding the shortcomings of the entire operations and ways to overcome them.

The purpose of this research study from Gagan Katiyar and Shubhneet Kaur in Chapter 21 is to analyse the customer perception and indentify the key attributes affecting the brand image in ceramic industry. Boom in the construction industry has lead to high scale sales in ceramic industry. In this highly competitive environment, brand attributes need to be mapped so that competitors can identify important brand aspects and customize their offerings. Information is collected through one to one interaction with respondents and using a structured questionnaire. The study concludes that major factors influencing the brand image are Design, Durability, Availability, Quality, Price and Product Range.

In a competitive world, SMEs have started realizing that they are not just selling products or services but a mass of branded products, services and people to sustain in the business. Therefore movement is captivating in the SMEs to introduce competency through branding for obtaining and enhancing market share. Auto-component is a great feeder industry in the Automobiles sector that has put India on Global map. Mukund Deshpande and Neeta Boparikar in their case in Chapter 22 on branding reveals significant marketing policies helping Pune SMEs become competitive.

PART: V: CREATING EXCELLENCE THROUGH PERFORMANCE EVALUATION

The main purpose of this paper by Sardana and Dasanayaka in Chapter 23 is to identify and analyze factors that affect business to business relationships between telecommunication operators and vendors in Sri Lanka. This study is based on two models developed in telecommunication operator and vendor perspectives, and through in-depth questionnaire surveys. Analysis shows that relationship is determined by trust, commitment, adaptation, communication and satisfaction in the perspective of operators. Satisfaction of operators is determined by product quality, service support, delivery performance, supplier know how and value for money. In the perspective of vendors, relationship strength is determined by trust, commitment and satisfaction.

Pallavi and G.N.Patel in case as described in Chapter 24 evaluate the performance of the Rashtriya Swasthaya Bima Yojna (RSBY) in the districts of Uttar Pradesh(India). The methodology applied includes the Charnes, Cooper and Rhodes (CCR) model of DEA as well as the Tobit regression model to find the key determinants of the efficiency. The methodology has been applied to all the districts of Uttar Pradesh except one district, Hathras for which data was not available. The results show that only a few districts are relatively efficient and the policymakers need to work to make the scheme efficient.

The sugar industry occupies a prestigious place in the predominantly agricultural economy of India. As a vital contribution to the agricultural development it offers economic activity and livelihood to nearly 25 million small and marginal farmers. An assessment of the sugar mills and setting targets for the relatively inefficient mills to improve their efficiency and productivity is crucial, as the interests of various stakeholders are largely dependent on its performance. Harjit Singh et al. in this case in Chapter 25 discuss the vital role played by Saraswati Sugar Mills, Jagadhari(India) in the employment generation and upliftment of the socio-economic status of the community. The study goes on to identify areas of improvement and performance evaluation.

Smriti Pande and G.N.Patel in Chapter 26 evaluate the performance of 46 pharmacy retail stores and to analyze the impact of non-discretionary variables on the efficiency of the stores through dividing the Decision Making Units (DMUs) into different categories. Basic Charnes Cooper Rhodes (CCR) and non-discretionary variable models are used to evaluate the efficiency of each store. First, efficiency is evaluated considering only the discretionary variables using basic CCR model. Second, non-discretionary variable model is used with categorical DMUs taking both discretionary and non-discretionary variables into consideration. Lastly, to analyze the impact of non-discretionary variables on the efficiency scores ANOVA is applied.

Silver Bird Group Bhd, a listed company, fails to issue its 2011 financial reports on time. The aims of the research case as developed by Tengku Akbar Tengku Abdullah and described in Chapter 27 are to determine whether its board with a majority of independent directors is in a better position to supervise the management, to assess the effectiveness of its audit committee and to determine whether its financial problems could be foreseen. The data for the study is obtained from publicly available information. The data for corporate governance is analyzed using SPSS Version 20.

A competent system of governance helps to balance the rights of both managers and owners and induce the management to make investment in the projects and schemes which are beneficial for overall business. The variables such as Ownership Structure, Accountability, Directors' Remunerations, Risk Management, Internal

Audit, Dividend Policy and Sustainability, have been reported to affect Corporate Governance/Performance. The objective of the study by Dinesh Kumar Likhi as described in Chapter 28 is to understand effect of these variables in unlisted companies (Public Sector Undertakings). The issues are taken up and implications discussed in the context of a hypothetical case of owner of small medium sized company who is ignorant about the subject of corporate governance.

PART VI: CRAFTING STRATEGY FOR SUSTAINABILITY

This case developed by Abha Rishi et al. in Chapter 29 is about Emmsons International Limited- a fast growing company, dealing in physical trading of farm and energy commodities, in India. It throws up the eternal dilemma of the entrepreneur- whether to focus on core business or think alternative growth markets. The case also discusses the need to set up trading centers in geographical proximity to the top and bottom of the trading chain. The case has learning objectives to understand how commodity traders have to balance global pressures with local demands and regional needs, and secondly to understand the need to diversify when dealing in volatile emerging markets.

Since 2004, the one hundred and thirty winegrowers of the Saumur-Champigny appellation d'origine controlee have been committed to biodiversity. For the first time in France, winegrowers have chosen more ecological weed control methods and concentrated on creating and maintaining plant hedges within zones écologiques reservoirs (ecological conservation areas. The aim of this case study in Chapter 30 from Jean-Pierre Noblet et al. is to show how some wine producers, in the quest for quality, have 'looked outside the box' for new information , assimilated that information and applied it to their own operation and production for improved commercial results.

The Dawei Industrial Estate is one of the principal means by which the newly-opening Burmese [Myanmarese] economy will engage with the world. It is being constructed largely by Ital-Thai Development (ITD), a company which has been involved with various controversies in large-scale infrastructure projects. In the teaching case as presented in Chapter 31 John Walsh mentions that Dawei faces concerns over forcible evictions and environmental concerns: how does ITD deal with these issues? There are other important issues which the author raises in this teaching case. These issues include, as to how should ITD approach the future development of the Dawei SEZ and how should ITD manage its relationship with the Myanamar government?

Over the course of the 20th century, the automobile rapidly developed from an expensive toy for the rich into the de facto standard for passenger transport in most developed countries. This case study from Pradip Pathak and Rahul Dayal in Chapter 32 focuses on automobile industry and finds out various environmental challenges/

pressures faced by them as well as to establish their adopted measures to counter/ curb these issues with excellence. The methodology of data collection includes use of structured questionnaire, face to face interaction wherever feasible and other secondary data available in public domain.

The importance of women-led enterprises for any country's economic growth, and competitiveness is well established. According to a 2009 study, in India female-run enterprises in recent years have performed significantly better than other enterprises in terms of productivity and export percentages. However, gender gap in business initiatives in India is among the highest in the world. Although accepted as crucial, the role of public policy towards addressing these barriers is under- researched in the entrepreneurship literature. The aim of this study presented in Chapter 33 developed by Debasree Das Gupta is to highlight this gap using the cases of Indian states of Gujarat and Kerala.

Swiftlet farming is not something new in Malaysia and has been a contributor to its agriculture industry since the 1980s. This case developed by A.K.Siti-Nabiha et al. in Chapter 34 is about swiftlet farming in Georgetown, a city which was conferred a world heritage status by UNESCO in 2008. Swiftlet farming is a lucrative industry in Malaysia and is considered one of the key projects under the Malaysian Economic Transformation Program. Thus, the issue that needs to be addressed is on how to balance the lucrative economic return versus the negative social, health impact arising from swiftlet farming which also poses a threat the heritage status of the city.

Katja Karinataus and Hanna Lehtimäki in Chapter 35 focus on the relational dimension of social capital and examine social connections in four internationally operating companies. The study is an empirical research to understand the ways by which social capital fosters collaborative advantage. it highlights the importance of understanding the fabric of inter-organizational social relations that facilitates action in the chosen strategic direction. The authors bring out the implications.

The last case tracks the story of Mr. Anil Agarwal, Chairman, Vedanta Resources. His move to Bombay and his amazing entrepreneurial run thereafter to the position of the Chairman of Vedanta Resources Plc, the number two global diversified mining company has been captured in this case; emphasis being on his last act, that of growth through the acquisition of Cairn India Ltd. The case from Sahay as described in Chapter 36 is a teaching case where issues related to entrepreneurship like idea, ambition, risk, financing, technology, growth etc. have been dealt with. The main objective of this case is to make students learn what corporate entrepreneurship is and how a corporate entrepreneur acts.

We trust that the cases presented will simulate environment for sharpening of analytical skills. It is hoped the cases will generate interest to think differently, think creatively, think 'out of the box' to reach different more efficient solutions for organizational transformation. We also carry hope that the reading will motivate the readers to share their experiences through management cases in the next volume. The case conference is our passion and an annual event.

REFERENCES

Blumenthal Barbara and Haspeslagh Philippe (1998). Toward a definition of corporate transformation. In Organizational Transformation through Business Process Reengineering, Edit. Vikram Sethi and William R. King. Pearson Delhi.

Collins, D.J. and Montgommery, C.A. (1998). Corporate Strategy. Boston.MA. Irwin-McGraw Hill.

Hall, R. (1992). The strategic Analysis of Intangible Resources. Strategic Management Journal, 13, 135-144.

Lapin Lawrence L. and Whisler William D. (2006). Cases in Management Science, Thomson Publishing Company, London.

Lynch, Richard (2006). Corporate Strategy, Pearson Delhi.

Prahalad, C.K. and Hamel, G. (1990) The core Competence of the Corporation. Harvard Business Review, 3, 79-91.

Wernerfelt, B. (1984). A Resources-based View of the Firm. Strategic Management Journal, 1, 37-47.

Venugopal R. (1999). Contemporary Strategic Management, Vikas Publishing House Pvt. Ltd., New Delhi.

PART I: Focus on Financial Management

PART I, the opening section of this volume is devoted appropriately to financial issues. Finance is considered as the prime resource for both setting up and operating a project. Its availability, the cost of availability, time of availability are of significance to an enterprise. The developing countries cry out for foreign investments even at the cost of sacrifice of social parameters as the capital availability is considered a key to future development and growth. This consideration of growth and development at the cost of non-inclusive growth, increase of unemployment and increase of poverty has foundations in coining of new concepts as conscious capitalism, or social capital. At grass roots level an enterprise looks for access to capital faster, as much demanded and at lower costs. Many an SME has gone into oblivision and faced a natural death as the same could not match its needs of financial requirements from the goods or services sold on credit.In another dimension the industry makes a forceful plea to the regulators to cut down the interest and encourage the consumer to go for loans from the banks/financial institutions to make purchases from a large number of choices as houses, automobiles, consumer durables, education etc. And this brings into focus the viability of the banks advancing loans . How do they secure funds for lending as advances? Of five cases selected for this conference three of them concern banking operations showcasing initiatives taken to improve their viability. Yet another also concerns banking operation, but this is an initiative to educate the investor. The last of the cases details a case of investment across two nations creating a plethora of conflicts concerning social issues.

Ifedapo Adeleye, in Chapter 1 provides a comprehensive history of First Bank of Nigeria and the problems it has faced in its journey to reach the present status.

The bank has over the decades maintained its position as the No. 1 bank in Nigeria. However in the last couple of years, a number of new-generation banks have posed a threat to FBN's jealously guarded position. The author showcases the initiatives undertaken by the bank.

In Chapter 2, Anju Arora explores the art of implementing benchmark practices relating to Credit Risk Management (CRM) operations and systems at portfolio level in commercial banks. The study also offers an empirical analysis based on current practices . The study concludes that Credit portfolio risk management practices in Indian banking system has not yet reached benchmark level in both: the methodology and the implementation, in terms of tools & targets.

Rajeeva Sinha et al in Chapter 3 paper discuss that effective financial literacy and education is a requirement for inclusive financial growth. The authors use a framework to evaluate program effectiveness of Sanchayan, a non-governmental organization, in India. The case shows that Sanchayan's success in providing financial literacy to the population segments draws largely from its ability to take the context and the needs of its clients into account.

Poverty in India remains to be one of the biggest policy concerns. The growth of economy at 9 percent is not inclusive with the economic condition of the people in rural areas and city slums worsening further. The research case by H.M. Jha Bidyarthi et al. as presented in Chapter 4 is based on a study of four sample villages drawn from two districts of Vidarbha region of India and a survey of 650 villagers regarding their financial needs, access to financial institutions, and availability of needed finance.

Chapter 5 presents a situation where a Finnish forest industry company, Metsä-Botnia Ltd , was caught in the cross fire of a heated debate between two countries, Uruguay and Argentina. Botnia decided to build a major pulp mill in the city of Fray Bentos. The Argentine government and local people on the Argentinian side voiced environmental concerns and to the negative effect on revenues from tourism. Anna Heininen et al. focus on the use of a stakeholder dialogue to avoid conflict.

Corporate Transformation and Restructuring at First Bank of Nigeria: From Geography to Markets

*Ifedapo Adeleye**

ABSTRACT

First Bank of Nigeria Plc (FBN), established in 1894, has over the decades maintained its position as the No. 1 bank in Nigeria. However in the last couple of years, due to modern aggressive marketing strategies and more sophisticated product offerings, a number of new-generation banks now pose a threat to FBN's jealously guarded position. Perceived by many as a traditional bank, FBN strives to be more aggressive than the traditional old-generation banks without losing its brand as a reliable, rock-solid organisation. In a bid to maintain its position amongst the 'big four', FBN engaged in a corporate transformation programme. In 2009, a new managing director, Stephen Onasanya, was appointed; his primary task was to steer FBN to the desired position it now occupies in 2012. The Onasanya-led corporate transformation programme saw the company's operational structure move from geography-based to market-facing as well as attract and maintain top talent. Like many noble change initiatives, there are often implications attached to such radical strategic moves. This case is designed to showcase the benefits of such initiatives and provide a platform for solutions to possible challenges or problems that could arise in implementing them. Research input was gathered through company reports, published articles, and interviews with company staff.

Keywords: Corporate transformation, corporate restructuring, organisational structure, geographic organisation structure, customer- or market-focused organisational structure, organisational change management.

On resuming as CEO in June 2009, Stephen Onasanya did not have much time to decide how to turn around First Bank of Nigeria (FBN) Plc. His predecessor, Sanusi Lamido Sanusi, had introduced an aggressive corporate transformation agenda premised on growth, operational excellence, and performance management. However, six months into his leadership of the bank, Sanusi resigned upon appointment as Governor of the Central Bank of Nigeria, joining an impressive list of First Bankers that had moved on

* Dr. Ifedapo Adeleye is Senior Lecturer, Strategy and Human Resource Management, Lagos Business School, Pan-African University, Ajah, Lagos, Nigeria.
  E-mail: iadeleye@lbs.edu.ng

to assume senior national assignments. By December 2009, Stephen had settled into his demanding role quite well, and had begun to propose and implement calculated steps towards actualising the bank's vision of becoming in every manner *'the clear leader and Nigeria's bank of First choice'* (Chairman, 2009). At the core of Onasanya's transformation programme, lay a radical new organisational design.

Based on the bank's historic beginnings, their appreciation of the diversity and richness of Nigerian cultures, and the notion that consumer behaviour could be delineated based on common geographic traits; the organisational structure of FBN placed their market-facing activities along geographic lines. Thus their chain of formal command put geography first, followed by product, and then function. As at 2009, FBN had five strategic business units (SBUs) – the corporate office which handled the bank's treasury activities and the Lagos, North, South, and West directorates. Each of the directorates was headed by an executive director who ensured that the various locations functioned effectively and operated in alignment with the overall practice and service standards of the bank. In addition, the bank's four strategic resource functions (SRF) namely the Group Managing Director, Chief Financial Officer, Chief Risk Officer and Operations directorates were responsible for providing back-end support and resources for the SBUs.

In the proposed design which was to be deployed in 2010, the bank would be structured as three interdependent global organisations, one organized by product category, one by geography, and one by business process. This new model would result in drastic yet essential changes in the bank's marketing and operations structures. For the market-facing business units, the focus moved from a geographic to a customer segment focus. Business units would focus on specific customer segments, enabling each unit to deepen its understanding of its customers' unique needs and thus develop tailored products and services. This was a clear case of corporate transformation under pressure as the bank's market leadership and market share was gradually being eroded after the Central Bank's consolidation exercise following the 2008 financial crisis and the aggressive competitive pressure from the newer banks.

Traditionally, First Bank had relied mostly on its sheer size and premium brand name recognition across all regions in Nigeria, however in the years leading up to 2009, focused competitors had been steadily taking away market share in many product lines and regions, suggesting perhaps that their corporate advantage was steadily withering away. One major challenge facing Onasanya was how the proposed organisational structure could be implemented with as little disruption as possible for both the customers and the employees of First Bank.

FIRST BANK OF NIGERIA: HISTORY AND BACKGROUND

The history of FBN dates back to 1894, when it was incorporated as a limited liability company under the name Bank of British West Africa with the head office in Liverpool.

The bank underwent several name changes and became known as First Bank of Nigeria Limited in 1979 and First Bank of Nigeria Plc in 1999. At inception, the bank focused principally on financing foreign trade with very little being done in areas of lending to indigenous Nigerians, especially those who had miniature offerings as collateral for loans. The situation however changed by Nigeria's independence in 1960; many more Nigerians were able to receive credit from the bank as the independent financial control mechanism allowed more citizens to patronise the bank.

Though the bank typically favours organic growth, it has also grown inorganically through a series of acquisitions and mergers. It acquired Anglo-African bank in 1912, FBN (Merchant bankers) Ltd and MBC International Bank in 2005, and had recently resumed its on-off talks about a proposed merger with Ecobank Transnational Incorporated (ETI). First Bank of Nigeria Plc, listed on the Nigerian Stock Exchange (NSE) in 1971, is the most diversified financial services group in Nigeria, providing services to over 6.9 million customers, through 717 business locations, has its headquarters in Lagos, Nigeria and presence in London, Paris, Johannesburg, Beijing, Abu Dhabi, and Kinshasha, DR Congo. Though the bank is keen on growing its presence in Sub-Saharan Africa in the long-term, its short to medium term focus is on creating an international footprint outside of Africa, particularly in markets that support trade financing and cross-border lending and investments.

Despite this system of growth, First Bank has continued to maintain its highly traditional and conservative company culture. The bank is known for its robust corporate governance structure which has been developed through years of strong institutional processes brought about by scrupulous systems and controls, well-balanced succession planning, thorough risk management frameworks, highly skilled management teams as well as a high regard for ethics, accountability and transparency (although the bank did not adopt the IFRS accounting standards until December 2009, it always had one of the highest disclosure levels on its audited accounts amongst quoted companies on the NSE). The brand is also largely perceived to be highly trustworthy and is viewed as a safe haven for customer deposits; this perception led to FBN's deposit liabilities growing by almost 71% during the 2008 and 2010 industry liquidity contraction.

THE CENTURY II ENTERPRISE TRANSFORMATION PROJECT

"...The Bank's brand transformation programme [is] aimed at fundamentally re-positioning First Bank from a perception of 'First' representing 'old generation' to 'First' meaning 'the very best'."

– Stephen Onasanya, GMD/CEO

First Bank, typically referred to as one of the 'Big Four' (along with the United Bank for Africa, Union Bank, and Afribank) due to their size and length of existence, was widely perceived as an 'old-generation' bank, synonymous with extreme conservatism, poor service delivery, lack of technological advancement, shoddy corporate behaviour, and dismal marketing capabilities to mention a few. After about a century of existence, much of which it remained the indisputable market leader, FBN found itself in a challenging situation which despite its size and reputation, threatened to displace it from its position as first among equals. As at 1996, the bank had over 400 branches operating nationwide, but due to a lack of technological presence almost all of these branches were operating as separate and disconnected 'piggy' banks making information extremely difficult to compile and disseminate. Customer requirements were becoming increasingly complex and rapid responses to these demands were becoming a necessity for being competitive in the business. More so, the regulatory requirements were more intense as the apex bank moved proactively to move up the industry to measure up with international banking practices. Thus a business transformation initiative, 'Century II', was launched in 1996, as the bank began to make concerted efforts to change the perception of its customers and the public. It was revalidated in 2001 under the theme, "Century II – The New Frontier".

Century II had three major objectives which were to modernise the bank's operations, strengthen the bank's brand and significantly improve customer experience, and project the bank as sophisticated, contemporary, and dynamic. Amongst other notable observations, Information Technology was clearly identified as an indisputable enabler for the bank's forward movement. In conjunction with the consulting firm, Accenture, FBN embarked on a global search for a strategic IT partner who would enable them make this quantum leap. This led to the choice of Indian IT consulting firm, Infosys's Finacle solution. The new generation architecture of Finacle – fully web-enabled, with powerful and unique capabilities such as Straight Through Processing (STP), workflow, scalability and true 24/7 banking across multiple delivery channels enabled the bank to streamline its operations. In 2004, its 110th year of existence, the bank launched a new corporate identity by changing its logo and official colours. The brand transformation initiative went beyond IT and corporate image as the bank also restructured its human capital development and talent management structures. In 2007, from a pool of 2000 highly graded brands, Superbrand Nigeria Council rated FBN a Superbrand.

FIRST BANK OF NIGERIA'S ORGANISATIONAL STRUCTURE

The 2009 organisational structure comprised five distinct geographic SBUs or directorates each headed by Executive Directors (apart from the Corporate Office which simply carries out treasury activities). The four geographic directorates – Lagos, North, South, and West – are each organised into about a dozen or so Business Development Offices (BDO), headed by Business Development Managers (BDMs). Branch managers provide all banking services at the various branches under each BDO. Through the branches, each directorate was able to offer wholesale/corporate banking products/ services to large corporate customers; retail banking products/services to small-sized businesses; consumer banking products/services to individual customers; and a mix of unique products/services for government ministries, departments and agencies.

The key economic sectors served varied significantly with each directorate. In Lagos, the key economic activities included telecommunication, aviation, shipping and ports, oil and gas (downstream), real estate, commerce and industry, power, transportation, banking and financial services, power and tourism. In the North, the focus was on the public sector, agriculture, mining and solid mineral extraction, and manufacturing. The South directorate was focused on oil and gas, public sector, and trading while in the West directorate the predominant economic activities in administrative, extractive, manufacturing, additive, agriculture, merchandising and services sectors thus wholesale/corporate banking is the main focus. In general, each of the directorates handled public sector, retail and wholesale banking in varying degrees depending on the level and type of economic activity within that area.

Table 1: Total Net Revenue per Directorate*

Lagos Directorate	27.66%
North Directorate	21.28%
South Directorate	29.83%
West Directorate	16.63%
Corporate Office	4.60%

Source: First Bank of Nigeria Plc Annual Report & Accounts, 2009.

The directorates received back-end support and provision of resource planning and administration from the bank's four strategic resource function (SRF) directorates namely the Group Managing Director's Directorate, Chief Financial Officer's Directorate, Banking Operations & Services Directorate, and the Risk Management Directorate.

THE NIGERIAN BANKING SECTOR

The Nigerian banking industry, arguably the second largest in sub Saharan Africa after South Africa, has experienced tremendous growth over the years from its modest start in the late 19th century with six predominantly foreign banks to over 20 locally owned banks by the early 21st century. By 2009, there were 24 commercial banks operating in Nigeria, three of which were foreign (fully) owned banks. All, but these three banks were operating with universal banking licenses which permitted them to float non-core banking subsidiaries. Of the 21 indigenous banks, 12 had established their presence internationally either by running fully owned subsidiaries or joint businesses with other international firms. This situation differed markedly from the situation in 2004 where the industry consisted of 89 banks of various sizes and questionable degrees of soundness. The industry structure, best described as oligopolistic, was highly concentrated as the 10 largest banks accounted for about 50% of the industry's total assets/liabilities (ILO, 2004).

Still, the largest bank in Nigeria had a capital base of about $240m compared with $526m for the smallest bank in Malaysia during the period under review. It was evident that the industry did not have the ability to support the Nigerian economy and calls were made for reforms to improve the situation of banking in Nigeria. In 2004, the CBN, under the leadership of Charles Soludo, introduced a banking sector consolidation programme whose primary objective with a series of reforms was to guarantee an efficient and sound financial system. On July 6th, 2004, he announced a policy to increase the minimum paid in capital of banks from ₦2 billion ($14 million) to ₦25 billion ($173 million) and gave the banks approximately 18 months (till December 2005) to obtain the capital required. The clear reason for this policy was to consolidate the highly fragmented and weakly capitalised industry into one with much fewer, but financially stronger banks. The policy resulted in a large number of mergers and acquisitions as well as the revoking of 13 licences resulting in 24 larger, better-capitalised banks by December 2005.

In 2009, still reverberating from the shock of the 2008 global financial crisis, the Nigerian banking industry, now under the leadership of Governor Sanusi Lamido Sanusi experienced yet another unprecedented shake-up. Following a two-stage assessment of the banks in terms of liquidity, corporate governance, and capitalization strength, eight banks were deemed to be distressed. The apex bank then spent ₦620 billion ($4.3 trillion) in the rescue of these eight banks. Their CEOs were relieved of their duties and a number of them along with other senior bank executives were charged with various financial crimes. For the first time in Nigeria, a list of debtors of non-performing loans was made public. Also, in March 2009, in a bid to address issues of low disclosure and year-end irregularities contributed to the industry's problems, the CBN introduced a mandate for all banks to adopt 31 December as the common year end for the industry. Tenure limits were also introduced for CEOs and directors. By 2011, the eight rescued banks had either been acquired, nationalised or rescued through private capital injections leaving the industry with a total of 20 operating banks.

In the face of these reforms, competition among the 20 operating banks has heightened as customer demands became increasingly sophisticated thus forcing banks to constantly re-evaluate and re-invent their mode of service delivery and operation strategies in order to remain competitive.

OVERVIEW OF FIRST BANK OF NIGERIA'S CORPORATE STRATEGY: 2009–2011

In 2009, the bank set itself a clear medium term target (2009 – 2011) of restoring the bank to a position of "clear leadership" of the Nigerian financial services industry by carrying out a number of calculated steps towards not only changing the consumers' perceptions of the bank but also by restructuring their internal processes and procedures. The bank focused on four strategic themes namely *growth, service excellence, performance management,* and *talent.* In order to successfully meet these targets, the bank's current operating structure was appraised following the realisation of a need to create more tailor-made services for the increasingly sophisticated demands of the modern and much younger generation of consumers than the bank was typically used to. Also, management realised that moving the bank forward could not be achieved without building a superior human capital base for the bank, thus a complete overhaul of the bank's performance and talent management systems was required in order to enhance staff productivity and improve the individual and collective performance of the staff. As a result of these changes, a *'Corporate Transformation'* department was established with the sole purpose of 'implementing the big-ticket cross-functional projects' such as the above-mentioned planned restructuring and centralised processing centre deployment. Their duties included the co-ordination and performance tracking of the bank's major transformation initiatives. The bank set itself a number of benchmarks including achieving industry leadership in total assets, achieving consistently high returns on assets, maintaining cost-to-income and non-performing loan/total loan ratios below industry average, and finally, obtaining a top quartile rating in the most authoritative annual customer ranking survey in the country.

In terms of *growth,* the bank set distinct targets for adopting organic growth by focusing on key segment penetration, cross-selling, value proposition enhancement, price optimisation, stimulating customer usage, and channel optimisation; inorganic growth through dedicated explorations of valuable and viable opportunities for consolidation; and international expansion in key markets first outside of Africa (in the short to medium term) and then within Sub-Saharan Africa in the (medium to long term). To improve *service delivery,* the bank put in place processes to continually monitor and enhance customer experience/issue resolution, brand recognition and optimisation, manning/frontline transformation, and centralisation and re-engineering of branch processes. For *performance management,* the bank introduced new performance pay initiatives (pay-for-performance for market facing roles and pay-for-role for non-market facing and back-office roles), adjustments to compensation along notches, and automation of its human capital development processes. Also, employee health and well being initiatives and remedial management frameworks were introduced as well as revised performance scorecards and quarterly performance evaluation sessions. Finally, FBN introduced a number of *talent* building and management initiatives such as FirstLearn (an online self-development tool), various capacity and management development programmes, and First Academy (a competency based learning and development system).

ALIGNING FBN WITH THE MARKET: THE 2009 PROPOSED PLAN

"Like many organisations, the facilitating forces for market alignment include: strategic emphasis on relational value, need for clearer accountability for customers, recognition of lack of sharing of market information, dissatisfaction with marketing productivity, and pressure from large customers."

– Day, 2006: 45

FBN's 2009 proposal to redesign the operating structure of the Bank, with an emphasis on market-facing business units was in response to the increasing demands of customers for an improvement of the typically generic services they were receiving due to bank's current geographic structure. Thus, the bank recognised the need to align its operations along market segments primarily with geographic segments now taking second place. The new structure would comprise the following strategic business units five independent SBUs namely *Corporate Banking, Institutional Banking, Private Banking, Public Sector*, and *Retail Banking*. The corporate banking group would focus on mid size and large corporate clients; its customers include private organisations with annual revenue greater than ₦500 million and midsize to large organisations with annual revenue greater than ₦5 billion but who had a key man risk. The institutional banking group would focus on multinationals and large corporate clients; customers would include organisations with well-structured management and annual revenue greater than ₦5 billion (which do not pose a key man risk), companies quoted on the NSE, multinational and multilateral companies as well as large NGOs and companies in specialised industries.

The private banking group would focus on high net worth individuals; customers include clients with investible income of at least ₦37.5 million. The public sector group (further subdivided into *Public Sector North* and *Public Sector South*) would focus on Federal and State establishments; customers include the Federal Government of Nigeria and its Ministries, Departments & Agencies (MDAs), State & Federal Tertiary Institutions, the Armed Forces, The Nigeria Police, Civil Defence organisations and Foreign Embassies. Finally, the retail banking group (also subdivided into *Retail Banking North* and *Retail Banking South*) would focus on individual customers with annual income below ₦50 million, businesses with annual turnover below ₦500 million and local governments. As before, retail banking would comprise 15 and 31 BDOs in the North and South respectively to manage a total of 611 branches while the other SBUs would be further divided into groups and/or locations. SRFs would continue to be shared amongst all 5 SBUs but would no longer follow the previous directorate style, instead, the bank introduced 15 SRFs namely Operations, Finance, Risk management, Company Secretary, Strategy and corporate development, Legal services, Human capital management, General services, Marketing and corporate communications, Corporate transformation, Project Implementation, e-business, Products and marketing support, Information technology, and Internal Audit.

The new structure would refocus the Bank's commercial activities along the five dedicated SBUs bringing the customers to the fore and centre of profitable operations. The new SRFs and independence of the 5 SBUs would enable each business unit to deepen its understanding of its customers' needs and thus continually innovate uniquely tailored products and services. *"We believe that this approach will enable us to increase our share of wallet and by extension market share, and also to improve profitability"*, Onasanya enthused in a 2009 statement.

RE-EVALUATING THE ROLE OF EXECUTIVE DIRECTORS

The bank's executive directors were geographically based and appointed on a single term of three years. In order to implement the new structure, current executive directors had to be changed and new ones appointed. The bank would also have to appoint new executive vice presidents as well as other senior executives hired as specialists to run the new customer segments and sub-segments as well as the new SRF units. The implications of this would mean an increase in overheads which could pose a big challenge to the bank's cost containment imperative. Some of the executive directors were in the final year of their second 3-year term with no option for renewal in line with First Bank's corporate governance policy and thus resigned immediately moving on to lucrative roles in other banks in the industry and the public sector.

IMPLEMENTING THE NEW OPERATING STRUCTURE: EMERGING ISSUES AND CHALLENGES

"New structures often create new organisational problems that are as troublesome as the ones they try to solve."   – Kaplan and Norton, 2006: 2

In implementing the new market structure, a key consideration was to ensure that the business units would be as effective as possible in realising the benefits of an improved customer focus. Issues such as disruption of services would have to be minimal so as not to frustrate the customers the bank was working so hard to please. Thus, it was imperative that the transition process was handled by highly competent individuals right from the heads of the SBUs to each and every member of staff involved in the process. Thus the bank was faced with the complex task developing its human capital to a desired level while simultaneously driving the restructuring process and effectively handling the change process. An experienced executive, Onasanya was very familiar with a challenge one of its contemporaries was experiencing. One of the other Big Four banks had changed its structure so many times within the last few years and it was obvious that the downsizing and restructuring was having a negative impact on staff morale. It was an open secret that the failures had created all sorts of problems and anxiety among workers, and was not producing the intended results. Rather, than solve the bank's problems it had resulted in instability and as a result, the loss of even more customers.

Thus careful attention was paid to the selection of personnel to staff each business unit, providing the required reorientation and training and ensuring that relationship management was not adversely affected. The bank's existing management information systems were reconfigured and Key Performance Indicators were adjusted to suit the new operating model. In addition, the financial management system was modified to enable profit and loss accounts to be generated at the business unit and group and team levels to enable the leaders of each level of the business to proactively and regularly monitor their business profitability. Also, the development of new independent SBUs could result in the loss of cross-selling incentives and the introduction of counter-productive internal competition amongst the different units particularly the corporate and institutional banking SBUs. Regardless of the issues and considerations highlighted above, FBN deployed the new structure in October 2010.

ALIGNING STRUCTURE, SERVICE DELIVERY MODEL, AND PEOPLE PRODUCES RESULTS

In order to ensure an alignment of the bank's new structure with its strategy and delivery model, FBN also reorganised its branch operations model. This reorganisation took the form of a centralisation of the branch operations function with Bank-wide branch operations functions now the responsibility of the group head operations. In this new operating model, rather than have the branch operations staff report to the branch manager, they reported to the branch operations managers, who in turn reported to area and regional operations managers with reporting lines to the group head operations. With this change, the branch operations function was separated from the marketing function, thus freeing relationship managers from all non-market-facing functions. The new model allows operations staff to focus purely on delivering the expected level of service to customers, while the centralised nature of the model allows the Bank to standardise the quality of service delivery across all branches. Sales/relationship management models were installed to cater for the customers such as high net worth individuals who were identified as a platform for a viable new business for the bank.

The change to the bank's operating structure in the 2009 - 2011 period required a review of existing incentives designed to align staff attitudes and performance with our strategic goals. Due to fundamental differences in the expectations and functions of the front-office/market facing personnel and the back office support/non-market facing staff, evaluation and reward systems were changed to realize a customer centric organisation. Pay-for-performance was introduced for front-end staff while for back-end staff, pay-for-role was introduced (pay-for-role differed form pay-for-performance as it has a significantly higher base pay). In addition, the staff underwent a series of training and development processes introducing a number of talent development and management initiatives as the bank realised the need to continually invest in building the specialist industry knowledge and relationship management skills required for each segment. The attention and development processes provided for staff during the transformation period appears to be successful as the bank was voted Employer of Choice by its staff in a 2011 Multi Talent survey and 2nd best place to work in Nigeria 2012 following a survey by Great Place to Work.

The bank's KPIs also allowed for effective monitoring of the progress being made following the restructuring. The KPIs were Net operating income growth which provided insight into the banks success at generating business – it grew by 35.5% to N161.5 billion in 2010 and by 50% to N244.7 billion in 2011; Net operating income mix which represented the relative distribution of relative distribution of revenue streams between net interest income, net fee and commission income, and other income thus assisting management in making business investment decisions; Cost to income which was a measure that indicated the consumption of resources in generating revenue; the bank's cost to income ratio grew from 58.8% to 65.8% in 2010 due to a decline in gross earnings and an increase in operating expenses as an immediate result of the restructuring and dropped to 55.1% in 2011; Credit performance which gauged whether credit was correctly priced; Shareholder returns (Return on Shareholders' Equity) – it rose by 500% from 0.4 to 9.7 in 2010 and by 35.42% to 13.2 in 2011; Brand perception – the bank did not have any brand awareness results for 2010 due to a discontinuation in the process by the research firm but ranked No 1 in Nigeria according to the 2011 interbrand report; IT performance which measured the reliability and effectiveness of the bank's IT systems – the bank improved almost all its markers to within a range of 99.58 and 99.67%; and Customer Satisfaction – according to the KPMG survey ranking, in retail banking, FBN climbed from 12th to 10th in 2010 and 8th in 2011, in corporate banking the bank went from 10th to 6th in 2010 and 3rd in 2011.

CONCLUSIONS

First Bank was in many ways successful in the implementation of their transformation judging from their financial and non-financial performance indicators. This was clearly due to the fact that they carried out a well-planned execution of the implementation and did not leave out the most important factor which was its people. Without providing adequate, continuous training and development programmes, their well-laid plans could not have been practicalised. Also, changing their brand perception had to work both on the outside and the inside, i.e. both their external customers (clients) and internal customers (employees) otherwise the desired outcomes could not have been realised. Hence, a lot of attention must be paid to change management and communication. The change process cannot be over-emphasised; s/he must be able to not only establish an agenda that focuses on results but also convince individuals and teams to pursue these targets energetically, intelligently, and realistically. It is also important to highlight that alignment is a continuous process in dynamic markets and environments. First Bank of Nigeria Plc. was able to achieve their restructuring and alignment goals and find ways to overcome the challenges it brought thanks to the visionary leadership of Stephen Onasanya and his management team.

QUESTIONS

1. How was First Bank's performance? What was First Bank's market position when Bisi became CEO?
2. What were its strategic priorities? Did they change? If so, how?
3. What was the Bank's business initial business model? How did it change?
4. What was its operating structure prior to 2010 and what changes were to be made?
5. What were the pressing challenges Stephen was confronted with?
6. How could these challenges be successfully managed?
7. In trying to unlock and create value, is structural change the right tool for the job?

ACKNOWLEDGEMENT

The author wishes to express thanks to the First Bank for the research assistance and permission in developing this case.

REFERENCES

Asikhia, O. (2010). Market-focused strategic flexibility among Nigerian banks. African Journal of Marketing Management, 2 (2): 18–28.

Boswell, W., Bingham, J. and Colvin, A. (2006) Aligning employees through "line of sight". Business Horizons, 49, 499–509.

BGL Banking Report, 2010.

Day, G. (2006). Aligning the organisation with the market. MIT Sloan Management Review 48 (1): 41–49.

First Bank of Nigeria Plc Annual Report & Accounts, 2009.

First Bank of Nigeria Plc Annual Report & Accounts, 2010.

First Bank of Nigeria Plc Annual Report & Accounts, 2011.

Frangos, C. (2004). Creating a strategy-focused workforce: aligning personal goals to the BSC. Balanced Scorecard Report. November – December 2004.

Kaplan, R. and Norton, D. (2006). How to implement a new strategy without disrupting your organisation. Harvard Business Review, March: 1–11.

Storey, J. (2009). New organisational structures and forms. In J. Storey, P. Wright and D.

Ulrich (Eds), *The Routledge Companion to Strategic Human Resource Management* (pp. 90–105), Oxon: Routledge.

Designing and Implementing Credit Risk Management Operations and Systems at the Portfolio Level: An Illustration of Indian Banking Sector

Anju Arora

ABSTRACT

This paper explores the art of implementing benchmark practices relating to Credit Risk Management (CRM) operations and systems at portfolio level in commercial banks. It also offers an empirical analysis based on current practices of commercial banks in India relating to CRM operations and systems at the portfolio level. It reports and evaluates current status of credit portfolio risk management practices in the Indian banking system on the basis of primary data collected from the 35 Domestic Scheduled commercial banks in India. For this purpose, a structured questionnaire was administered on the sample banks in the year 2007-08. The findings regarding CRM operations and systems at portfolio level primarily focused on credit portfolio risk assessment, analysis of portfolio risk, and risk monitoring. The study observed that Credit portfolio risk management practices in Indian banking system has not yet reached benchmark level in terms of both: the methodology and the implementation (in terms of tools & targets). The paper clearly brings out that the various implementation challenges in designing and implementing credit portfolio risk operations and systems center on four issues, namely, data availability, standardization of information, in-house staff training and system integration.

Keywords: Credit risk management operations and systems, commercial banks, credit portfolio risk modeling, portfolio risk estimation, stress testing.

INTRODUCTION

The commercial banks in their normal course of business lend to a variety of clients belonging to varying types of industry/sector, forms of business enterprise and

* Dr. Anju Arora is Associate Professor with Keshav Mahavidyalaya, Department of Commerce, University of Delhi, Delhi.
  E-mail: puruanju@yahoo.co.in

levels of risk, etc. Each category of client/counterparty may have a unique risk-return profile. For instance, some may belong to high credit risk profile, and therefore, may provide the bank a higher interest income, whereas others might belong to low credit risk profile and provide a stable, yet low return on credit. This collection of various types of investments in loans/credit facility is known as a bank's credit portfolio. By managing the credit portfolio risk, a bank can help manage its overall risk. The Credit Risk Management (CRM) operations and systems provide the tools, strategies and techniques to effectively identify measure, manage and control credit risk-both at the transaction level and at portfolio level in accordance with the bank's CRM policy. The focus of a given CRM operation or system may be individual credit transaction or aggregate credit portfolio. At the transaction level, the CRM operations and systems relate to credit-risk rating framework, monitoring individual transactions risk and assessment of risks underlying each transaction. However, the risk and returns from the individual borrowers correlate due to varied economic, technical, financial and/or managerial factors. These complex correlations and diversification effects between random individual transaction values or returns are difficult to measure leading to exposure to aggregate credit portfolio risk. Thus, there lies a case for designing and implementing CRM operations and systems at portfolio level for the lending activities of banks. Such CRM operations and systems at portfolio level encompass identification, measurement, monitoring and control of credit portfolio risk and the risks underlying it, namely, concentration risk and intrinsic risk. The underlying objective being that bank management is in a better position to manage and control obligor and portfolio concentrations, default correlations, maturities, and loan sizes, and to address and even eliminate problem assets before they create losses.

NEED FOR STUDY

The CRM practices have evolved, from the times, when the CRM operations were generally limited to reviews of individual loans and banks kept most loans on their books to maturity to active credit portfolio risk management in recent times. The growing popularity of credit risk modeling, new markets for credit derivatives and the increasing marketability of existing loans through securitisation/loan sales market has added a new dimension to operations and systems at the portfolio level. The present study that attempts to provide an inventory of benchmark practices in this regard shall assist bank management in designing, implementing and strengthening its CRM operations and systems at the portfolio level. Such study shall also help bank management in assessing the current level of maturity and strength of their CRM framework.

Further, an evaluation of CRM operations and systems at the portfolio level has always been a fundamental part of bank supervision. Nowadays, in light of Basel norms (Basel2003), regulators are increasingly concerned to improve the bank capital requirements especially as it relates to credit risk. Therefore, a comprehensive study on practices relating to CRM operations and systems at the portfolio level shall assist regulatory authority in exercising risk management based supervision.

Further, as already observed the challenge underlying credit portfolio level operations and systems is the necessity to optimize the benefits associated with diversification and reduce the potential adverse impact of concentration of exposures to a particular borrower, sector or industry. So a study that improves an understanding of the complex interplay of various issues/risks underlying credit portfolio risk shall be immensely useful for academicians and bank practitioners, both.

RESEARCH METHODOLOGY

The present paper offers a broad list of inventory of benchmark practices relating to requisite CRM operations and systems at the portfolio level for the commercial banks in a developing economy, where the majority of the banks have only recently begun to collect the relevant data in a systematic manner so complex risk modeling may not be applied. The major benchmarks used for this inventory are the various documents released by the Risk Management Group of the Basel Committee on Banking Supervision, by RBI and regulatory authorities of other countries in this regard. It offers empirical evidence of CRM practices of commercial banks in India relating to CRM operations and systems at the portfolio level. Another objective of the study is to evaluate these practices against the benchmark practices in this regard to identify the potential areas of improvement. For this purpose, a structured questionnaire consisting a series of questions on various processes/procedures and tools put in place to manage credit portfolio risks was personally administered on the sample banks in the year 2007-08. The analysis is based on responses received from the 35 Domestic Scheduled commercial banks in India, nearly 70% of then population size.

CRM OPERATIONS AND SYSTEMS AT THE PORTFOLIO LEVEL

For CRM operations at portfolio level to be effectively implemented, firstly, it is necessary to understand risks underlying credit portfolio risk and then design all the necessary operations and systems. They need to be also harmonized with the relevant regulations in the country and be consistent with the nature, size and complexity of operations at the bank. CRM operations and systems at the portfolio level primarily relate to credit portfolio risk analysis, portfolio risk modeling and monitoring credit portfolio risk as elaborated further. The practices of sample banks with regard to each of these are also discussed in this section.

CREDIT PORTFOLIO RISK ANALYSIS

Credit portfolio risk analysis focuses on the interdependencies or correlations between the individual transactions and the diversification effects. The correlation measures the extent to which credit risk of individual transactions change together or not and if change, whether in the same direction or in opposite directions. A banker generally builds up such individual loan assets in its portfolio which have negative correlation between themselves with an aim to reduce aggregate credit portfolio risk. However, the entire risk can not be diversified away because of dependence of each client/counterparty on macro economy. Thus, every banker should attempt to diversify its credit portfolio so as to reduce aggregate credit risk to its systematic risk component. To design operations and systems at portfolio level, it is necessary to understand following issues; each individual asset's risk, its weight in the portfolio and the correlation between the assets. Thus, two risks underlying credit portfolio risk, namely, concentration risk and intrinsic risk have to be analyzed.

The *concentration risk* refers to the risk that arises as a result of undertaking exposure in only few industries/sectors/borrowers/ borrowing group. In general, the greater the diversification achieved in a bank's credit portfolio, the smaller is the probability of losses on all loans at the same time. But some banks may not prefer to diversify across various industries/sectors since the bank managers are usually expert in credit analysis of specific industries and sectors of the economy.

The *Intrinsic risk* is the risk that is inherent in the activity due to its operating environment. If a portfolio is fully diversified, (i.e. diversified across geographies, industries, borrowers, markets etc.), then the portfolio risk is reduced to a minimum level. This minimum level corresponds to the risks in the economy in which it is operating. This is systematic or intrinsic risk. If the economy as a whole does not perform well, the portfolio performance will be affected. Some of the relevant macro-economic parameters that may be analyzed by the banks include overall growth rates, growth in exports / industrial / agricultural sectors, interest rates, exchange rates, import duties, equity market and liquidity conditions. An ability to understand the impact of macro-economic environment on portfolio risk shall be valuable in drawing appropriate strategies and also allows for use of stress testing models.

Credit portfolio risk estimation is data intensive requiring granular level transaction data and reference data base for sufficient number of years. Various statistical measures that may be commonly employed are discussed further.

Lutkebohmert (2008) observes that the simplest method to quantify concentration in credit portfolio is to compute the *concentration ratio*, which is the ratio between the sum of largest loan exposures (K) and total credit portfolio exposures. However, this ratio has a limitation in that the choice of K is arbitrary, although it has strong impact on the outcome. Moreover the ratio considers only size distribution of K largest loans and does not take into account full information about loan distribution.

Another measure, namely *Herfindahl- Hirschman Index (HHI)* gives an estimate of concentration ratio, diversification quotient and incremental portfolio risk due to the addition of fresh loan to the loan portfolio. Herfindahl-Hirschman Index (HHI) is defined as the sum of squared market shares (measured in fraction of total portfolio) of each loan. Value of HHI ranges between 0 and 1, representing 100% and 0%, diversification respectively. All other things equal, the closer the HHI of loan portfolio is to 1, the more concentrated the bank's loan portfolio is. The concentration ratio is a very simple and adequate tool. It not only helps to assess the extent of credit risk in a loan portfolio but also for computing the credit risk contribution of adding fresh loans to the existing portfolio. However, neither of these measures incorporates the effects of counterparty specific credit qualities.

Default Correlations measures the strength of default relationship between two borrowers. In other words, a default in one asset may or may not cause another asset to become defaulted. Reserve Bank of India in its Guidance Note on CRM, (Reserve Bank of India ,2002) defines it in statistical terms, "credit portfolio correlation would mean the number of times companies/counter-parties in a portfolio defaulted simultaneously". If the defaults are independent, correlation is zero and the probability of extreme events (large number of defaults or zero default) is low. However, when two borrowers are correlated, the probability of both defaulting at the same time is heightened or is larger than it would be if they were completely independent.

Probability distribution of losses for entire credit portfolio is another useful tool for ascertaining portfolio credit risk. To arrive at the portfolio distribution, one has to first look at the returns on individual loan transaction. If the borrower does not default, the loss is zero. However when default occurs, the loss is usually substantial. In other words, individual debt assets have very skewed loss probabilities or for entire credit portfolio, there is always a large probability of relatively small losses and a small probability of rather large losses. As shown in the Figure: 1,where X-Axis measures the magnitude of the loss and the Y axis measures the probability; that the bank can suffer from large potential downside because of high probability of large losses due to default (fat tail) whereas, there is no chance of earning more than contractual rate of interest. It also indicates Expected Loss (EL) and Unexpected Loss (UL). The frequency distribution of portfolio losses may be used (Glantz, 2003, pp476) to compare the extent of diversification achieved in the credit portfolio.

Maximum portfolio loss or Credit value at risk is the summation of Expected Loss (EL) and unexpected loss. EL is given as the average of all the credit losses on the portfolio that a bank may incur during its ordinary business. "The expected loss of a portfolio of say, N counterparties is the sum of the expected losses on the constituents of the portfolio" (Servigny & Renault, 2004, pp 237). In principle, the EL should be perceived as a cost at par with staff and IT costs, etc. The banks must cover this cost by requiring an appropriate interest premium which is added to the funding and administration costs, etc.

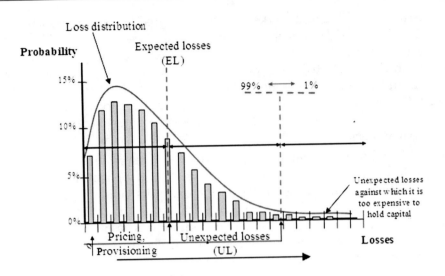

Fig. 1: Expected loss and Unexpected Loss
Source: Adapted from, Altman, "Managing credit risk: The next great financial challenge", John Willey& Sons, 1998.

On the other hand, Unexpected Loss (UL) is the loss that a bank may face under extremely rare but possible events such as, stock market crash, wave of defaults, etc. UL is simply defined as the standard deviation of portfolio losses. The UL in the credit portfolio arises due to the probability that the actual credit loss may be greater than expected. This measure indicates the bank's risk as the maximum credit loss which will occur with a given probability. As shown in Figure 1, UL may be set as the 99th percentile, in which case there is a maximum 1 per cent probability of a loss that exceeds UL.

The credit portfolio risk analysis may be executed by CRM practice of estimation of credit portfolio risk and stress testing. The CRM practices(Arora 2010) followed by sample banks in this regard are examined further under following heads;

Estimation of Credit Risk at the Portfolio Level

An estimate of aggregate credit portfolio risk is necessary for estimating risk-adjusted capital adequacy ratio. So CRM practice of estimating aggregate credit portfolio risk at the head office level may be followed. In addition, the aggregate portfolio risk may be also measured at the branch level or at the zonal/regional office level or at all of these levels. The survey analysis showed that all sample banks estimated it at head-office level but only six sample banks (less than 20%) were following the practice of aggregating credit risk at more than one level. The investigation into practices followed with regard to estimation of other measures of credit portfolio risk revealed that estimation of these statistical measures was made usually at head office; therefore some of the officials (13 out of 35) in the Zonal office were not aware of the measures estimated. Various parameters that were commonly employed by the remaining 22 sample banks are listed in Table 1.

Table 1: Estimation of Credit Portfolio Risk

Parameter Employed	Number of Banks (Overall)
Default correlations	13 (59.09)
Diversification ratio	15 (68.18)
Probability distribution of losses	11 (50.00)
Credit value at risk	10 (45.45)
Total*	22

Note: Figures in brackets indicate percentages of total. Also * represents that total percentage do not add to 100 due to multiple responses.

As may be observed from the table, some of the sample banks were using multiple measures to estimate portfolio credit risk. Diversification ratio followed by Default correlation measures were commonly deployed by the sample banks for portfolio risk analysis. Less than half of the sample banks were estimating Credit value at risk. It indicates that commercial banks in India were lagging behind benchmark practices regarding portfolio risk estimation.

Stress Testing of Credit Portfolio

As per Reserve Bank of India draft guidelines to banks on stress testing, issued on July 3, 2006, banks may use stress tests for understanding their risk profile. Stress testing involves projecting the performance (volatility) of a credit portfolio under altering macro-economic environments. In specific terms, stress testing would involve a test of the debt-servicing ability of a portfolio under alternative scenarios or a specific adverse event, which though exceptional can cause large losses. Adverse events commonly taken include interest rate increases, stock market decline, and foreign market downturns. The quantitative outcome of stress testing can be used in several issues of portfolio risk analysis, such as; determining risk buffers, testing the risk capacity of a bank against extreme losses, fixing limits for sub-portfolios to avoid given amounts of extreme losses, etc. The CRM practices followed by the sample banks with regard to the stress testing of advances portfolio are presented in Table 2.

Table 2: Stress Testing of Credit Portfolio

Stress Testing Made	Number of Banks (Overall)
Yes	23 (65.71)
Not done	9 (25.29)
Do Not Know	3 (8.50)
Total	35

(Figure in parentheses represen ts percentages of Total)

As may be observed from the Table 2, nearly one-fourth of sample banks were not following the practice of stress testing their advances portfolio, clearly indicating that Indian banks were lagging behind international benchmark practices regarding credit portfolio risk analysis.

The CRM practices of the commercial banks regarding stress testing may range from relatively simple alterations in assumptions about one or more macro variables to the use of highly sophisticated models. BIS norms further stipulate that following three areas could be usefully examined for stress testing, namely industry downturn, market risk events and liquidity conditions. The Table 3, below shows the type of change evaluated in stress testing by the sample banks.

Table 3: Variables Evaluated in Stress Testing

Variable Evaluated	Number of Banks (Overall)
Economic/Industry downturn only	2 (8.70)
Market risk events only	3 (13.05)
Liquidity conditions only	0 (0)
Economic/Industry downturn and Market risk events both	3 (13.05)
Economic/Industry downturn and Liquidity conditions both	1 (4.35)
All three variables	14 (60.90)
Total	23

Note: Figures in brackets indicate percentages of total.

As may be observed from the table, only 61% of the sample banks were evaluating all the three variables, namely, economic/ industry downturn, market risk events and liquidity conditions, while stress testing their advances portfolio, indicating huge gap between practices followed in Indian banking sector and internationally accepted practices in this regard. None of the sample banks analyzed change in liquidity conditions only. In informal discussion with bank officials, it was observed that majority of the sample banks did not have the necessary historical data base or the sophisticated models/software or the infrastructure required for risk analysis. To better implement portfolio risk analysis procedures, bank management in first instance need to make consistent efforts to up-date, process and standardize the data across all branches which may be at varying levels of standardization.

CHOICE OF CREDIT PORTFOLIO RISK MODEL

The credit portfolio risk models offer banks framework for understanding credit risk exposures classified across various base (such as, geographical locations and product lines), centralizing data and analyzing marginal and absolute contributions to credit risk. These models may be categorized into default mode models and mark to market models. Default mode models distinguish only two states: default and non-default of the borrower. These two states are assessed in terms of their probability of occurrence to determine the loss given default. For implementing default mode models important input parameters requires are; the loan amount, the default rate of the loan and its fluctuation, the recovery rate, i.e. the proceeds that can be achieved when selling the collateral used for cover; and the correlations (assumed to be constant) between the default risks (Jorion, 2003). The advantages of default mode models are their ease of implementation and the relatively low data requirements.

Mark-to-market models evaluate credit portfolios in terms of their market value and the risk the bank incurs if the market value changes. Thus, the evaluation here takes into account the changes in the borrower's credit standing and often also in the recovery rate over time, as well as the correlations of the credit risks. To implement the mark to market models the changes in rating and value of collateral are modeled on the basis of various procedures, by using internal historical data, a Monte Carlo simulation, or procedures based on option pricing theory. The most commonly used mark to market portfolio risk measurement models are Portfolio Manager by Moody's KMV, Credit Portfolio View (CPV) by McKinsey. The advantage of the mark-to-market model is that due to the various parameters and the fact that they can easily be modeled, the actual portfolio risk can be shown far more accurately than is possible using default mode models. However, it is not always easy to apply mark-to-market models as it is time consuming and all the data required are not easily available.

Further, a bank may devise appropriate portfolio risk model as per its special features such as geographical concentration, maturity profile, term structure of advances and degree of diversification in the portfolio. Reserve Bank of India (RBI) in its Guidance Note on CRM suggests that banks may adopt any model depending upon their size, complexity, risk appetite, etc.

The survey findings with regard to the portfolio risk model implemented by the sample banks are summarized in Table 4. As may be observed from the table, that 43% of the sample banks were still not using any portfolio risk models, clearly indicating a potential area of concern and improvement in Indian banking system.

Credit risk+ which is a default mode model was being used by 20% of the sample banks and CPV model was used by another 20% sample banks. Further, 17.1% of sample banks were using a portfolio risk model, developed in-house by these banks. Devising and employing self made credit portfolio risk models by these sample commercial banks may be taken as an indicator of higher expertise and maturity in designing credit risk management practices followed by them.

Table 4: Choice of Credit Portfolio Risk Model

Choice of Credit Portfolio Risk Model	Number of Banks (Overall)
Self -designed	6 (17.1)
Credit risk +	7 (20.0)
Credit portfolio view	7 (20.0)
Not employed	15 (42.9)
Total	35

(Figure in parentheses represents percentages of Total)

MONITORING CREDIT PORTFOLIO RISK

A working paper[1] Mckinsey & Company (2008) listed portfolio monitoring as a key issue in credit portfolio management. Monitoring procedures need to be designed with aim at ensuring actual composition of credit portfolio in compliance with the risk strategy, detecting early warning, provisioning for loan loss, identifying the parts of the credit portfolio vulnerable to specific external/systematic risks which in turn serves

---

[1] Gunnar Pritsch, Uwe Stegemann, and Andrew Freeman. September 2008 "Turning risk management into a true competitive advantage: Lessons from the recent crisis"., McKinsey & Company, Working Paper. Number 5.

as vital inputs for following the approach of risk mitigation and risk control. But a big practical issue in this regard is to determine the basis of classification of advances. The advances portfolio may be also classified on the basis of size / geographical region / credit facility and on the basis of rating migration. Each base serves a distinct purpose. For instance, monitoring on the basis of type of credit facility / product wise classification of advances portfolio reflects whether the bank is primarily lending working capital funds or focusing on the long term finance. Monitoring on the basis of size of advances provides input for estimating diversification ratio/ concentration ratio of the bank and monitoring geographic region wise classification of advances portfolio may help in identifying the potential markets. A comprehensive study on migration (upward – lower to higher and downward – higher to lower) of borrowers in the ratings categories shall lead to accuracy in expected loan loss calculations. A bank may also follow multiple base of classification to have more in-depth monitoring of advances portfolio.

The credit portfolio monitoring practices implemented by sample banks are summarized in the Table 5 below. As may be observed from the table, the sample banks were monitoring portfolio credit risk on multiple bases in agreement with Basel norms.

Table 5: Basis of Monitoring Credit Portfolio Risk

Basis of Classification of Credit Portfolio	Number of Banks (Overall)
Rating category	26 (75.30)
Type of Industry / Sector	28 (80.0)
Type of Credit facility	13 (37.15)
Size of Advances	22 (62.86)
Geographical Region	13 (37.15)
Total*	35

Note: Figures in brackets indicate percentages of total. Also * represents that total percentage do not add to 100 due to multiple responses.

It is further observed that three most important classification bases for monitoring credit portfolio included type of industry/sector, rating categories and size of advances. This reflects that the banks were implementing monitoring portfolio credit risk practices largely to maintain actual exposure in each industry / sector against the defined exposure norms in CRM policy.

CONCLUSION

The study observed that some commercial banks in India have reached fair level of maturity in designing and implementing CRM operations and systems at portfolio level, while some banks are still in nascent stage. This reflects the growing familiarity with CRM operations and systems at portfolio level and evolution towards increasing maturity/sophistication in the banking industry in India. There is still a fair good amount of scope for improving upon these operations and systems in Indian banking sector. The focus of such improvement may be on finer analysis of portfolio risk, increasing the use of credit portfolio risk model and close monitoring of portfolio risk. During personal interviews, respondents reported "data insufficiency" to be a key impediment to design and implementation of operations and systems at the portfolio level. Banks must, therefore, as a first step, endeavor building adequate database for implementing portfolio credit risk modeling over a period of time. To conclude, credit portfolio operations and systems need to be designed with a sound combination of both the, statistical /quantitative skills and management skills.

MANAGERIAL IMPLICATIONS

The study has implications for bank management and regulatory authority alike by offering evidence that credit portfolio risk management in Indian banking system has not yet reached its sophistication level in terms of both: the design and the implementation (in terms of tools & targets). The study has brought in focus the need to address various implementation challenges in designing and implementing credit portfolio risk operations and systems. These challenges primarily center on three issues, namely, data availability, standardization of information and system integration.

REFERENCES

Arora.Anju. (2010). "Credit risk management practices: Indian banking experience". Prajann, Journal of social and management sciences, Oct-Dec 2010 issue. National Institute of Bank Management, Pune, India.

Basel Committee on Banking Supervision(2003), The New Basel Capital Accord, Consultative Document, April 2003, Bank for International Settlement, Basel. (www. bis.org).

Glantz,Morton (2003). Managing bank risk, Academic press, London.

Jorion. Philippe, (2003) Financial risk manager handbook, pp561, Willey finance, III edition.

Llutkebohmert, Eva (2008) Concentration risk in credit portfolio, Springer publications.

Reserve Bank of India(2002). Guidance note on Credit Risk Management, issued on 12, October,2002, downloaded from website, www.rbi.org.in

Servigny & Renault, (2004). Measuring and managing credit risk, pp237, McGraw Hill.

Financial Literacy and Program Design: Sanchayan and Service Innovation

Rajeeva Sinha*, Bharat Maheshwari** and Avik Kedia***

ABSTRACT

Effective financial literacy and education is a requirement for inclusive financial growth. Effectiveness of programs cannot be easily assessed as success in financial literacy and education is a combined outcome of skill development and behavioral changes. In this paper, we use a framework from the service innovation literature to evaluate program effectiveness of Sanchayan, a non-governmental organization, in India, that delivers financial literacy and services to low-income adults and youth. The analysis based on insights from the service innovation literature and the case method shows that Sanchayan's success in providing financial literacy and services to these population segments and create a new market for services draws largely from its ability to: (a) take the context and the needs of its clients into account and (b) deliver the services to its clients in their own comfortable environment.

Keywords: Financial inclusion, Sanchayan, service innovations, financial literacy, social entrepreneurship.

INTRODUCTION

The importance of finance cannot be over-emphasized. Much of what we equate with economic progress would not have been possible without the enabling role of finance and more specifically credit (Ferguson 2008). Development economists have identified credit as the single most significant factor that separates the poor from the rest of the society (Soto 1989). Increasing longevity and rising healthcare costs coupled with declining fertility and the breakdown of the extended family support system has increased the urgency for pensions and asset accumulation at all levels of income and more so for low income households (WEF 2010). The capability to engage and interact

* Associate Professor of Finance, Odette School of Business, University of Windsor.

**Associate Professor of Management Information Systems; Odette School of Business;University of Windsor.

***CEO, Sanchayan, Delhi, India.

E-mail: rsinha@uwindsor.ca, bmaheshw@uwindsor.ca, avik@sanchayansociety.or

with the financial system will be a function of a number of influences such as social standing, education, property rights, etc. A significant influence is financial literacy and education or the individual's ability to comprehend the financial system, the rewards and risks it represents, and the ability to take financial decisions. Global studies in a number of countries are documenting the lack of financial literacy in developed and developing countries. These studies are also documenting consistent patterns in the lack of financial literacy based on income levels, gender and age.

Governments and organizations all over the world are taking a number of initiatives and implementing programs to address the significant expertise gap in understanding and implementing financial literacy and education. Sanchayan, through its innovative program design and social entrepreneurship, is an interesting example of a social venture that strives to equip the young and low income population to take individual responsibility of their future needs in healthcare and retirement.

In this paper, we analyse Sanchayan's program design and assess its effectiveness. We base this evaluation of program design in the substantial literature on financial literacy and education delivery models and the literature on service design and innovation.

The paper is organized as follows. In Section 2 we provide an overview of Sanchayan[1], its background, and its program structure. Section 3 is a review of literature on delivery models for financial literacy and education and a selective view of the service design literature. Section 4 discusses the findings of the paper, including important insights into service innovation, design, and delivery of effective financial literacy, education, and access programs. Section 5 concludes the study.

CASE BACKGROUND

Sanchayan was co-founded by two young professionals in 2009 that brought together their individual expertise and zeal to contribute to society. One of them was a chartered accountant and a financial expert, who brought his understanding of finance to the team; the other co-founder managed the outreach programs given her experience and understanding in delivering literacy programs. Sanchayan perceives itself as a neutral and independent organization promoting financial literacy to youth and lower income adults. Its core area of concern is the bottom of the base of the pyramid; young and adult Indians that have a daily income of $2 or less. In India, the wider population mistrusts government organizations (including banks) and continues to rely on money-lenders and informal saving mechanisms. Sanchayan leverages a multitude of synergistic partnerships with a number of agencies in the government, private and the non-profit sectors to design and deliver financial literacy programs to youth and lower income adults in both urban and rural areas in India[1].

---

[1] Sanchayan is Sanskrit for 'To accumulate'. For more on Sanchayan's profile go to www.sanchayansocirty.org

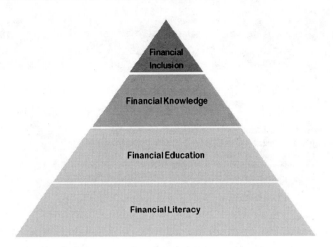

Fig. 1: Financial Empowerment Pyramid

Sanchayan's key value proposition lies in its innovative financial literacy programs and services. In the new environment of fast economic growth, organizations like Sanchayan can play a significant role in promoting financial inclusion of youth and lower income population segments through financial literacy. Financial literacy enhances the financial capability of the poorer population, thus increasing the potential for their inclusion in the mainstream financial systems and getting them access to financial services and products. Prominent development economists have identified access to finance as a key requirement for enabling participation of people in economic growth (Soto, 1989).

Fig. 1 illustrates what Sanchayan describes as the interconnectedness of financial literacy, financial education, financial knowledge and financial inclusion. Their newsletter of May 2011 elaborates on this interconnectedness as follows:

> *"We believe that once the process of financial literacy starts at the elementary level, this will lead to the second step of financial education being inculcated into the educational curriculum. This will further serve as a platform for the spread of informal financial knowledge sharing among the common man. Literacy, education and knowledge would empower the common man to be included in the financial system. Therefore, financial literacy is only the first step to this entire process and is the foundation for creating financial inclusion."*

Sanchayan's program delivery is organized around three verticals; youth, the urban poor and the rural poor. Specific programming for each of these verticals is shown in Fig 2 and details of each program can be found in Exhibit 1.

Youth	Urban Poor	Rural Poor
• Money Smart	• Sanchayan Suraksha	• Arthaniti
•Financial Education for the privileged as well as disadvantaged youth to encourage prudent financial decisions	•One stop shop for the urban poor for financial inclusion and asset accumulation	•Financial education programmes for the farmers and rural poor

Fig. 2: Sanchayan Program Verticals

Guided by a number of other prominent professionals from different fields who constitute the advisory panel, Sanchayan today partners with a number of other stakeholders (such as governments, education institutions, financial institutions, corporate foundations, and other NGOs) in offering several financial literacy programs for youth and low income adults. Partnering with VISA, Sanachayan is targeting to offer its youth and adult financial workshops, "MoneySmart," to 52,500 students this year. Its rural financial literacy program "Arthniti" is delivered in partnership with banks that have a mandate to disseminate financial knowledge in rural areas.

Sanchayan claims its approach to financial literacy is independent and neutral which brings value to both its clients and partners. The clients can trust Sanchayan as it does not drive the agenda of a particular institution. On the other hand, its partners can use its reach in delivering their policy mandates and programs. The organization is technologically savvy and innovative. It uses both traditional and emerging methods to reach its clients. While the traditional methods are more effective in rural and low income adult setting, virtual mediums such as Facebook and Twitter are becoming popular ways to reach the youth.

LITERATURE ON FINANCIAL LITERACY DELIVERY AND SERVICE INNOVATION

Sanchayan in its annual report of 2009-2011 identifies some very core issues in the quest for financial inclusion in India. Policy recognition exists in India that growth to be sustainable has to be inclusive, and a key requirement for inclusive growth is inclusive finance (Mukherjee, 2010). The literature on financial literacy and education also identifies a huge latent demand for financial inclusion and access among all sections of the population and particularly amongst the lower income groups. Sanchayan in its survey of unorganized workers in three Indian states found that more than 75% of the respondents wanted to save for their future needs in order to avoid approaching local money-lenders during financial emergencies (GIZ-IGSSP Study, 2012).

A major constraint in the promotion of financial inclusion is insufficient financial literacy in general and more specifically amongst low income population segments (Buckland, 2010). While the need for financial literacy is recognized, there are serious supply side deficits in financial education and this in turn constraints prospects for financial inclusion. This supply side deficit exists in a number of countries, and it is true for India as well. Government policy and the market come up short in capacity building for financial inclusion. Financial literacy and education program design in India lacks coordination and is driven by a number of major players including the Reserve Bank of India, the Ministry of Corporate Affairs, and the various stock exchanges and its regulator, the Stock Exchange Board of India. There is no dedicated organization in charge of the design and delivery of financial literacy and education programs[1]. Development of capacity could greatly benefit from the experience of other countries in designing financial literacy and education programs. A review of the literature identifies four templates for the design of financial education and literacy programs (Buckland, 2010). A brief synopsis of these approaches, their scope, strengths and limitations is provided in the Table1 below:

Table 1: Delivery Models Financial Literacy And Education Programs

Program	Stand-Alone Program with General Literacy Goals	Stand-Alone Program with Specific Literacy Goals	Component of Financial Inclusion Program	Component of an Asset Building Program
Scope	Improving participants' general financial literacy levels with curriculum: Budgeting, Planning and Investing.	Limited to educating or training of focused literacy goals e.g., boosting savings for retirement or house purchase, repair and extension.	Contains financial literacy education + inclusion component (e.g. access to credit + bank account); how banks can profitably offer small dollar loans vs. high cost products (pay day loans & overdraft protection) programs.	All aspects of earlier three delivery models plus asset building programs like matched savings as in the Pension Scheme (NPS – Lite) introduced by the Government of India and the Indian Bankers Association, in the 'Swavlamban Scheme.

---

[1] The Government of India has recently set up the "Financial Stability and Development Council (FSDC)" in its effort to develop an integrated national approach to financial literacy. This high powered council has representatives from the government, the finance ministry and is headed by the prime minister. Given the high powered composition of the committee expectations have been raised for a successful national financial literacy policy, however, turf wars have already surfaced putting the outcome in doubt (Economic Times, July 31, 2012).

Strengths; Outcomes	Simple program design; Creating a framework that provides an understanding of institutions, economy, financial services, and changes in life circumstances; Increased financial planning, management & savings; stimulates pensions and savings and lower delinquency rates	Prevents workers from saving at sub-optimal rates; Lowered mortgage delinquency rates; Improved savings amongst low-income groups; Work based retirement savings seminars have stronger effects on low-income and less educated groups;	Lowered default rates; Improved access to banking & lower cost loans; Improved money management skills & financial knowledge; Decreased use of fringe banks; Appropriately discounted the future	Effectively supports savings and boosts financial literacy; induces change in participant attitudes towards education and financial institutions; Proves to be more effect as a combination of matched savings and financial literacy training; Particularly, effective in targeting low-income groups
Caution; Limitations	One-time literacy training can quickly lose its benefits; Deficiency in addressing low-income youth; Youth education should occur in earlier life stages; Need to highlight the importance of human capital among youth	Need to strike a balance between Universality and addressing social context needs; Expensive to provide participant tailored advice	most effective when offered in collaboration through local non-profits & financial institution; Success depends on clearly defined program goals	Commitment by stakeholders and motivating content; Finding a balance between comprehensiveness and flexibility;

The literature on the design of delivery models for financial literacy and education programs summarized in Table 1 provides an overview of program scope; outcome and limitations under differing objective and conditions. However, it is difficult to use the experiences of these financial literacy and education program models to develop other program delivery models. We do not have evidence on the relative effectiveness of financial literacy and education program delivery models. The outcome of financial literacy programs and their relative effectiveness is difficult to measure and evaluate. Financial literacy programs can lead to skill development and behavioral changes. While the changes in the level of skill developed can be measured, it is difficult to measure the changes in behavior and establish attribution to financial literacy and education programs. This makes it difficult to develop templates for an effective financial literacy and education delivery model design.

In the absence of empirical evidence on the relative effectiveness of program delivery and design for financial literacy and education, we develop an ex ante rationale for financial literacy and education model design. For this design, we turn to the literature on service innovation and design (Miles 2005; Mansharmani, 2005; Bitran and Logo, 1993). The design rationale is based on the understanding that financial literacy and education delivery design is a service sector activity, and moving beyond the non-profit framework and adopting the social enterprise and social entrepreneurial approach, we consider it to be a social venture in the service sector. This literature in the discussion below provides some useful insights and frameworks to better understand the rationale for financial literacy and education program delivery design.

SELECTIVE OVERVIEW OF SERVICE DESIGN AND INNOVATION LITERATURE

Service innovation is a topic of great interest and a major source for employment in most developed countries. Progressive organizations around the world are consistently seeking ways to improve their service offerings and make them more useful and/ or more convenient (Miles, 2005). Like product innovations, managing service innovations is a complex task. However, service innovation is often more complex than product innovation, as service components are often not plain physical entities but a combination of processes, people skills, and materials. People and processes in services are part of the customer experience and thus an integral part of the innovation and it is not possible to separate production and consumption (Mansharamani, 2005).

Bitran and Lojo (1993) identify six distinguishing and unique characteristics of service operations (vs. products): (1) intangibility, (2) perishability, (3) heterogeneity, (4) simultaneity, (5) transferability, and (6) cultural specificity. These characteristics affect the way service innovations are resourced and managed. For example, intangibility makes it particularly difficult for firms to appropriate resources to service innovations and limits their ability to seek intellectual property protection. Often intangibility of services in many sectors has been illustrated by the example of a lighthouse where most stakeholders do not value the service until things go wrong. Similarly, the perishable nature of services makes it impossible to store them during peak demand, and firms have to formulate creative ways to smoothen the consumption patterns, particularly in high capital-intensive industries such as airlines and hospitals.

Berry, Shankar, Parish, Cadwallader and Dotzel (2006) propose that most of organizations make incremental innovation to their services. Very few organizations develop services that create a new market or reshape a market completely. In a study based on multiple case studies of firms introducing new market-creating service innovations, the authors propose a taxonomy of service innovations classifying market-creating service innovations on two dimensions: (a) the type of benefit offered and (b) degree of service 'separability'.'

On the benefit dimension, Berry et al (2006) show that firms can innovate by offering services with new core benefits (e.g., Cirque du Soleil which created a new market for live entertainment) or new delivery benefits which offer an established core benefit using a new and more convenient delivery system (e.g., University of Phoenix which has become the largest US institution of higher education using the Internet as the new delivery mode).

The separability dimension examines whether the service must be produced and consumed simultaneously. Technology plays a major role in separating production and consumption of services which was largely inseparable before. For example, doctors and nurses can use telemedicine to advise patients. Berry et al (2006) combine and use these two dimensions to create a 2 x 2 matrix to classify innovative companies into four categories (Figure 3). The authors further identify nine success drivers behind creating service innovation.

1. Scalable business model
2. Comprehensive customer-experience management
3. Investment in employee performance
4. Continuous operational innovation
5. Brand differentiation
6. An innovation champion
7. A superior customer benefit
8. Affordability
9. Continuous strategic innovation

CREATING NEW MARKETS THROUGH SERVICE INNOVATION

In this section, we evaluate Sanchayan's service design from the perspective of the above-discussed financial literacy and innovation literature. The matrix and service innovation drivers proposed by Berry et al (2006) are used to position and analyze Sanchayan's service innovation efforts

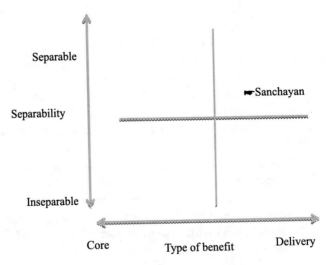

Fig. 3: Sanchayan on the Service Innovation Matrix

We find that Sanchayan is positioned as an organization innovating its services on both delivery and separability dimensions. On the benefit dimension, Sanchayan through its Sanchayan Suraksha Points (SSPs) extends access to core financial services of a multitude of partner organizations such as banks, insurance companies, government offices (e.g., for obtaining permanent account numbers) to lower income population segments in their neighborhoods. Sanchayan strategically leverages the existing client-vendor relationships by strategically selecting franchises for their SSPs. They select and train mobile telecom service providers who have a prominent position in lower income neighborhoods given the massive adoption of phone services. The SSPs also act as a one-stop and dignified access point for the low-income population who tend to find it difficult to access these services from original providers such as banks and a number of other government agencies and departments.

On the separability dimension, Sanchayan provides these services at time slots that are comfortable for their clients such as after work hours. Before Sanchayan, their clients often found it difficult to go to banks and other agency offices to avail services during the day or do it at the cost of missed wages for the hours spent in availing those services. The challenge Sanchayan faces includes cognitive dissonance. As substantiated by the survey of low-income workers from the unorganized sectors in India (INZ-IGSSP, 2012), lower income people continue to prefer working with local money-lenders and high risk prone methods such as the "committee or "matka" for their financial needs. The survey found a strong preference for keeping savings in the form of cash at home. Sanchayan's role in increasing financial inclusion includes addressing the cognitive dissonance and building the required trust with their clientele.

Sanchayan's Success Drivers

Sanchayan by taking the services to the consumers in their own comfort settings is an example of service innovation that creates both separability of services and provides a new benefit by delivering financial literacy and eventually services to lower income population segments leading to their financial inclusion. Sanchayan's service design and delivery approach to creating new markets can also be appreciated in their ability to address several key issues through their innovative approach

Comprehensive Customer-experience

Sanchayan's role in creating new markets is larger than just providing financial literacy. The organization through its array of programs and variety of services provides a comprehensive experience to its clients. It is able to build financial capability of the lower income people and then lead them to financial inclusion by providing them financial services offered by multiple other players in the financial sector through the SSPs. It has a continuing education approach for their clients, leading to financial literacy and behavioral change. The success of Sanchayan lies not just in providing financial products and services which is something other agencies have been able to do, but in building up the financial capability of their clients so that they can continue to use and avail the services. It is not very uncommon in India to find people falling into loan trap by taking loans from another lender to return money borrowed from a previous one (WSJ, August 13, 2008).

Scalable Business Model

Sanchayan's approach to providing services is scalable as it employs the franchisee model for expanding its SSPs. The approach does carry the risks associated with agency development. However, by carefully selecting the franchisee, training, and taking an approach which leverages the existing relationships and strengths of the franchisee, Sanchayan's mitigates this risk. Sanchayan has been quite successful in this by selecting mobile telecom vendors as their SSP franchisees. They find that young adults are technologically advanced and quick learners and also have a significant recommender power because people in lower income neighborhoods listen to them.

Continuous Operational Innovation

The continuous extension and improvement of services is important to take into account the changing needs of the clients as they evolve and are included into the financial systems. Carpenter (2008) and Friedman (2005) emphasize the need for financial literacy and education programs which are relevant to the participants' needs. Sanchayan continuously invests in improving its operations. Further, by building synergistic partnerships with other stakeholders including financial institutions, government programs, educational institutions, and other NGOs, Sanchayan is able to provide a full set of services to its clients through its SSPs.

Investment in Franchisee Performance

Sanchayan's model depends on the franchisees and their relationship with their clients. Sanchayan has no direct employees other than the founders, but its success depends on incorporating its franchisees into its mission. The key to achieving this depends heavily on training its franchisees. These trained Sanchayan's franchisees also are its innovation champions, and the organization leverages their training as they provide education at the point of sale to its clients. This allows them to leverage sales across its programs and services such as asset accumulation, credit and asset building, and pensions, and they can lead to long-term benefits as identified in the literature (Sherradan and Boshara 2008).

Brand Differentiation

Sanchayan has been systematically branding its services for greater retention and trust. Their brand Sanchayan Suraksha has been developed to exhibit the trust in their services. The branding also provides the organization better negotiation powers when dealing with larger partners such as banks in the long term.

A Superior Customer Benefit

The model extends some very direct benefits to their clients. For example, a large number of Sanchayan's clients in rural slums of New Delhi are migrant laborers, who need to send money back to their villages and need micro-loans and advances in times of agriculture cropping seasons. Through financial inclusion, these clients right away can access services like money transfer and micro-loans at times of need.

Affordability

Affordability is a key parameter in service design for lower income population segments. Sanchayan's service selection and partnerships with micro-finance and micro-insurance companies makes its products affordable.

Continuous Strategic Innovation

Sanchayan depends on its partners whose programs it helps in implementing for resources. Primarily, its activities are guided by government programs and priorities. It often finds through its interactions with clients at the ground level the programs it helps in implementing are not aligned well to the needs of the lower income people. As Sanchayan grows, it is important for the organization to keep improving its position in value chain. Sanchayan can specially provide inputs in the area of new program design.

CONCLUSION

We found that Sanchayan's success in providing financial literacy and services to two prime population segments – youth and lower income adults – draws largely from its ability to take the context and the needs into account and deliver the services to their clients in their own comfortable environment. The youth-oriented programs are delivered in schools and adult-oriented programs are delivered in the neighborhoods. The difference is made through positive client experience and convenient delivery of service. The organization has adopted a lean business model where the founders are mainly providing training and mentorship to franchisees. The organization leverages its synergistic partnerships and innovative service design. Going forward, Sanchayan faces some of the common challenges associated with growth including intense competition. However, Sanchayan enjoys the first mover advantage and continues to innovate.

This case study illustrates some of the key service design issues and challenges and how organizations can leverage partnership. Importance of service innovation in creating new markets is highlighted. The model currently relies heavily on the co-founders who are looking forward to hiring people to assist them as the number of SSPs grows. In fast-growing economies like India, hiring and retaining talented people can be a challenge. The study also provides an additional insight into an aspect of financial literacy not addressed well in the literature. The literature on financial literacy is limited to outcome driven models and does not provide much guidance on service design. Sanchayan's case also provides some insight into how the financial literacy and education delivery should be designed for better uptake among the young and lower income population segments.

REFERENCES

Berry, L. L., Shankar, V., Parish, J. T., Cadwallader, S., & Dotzel, T. (2006). Creating New Markets Through Service Innovation. MIT Sloan Management Review, 47(2), 56-63.

Bitran, G. R., & Logo, M. (1993). A Framework for Analyzing Service Operations. European Management Journal, 11(3), 271-282.

Buckland, J., (2010). Money Management on a Shoestring, A critical literature review of financial literacy & low income people,. 2010. Research paper prepared for the Taskforce on Financial literacy, Available at: *www.financialliteracyincanada.org*

Carpenter, E. (2008). "Major Findings from IDA Research in the United States." CSD Research Report No.08-4. St. Louis, Missouri: Washington University Center for Social Development.

Ferguson, Niall. (2008)., The ascent of money: a financial history of the world, New York: Penguin Press.

Friedman, Pamela, 2005. "Providing and Funding Financial Literacy Programs for Low-Income Adults and Youth." Strategy Brief. Washington, D.C.: The Finance Project. Available at *www.financeproject.org*

Hayashi, C., Heli, O., Brend, J. S. & Juan, Y., (2010). Transforming pensions and healthcare in a rapidly ageing world: opportunities and collaborative strategies Pensions, Vol. 15(3) pp. 161-174

INZ-IGSSP, (2012). Pre-Study on the Ability and Willingness to Contribute to Social Security Schemes, Study conducted by Sanchayan for the GIZ and Indo German Social security Program; available at *www.Sanchyansociety.org*

Lusardi, A., (2008). Financial Literacy: An Essential Tool for Informed Consumer Choice? Working Paper, Center for Housing Studies, Harvard University.

Mansharamani, V. (2005). Towards a Theory of Service Innovation: An Inductive Case

Study Approach to Evaluating Uniqueness of Service. MIT.

Miles, I. (2005). Innovation in Services. In J. Fagerberg & D. C. Mowery & R. R. Nelson (Eds.), Oxford Handbook of Innovation (pp. 433-458). Oxford: Oxford University Press.

Mukherjee, P., (2010). National Strategy for Financial Education, Speech delivered by Union Finance Minister, Government Of India, at the RBI-OECD Workshop, on Delivering Financial Literacy

Sanchayan, (2011). Annual Report 2010-2011. Available at: *http://sanchayansociety.org/*

Soto, Hernando de, (1989). The other path: the invisible revolution in the Third World, foreword by Mario Vargas Llosa; translated by June Abbott. New York: Harper & Row.

WSJ, (2008)., A Global Surge in Tiny Loans Spurs Credit Bubble in a Slum, The Wall Street Journal , retrieved on August 11, 2012 from *http://online.wsj.com/article/SB125012112518027581.html*

Wolfe, A. (2005). The Service Economy in OECD Countries.: OECD STI Working Paper 2005/3. Available at SSRN: *http://ssrn.com/abstract=1690930* or *http://dx.doi.org/10.2139/ssrn.1690930.*

Exhibit 1: Sanchayan Programs for the Youth and Low Income Populations (Urban and Rural), Available at: http://sanchayansociety.org/

MoneySmart – Are You?

Financial Inclusion

- Opening No Frills Bank Accounts

- Opening Recurring Deposits / Fixed Deposits / Auto Sweep

- Obtaining Financial Identity (PAN card, UID)

- Micro-insurance (LIC health insurance for Rs.300/- pm)

- Enrolling for New Pension Scheme

(On saving Rs. 1000/- pm, Government of India contributes Rs. 5000/- Free in 5 years under 'Swavalamban scheme')

Financial Literacy

- Planning & Budgeting Family Finances

- Importance of Savings

- Basics of Banking

- Credit Cards & Debt

- Indian Economy

- Markets and Investing

- Entrepreneurship & Micro-finance

- Careers in Financial Services

Sanchayan Suraksha Point [SSP]

Sanchayan Suraksha Points (SSPs) are one-stop outlets designed for delivery of right financial products and services to the urban and rural poor. The products and services on offer are:

- Bank Savings A/c

- Micro – Insurance

- Micro – Pension (NPS Lite)

- PAN Card

- Financial Planning for Poor

- Other Services

ARTHNITI – Sanchayan's Rural Financial Literacy Program

Sanchayan's Rural Financial Literacy Programs are non-allied with any financial service provider and are independent, neutral programs, creating awareness about the right kind of financial products and services, dispelling common myths regarding money and institutions, protecting women from pyramid schemes, chit funds, matkas, loan sharks, and offering them a larger view of the financial services industry.

- Inclusion of excluded

- Building Individual Capability

- Basics of Banking

- Importance of Savings & Growth

- Financial Identity for All

- Consumer Protection

- Financial Planning

- Group Experiences

- Financial Awareness

- Money Transfers

- Social Security

Banking Upon Unbanked Through UID-Enabled Banking: A Case Study of a Multinational Bank

H.M. Jha "Bidyarthi"", *S.M. Mishra""*, *N.Y. Kasliwal""*
*and Ashish K. Srivastava""**

ABSTRACT

This research is based on a study of four sample villages drawn from two districts of Vidarbha region and a survey of 650 villagers regarding their financial needs, access to financial institutions, availability of needed finance and its terms and conditions and the possibility of connecting them with a multinational bank through UID-enabled 24-hour door-step banking using business correspondence model. Though this seems to assure financial inclusion but a host of regulatory limitations impede its scope which this paper attempts to address and answer.

Keywords: Financial inclusion, micro-finance, UID-enabled banking, micro-ATM.

INTRODUCTION

For a country like India, poverty remains to be one of the biggest policy concerns. Though our country's economy is growing around 9 percent, still the growth is not inclusive with the economic condition of the people in rural areas and is worsening further. One of the typical reasons for poverty is being financially excluded (www.economictimes.indiatimes.com). Banking services are central to the challenge of financial inclusion. Financial exclusion can impose significant costs on individuals, families and society as a whole. Lack of access to a bank account can be a significant

---

[*] Professor and Head, Department of Business Administration and Research, Shri Sant Gajanan Maharaj College of Engineering, Shegaon, India.

[**] Asstt. Professor, Department of Business Administration and Research, Shri Sant Gajanan Maharaj College of Engineering, Shegaon, India.

[***] Associate Professor, Institute of Management, Pt. Ravishankar Shukla University, Raipur, India.

E-mails: hmjhabidyarthi@rediffmail.com, satyamohan84@gmail.com, nneelam-yk@rediffmail.com, ashish1@rediffmail.com

barrier to employment and enterprise. The unbanked can also face higher charges for cheque cashing and utility bills. Providing access to a bank account needs to be the foundation of the Government's strategy for promoting financial inclusion (Rural Labour Enquiry 1990). The worldwide unbanked market is estimated to be in excess of 2.6 billion people. *Millions of Americans -- 60 million, in fact -- conduct their day-to-day financial business outside the banking system, leaving many to be preyed upon by payday-loan companies, rent-to-own establishments and other non-bank institutions. Banks have largely ignored the unbanked and under banked, arguing that it's difficult to figure out how to make money off them* (http://www.articlesbase.com/credit-articles/ajo-banking-for-the-unbanked-and-financially-underserved-populace-at-the-bottom-of-the-pyramid-bop-2691490.html). In India, the traditional banking remains out of reach for many people due to logistics, cost and lack of financial literacy and the absence of compatible products (Elizabeth Rowe, http://www.packagedfacts.com/Unbanked-1383052/). India is a home of more than 120 billion people and out of these 120 billion populations more than 70 percent population is still living in villages. Historically, in India, financial inclusion of under-served people has been sought to be achieved through three different financial institutions—rural cooperatives, SCBs and RRBs—although the success of their operations has been limited and they have been criticized for having a non-aggressive business profile. Several major initiatives have been rolled out in India, which would have implications for the microfinance sector. Following the recommendations of the Committee on Financial Inclusion, a nation-wide programme of financial inclusion, utilising the banking network to include all the excluded with a financial service need, has been initiated.

FINANCIAL INCLUSION THROUGH MICRO FINANCE – LITERATURE REVIEW

Professor Muhammad Yunus, the father of microcredit, started the Grameen Bank Project in 1976, which became a bank in 1983. The Grameen Bank is a bank for the poor and of the poor. It has grown through a process of learning by doing. It is a highly innovative institution. It has developed unique inclusive financial products and services, its own criteria of targeting and a system of credit delivery and recovery, as well as training and technical assistance. If one is interested to know the key to the tremendous success that Grameen Bank has achieved, one needs to learn its philosophy and methodology (Hossain, M. 1993). There is one single term that the philosophy of Grameen Bank can be broken down into. That is "Financial Inclusion". Financial inclusion is a matter of great consideration in the world today. It has become a policy priority in many countries including USA, UK, France, China, India, Bangladesh, South Africa, Zambia, Uganda, and Brazil (http://www.reportlinker.com/p057872/Non-traditional-Financial-Services-Markets-in-the-U-S-Unbanked-and-Underbanked-Consumers.html). Given the poverty situation worldwide and the consequences of financial exclusion, the importance of financial inclusion is being realized in every country. With the belief that "Credit is a human right" and "There is an inbuilt capacity in every person", Professor Muhammad Yunus framed the Grameen Bank model in order to serve the poorest of the poor with microcredit to provide them with opportunities to engage themselves in income generating activities (Hulme, D and Mosley, P. 1998).

While the Indian economic structure is dominated by the massive poor and vulnerable groups, the financial system is geared to serve, directly or indirectly, the relatively small number of middle and high-income categories. This dichotomy has considerably widened after the 1990s. Even the nation-wide surveys on household indebtedness seem to underestimate the extent of financial exclusion of the hierarchy of the vastly neglected sections of society. Estimates have placed the poor and vulnerable groups at 76.7% of the population (or 836 million) in 2004-05. Financial inclusion is providing banking services at affordable costs to the weaker sections of society or the unbanked segment, which does not have any access to the formal banking system (http://www.rediff.com/money/2005/dec/01guest3.htm). India - the world's second fastest growing economy presents a very uneven picture when it comes to banking. The unbanked population is the highest in the North-East. When it comes to accessing bank loans, the scene is worse. The credit market is very small with the number of loan accounts constituting only 14% of adult population in India. In rural areas, the coverage is 9.5%. Regional differences are glaring with the credit coverage at 25% for the southern region and as low as 7%, 8% and 9%, respectively, in north-eastern, eastern and central India (Hulme, D and Mosley, P. 1996).

Out of 203 million Indian households, three-fourths, or 147 million, are in rural areas and 89 million are farmer households. In this segment, 51.4% have no access to formal or informal sources of credit, while 73% have no access to formal sources of credit (http://www.livemint.com/2007/10/08021019/Targeting-the-unbanked-in-Indi.html). The share of non-institutional sources for finance reduced from 70.8% in 1971 to 42.9% in 2002, but strangely, after 1991 when India opened up its economy, the non-institutional sources' share has increased. The share of moneylenders in the debt of rural households increased from 17.5% in 1991 to 29.6% in 2002. This has happened despite the growing reach of bank branches. (Narayana, D. 2000) There were 8,321 branches of commercial banks and regional rural banks in 1969. Now, there are close to 69,000 branches. With this, the size of average population covered by each bank has been cut drastically—from 64,000 per bank branch to 16,000. While banks tend to avoid small-ticket deposit and loans for fear of rising transaction cost, availability makes informal credit sources popular despite their higher cost. The first serious attempt to spread the message of banking was seen when banks were allowed to utilize the services of non-governmental organizations and microfinance institutions as intermediaries in offering banking services through use of business correspondent model. This essentially allows branchless banking. Meanwhile, between March '06 and '07, banks opened six million no-frill accounts with low or zero minimum balances (http://www.chillibreeze.com/articles_various/Indian-Finance.asp).

Under the National Rural Employment Guarantee Act (NREGA), more than twenty million saving bank accounts have been opened in banks and post offices across the country. This is the largest number of bank accounts linked to a development program across the globe. Of these, more than 1.1 lakh accounts have been opened with post offices and the rest, with public sector or cooperative banks across the rural belt. However, the number of saving accounts would go up even further, if states, which lag in opening accounts, speed up efforts in this regard (Johnson, S and Rogaly, B. 1997). The rural development ministry officials state that despite the spread of rural bank branches, more than 50% of rural households have been deprived of banking services for many years. "This has resulted in the inclusion of a large number of people under the poverty line, with the formal banking system"(www.financialexpress.com).

The banks are looking at several low-cost delivery models such as smart card, mobile banking and point of transaction device and also to set up separate financial inclusion team. The RBI has already asked all private and public sector banks to chart out three plans on a road map on financial inclusion. The plan should cover issues like the number of branches they plan to open in rural India, the number of no-frill accounts they plan and the number of business correspondents they would appoint to achieve the target. (Bhat, N. and Tang, Shui-Yang. 1998).

METHODOLOGY OF STUDY

As a proxy for the class of landless households whose income comes mainly from the earnings of its members from hired labour the investigator picked up for the purpose of this research three sets of households. The first set consists of those households that are landless and whose entire income is derived from hired labour on agricultural or non-agricultural tasks. This set of respondents are called as "landless labour households with no other sources of income" The second set consists of landless households whose members are hired labourers, but also gain income (however small) from self-employment, salaries or remittances. These households' respondents are called "landless labour households with other sources of income". The third set consists of farmers having land and earning income from agriculture. In addition were those respondents who were villagers linked with government schemes as beneficiaries particularly NAREGA etc., some bank officials and members of local NGOs and micro finance institutions and also local money lenders. Thus the following categories of respondents were included under this study.

1. Landless labour households with no other sources of income
2. Landless labour households with other sources of income
3. Farmers having land and farming income
4. Schemes-linked rural people of Vidarbha
5. Private money lenders in rural and urban Vidarbha

6. Bank officials
7. NGOs
8. Members of micro-finance institutions in the area

Stratified sampling method was used for picking up the respondents. They were approached personally for collecting data through verbal interviews in case of primary respondents and through structured questionnaire in other cases. The number of sample respondents, because of the diversified nature of respondents was kept at 650 (which included one third household population of the sample villages and members of other categories of respondents) to facilitate the completion of the research without risking its representativeness. 157 members of a local NGO were involved in facilitating the survey besides 11 students' investigators. The local money lenders were however found to be very cautious in responding to the investigators.

CHRONOLOGY OF EVENTS

It was during an informal chat with top executives of a multinational bank that the idea of a study on micro finance in the rural areas of Vidarbha region of Maharashtra was mooted. It subsequently followed with detail discussions with other executives from this multinational bank to explore the possibility of such study and an intervention by the multinational bank. Accordingly, in coordination with the local NGO four villages from two districts of Vidarbha were so picked up as to comply with the Reserve Bank of India guidelines to a foreign bank for starting any banking business with clients falling within 40 Kilometers range from its local branch. The authors along with a team of eleven student investigators from authors' institution discussed and designed questionnaire for the said study. Two executives from the concerned multinational bank also joined the survey which was conducted later on with support from the local NGO and an NGO from nearby area and another NGO from Ahmedabad. As the analysis of the study came out so the multinational bank moved for clearing the regulatory bottlenecks. One of the regulatory requirements was to seek approval from the District Coordination Committee for stepping into similar type of banking business by it and was obtained in the due course of time. It then followed testing of the equipment (micro-ATM) to be used for providing door-step banking to the villagers. These works took several rounds of visits to the selected villages and consultations with the villagers, Pradhans and also some retail shopkeepers of these villages. It was realised that the Business Correspondent model would be more appropriate to execute the proposed micro banking project. Now came up the question of identity of the clients and it was considered that Unique Identity (UID - Aadhar) would be the best way to sort this issue out. This required Aadhar scheme implementation. The executives of the multinational bank took up the matter with the district authorities in this connection for early Aadhar registration of the natives of the selected village. The Aadhar registration began and in the process two years have passed by for the

UID-enabled banking system to be implemented by the concerned multinational bank for the unbanked community of the area so that they are brought under the gamut of the financial institutions for their economic development. Meanwhile another RBI directives relating to uplinking of hand machines for banking transaction and the cost per transaction cropped up as another impediments on way to implementing this financial inclusion scheme by the bank.

RESULTS AND ANALYSIS

One of the four villages under study has banks within village area where as for the remaining three villages the banks are located at a distance of minimum 3 kms. However household average income of these villagers range from minimum of Rs. 3000 to maximum of Rs. 8000 per month coming from farming, farm labour, other labour (including NAREGA), self employed and pension sources. From 40% to 50% household belong to BPL (below poverty line) families having working women population ranging between 10% and 70%. It is surprising to find that the mobile penetration in these villages is from 80% to 100% and this fact goes in favour of establishing micro-banking system in these villages. Villagers are linked with government schemes and grants and hence have accounts with local banks and the percentage of households with bank account ranges from 50% to 85% with their average banking transaction per month ranging from less than one time to 4-5 times. The noteworthy fact here is that the village with higher average income has higher percentage of household with bank account and has also comparatively higher number of banking transactions per month. They have different types of transactions with their banks such as saving bank accounts, recurring deposit accounts, fixed deposit accounts, agricultural loans, NAREGA disbursement accounts etc. indicating their diversified nature banking transaction requirement. It was also reported that the farmers have to compulsorily open certain types of accounts with the local banks preferable saving bank account and recurring deposit account in order to avail of agricultural loan facilities. Some of the recurring deposits are made by the farmers on daily basis without earning any interest on it from the concerned bank as that bank has put this as a condition for obtaining loans from them. The poor and needy farmers have no choice than to succumb to these conditions of the bank. Inspite of this, the money lenders enjoy robust business with these helpless farmers of the villages.

The villagers are found to have average to good financial literacy. Many of the villagers did not know calculating interest rate payable on the loans received by them and they blindly relied on the bank officials' version of implied interest rate which is simply a disillusion for them. The farmers got surprised when the investigators calculated and showed to them based on their loan and receipts against payment of loan instalments the effective rate of interest paid by them.

The villagers were found to be very enthusiastic about the scheme and hoped that its implementation shall not only sort their host of financial issues but shall also be convenient for them as the banks are located miles away from their villages. The present situation is very pathetic where they mostly approach private lenders for their financial requirements who charge interest rates on the loans as high as 3% per month calculating to 36% per annum. The local cooperative and nationalized banks are also inert towards the villagers' financial requirements that get exploited by the bank officials due to their ignorance in general and lack of financial literacy in particular. It is found that farmers have lot of productive investment requirements and they are capable of refunding their loans even at the exorbitant rate of 36% per annum but they are still under the grip of poor economic conditions simply because of the lack of their connectivity with a genuine financial and / or banking institution. Disconnection from the source of finance to these people having the need of finance appears to be basic cause of the economic backwardness in this region. On the other hand, the banks are looking for profitable advances and loans which these villagers provide but are helplessly away for the reasons of a host of administrative and regulatory impediments in implementing tailor-made financial schemes.

Table 1 shows the details of the villages under study indicating the dire financial requirements by them and also the disconnect between the farmers and the banking organizations in the region.

Table 1: Showing data collected from respondents of sample villages

Criteria / Village	Village			
	Manatri	*Manabda*	*Jawala Palakshed*	*Tintrava*
Area(In Acres)	40	40	35	15
Distance From District HQ	40 km	37 km	35 km	45 km
Major Occupation	20% - Farming	80% - Farming	60% - Farming	95% - Farming
	70% - Farm Labors	15% - Farm workers	35% - Farm workers	5% - Farm workers
	10% - Labors	5% - Others	5% - Others	
No. of Households	300	400	400	400
% of Household below BPL	Approx 50%	40%	45%	50%
Average Household Income	<3000	5000	5000 -7000	5000 -8000
% of Households with Bank A/c	50%	80%	85%	75%
% of Working Women	60%	10%	70%	15%

% of Women having Bank A/c	10%	5 -10%	40%	15%
Name of the nearest Bank	District Coop. Bank	Coop. Bank, Union Bank	Coop. Bank, Credit Societies	Cooperative Bank
Distance from the nearest bank	3 km	5 km, 12 km	Within the village	3 km
Banking Facilities Availed	SB, Agri Loan	SB,RD,FD, Loan	SB,RD,FD, Loan	SB,RD,FD, Loan
Bank Working Hours	11 am - 5pm	11 am - 5pm	11 am - 5pm	11 am - 5pm
Avg no. of Transactions per month	<1 in a month	3-4 in a month	4- 5 in a month	<1 in a month
Govt Grants received	Yes (Minimal)	Yes - NAREGA/ Pension	Yes - NAREGA/ Pension	Yes - NAREGA/ Pension
Financial Literacy	Average/Poor	Good	Good	Average
Interest in Micro Sanchay Program	Highly Interested	Highly Interested	Highly Interested	Highly Interested
Mobile Phone Penetration	85%	80-90%	100%	100%
No. of Kirana Store	5 shops	8 shops	10 shops	9 shops
Avg Daily Turnover(Kirana Store)	Rs 600-700	Rs 1500- 2500	Rs 500 – 2500	Rs 500 - 1500
No. of Local NGO Members	48	43	45	21

CONCLUSIONS

The return from an industrial or business or financial investment comes in two ways – through dividend earning or through price differential earning. The later is the part of speculative business while the former is the mostly preferred option by many individuals and institutions. There is hardly any dividend earning given by a company as high as 36% as the villagers under the case study are able to repay to their financers. If still, these individuals are economically backward, the financial exclusion of this community alone can be blamed for it. The case aptly suggests the immediate need for banking upon the unbanked community of our nation for the benefit of all. Micro-ATM appears to be the answer for quick and convenient linking of the unbanked Indian community with banking and financial institutions. There is a need of government intervention to amend and pass regulatory and legal provisions to facilitate the micro-ATM based micro banking and subsequently micro financing facilities to remote villages for financial inclusion.

ACKNOWLEDGEMENT

The authors express sincere thanks to the All India Council of Technical Education, New Delhi for approving (vide F.No.- 8023/RID/RPS-125(Pvt.)/2011-12)a research proposal under its Research Promotion Scheme for the years 2011-2013 as part of which the present case research has been undertaken. The authors also express their gratitude to 157 members of local NGOs for their help in conducting surveys and the students of their employer college for conducting these surveys. The support of executives of the multinational bank and those of NGOs from Ahmedabad is also acknowledged. The cooperation extended by the framers of the four villages in responding to the queries of the students investigator in filling up the questionnaire for this project is sincerely acknowledged.

REFERENCES

Hossain, M. 1993. "Credit for Alleviation of Rural Poverty: The Grameen Bank in Bangladesh", in Tropicultura, 11, 3, pp. 115-121.

Hulme, D and Mosley, P. 1996. Finance against Poverty, London, Routledge.

Hulme, D and Mosley, P. 1998. "Microenterprise Finance: Is There a Conflict Between Growth and Poverty Alleviation?", in World Development, 26, 5, pp. 783-790.

Johnson, S and Rogaly, B., 1997. Microfinance and Poverty Reduction, OXFAM (UK and Ireland) and ActionAid (UK)

Rural Labour Enquiry(RLE), 1990. Indebtedness Among Rural Labour Households 198,3 Labour Bureau, Government of India

Narayana, D. 2000. "Banking Sector Reforms and the Emerging Inequalities in Commercial Credit Deployment in India" (Thiruvanthapuram, Centre for Development Studies), Working Paper No 300, March.

Bhat, N. and Tang, Shui-Yang. 1998. "The Problem of Transaction Costs in Group-Based Microlending: An Institutional Perspective", in World Development, 26, 4, Apr., pp. 623-637.

http://economictimes.indiatimes.com accessed on 5.12.2011

http://www.financialexpress.com accessed on 24.6.2012

http://www.livemint.com/2007/10/08021019/Targeting-the-unbanked-in-Indi.html accessed on 7.7.2010

http://www.rediff.com/money/2005/dec/01guest3.htm accessed on 19.3.2012

http://www.washingtonpost.com/wp-dyn/content/article/2009/12/04/AR2009120405116.html accessed on 2.8.2011

http://www.articlesbase.com/credit-articles/ajo-banking-for-the-unbanked-and-financially-underserved-populace-at-the-bottom-of-the-pyramid-bop-2691490.html#ixzz0tGO24ceC accessed on 16.6.2010

http://www.packagedfacts.com/Unbanked-1383052/ accessed on 27.1.2012

http://www.reportlinker.com/p057872/Non-traditional-Financial-Services-Markets-in-the-U-S-Unbanked-and-Underbanked-Consumers.html accessed on 3.12.2010

http://www.chillibreeze.com/articles_various/Indian-Finance.asp accessed on 14.9.2011

Stakeholder Dialogue: MNE Green Field Investment in Uruguay

Anna Heikkinen* Johanna Kujala** and Hanna Lehtimäki***

ABSTRACT

This case focuses on the use of stakeholder dialogue in a situation where a multinational company's foreign green field investment raises both opposing and supporting views among the local interest groups. By engaging in this case, the students will deepen their understanding of the multitude of stakeholder interests and learn to facilitate a dialogue, which seeks to find solutions and avoid conflict in a situation of a stakeholder dispute.

Keywords : Stakeholder relationships, stakeholder dialogue, multinational business, foreign investment, conflict.

INTRODUCTION

The values affecting corporations are increasingly pluralistic, and the political and ethical responsibilities are ever more pressed upon corporations (Calvano, 2008; Burchell & Cook, 2008; Hendry, 2005). Multinational enterprises (MNE's) face growing challenges managing the complexity and intensity of interactions across local and global contexts (Meyer, Mudambi, & Narula, 2011). Recent research on MNE's question the established argument that superior performance can be obtained by implementing centralized global strategies, and claims, that a deep understanding about local context is a necessary requirement for success (Ghemawat, 2007). To sustain competitive advantage in a complex business environment, firms are required

*   Anna Heikkinen is a Ph.D. Student, University of Tampere, Finland.
**   Johanna Kujala is Professor, University of Tampere, Finland.
*** Hanna Lehtimäki is Professor, University of Eastern Finland, Kuopio, Finland.
E-mail: Anna.Heikkinen@uta.fi, Johanna.kujala@uta.fi, Hanna.Lehtimäki@uta.fi

to exercise competitive imagination and to reconcile the perspectives of diverse, dispersed and even adversarial actors (Hart & Sharma, 2004).

To better understand the pluralism related to international business, we adopt a stakeholder view to a greenfield investment of a globally operating company.Stakeholder theory concerns defining and exploring important stakeholders, and analysing the nature of stakeholder relationships, firm-stakeholder interaction processes, and the outcomes of these relationships to organisations and their stakeholders (e.g. Freeman & Evan, 1990; Freeman, Harrison & Wicks, 2007; Jones & Wicks, 1999; Mitchell, Agle & Wood., 1997; Rowley, 1997; Savage et al., 1991) Stakeholders are identified based on the stakeholders' stakes, including interests, values, expectations, and claims towards the focal company (Donaldson & Preston, 1995; Näsi, 1995).

In the most recent stakeholder literature, a lot of effort has been placed on understanding stakeholder dialogue (Burchell & Cook, 2006, 2008; Kaptein & van Tulder, 2003; van de Kerkhof, 2006; O'Riordan & Fairbrass, 2008; Payne & Calton, 2004; Pedersen, 2006). It has been argued that a company does not respond to individual stakeholder demands, but rather, to the simultaneous demands of multiple stakeholders (Rowley, 1997) and that a stakeholder may influence and align itself with other stakeholders who have power in order to indirectly impose their will on managers (Zietsma & Winn, 2008). Thus, it is important to understand the multitude of stakeholder interests and learn to facilitate a dialogue, which seeks to find solutions and avoid conflict in a situation of a stakeholder dispute.

THE CASE

The case presents a situation where a Finnish forest industry company, Metsä-Botnia Ltd (hereafter Botnia), was caught in the cross fire of a heated debate between two countries, Uruguay and Argentina. The situation erupted when Botnia decided to build a major pulp mill in the city of Fray Bentos by the Rio Uruguay River in Western Uruguay. Before the investment decision in 2003–2004, Botnia had examined possibilities for starting pulp production in Uruguay. The company carried out studies assessing the prospective environmental and social impacts of the mill, arranged conferences and meetings for the media, local communities and NGOs, invited Uruguayan reporters and politicians to visit Finland, and held local information dissemination sessions in both Uruguay and Argentina. Despite Botnia's efforts to ensure smooth progress of the project, a disagreement arose regarding the mill's location. The Argentine government and local people on the Argentinian side of the Rio Uruguay River voiced environmental concerns related to the pollution of the river and to the negative effect on revenues from tourism. The dispute began as a disagreement between Uruguay and Argentina. Soon, however, it was politicized into an open conflict between the two nations. Argentina decided to take the case to The Hague International Court of Justice. The conflict also erupted into a public issue that attracted various sets of stakeholders, including civic and environmental organizations, local people, workers, financiers, and the governments of Uruguay, Argentina, and Finland. Figure 1 presents the timeline of the conflict with main events.

KEY STAKEHOLDERS

Botnia

The Finnish forest industry group Metsä-Botnia Ltd is Europe's second biggest manufacturer of chemical pulp, with an annual production capacity of 2.4 Million tonnes of bleached softwood and hardwood pulps. The company was founded in 1973 and before the pulp mill investment in Uruguay the company had four pulp mills located in Finland. In 2004, the company had some 2,000 employees and a turnover of over EUR 1 Billion. At the time, Botnia's owners were UPM-Kymmene Corporation (47 per cent), M-real Corporation (47 per cent) and Metsäliitto (6 per cent).

In 2003, Botnia set up a company called Botnia S.A. to investigate prospects for starting pulp production in Uruguay and later to implement the pulp mill project. In 2003, the cost of the investment was estimated USD 1.1 Billion (EUR 830 Million). Once the project was completed, Botnia S.A. began pulp production and related activities in Uruguay. The pulp mill had an annual capacity of one Million tonnes of bleached eucalyptus pulp. Botnia S.A.'s agreed ownership is Botnia (82%), UPM (12%) and Metsäliitto (6%). The other Uruguay based subsidiary is called Compaña Forestal Oriental S.A. (FOSA) whose agreed ownership is Botnia (60%), UPM (38%) and Finnfund (2%). Founded in 1990, FOSA specialises in eucalyptus plantations and in 2005 the company owned 90,000 hectares of land and forest areas in Uruguay, of which 40 per cent was preserved as pastures and sanctuaries. FOSA's plantations received FSC (Forest Stewardship Council) certification.

Uruguayan Government

The Uruguayan government welcomed the pulp mill investment, as it was estimated to boost the country's gross national product (GNP) by more than USD 200 Million a year, accounting for 1.6% of Uruguay's GNP. The mill was estimated to employ about 300 people and to provide direct or indirect jobs for about 8,000 people. Uruguay granted the mill free trade zone status in 2004 for 30 years, during which the company would not pay taxes to the government. Uruguay and Argentina had signed a bilateral agreement, the Uruguay River Statute, in 1975 to protect the use of the Rio Uruguay river requiring both parties to agree on any issue concerning the river.

Argentine Government

The Argentine government opposed the mill claiming that it would cause environmental damage. Further, it claimed that Uruguay had violated the Uruguay River Statute by

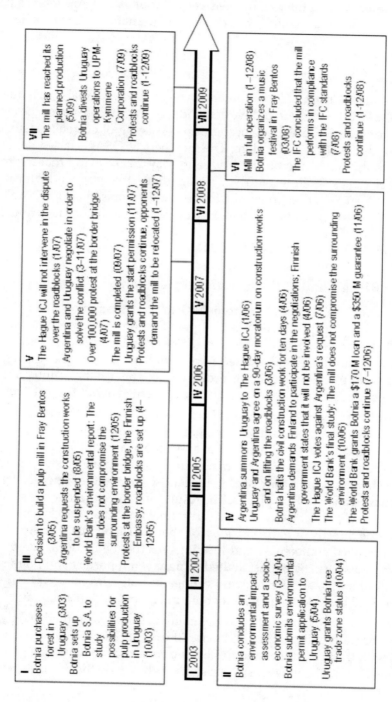

I

Botnia purchases forest in Uruguay (3/03)

Botnia sets up Botnia S.A. to study possibilities for pulp production in Uruguay (10/03)

II

Botnia concludes an environmental impact assessment and a socio-economic survey (3–4/04)

Botnia submits environmental permit application to Uruguay (5/04)

Uruguay grants Botnia free trade zone status (10/04)

III

Decision to build a pulp mill in Fray Bentos (3/05)

Argentina requests the construction works to be suspended (8/05)

World Bank's environmental report: The mill does not compromise the surrounding environment (12/05)

Protests at the border bridge, the Finnish Embassy, roadblocks are set up (4–12/05)

IV

Argentina summons Uruguay to The Hague ICJ (1/06)

Uruguay and Argentina agree on a 90-day moratorium on construction works and on lifting the roadblocks (3/06)

Botnia halts the civil construction work for ten days (4/06)

Argentina demands Finland to participate in the negotiations, Finnish government states that it will not be involved (4/06)

The Hague ICJ votes against Argentina's request (7/06)

The World Bank's final study: The mill does not compromise the surrounding environment (10/06)

The World Bank grants Botnia a $170 M loan and a $350 M guarantee (11/06)

Protests and roadblocks continue (7–12/06)

V

The Hague ICJ will not intervene in the dispute over the roadblocks (1/07)

Argentina and Uruguay negotiate in order to solve the conflict (3–11/07)

Over 100,000 protest at the border bridge (4/07)

The mill is completed (09/07)

Uruguay grants the start permission (11/07)

Protests and roadblocks continue, opponents demand the mill to be relocated (1–12/07)

VI

Mill in full operation (1–12/08)

Botnia organizes a music festival in Fray Bentos (03/08)

The IFC concluded that the mill performs in compliance with the IFC standards (7/08)

Protests and roadblocks continue (1-12/08)

VII

The mill has reached its planned production (5/09)

Botnia divests Uruguay operations to UPM-Kymmene Corporation (7/09)

Protests and roadblocks continue (1-12/09)

I 2003 | II 2004 | III 2005 | IV 2006 | V 2007 | VI 2008 | VII 2009

Fig. 1: Timeline of the main events of the case

allowing Botnia to build the mill by the river without asking Argentina's permission. In 2006, Argentina sued Uruguay to The Hague International Court of Justice (ICJ) to solve the dispute.

CEAG

The Argentinian Citizens Environmental Assembly of Gualeguaychú (hereafter referred to as CEAG) presented their demands for the suspension of the construction works in spring 2005. CEAG is a local group consisting of citizens of Gualeguaychú, a city across the river from the plant. The members of CEAG started demonstrations against the pulp mill at the border bridge in May 2005, saying that the mill would, among other things, pollute the river, contaminate the area, and ruin the tourism business in the area. Further, demonstrations were organised also outside the Finnish Embassy in Buenos Aires and roadblocks were set up on the border bridge.

EVENTS OF THE PULP MILL PROJECT

2003–2004: Background of the Investment Decision

Prior to the investment decision, from 2003 to 2004, Botnia had completed studies on commencing pulp production in Uruguay and on the environmental and social impacts of the proposed mill. Both the environmental impact assessment and the socio-economic survey included interviews with local people in Uruguay, who were mostly in favour of the project for its economic benefits for the country and the jobs it would create. The interviewees were mainly concerned about the local environment.

The results of the environmental impact assessment stated that the pulp mill would have little noticeable effect on the immediate environment or on the quality of water in the Rio Uruguay River and would not affect the health of fish, algae or people. The smell problems would be rare, occurring during start-up and disturbances. The only significant changes would be related to the landscape and the increased traffic during the construction and start-up phases. The results of the socio-economic survey showed that the pulp mill project would have a substantial impact on the Uruguayan economy and to provide directly or indirectly jobs for about 8,000 people. (See Appendix 1.) The company arranged conferences and meetings for the media, local communities, and nongovernmental organizations; invited Uruguayan reporters and politicians to visit Finland; and held local informative meetings in both Uruguay and Argentina. The project received considerable publicity both in Finland and in Uruguay.

In February 2005, Uruguay's environmental authority granted an environmental permit for the pulp mill project. In March 2005, Botnia's Board of Directors decided to go ahead with the investment and to start the construction work of a pulp mill in the city of Fray Bentos. The investment decision was based on the needs of the company's owner-customers; they required eucalyptus pulp to maintain and to improve the quality and competitiveness of their fine paper products. The project was funded mainly through capital investments by Botnia S.A.'s shareholders and by external loans. The loans were provided by the Nordic finance group Nordea, the French investment bank Caylon and the World Bank. The World Bank provided Botnia a EUR 55 Million credit and securities for, inter alia, political risks.

A number of reasons favoured the choice of Uruguay, and the city of Fray Bentos, to be the site for the pulp mill. The fast growing eucalyptus is affordable in Uruguay, where pasturelands have been turned into eucalyptus plantations and trees have been planted since 1980's with the support of the World Bank and the Uruguayan government. The city of Fray Bentos lies close to large eucalyptus plantations and provides logistic and other advantages for pulp production. The mill covers approximately 550 hectares and will use annually 3.5 Million cubic metres of wood raw material. Majority of this wood will be supplied from FOSA's plantations and the remaining 40 per cent of the wood will be purchased through long-term contracts from private forest owners, funds, foundations or cooperatives. In addition, crucial factors for the investment decision were Uruguay's well-developed legislation, clear land ownership rights, and the political stability of the nation. The Uruguayan government had been favourable to foreign investments and the company was granted free trade zone status in 2004.

When the project was kicked off, Botnia expected the pulp mill to start operating in autumn 2007 and estimated that the total cost of the project would be USD 1.1 Billion. Thus, the pulp mill project was going to be the biggest Finnish private sector foreign industrial investment and the biggest industrial investment in the history of Uruguay.

2005: Project launch facing headwind: Construction Works Begin, First Signs of Opposition

The construction work began in September 2005. The city of Fray Bentos used to live on meat processing, whereas nowadays the refinery served as a museum. The citizens were in favour of the mill for the promised job prospects:

'Never mind the pollutants and smells, as long as we get jobs, is the public opinion in Fray Bentos, the home town of Botnia SA, the subsidiary of Metsä-Botnia. This opinion becomes clear from the city's opinion poll and a street poll conducted in the city centre.

"People need jobs and it doesn't matter if the mill pollutes a bit," Maria Acuna says.' (Iivonen, 2005a)

Environmental and civic organisation, Greenpeace and the local CEAG, opposed the project from day one. Greenpeace demonstrated at the mill claiming that the construction work were illegal on the grounds of the Uruguay River Statute. They criticized the company for polluting the environment and demanded the mill to be relocated to an area where it would not harm local livelihoods. Similarly Argentinians feared that the mill would pollute the river, foul the area, and ruin the tourism business. The first anti-pulp mill protests on the border bridge were already organised in spring 2005. In autumn, a massive protest brought together 15,000 people to oppose the pulp mill. The protest was called Grito Blanco (White Cry) after the participating pupils' white uniforms and it was one of the first events to receive international media attention. The protestors also set up roadblocks on the border bridge. The first protest at the Finnish Embassy in Buenos Aires, Argentina, was organised in December 2005 and the protestors strove to appeal to the decision-makers emotions:

> '"We do not want death upon the Rio Uruguay River. We demand the mills to be shut down immediately, for they will pollute our children's future. This is a protest for peace, environment and life," clarifies Gualeguaychúan Alejandro Gahan.' (Pohjola, 2005)

The Argentinean protestors claimed that Botnia would use technology that was prohibited in Europe. The company felt that their efforts to enclose information were unfruitful:

> 'Botnia has not been able to influence Argentinians' opinions, even though the mill's environmental impact assessment is a public document. "I doubt that anyone in Argentina has read it or that the general public has the faintest idea of this industry. And if they do, it is an image of the old industry," Varis [Botnia's CEO] states.' (Iivonen, 2005b)

Quarrel between Argentina and Uruguay

The governments of Argentina and Uruguay disagreed about the pulp mill as Argentina criticized the environmental impact assessment concluded by Botnia and demanded the construction work to be suspended until a new environmental assessment was concluded. In addition, Argentina claimed that the Uruguayan government had not asked its permission to build the mill on the border river, even though the use of the Rio Uruguay River was protected by a 1975 bilateral agreement. When Argentina demanded the construction work of the mill to be suspended, Uruguay was stuck between a rock and a hard place – the continuation of the construction work and the operations of the mill would bring significant economic benefits to the area and the country. However, Uruguay did not want to risk the long-standing relations to

Argentina or harm the economy, as the roadblocks were inflicting losses especially for the tourism industry.

In June 2005, the presidents of the neighbouring countries agreed to set up a joint committee to assess the environmental impacts. Additionally, the main financier of the mill, the World Bank Group's International Finance Corporation (IFC), started a cumulative impact study in July. In August, Argentina stated that the project had to be suspended pending the completion of the environmental report and threatened to summon Uruguay to The Hague International Court of Justice (ICJ) to resolve the dispute. In November 2005, the IFC published the results of the cumulative impact study announcing that the mill would not harm the environment. The Argentine government declared that the report was preliminary and inadequate. In December, the Uruguayan government refused an official request by the Argentine government to suspend the construction works.

2006: The storm is rising : Suspension of the construction works

During spring 2006, the quarrel between Uruguay and Argentina turned into a raging storm. The Argentine government and CEAG had demanded the construction work to be suspended already in 2005 until the arrival of the new environmental report. In December 2005, Argentina officially requested that Uruguay halt the construction work, but as the Uruguayan government refused, the dispute inevitably erupted. In March 2006, however, the presidents of Uruguay and Argentina appealed for a 90-day moratorium on construction works until a new, independent environmental impact study had taken place. They also agreed that the roadblocks damaging to the Uruguayan economy and free movement of people and goods would be lifted. The employees and residents of Fray Bentos opposed the suspension, as they feared job losses and the loss of the economic benefits of the pulp mill project. A demonstration in favour of the mill was organised in Fray Bentos to object to the demands to suspend the construction work.

After the appeal for suspension, the representatives of Botnia stated that the construction would go ahead in spite of any appeal:

'Botnia is expecting an official statement from the Uruguay government concerning a request that the work be suspended.'

"We are waiting for the government's proposal before we take a stand on the issue," explains Botnia's President and CEO Erkki Varis.

"There are no legal grounds for suspending construction work. We shall assess the situation once we know the contents of the government's proposal. We will then be in a position to make an announcement."' (Oy Metsä-Botnia Ab, 2006b)

Later Botnia halted the works for ten days instead of the 90 days required by the presidents in order to help find a solution to the dispute between Uruguay and Argentina:

'With the purpose of contributing to opening a space for dialogue between the republics of Uruguay and Argentina and answering the requests made by Presidents Tabaré Vazquez and Nestor Kirchner, Botnia is willing to suspend, during a maximum period of 10 days, the works of installation of the pulp mill that is being built in the city of Fray Bentos, Department of Rio Negro in Uruguay.

The Uruguayan government has informed that in this period of time both countries will study the environmental impact that the mills could generate in the region. To facilitate this, the company will give all the information needed in order to clarify the doubts that might exist and to ensure the correct conditions of operation and control of the pulp mills.' (Oy Metsä-Botnia Ab, 2006a)

The presidents had already agreed that they would negotiate during the moratorium, but as Botnia refused to cooperate, relations were broken off. The quarrel caused frustration in Botnia:

'Metsä-Botnia's CEO Erkki Varis can't figure out why the presidents of Uruguay and Argentina won't meet in order to solve the dispute related to the Fray Bentos pulp mill project. Botnia has been accused of having an attitude that has so far prevented the meeting of the presidents.

"There always has to be someone to blame. If that someone has to be us, then so be it," Varis snorts.' (STT, 2006)

Proceedings in The Hague ICJ

In January 2006, Argentina declared that it would take the case to The Hague ICJ. Argentina accused Uruguay of violating the Uruguay River Statute by authorising the construction project without prior consultation with Argentina and demanded the project to be suspended. The court proceedings were closely followed by the international press and turned the conflict into an internationally notable issue. Botnia's CEO commented on the court proceedings:

'"Taking the dispute to The Hague was no surprise," says Metsä-Botnia's CEO Erkki Varis. He emphasizes that Metsä-Botnia is not a party in the court case involving Argentina and Uruguay.

Varis assesses that it is not very likely that the court should demand the construction work to be suspended.

According to Varis the recent developments of the dispute may even ease the tense situation. "Acute quarrelling may decrease. Argentina has now removed the roadblocks because a process like this makes it difficult to perform illegal operations," Varis states.' (Width, 2006)

In response to this, Uruguay took the case to Mercosur, claiming that Argentina had prevented the free circulation of goods and services by allowing the roadblocks to be set up. In July 2006, The Hague ICJ ruled that there were no grounds for imposing suspension on the work of the pulp mill project. Argentineans were dissatisfied with the ruling.

Demands for the Finnish Government to Intervene

In spring 2006, the Argentine government requested the Finnish government to help to resolve the conflict. The government, however, responded that they would not intervene. The Finnish Minister of Foreign Trade and Development stated that Uruguay, Argentina and Botnia as a private company should resolve the conflict.

Demonstrations were organised outside the Finnish Embassy in Buenos Aires, and the demonstrators called for Finland to bear its responsibility:

"'Finland, listen to the voice of the peoples!" "Finland, stop the lies!" urged the signs of the protestors opposing Metsä-Botnia's pulp mill in Uruguay at the Finnish Embassy in Buenos Aires on Tuesday morning.

Approximately 200 protestors wearing gas-mask demonstrated against the Finnish government, in order for it to 'bear its responsibility' in the pulp mill conflict.' (Pohjola, 2006)

In August 2006, the representatives of civic and environmental organisations visited Finland and delivered a petition of over 40,000 signatures from Gualeguaychú to the Finnish Minister of Foreign Trade and Development. The Minister reiterated that the Finnish government is not a party to the conflict.

The IFC's decision-making process

The World Bank's IFC had commenced an independent environmental impact assessment in September 2005, as Argentina had criticized the initial assessment carried out by Botnia. The draft impact assessment was published in December 2005, and it stated that the technical requirements for the pulp mill had been fulfilled and that the quality of water and air should not be impaired. The Argentine government sent an official letter to the IFC protesting against the study in January 2006 and the IFC embarked on another assessment. In response, Botnia publicly accused Argentina of delaying the financing decision. The members of CEAG endeavoured to influence the financing banks by demonstrations and roadblocks, as well as by writing letters to the banks.

The new impact assessment was completed in April 2006, and the IFC stated that it needed further consultations. The interest of Botnia's management was to provide the IFC with the best available information to ensure fair decision-making, and thus they agreed to participate in another assessment.

In October, the members of CEAG set up the roadblocks again, despite Argentina's objection:

> 'According to Argentina it is a mistake to close the roads for it impairs the country's standing in the Hague ICJ.
>
> The new protests are spurred by the recent environmental report released by the World Bank's IFC. Many of the local residents feel that the roadblocks are their only means to influence the World Bank for deciding not to fund the Botnia mill.' ('Botnian vastustajat', 2006.)

The final version of the environmental study was released in October and it stated that the pulp mill would not harm the environment and that it would benefit the Uruguayan economy.

In November, Botnia announced that will utilise its know-how to improve the quality of the water of the Rio Uruguay River. The company stated that it will work together with relevant authorities and companies in Uruguay to enable the treatment of domestic sewage from the city of Fray Bentos in the mill's effluent treatment plan.

Despite fierce criticism from Argentina, the IFC and MIGA (Multilateral Investment Guarantee Agency) granted a USD 170 Million loan and a USD 350 Million guarantee for the project in November. The Argentine president responded by emphasising that they would not prevent the roadblocks, which compelled Uruguay to take the case to The Hague ICJ. In December the installation work begun at the mill and the number of workers peaked with 4,000 people.

2007: Start-up in the Midst of Continuing Controversy

In spring 2007, Argentina and Uruguay tried to resolve the conflict in negotiations led by the King of Spain and his representatives. The negotiating parties expected the Finnish government and Botnia to participate in these negotiations. A lot was expected of these negotiations, but they turned out to be unsuccessful. At the same time, the opponents demanded that the construction work should be suspended in order to maintain peace in the society and they stated that if the mill began its operations, they would regard it as a declaration of war. A massive demonstration of over 100,000 participants was organised in April 2007.

The construction and installation works were completed by September 2007. Uruguay gave authorisation for the plant to start operations in November. A few days before the start-up, Botnia released a pre-start-up audit report confirming that the mill would operate according to Best Available Techniques (BAT). The main conclusions of the report were:

- The mill project organization met with the operational objectives including the environmental management goals.
- All process equipment and technology installed or planned to be installed was similar or equivalent to best available techniques as described in the CIS.
- The mill management team had an appropriate level of environmental awareness for a project of this type.
- There was a comprehensive personnel training programme in place and experienced staff were being used for start-up.
- The overall impression was gained of a well designed and generally well executed project, with competent and motivated staff. Modern process technologies were used that promised to perform with low emission and world-leading environmental performance. (Oy Metsä-Botnia Ab, 2007)

The mill started its operations on November 9, 2007. See Appendix 2 for project fact sheet.

2008–2009: Production in Full Speed

In early 2008, the mill was in full operation and deliveries to customers in Europe and China commenced. In March, Botnia organized a music festival in Fray Bentos with the local authorities, and in April 2008, Botnia launched an educational, travelling exhibition on pulp production process in Fray Bentos. The activists continued their protests, insisting that they would not lift the roadblocks unless the mill was relocated. In July 2008, the IFC publicly released the first environmental monitoring report of the pulp mill. According to the report, the mill was performing in compliance with the air and water quality standards required by the IFC.

In May 2009, Botnia announced that the mill had reached its planned production and had produced to date more than 1,300,000 tons of pulp. In July 2009, Botnia announced that the Uruguay operations would be divested to UPM-Kymmene Corporation, another Finnish forest industry company and that Botnia would focus on being the premier supplier of Finnish pulp through its' Finland based mills.

The protests and roadblocks continued through 2008 and 2009. Some of the protestors were disappointed that the roadblocks had no effect on the mill, while others feared that the removing of the roadblocks would result in the opposition dying out of the public eye.

CONCLUSIONS

This case presents a situation were a Finnish forest industry company's investment project in Uruguay was caught in a heated debate between two nations – Uruguay and Argentina. The case discusses the background of the investment decision and Botnia's efforts to ensure the smooth operations of the project. Project assessments concluded before the investment decision showed that the pulp mill project would bring economic benefits to the area and that it would not harm the environment. However, environmental organisations and the Argentine government opposed the project fiercely, which caused a great deal of tension surrounding the project and brought international media attention to the case. Despite the opposition, the construction work was concluded by the end of 2007 and the mill started its operations.

From a stakeholder dialogue point of view, this case raises an intriguing issue. The company strove to ensure that all stakeholders are taken into consideration during the decision-making process, and yet it faced fierce opposition hampering the project. When Botnia and the Finnish Embassy tried to inform the opposing groups during the project, they did not want to listen.

Interactive or multi-voiced dialogue is seen as a more efficient and satisfactory way of communicating than ad hoc or one-way communication (Crane & Livesey, 2003). In a conflict situation, a company could increase stakeholder involvement, provide stakeholders with more information on its strategic plans and operations, and engage in more communication with different stakeholders. The company could, for instance, set up discussion forums for the different stakeholders to voice their views or provide messages tailored to different stakeholders. Key to the communication is to identify with the stakeholders and seek an understanding and appreciation of the stakeholder concerns. This would require adopting a stakeholder viewpoint to the operations of the company.

We conclude that stakeholder dialogue is an aspect of relationship management and a process where the firm and its stakeholders learn to live with multiple realities. The case shows how a dispute of this magnitude is about a company's investment policy and strategy, local politics and global politics, and the same situation can be presented both as a question of foreign investment creating work and wealth and as a political question where two countries are disputing with each other and seeking international support for their views. Each different construction of the situation builds and legitimizes the identities of different stakeholders, and thus also legitimizes the interests and actions of each stakeholder. The challenge both for academic researchers and business managers lies in developing tools and methods for stakeholder dialogue that help the company to understand the multi-voiced nature of this dialogue and lead it to take responsibility in the process.

QUESTIONS

1. In the case introduction, Botnia, the Uruguayan and Argentine governments and the environmental organization CEAG are introduced as key stakeholders. What interests in the case do these stakeholders have, and how do these interests evolve throughout the conflict?

2. What other stakeholders are involved in the case, what are their interests and how they change during the conflict?

3. What kinds of arguments do the stakeholders opposing the pulp mill project present to support their view? How about the defensive stakeholders? What hopes, fears and demands do these stakeholders have as groups or individuals, and why?

4. What kinds of solutions could there be to solve the conflict? Is there any room for a compromise? How could Botnia engage with finding a way out? What other possibilities are there?

5. Would it be possible to build a stakeholder dialogue between the company and its stakeholders? How would you do it?

REFERENCES

Botnian vastustajat sulkevat taas tien. [Botnia's opposers block the road again]. (2006, October 12). *Helsingin Sanomat*. Retrieved from http://www.hs.fi

Burchell, J. & Cook, J. (2008). Stakeholder dialogue and organisational learning: changing relationships between companies and NGOs. *Business Ethics: A European Review*, 17 (1), 35–46.

Calvano, L. (2008). Multinational Corporations and Local Communities: A Critical Analysis of Conflict. *Journal of Business Ethics*, 82 (4), 793–805.

Crane, A., & Livesey, S. (2003). Are You Talking to Me? Stakeholder Communication and the Risks and Rewards of Dialogue. In J. Andriof, S. Waddock, B. Husted & S. Sutherland Rahman (Eds.), *Unfolding Stakeholder Thinking 2: Relationships, Communication, Reporting and Performance*, 39–52. Sheffield: Greenleaf Publishing Limited.

Donaldson, T. & Preston, L.E. (1995). The Stakeholder Theory of the Corporation: Concepts, Evidence, and Implications. *Academy of Management Review* 20(1), 65–91.

Freeman, R. E. & Evan, W. M. (1990). Corporate Governance: A Stakeholder Interpretation. *The Journal of Behavioral Economics*, 19, 337–359.

Freeman, R. E., Harrison, J. & Wicks, A. (2007). *Managing for Stakeholders. Survival, Reputation, and Success*. London: Yale University Press.

Ghemawat,P(2007)*Redifining Global Strategy*,Boston,MA:Harvard Business School Press.

Hart, S. & Sharma, S. (2004). Engaging fringe stakeholders for competitive imagination. *Academy of Management Executive*, 18 (1), 7–18.

Hendry, J. R. (2005). Stakeholder Influence Strategies: An Empirical Examination. *Journal of Business Ethics*, 61, 79–99.

Iivonen, J. (2005a, May 22). Fray Bentosin pikkukaupunki toivottaa sellutehtaan työpaikat tervetulleeksi. [The small town of Fray Bentos welcomes pulp mill jobs]. *Helsingin Sanomat*. Retrieved from http://www.hs.fi

Iivonen, J. (2005b, August 11). Argentiina vaatii Botnian selluhankkeen keskeyttämistä. [Argentina demands Botnia's pulp mill project to be suspended]. *Helsingin Sanomat*. Retrieved from http://www.hs.fi

Jones, T. M. & Wicks, A. C. (1999). Convergent stakeholder theory. *Academy of Management Review*, 24 (2), 206–221.

Kaptein, M. & van Tulder, R. (2003). Toward Effective Stakeholder Dialogue. *Business and Society Review*, 108 (2), 203–224.

van de Kerkhof, M. (2006). Making a difference: On the constraints of consensus building and the relevance of deliberation in stakeholder dialogues. *Policy Sciences*, *39*(3), 279–299.

Meyer, K. E., Mudambi, R. & Narula, R. (2011). Multinational Enterprises and Local Contexts: The Opportunities and Challenges of Multiple Embeddedness. *Journal of Management Studies*, 48 (2), 235–252.

Mitchell, R. K., Agle, B. R. & Wood, D. J. (1997). Toward a Theory of Stakeholder Identification and Salience: Defining the Principle of Who and what really Counts. *Academy of Management Review*, 22 (4), 853–886.

Näsi, J. (1995). What is Stakeholder Thinking? In Näsi, J. (ed.) *Understanding Stakeholder Thinking*. Helsinki: LSR-Publications.

O'Riordan, L. & Fairbrass, J. (2008). Corporate Social Responsibility (CSR): Models and Theories in Stakeholder Dialogue. *Journal of Business Ethics*, 83, 745–758.

Payne, S. L. & Calton, J. M. (2004). Exploring Research Potentials and Applications for Multi-stakeholder Learning Dialogues. *Journal of Business Ethics*, 55 (1), 71–78.

Pedersen, E. R. (2006). Making Corporate Social Responsibility (CSR) Operable: How Companies Translate Stakeholder Dialogue into Practice. *Business and Society Review*, 111 (2), 137–163.

Pohjola, J. (2005, December 8). Botnian sellutehtaan vastustajat osoittivat mieltään Argentiinassa. [The opposers of Botnia's pulp mill demonstrated in Argentina]. *Helsingin Sanomat*. Retrieved from http://www.hs.fi

Pohjola, J. (2006, April 26). Botnian vastustajat protestoivat Argentiinassa. [Botnia's opposers protested in Argentina]. *Helsingin Sanomat*. Retrieved from http://www.hs.fi

Oy Metsä-Botnia Ab. (2006a). *Botnia willing to suspend installation* [Press release]. Retrieved from http://www.botnia.fi

Oy Metsä-Botnia Ab. (2007). *Pre-start-up audit report confirms that Botnia's Fray Bentos mill will operate according to Best Available Techniques (BAT)* [Press release]. Retrieved from http://www.botnia.fi

Rowley, T. J. (1997). Moving Beyond Dyadic Ties: a Network Theory of Stakeholder Influences. *Academy of Management Review*, 22 (4), 887–910.

Savage, G. T., Nix, T. W., Whitehead, C. J. & Blair, J. D. (1991). Strategies for assessing and managing organizational stakeholders. *Academy of Management Executive*, 5 (2), 61–75.

STT. (2006, April 8). Botnia keskeytti työt väliaikaisesti Uruguayssa. [Botnia suspended works in Uruguay]. *Helsingin Sanomat*. Retrieved from http://www.hs.fi

Width, T. (2006, May 6). Argentiinan valtio vei sellutehdaskiistan Haagiin. [The Argentine government took the pulp mill dispute to The Hague]. *Helsingin Sanomat*. Retrieved from http://www.hs.fi

Zietsma, C. & Winn, M. I. (2008). Building Chains and Directing Flows: Strategies and Tactics of Mutual Influence in Stakeholder Conflict. *Business & Society*, 47 (1), 68–101.

APPENDIX 1 Press release 3 May 2004

BOTNIA   1 (2)

Communications
Annikki Rintala   3 May 2004

**BOTNIA'S ENVIRONMENTAL PERMIT APPLICATION SUBMITTED TO URUGUAY EN-
VIRONMENT AUTHORITIES**

Towards the end of last year Botnia began investigating the possibility of starting pulp production in Uruguay. The related environmental impact assessment that began last November
were completed at the end of March and the socio-economic evaluation at the end of April.
Botnia has submitted the findings to the Uruguay environment authorities. Processing of the
environmental impact assessment will take roughly five months, following which the Uruguay
authorities will issue their decision.

The results of the socio-economic survey show that the construction and operation of a pulp
mill will have a substantial impact on the Uruguayan economy. The project will permanently
boost the country's gross national product (GNP) by more than USD 200 million a year,
which represents 1.6% of Uruguay's present GNP. The mill will bring the government around
USD 25 million in annual tax revenues.

The pulp mill will create a total of more than 8,000 new jobs, the direct impact on employment
being around 5,000 jobs. Most of these will be in forestry and transport. The mill itself will
employ 300 people.

The both surveys included interviews with local people. Most of those interviewed were in
favour of the project because it would create jobs and boost the economy. The main area of
concern was the environment.

According to the results of the environmental impact assessment, the pulp mill would have
little noticeable effect on the immediate environment or on the quality of water in the river
Uruguay. The only significant change environmentally would concern the landscape. A substantial increase in traffic is also expected both during the construction phase and after the
mill goes into production. The mill will only rarely cause smell problems, which may occur
during disturbances and during start-up.

The mill will employ the best available technology and this, together with the high volumetric
flow of the river Uruguay (c. 6,000 m^3/s), means wastewaters from the mill would have no
material impact on the quality of the river's water.

None of the changes attributable to the mill will be visible in the area's biological environment
and will therefore not affect the health of fish, algae or people.

The site chosen for the mill, which will produce one million tonnes a year of bleached eucalyptus pulp, is the town of Fray Bentos. The town has 20,000 inhabitants and stands on the
river Uruguay in the west of the country. A decision on the USD 1 billion investment will be
possible towards the end of this year once all the necessary permits have been obtained.
The timing of the decision will also be affected by the fibre needs of Botnia's owners and by
the general economic situation.

APPENDIX 2 Fact sheet November 2007

BOTNIA

BOTNIA'S PULP MILL PROJECT IN URUGUAY

General
- Location   City of Fray Bentos in Western Uruguay
- Cost estimate   USD 1.2 billion
- Capacity   1 million tons of ECF bleached (elemental chlorine free) eucalyptus pulp/year
- Used technology   Best available techniques (IPPC-BAT) with minimal environmental impact

Milestones
- Investment treaty ratified between Finland and Uruguay in 2004
- Free Trade Zone status granted in 2004
- Environmental permit granted in February 2005
- Investment decision made in March 2005
- Excavation works started in April 2005
- Construction works began in September 2005
- Start-up in November 2007

Socioeconomic impacts in Uruguay
- Impact on Uruguay: GDP increase by estimated 1.6%
- Employment effect during construction period
  - Max. 5,300 at the site
- Employment effect during pulp mill operations
  - Direct new jobs 3,000 (mill, forestry, logistics)
  - Indirect new jobs 5,000
  - Total job creation approximately 8,000

Largest ever construction project in Uruguay
- Total manhours worked during construction: 15.000.000.
- Total cargo transported: 58.000 tons
- Participation of 64 companies

In commissioning and testing:
- More than 100 people coordinating the commissioning activities
- 25 work teams operating in different areas
- Tests completed on 150 km pipelines, 2,000 motors and 1,200 km cable
- Inspections conducted in more than 150 tanks and daily approximately 200 X-ray inspections done for tanks and pipes

BOTNIA

Environmental impacts
as defined in CIS (Ecometrix) and Experts Report (Hatfield Consultants)
- No biological impacts on the Uruguay River
- Occasional and minor local odour problems
- No significant noise problems
- No health impacts in the environment
- Main impacts in traffic and landscape
- No impacts on present livelihoods in the area (agriculture, tourism)

European suppliers
- Main supplier Andritz AG
- Other suppliers Siemens AG, Degremont S.A., Butting GmbH, ABB, DHL, Alstom

Machinery
Fibreline:
- 3,200 t/d digester with Lo-Solids process resulting in high cooking yield
- 9 DD washers
- ECF bleaching with hexenuronic acid removal -> lowest bleaching chemical consumption in the reference mills around the world
- Two drying machines ensuring continuous productivity with 3,600 admt/d capacity
- 4 baling lines

Chemical recovery:
- 7-effect evaporation plant
- 4,450 tds/d recovery boiler
- 10,000 m^3/d white liquor plant

Energy self-sufficiency 165 %

Financing
- Ca. 60% as equity from Botnia and other stakeholders
- Ca. 40% debt financing through World Bank, export credit agencies, NIB and commercial banks

PART II: Innovations and Technology

It is not easy to define innovation, although it is recognised as a buzzword to every bodys liking. There is hardly any course in the omni- programme of management studies where the virtues of innovation are not counted . Innovation is cited as the mantra of reviving sickness in any functional area or management process. Majorly it is referred to an idea which is non-obvious, a concept which suggests new function or 'jugad' in India's wisdom which makes an existing operation more efficient. It may or may not have technology element coming from a disciplined technology education. Technology on the other hand is usually considered to emanate from labs, educational programmes and carries newness of product, process or approach. Because of the synergy of approach and benefits that accrue, the cases have been grouped together . There are a total of five cases. Three of them focus on application of new technology. One of them refers to attempts to find funds for innovative projects. One of them concern management of innovation.

Geographical Information Systems (GIS) has emerged as a very useful tool for analyzing public health data. Uma Kelekar and Xiang Liu in Chapter 6 review the use of visualization techniques and spatial analysis generated in GIS for decision support in the field of public health by some of the developing countries. It extends the study by examining the potential uses of GIS applications for public health decision-making, specifically disease surveillance in the Philippines.

Crowdsourcing has been the core model behind many Internet success stories. Mini War Gaming uses this model for raising funds through many small donations from its eager supporters. Daniel Roy in Chapter 7 explores successful use of a new and innovative approach for financing NPD projects by a Canadian small business.

Enterprise Resource Planning is an enterprise solution software system that allows a company to automate and integrate the majority of its business processes, and share common data and practices across the enterprise through integration of various functions in the organization. Resmi et al in Chapter 8 discuss an application at Food Corporation of India and bring out comparison of ERP software with bespoke software.

Marketing of software firm is a challenging task. This requires constant analysis of customer needs and technology upgradation. Surabhi Singh in Chapter 9, identifies the marketing challenges small software firms face during the growth process. This case illustrates the determinants of successful marketing strategy for the software firm and how it impacts the future of the firm.

P&G has a long history of envisioning sustainability as a responsibility to do the right things for the environment and for human safety. P&G strives to ensure that consumers need not make a choice between sustainability, performance, and value. Raveesh Agarwal and Monica Thiel present a study in Chapter 10, on Life Cycle Assessment (LCA) adopted by P & G to deliver sustainable innovations.

Geographic Information System Applications in Public Health – A Decision-making Tool for Public Health Managers in the Philippines

Uma Kelekar* and Xiang Liu*

ABSTRACT

Geographical Information Systems (GIS) has emerged as a very useful tool for analyzing public health data. However, the application of GIS in the developing countries is not as widespread as in the developed world. This paper reviews the use of visualization techniques and spatial analysis generated in GIS for decision support in the field of public health by some of the developing countries. It extends the study by examining the potential uses of GIS applications for public health decision-making, specifically disease surveillance in the Philippines. It particularly explores the spatial aspects of diarrhea incidence among provinces in the Philippines – its spatial distribution and dependence with neighboring provinces. The uses of exploring the geographic aspects of the disease from the perspective of planning and management are also discussed.

Keywords: Public health management, disease surveillance, spatial analysis.

INTRODUCTION

Infectious or communicable diseases have a significant spatial component associated with them, where people, place and time constitute basic elements of outbreak investigations and epidemiology (Moore & Carpenter, 1999). Infections may be easily transmitted within a network of individuals in close geographic proximity to one another. In order to control and manage the outbreaks as well as minimize the associated direct and indirect costs, epidemiologic surveillance and response (ESR) is a critical function of the national and local public health managers. Epidemiologic surveillance and management require a standardized methodology, relevant tools

---

* Marymount University, USA.
E-mail: ukelekar@marymount.edu

for data collection, and timely dissemination of information to the public health managers. Historically, the importance of geography has been demonstrated in several epidemiological studies (Moore and Carpenter, 1999)[1]. And in the last decade, Geographic Information System (GIS) (will be referred to as GIS now onwards), a computer program used to store, manipulate, analyze and display data in a geographic context has proved to be one of the very useful tools for health care research and epidemiology (Law & Wilfert, 2007; Moore & Carpenter, 1999).

GIS has emerged as an effective evidence-based technology for the early detection, communication and timely response to disease outbreaks. The standardized geo-referenced epidemiological or socio-demographic data may be collected, mapped and analyzed using GIS to reveal significant trends or interrelationships that may not be easily understood in a tabular format[2]. Mapping of data depicts the spread or intensity of hosts/vectors or diseases across regions. This information in turn might be related to the potential sources of the diseases and consequently be used to eradicate the disease in a more focused and cost-effective way (Law & Wilfert, 2007; Moore & Carpenter, 1999; Wiafe & Davenhall, 2005). Global positioning systems (GPS) add an additional functionality to GIS in detecting and addressing outbreaks. It offers a tool to precisely identify the location of research subjects and their distances to specific geographic features that are likely to be associated with an outbreak (Law & Wilfert, 2007).

Recently, an experimental tool launched by Google called Google Flu Trends (available at *http://www.google.org/flutrends/*) shed light on 'near real-time detection of influenza outbreaks' in the United States (Carneiro & Mylonakis, 2009). Distinct from the traditional disease surveillance system that relies on clinical data, this tool utilizes and analyzes care-seeking information sought by individuals through online Google queries (Carneiro & Mylonakis, 2009, p.1557; Ginsberg et al., 2009). Although this system is better suited to track diseases in developed countries due to a large volume of Internet users, inventors and developers of the Google Flu Trends will eventually aim at applying these models in global settings.

This study aims at highlighting the uses of GIS in disease surveillance and management, one of the key functions of public health managers in the Philippines. The applications of GIS are demonstrated through maps that help to visualize the incidence of a disease and analyze the spatial dimension with the help of spatial regressions. From a public health management and policy perspective, the goal of this analysis is to highlight the benefits of mapping disease incidence and analyze the

---

[1]   The earliest epidemiological investigation in 1854 by John Snow mapped cholera incidence spatially. The spatial aspects of the outbreak led him to hypothesize that one particular water supply could be the source of the outbreak (Law & Wilfert, 2007). Another spatial investigation was that of Burkitt's lymphoma of children in Africa in 1950s (Moore & Carpenter, 1999).

[2]   GIS displays different kinds of information in map "layers".

spatial relationship of the incidence of diarrhea with that in the neighboring provinces. Further, it also demonstrates the need for public health managers to coordinate with their neighbors in the Philippines to work together in an effort to control and manage the spread of infectious diseases. By exploring the spatial dimension of a disease in addition to the other determinants, public health managers will be able to allocate and manage resources more efficiently.

The paper is organized as follows. Second outlines some of the relevant applications of GIS in the public health management field, specifically disease surveillance and management in several developing countries, followed by the existing applications of GIS in the Philippines in the next section. The research methods, specifically the spatial techniques are discussed in the next section. The results of the analysis are presented in the next section. Conclusion next discusses the policy implications and recommendations to public health managers.

BACKGROUND

The GIS technology has been widely used in areas of health care research, forecasting and planning in the context of the developing world by international organizations (e.g., (e.g., Clarke, McLafferty, & Tempalski, 1996; Moore & Carpenter, 1999; Myers et al., 2000). In an effort to eradicate Guinea worm disease in 1993, the World Health Organization and United Nations Children's Fund (UNICEF) developed a Public Health Mapping Programme using GIS to visualize, monitor and curb the spread of the diseases. Since the Guinea worm disease project, there were other disease control initiatives set up to eradicate diseases including river blindness, sleeping sickness, or elephantiasis using some of the GIS applications. Of particular interest to developing countries, WHO and its partners adopted software applications called the Health Mapper and Roll Back Malaria for mapping and surveillance of lymphatic filariasis and malaria respectively (Law & Wilfert, 2007).

Although GIS applications have been widely used in the developed world, they remain an under-utilized analytical tool in the developing countries (Tanser, 2006). Limited access to infrastructure, technology and cost constraints pose challenges for the developing countries to collect reliable data, monitor and detect epidemics, or manage disease outbreaks (Tanser, 2006). However, the recent outbreaks of infectious diseases, particularly severe acute respiratory syndrome (SARS), H5N1 avian influenza, and drug-resistant tuberculosis, have brought the relevance of GIS to the attention of public health managers and policy-makers in order to carry out efficient and timely disease surveillance in the developing world.

Despite its various obstacles, more and more developing countries have taken first steps in applying GIS towards public health management. For example, GIS was used in Thailand to analyze data of infectious diseases and their sites of occurrence. Both spatial and statistical analyses were applied in order to visualize disease distribution and obtain information critical to health care decision-making processes (Keola et al., 2002). In rural South Africa, a spatial epidemiologist used GIS as a research and planning tool to design and plan health service in the Hlabisa subdistrict in order to maximize the population having access to primary health care facilities (Tanser, 2006). A similar project was accomplished in the state of Karnataka in India in 2002. The major goal of this project was to optimize health resources and to cover clients' needs (Mesgari & Masoomi, 2008).

In Egypt, a project used satellite data to develop a GIS environmental risk model, which increased the accuracy of schistosomiasis control program decisions (Abdel-Rahman et al., 2001). In Iran, GIS was used to analyze geographical data and the linked statistical and attribute data to monitor and control diseases (Mesgari & Masoomi, 2008). The geo-statistical model was built to capture the relationship between diseases and their explanatory factors.

GIS APPLICATIONS IN THE PHILIPPINES

The Philippines comprises of 7,000 islands categorized into three groups: Luzon, Visayas and Mindanao. It is composed of 80 provinces and the National Capita Region that is comprised of 17 cities/municipalities. As of 2011, the Philippines is the world's 12th most populous country and the 7th most populated Asian country, with a population of over 94 million (National Statistics Office of the Republic of the Philippines, 2012). Due to its geographical location (on the western fringes of the 'Pacific Ring of Fire'), the Philippines experiences frequent natural disasters such as typhoons, landslides, volcanic eruptions and earthquakes (World Health Organization). The country is not only susceptible to natural disasters but also infectious diseases. The Philippines was classified as one of 22 high-burden countries by the World Health Organization (WHO). The high incidence of communicable diseases makes public health a challenging issue for the Philippines government (WHO).

Since the value of GIS capability to decision-making became increasingly evident, the Department of Health (DOH) of the Philippines launched several GIS projects in health planning and disease surveillance (Department of Health, 1999). One of the GIS pilot studies was conducted in Cavite within the Greater Manila Area aimed at setting up an Infectious Disease Data Management System to collect data on the spread of two diseases namely rabies and pulmonary tuberculosis (Leonardo et al., 2007).

The DOH agencies, specifically the National Epidemiology Center (NEC) and National Center for Disease Prevention and Control are responsible for disease surveillance and management. These agencies primarily develop and evaluate surveillance and other health information systems. While the National Epidemiology Center investigates disease outbreaks and monitors the health status of the population, the National Center for Disease Prevention and Control develops plans, policies, programs, projects and strategies for disease prevention and control. It also provides technical assistance and co-ordination and advisory services when necessary (DOH Philippines).[3], [4]

The Department of Health (DOH) has implemented several GIS-based projects in health planning and disease surveillance.[5] The National Epidemiology Center (NEC) of the DOH is increasingly using more powerful visualization and analytical tools for surveying and monitoring the extent and magnitude of diseases (Leonardo et al., 2007).

The first successful attempt of using GIS and remote sensing (RS) was carried out by UP Manila in order to determine the environmental factors associated with malaria and schistosomiasis (Leonardo et al., 2005). The GIS technology was used to update prevalence maps and other data collected during a pilot study of municipalities in the Davao del Norte and Mindanao provinces. The application of the GIS technology was extended to monitor malaria prevalence and evaluate the effectiveness of the control programs. The maps were used in recommending ways to respond and manage malaria during disasters and other emergencies (Bloland & Williams, 2001; Leonardo et al., 2007). Another major GIS application in the Philippines is the Maternal GIS Project initiated under the Women's Health and Safe Motherhood Programme in December 1999 (Leonardo et al., 2007). The provincial government of Capiz also depends on GIS in tracking of dengue cases (Leonardo et al., 2007). Despite the widespread applications of GIS in the Philippines, as suggested by a formal assessment by the DOH, there is still a need to improve or strengthen coordination between various programs, projects, standards, systems, and policies in the Department of Health (Pacific Rim Innovation and Management 2008).

RESEARCH METHODOLOGY: SPATIAL ANALYSIS TOOLS USED IN IDENTIFYING SPATIAL PATTERNS OF A DISEASE

Spatial Techniques

Several spatial methods using GIS may be employed for disease surveillance. Some of the common spatial techniques used in health research and epidemiology are disease mapping, clustering techniques, diffusion studies, and identification of risk factors through mapping and regression analyses (Moore & Carpenter, 1999).

---

[3] Source URL: http://dev1.doh.gov.ph/content/national-epidemiology-center
[4] Source URL: http://dev1.doh.gov.ph/content/national-center-disease-prevention-and-control
[5] The major software products used in the GIS projects in the Philippines are Arc/Info and ArcView (Leonardo et al., 2007).

Disease Mapping

In disease mapping, disease incidence may be presented with the help of choropleth maps, where each of the polygons has a value associated with it that may be a number of cases, rate of a disease, or mortality ratios displayed by colors, patterns or other areal features (Leonardo et al., 2007; Moore & Carpenter, 1999). Visual communication through maps however might be over-simplified since all values appear evenly distributed within a polygon. Some other limitations include the visual dominance of larger states over smaller states. In addition, there is no statistical reliability associated with reported incidence. Moreover, the relationship between disease incidence and environmental factors cannot be established with the help of maps (Croner & Cola, 2001; Moore & Carpenter, 1999).

Disease Clusters

Events in space may either be randomly or uniformly distributed. If a number of health events are located together in space or time, they are referred to as clusters (Moore & Carpenter, 1999)[6]. Spatial clustering for continuous data such as disease patterns can be detected by estimating spatial autocorrelation specifically Moran's I, a measure that has successfully been used in the field of epidemiology for detecting cancers and stroke mortality rates (Moore & Carpenter, 1999). Getis (2010) defines spatial auto correlation as the relationship between nearby spatial units. A systematic relationship between spatial units denotes that a specific attribute associated with a specific area is related to the value of these attributes in the neighboring areas. There are two kinds of spatial autocorrelation: global and local. A global spatial autocorrelation estimate provides a single value for all the spatial units taken together, where as a local spatial autocorrelation estimate is a more local measure that focuses on one particular spatial unit(Aksioma & Iriawan, 2010).

Spatial patterns can be described in three ways: clustered, scattered or random. When the measure of spatial autocorrelation is positive, a given region as well as its neighbors has similar values, resulting in a clustered spatial pattern. On the other hand, a chessboard or a scattered spatial pattern is formed when adjacent areas do not have similar values as its region. In other words, there is negative spatial autocorrelation between regions. Third, the spatial pattern is random in the absence of any spatial autocorrelation (Aksioma & Iriawan, 2010).

---

[6] Clusters may be identified from various forms: point-pattern, nearest neighbor, quadrat analysis. A simple point-pattern analysis entails an inspection of a dot map which displays a geographic distribution of events. The strength of clustering of point data may also be gauged from the nearest-neighbor analysis that uses distances between events. A quadrat analysis, on the other hand is a cell count method that observes point density in a grid format (Moore & Carpenter, 1999).

Diffusion Studies

Third, patterns of diffusion in space or time can be observed using line, network or trend-surface analysis (Moore & Carpenter, 1999).[7]

Prediction Methods

Interpolation

Kriging is one such spatial technique used to estimate point values by using surrounding known point values. It is a prediction method that uses moving average interpolation to interpolate spatial points, where the weights are the distances between the location for which the value is being predicted and the locations with measured values (Moore & Carpenter, 1999). Kriging has been used to map public health data and valued for its ability to communicate event patterns over space or time (Croner & Cola, 2001).

Regression Analysis

Due to the nature of the infectious diseases, geographical proximity may be critical in explaining disease clusters. For instance, a high incidence of diarrhea in one province may affect the incidence of diarrhea in the neighboring provinces due to the movement or communication of people from geographically close provinces as compared to distant provinces. Further, disease clusters may also be explained as a result of environmental hazards or exposure of a group of provinces to a factor that is linked to a certain health outcome (Glavanakov et al., 2001). Alternately, disease clusters may be completely random and not related to any specific spatial factors. Therefore, a regression analysis may be used to determine whether the disease clusters are attributed to a specific spatial factor, while controlling for other socio-economic and demographic factors predictors. Further, the nature of the spatial relationship might vary between groups of regions. While in some regions, the incidence of diarrhea in one region might positively influence the incidence of diarrhea in the neighboring regions. However, the relationship might be inversed for another group of regions. The spatial dependence in the incidence of a disease may be captured with the help of several models including spatial lag, spatial error or a combination of both (Anselin 1988).

Unlike the traditional regression analyses methods, one of the complexities faced in the use of spatial econometric models is an endogenous dependent variable. Endogeneity refers to the simultaneity in the relationship between spatial neighbors. If diarrhea incidence in province i affects the diarrhea incidence in province j and vice

---

[7] In a line analysis, vectors or lines are used to describe disease flow through an area. Alternately, a trend analysis is a least square regression technique that is used to study diffusion in space and time (Moore & Carpenter, 1999).

versa, the results in the dependent variable are likely to be correlated with the error terms. In order to obtain consistent estimates, a simultaneous estimation procedure is recommended such as instrumental variables (IV) or non-parametric maximum likelihood estimation (MLE) approaches (Anselin, 1988).

The "neighboring regions" may be identified in several ways: either contiguity-based or distance-based. Contiguous regions are those that share a common edge to the immediate right or left of the unit of interest (Aksioma & Iriawan, 2010). Alternately, an inverse distance weight matrix may be used to assign weights to neighbors that decline as distance between them and the region under consideration decreases (Anselin et al. 2007).

Diagnoses and Analysis

Description of the data

This section develops a case study of the application of GIS to map the incidence of diarrhea in the Philippines along with some infrastructure variables and demonstrate a spatial regression analysis to determine whether the incidence of diarrhea correlates spatially with its neighbors. Diarrheal disease is the second leading cause of morbidity and sixth leading cause of mortality for all ages in the Philippines (Carlos & Saniel, 1990). The DOH reports indicate that it was the second-highest cause of morbidity from 2002 to 2008, following pneumonia.[8] In 2007, there were 640 cases of acute watery diarrhea per 100,000 reported in the country. Diarrheal disease can be spread through contaminated food or drinking water, or transmitted through human contact (Carlos & Saniel, 1990). Appropriate interventions such as improved sanitation and hygiene practices can significantly reduce diarrhea cases as well as morbidity and mortality rate in children (Fewtrell et al., 2005; Luby et al., 2005).

The morbidity rate of diarrhea - the primary variable of analysis - denotes the number of diarrhea cases per hundred thousand residents in a province. This province-level (including 70 provinces and the National Capital Region that comprises of 17 highly urbanized cities/municipalities), cross-sectional study uses data of the year 2007 to investigate the spatial dependence in the incidence of diarrhea among provinces. While spatial autocorrelation and dependence is usually evident in smaller spatial units such as municipalities or counties, due to lack of municipality-level data in this case, it could not be demonstrated for municipalities. Instead, the study uses province as the unit of analysis.[9]

The data for this analysis came from various sources. The diarrheal morbidity and the environmental data were taken from the Field Health Service Information System (2007) of the National Epidemiology Center at the Department of Health. The socio-

---

[8] The statistics data was retrieved from http://www.nscb.gov.ph/secstat/d_vital.asp.
[9] Ten provinces were excluded from the analysis due to missing data.

economic and demographic variables were collected from the Census of 2007 (Refer to *http://www.census.gov.ph/*).The geographic shapefile has been obtained from PhilGIS. Estimates of household income are obtained from a survey.[10]

DATA ANALYSIS AND RESULTS

A set of choropleth maps provides a visual distribution of households with safe water and the incidence of acute diarrhea across provinces in the Philippines. These maps are displayed in Figures 1 and 2. In each of these maps, a darker shade indicates a higher number/percentage/incidence while a lighter shade denotes a lesser number/ percentage or incidence of a phenomenon. It is clear that there are groups or clusters of provinces in the northernmost and middle islands specifically Luzon and Visayas that exhibit a high incidence of diarrhea denoted by a darker shade of color. Conversely, there is a cluster of provinces in the southern-most region of Mindanao that exhibits a lower incidence of diarrhea denoted by a lighter shade of color. A measure of spatial autocorrelation is estimated in order to address whether the spatial disease clusters are systematic or random. In other words, the measure of spatial autocorrelation identifies whether high diarrheal occurrence in one province is associated with diarrheal occurrence in the neighboring provinces. The statistical significance of spatial autocorrelation for the entire country as well as specific regions is tested using global and local Moran's I respectively. The positive and statistically significant (at 0.05 level of significance) global Moran's I estimate of 0.2442 indicates presence of spatial autocorrelation in the incidence of diarrhea among provinces in the Philippines. Further, clusters of provinces are identified with high-high, low-low, low-high and high-low estimates. Provinces marked by high-high indicate that that a province with a high diarrheal incidence is also surrounded by provinces with high diarrheal incidence and therefore it denotes presence of a positive spatial autocorrelation. Conversely, if the spatial relationship is denoted by high-low/low-high, it indicates that a province with a high diarrheal incidence has neighboring provinces with a low diarrheal incidence. This denotes negative spatial autocorrelation. In addition, the statistical significance of these clusters may also be noted.

Figures 1 and 2 Choropleth maps showing visual distribution of households with sanitation and the incidence of acute diarrhea across provinces.

As discussed earlier, the statistically significant spatial clusters might be the result of specific spatial factors such as exposure of a group of provinces to a shared environmental hazard, or may be completely random. The regression analysis, therefore, is used to determine whether the disease clusters can be attributed to a spatial spillover effect, while controlling for other socio-economic and demographic predictors. In order to test for spatial dependence of diarrheal occurrence among provinces, a spatial autoregressive model (with a spatial autoregressive error term) is

---

[10] Source: *http://www.census.gov.ph/data/sectordata/2006/2006SE_prv-income.pdf.*

used in which the dependent variable, diarrhea morbidity (zi) of a region is a function of the weighted diarrhea morbidity of neighboring regions given by, $\sum W_{ij}z_j$ where every neighboring province gets a weight inversely proportional to the distance from a given province (Anselin, 2007) (Equation 1). The parameter λ in Equation 1 denotes the sign and magnitude of the interaction between provinces. An inverse distance weight matrix given by $\sum W_{ij}$ is used to define the neighborliness between provinces. The presence of a spillover of diarrhea from the neighboring province to a given province is tested using a regression analysis while controlling for other socio-economic and infrastructure variables that may influence incidence of diarrhea.

$$z_i = \lambda \sum W_j z_j + \beta_k x_i + u_i - \text{Eq. 1}$$

$$u_1 = \rho \sum m_j u_j + e_i$$

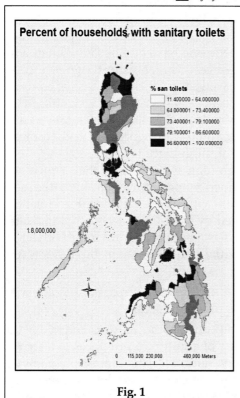

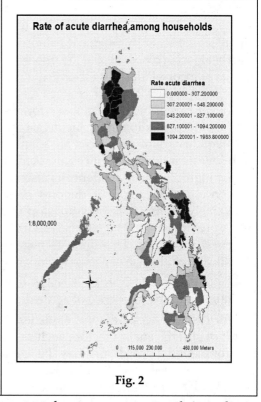

| Fig. 1 | Fig. 2 |

By using the instrumental variables two-stage least square approach in order to address the endogeneity problem, the spatial autoregressive model indicates that there is positive spatial dependence among provinces in the incidence of diarrhea in the Philippines after controlling for independent variables including population density, income and availability of safe drinking water and sanitary toilet facilities.[11], [12]

The regression results indicate that if the incidence of diarrhea in the neighboring provinces increases by 10 per 100,000 residents, a given province also experiences an increase of 9.566 per 100,000 residents (Model 1 in Table 1). Therefore, this implies that the incidence of diarrhea in a given province is spatially dependent on the incidence of the disease in the neighboring provinces.

Following from the high-high disease cluster in the Luzon region, the analysis was separately carried out for the Luzon region comprising of 26 provinces and 17 cities/ municipalities of the National Capital Region (Model 2 in Table 1). The results were consistent in this case -- spatial dependence was positive and statistically significant at 5 % l.o.s.

Table 1. Regression results

Dependent Variable/Independent Variables	Model 1	Model 2
Lag of Diarrhea Incidence	0.9566***	1.3737**
	(0.3307)	(0.5920)
Population density	-0.1875***	-0.1879***
	(0.0532)	(0.0573)
Income	0.5330*	0.5073**
	(0.2774)	(0.3700)
Availability of safe drinking water	0.0248	0.6590
	(0.955)	(0.6844)
Availability of sanitary toilet	0.0561	0.3180
	(0.901)	(0.7082)
Number of observations	87	43

Notes: All the variables are logged.
The standard errors are in the parenthesis.

POLICY IMPLICATIONS AND RECOMMENDATIONS

The geography of a disease and its relationship with individuals can convey important information to public health managers about how to tackle the outbreak. As discussed earlier, various GIS applications provide means for presenting and analyzing the spatial dimension of a disease that can consequently help public health managers

[11] As Anselin (1988) suggests, the spatially lagged exogenous variables are used as appropriate instruments.
[12] The model was run using the generalized 2SLS model found in Drukker, Prucha and Raciborski's work (2011)

make more informative and comprehensive public health decisions.

Visualization of disease incidence or identification of disease clusters through maps can be useful to public health managers for planning disease control, prioritizing local resources and allocating them vis-à-vis the spread of the disease and the affected communities, in developing information and advisory packages for residents and assessing risk. (Johnson & Johnson, 2001; Leonardo et al., 2007; Moore & Carpenter, 1999; Tanser, 2006).

Second, GIS applications allow public health managers to monitor the impact and control the transmission of infectious diseases in conjunction with environmental data (Tanser, 2006) . Third, due to the continuous technological advancement in GIS, it is not uncommon for people to manipulate spatial data or display the results in real time or rapid speed when using GIS. More advanced GIS analysis and modeling from high-end systems can take place at a centralized level, and the results can be fed into the district-level GIS systems, where local decisions are made (Tanser, 2006).

Due to spatial dependence in the incidence of diarrhea among geographically close provinces, a more focused and active co-operation zone among provinces might be necessary. Working together in co-ordination with neighbors might be more efficient in terms of conserving resources as well as producing the desired output (PIDS, 2009; Kelekar, 2012). As demonstrated in the case study, GIS has the ability to compare and contrast spatial data from different sources. It can also handle and manipulate a large amount of data at a time at a good speed. Furthermore, it can perform various organizational, descriptive and analytical functions that can help public health managers to carry out their disease surveillance activities successfully (Moore & Carpenter, 1999).

However, there are also some functional and managerial disadvantages associated with the use of GIS in the developing countries. The costs of implementing the necessary hardware and software can be high. Additionally, manpower training and maintenance can also be costly. There might be additional challenge in obtaining relevant and accurate data from various agencies. Despite some of these limitations, GIS offers significant advantages to public health managers monitoring disease outbreaks.

CONCLUSION

This paper demonstrates some of the applications of GIS in disease surveillance among provinces in the Philippines. GIS is used to map the incidence of a diarrheal across Filipino provinces and a spatial regression is performed to identify spatial dependence of diarrheal incidence among provinces while controlling for socio-economic and infrastructure variables. The analysis shows that there is a significant positive spatial dependence in the occurrence of diarrhea among provinces. Further, the benefits of GIS for public health managers are discussed. In this study, GIS is used to visualize the incidence of a disease vis-à-vis the budget and available resources. Additionally, examining the spatial dimension of the disease incidence, and identifying spatial dependence may call for coordination among public health managers of neighboring provincial governments for effective disease surveillance and management.

BIBLIOGRAPHY

Abdel-Rahman, M. S., El-Bahy, M. M., Malone, J. B., Thompson, R. A., & El Bahy, N. M. (2001). Geographic information systems as a tool for control program management for schistosomiasis in Egypt. *Acta Tropica, 79*(1), 49-57.

Aksioma, D. F., & Iriawan, N. (2010). Spatial Autocorrelation of the DHF Outbreaks in the city of Surabaya. *Proceedings of the Third International Conference of Mathematics and Natural Sciences*.

Anselin, L. (1988). *Spatial Econometrics: Methods and Models-Studies in Operational Regional Science* (1 ed.): Springer.

Anselin, L., Gallo, J. L., & Jayet, J. (2007). Spatial Panel Econometrics. In L. Matyas & P. Sevestre (Eds.), *The Econometrics of Panel Data, Fundamentals and Recent Developments in Theory and Practice* (3rd ed.). Dordrecht: Boston: Kluwer Publishers.

Bloland, P. B., & Williams, H. A. (2001). *Malaria control during mass population movements and natural disasters*. Washington, DC: National Academies Press.

Carlos, C. C., & Saniel, M. C. (1990). Etiology and Epidemiology of Diarrhea. *Philippine Journal of Microbiology and Infectious Diseases, 19*(2), 51-53.

Carneiro, H. A., & Mylonakis, E. (2009). Google trends: A web-Based tool for real-time surveillance of disease outbreaks. *Clinical Infectious Diseases, 49*(10), 1557-1564.

Clarke, K. C., McLafferty, S. L., & Tempalski, B. J. (1996). On epidemiology and geographic information systems: a review and discussion of future directions. *Emerging Infectious Disease, 2*(2), 85–92.

Croner, C. M., & Cola, L. D. (2001, September). *Visualization of Disease Surveillance Data with Geostatistics*. Paper presented at the UNECE (United Nations Economic Commission for Europe) work session on methodological issue involving integration of statistics and geography, Tallinn.

Department of Health. (1999). National Objectives for Health (Philippines 1999-2004).

Drukker, D. M., Prucha, I. R., & Raciborski, R. (2011). Maximum-likelihoodand generalized spatial two-stage least-squares estimators for aspatial-autoregressive model with spatial-autoregressive disturbances, Working paper, University of Maryland, Department of Economics. Retrieved from *http://econweb.umd.edu/~prucha/Papers/WP_spreg_2011.pdf*.

Fewtrell, L., Kaufmann, R. B., Kay, D., Enanoria, W., Haller, L., & Colford Jr., J. M. (2005). Water, sanitation, and hygiene interventions to reduce diarrhea in less developed countries: A systematic review and meta-analysis. *Lancet Infectious Diseases,, 5*(1), 42-52.

Field Health Service Information System. (2007). National Epidemiology Center, Department of Health, Manila, Philippines.

Getis, A. (2010). Spatial Autocorrelation. In M. M. Fischer & A. Getis (Eds.), *Handbook of Applied Spatial Analysis* (pp. 255-275): Springer.

Ginsberg, J., Mohebbi, M. H., Patel, R. S., Brammer, L., Smolinski, M. S., & Brilliant, L. (2009). Detecting influenza epidemics using search engine query data. *Nature, 457*.

Glavanakov, S., White, D. J., Caraco, T., Lapenis, A., Robinson, G. R., Szymanski, B. K., & Maniatty, W. A. (2001). Lyme disease in New York state: Spatial pattern at a regional scale. *The American Journal of Tropical Medicine and Hygiene, 65*(5), 538-545.

Johnson, C. P., & Johnson, J. (2001). *GIS: A tool for monitoring and management of epidemics*.

Paper presented at the Map India 2001 Conference, New Delhi, India.

Kelekar, U. (2012). Do Local Government Units (LGUS) Interact Fiscally While Providing Public Health Services In The Philippines? *World Medical & Health Policy, 4*(2), Article 6.

Keola, S., Tokunaga, M., Nitin, K. T., & Wisa, W. (2002). Spatial surveillance of epidemiological disease: A case study in Ayutthaya Province, Thailand. *GIS development Magazine.*

Law, D. C. G., & Wilfert, R. A. (2007). Mapping for surveillance and Outbreak Investigation. *Focus, 5*(2), Available at *http://cphp.sph.unc.edu/focus/vol5/issue2/5-2Mapping_issue.pdf.*

Leonardo, L. R., Crisostomo, B. A., Solon, J. A. A., Rivera, P. T., Marcelo, A. B., & Villasper, J. M. (2007). Geographical information systems in health research and services delivery in the Philippines. *Geospatial Health, 2*, 147-155.

Leonardo, L. R., Rivera, P. T., Crisostomo, B. A., Sarol, J. N., Bantayan, N. C., Tiu, W. U., & Bergquist, N. R. (2005). A study of the environmental determinants of malaria and chistosomiasis in the Philippines using remote sensing and geographic information systems. *Parassitologia, 47*, 105-114.

Luby, S., Agboatwalla, M., Feikin, D., Painter, J., Billhimer, W., Altaf, A., & Hoekstra, R. (2005). Effect of handwashing on child health: A randomized controlled trial. *The Lancet, 366*(9481), 225–233.

Mesgari, M. S., & Masoomi, Z. (2008). GIS applications in public health as a decision making support system and it's limitation in Iran. *World Applied Sciences Journal, 3*((Supple 1)), 73-77.

Moore, D. A., & Carpenter, T. E. (1999). Spatial analytical methods and geographic information systems: use in health research and epidemiology. *Epidemiologic Reviews, 21*(2), 143-161.

Myers, M. F., Rogers, D. J., Cox, J., Flahault, A., & Hay, S. I. (2000). Forecasting disease risk for increased epidemic preparedness in public health. *Advances in Parasitology, 47*, 309-330.

National Statistics Office of the Republic of the Philippines. (2012). Philippines population. Retrieved from *http://www.census.gov.ph/data/pressrelease/2012/pr1227tx.html*

Pacific Rim Innovation and Management (2008). Technical Assistance Consultant's Report- Regional: Strengthening Epidemiological Surveillance and Response for Communicable Diseases in INO, MAL, PHI.

PIDS (2009). Improving local service delivery for the MDGs in Asia: the Case of the Philippines. Philippines Institute for Development Studies. Discussion Paper Series No. 2009-34.

Tanser, F. (2006). Geographical information systems (GIS) innovations for primary health care in developing countries. *Innovations: Technology, Governance, Globalization, 1*(2), 106-122.

Wiafe, S., & Davenhall, B. (2005). Extending Disease Surveillance with GIS. *Esri ArcUser, 8*(2).

Employing Crowdsourcing for Funding Innovation Projects: The Case of Mini War Gaming

Daniel Roy*, Kalinga Jagoda* and Bharat Maheshwari**

ABSTRACT

Crowdsourcing has been the core model behind many Internet success stories. Mini War Gaming uses this model for raising funds through many small donations from its eager supporters. This case study explores and examines the successful use of a new and innovative approach for financing NPD projects by a Canadian small business. We analyze the necessary steps taken to formulate a successful crowd funding campaign and deliver a model which can be applied to other businesses wishing to raise capital from supporters of a small business in exchange for perks or rewards.

Keywords: Crowdfunding, innovation, Mini War Gaming, fund raising, NPD, innovative approach.

INTRODUCTION

Innovation is a resource intensive and uncertain process (Schumpeter, 1942). Shorter product life cycles, hyper global competition and the fast pace of technological development and obsolescence, makes new product development (NPD), a pre-requisite for survival of modern firms, particularly, for those in new media1 businesses such as entertainment and gaming. Firms in these businesses continuously strive to create new and innovative content which is important for their survival and requires dedication of their best talent and resources. However, as the return on investment in this process cannot be assured, it is not very easy for the entrepreneurs to find investors

---

[1] The term new media has been has been coined in the literature to represent creative businesses involved in developing entertainment and knowledge tools and practices that exploit the potential and reach of the Internet (e.g. Pratt, 2000).

---

[*] Bissett School of Business, Mount Royal University, Canada.
[**] Odette School of Business, University of Windsor, Canada.
E-mail: kjagoda@mtroyal.co, bmaheshw@unwindsor.ca., brraheshw@unwindsor.ca.

for NPD projects in new media business. This case study examines the experience of "Mini War Gaming," a Canadian small business that decided to choose an innovative non-traditional approach for raising capital, for their NPD project "Dark Potential."

Businesses can use several traditional options for raising capital when it comes to funding NPD projects. However, most of these traditional options rely on leveraging assets or relationships for loans or using retained capital in the business or employing personal savings of the entrepreneurs. In theory, small business can also sell equity through a stock exchange but, in practice it is exclusively a resource for larger companies as far too many expenses and government regulatory restrictions make it impractical for small businesses (Kaplan, 2012).Given that retained earnings take several years to accrue, an average small start-up in search of capital is often restricted to privately issuing debt or securities to angel investors or banks (Kaplan, 2012). None of these options favor the small business owners who may not possess the necessary collateral to back their business plans or secure them a reasonable loan with a relatively low interest rate. The old adage still holds true today, "it takes money to make money".

Crowdsourcing, with the rise of social media and the Internet has emerged as viable mechanism for raising capital for social projects and is now behind the rise of many success stories within the past few years such as Wikipedia which rely on voluntary contribution of its users for funding. Small businesses have much to benefit from it over traditional mechanisms to raise capital. Crowd funding is a derivative of crowd sourcing illustrated in this case. It allows entrepreneurs the chance to not only display their ideas to the world but also receive financial support through small contributions by numerous investors who are interested in the success of the proposed new product or business idea. This can be done with the added benefit of a zero percent interest rate attached to the newly acquired funds. This paper describes and analyzes the necessary steps taken by Mini War Gaming to formulate a successful crowdfunding campaign for supporting the development of its new game. The model which emerges can be applied to other businesses wishing to raise capital from many contributors in exchange for perks or rewards given back to these contributors.

We find that unlike traditional methods which are often limited in their reach and often put multiple constraints on the entrepreneurs, this approach comes with fewer constraints. However, the approach has its own challenges and issues. Understanding the mechanism, identifying the medium (right portal), and following through with the expectations of the supporters can be very challenging. The paper is organized into five sections. This case study provides deeper insights into the crowdfunding approach and guidance for managers seeking to use it for their own businesses. The next section of the paper provides a brief understanding of Crowdfunding. The third section provides background of the case study organization. We discuss the crowdfunding experience and process in the fourth section and a brief conclusion to the case is provided in the last section.

CROWDFUNDING

Crowdfunding at its core has existed in modern society for many years, taking many different forms that have ranged from humanitarian relief projects to political campaign donations. The overall goal of crowdfunding is to gather support from as many individuals as possible. These individuals would donate their support through varying contribution sizes of money, with those who are most committed to the cause donating usually more than the average person. This collective form of fund raising has its roots traced back to the year 2000 with internet startup sites for artists looking to finance their work through the means of "fan-funding". [1]

This concept was carried over into other creative fields such as indie film making, videogame production, comic book creation, software development, fashion and food creation, as well as startup company/product ideas. These crowdfunding sites were no longer only for musicians or humanitarian relief projects, but available to creative people everywhere who wanted their ideas backed by vast number of supporters. This shift in purposes was backed by the changes to the internet during the same time. Web 2.0 ushered in a new way of interacting with the internet and its users through social networking sites. Users could now have information shared and displayed to targeted groups of similar individuals with a few shared links through these social networking tools which would take the interested supporters to crowdfunding portals. Many crowdfunding portals have emerged in the last few years. Some examples include Kickstarter and IndieGoGo which were formed in 2008, GoFundMe and Sponsume in 2010, and PleaseFundUs in 2011.

Crowdfunding portals invite donors to contribute to projects through funding campaigns, which inform the donors about the projects and promise tangible or intangible reward. The successful campaigns receive contributions when they have enticing rewards that adequately reflect the donor's contribution size, larger donations promise greater rewards. Rewards can range from recognition and thanks, to a form of pre-order for the finished product when production is under way. As with anything newly developed on the internet there always is a risk of internet fraudsters. Crowdfunding portals provide a level of transparency and open communication to everyone involved in the campaign. By having a trusted and secure crowdfunding portal supporters feel comfortable contributing to the through their platform and will continue to grow in popularity. Since 2007 crowd-funding support has increased 452% in 2011, with projections in increase up to 557% for 2012 (Crowdsourcing, LLC, 2012).

---

[1] Wikipedia page on crowd funding (http://en.wikipedia.org/wiki/Crowd_funding) identifies ArtistShare.com as the first recorded website where individuals could contribute to the development of a musician or group of musician's record release. Later many similar fan supporting websites emerged, Sellaband in 2006, Pledge Music and Rockethub in 2009, and Rock the Post in 2011.

The 2008 recession has caused a lot of changes to the capital lending industry and it appears that these changes are here to stay (Crowdsourcing, LLC, 2012).

CASE BACKGROUND

INITIATION

"Mini War Gaming"is an online store which was established in 2007 by friends, Matthew Glanfield and David Nordquist. The immediate fascination of these two friends with the assortment of finely painted miniature models led them to want to pursue a new business. The two co-founders, in addition to pursuing the collection of models sold by "Games Workshop" as a hobby, decided to create their own business venture of distributing Games Workshop's products through an online store. Mini War Gaming started with an initial goal of selling war gaming products from "Games Workshop" through an online community of hobby enthusiasts which the co-founders felt would grow as they explored the details of the hobby for themselves.

The miniature table-top war-gaming hobby market is a niche market where the United Kingdom based company Games Workshop is an established industry leader. Founded in the mid 1970s, Games Workshop produces a vast catalogue of table-top miniatures to be used in their war game scenarios. Their retail stores are located around the world and are designed to not only as a place for customers to come in to purchase their hobby materials, but also as a place for learning how to play the games. In a way, these retail stores also act as a form of marketing, in that they are designed to draw in potential hobbyists, to become educated about the hobby itself. Mini War Gaming was supposed to be an online store only. However, in order to comply with Games Workshop's franchising agreements and distribution rules which itself had an online store also, the company were required to establish a local physical store as well. Their store grew from a small circle of friends and family using Matthew's basement as the business storefront, but soon operations from online orders required the acquisition of a more accommodation for storage and retailing.

GROWTH

Mini war gaming was relocated to the old city hall building in Welland, Ontario, which had enough space to store larger quantities of products, as well as introduce a club area for their patrons. This common club area was designed in a way that would reflect many of the aspects of the Games Workshop stores found in major cities. These aspects are used to keep customers in the store longer and to keep returning to the store.

Around the same time that operations improved at the store level, Mini War Gaming started to really push for the development and production of their online hobby videos. This innovation also aligned with their original goal to become an online store exclusively, from which Mini War Gaming would be able to reach a larger target market. The content of these videos ranged from everything from getting started with the hobby, to various painting and modeling techniques critical to the development of the hobby. At first, the videos were designed to give other war-gamers the necessary tools and information to explore the hobby further and were originally produced about once per week. With more and more viewers watching the videos on their website the demand for more videos grew as well as their production quality. Soon the number of videos and the number of projects and types of videos increased with the hiring of additional staff members. Mini War Gaming launched an exclusive membership with a paid subscription to view exclusive video and other tutorial content made available first to their "vault members", then released one month later to the general public.

This video marketing helped to establish a loyal following of supporters from North America and Europe. Mini War Gaming's website became frequently visited by fans who wanted to watch the latest turn-by-turn (play-by-play) "battle report" played by the experts at Mini War Gaming, and then would place an order through their online store. Mini War Gaming's customers also more frequently chose to purchase their Games Workshop models through Mini War Gaming because of the percentage discounts they received through the store, instead of another online or retail store, including Games Workshop's own online store. Buying items this way was greatly preferred by many customers who already deemed the hobby to be expensive, especially for newcomers. With these financial enticements offered to customers, combined with a frequent video production of additional gaming content, Mini War Gaming had successfully positioned themselves in a firm position within the value chain of this niche market.

TRANSFORMATION: DISTRIBUTOR TO NEW GAME DEVELOPER

Having developed a successful retail and e-tail business and a dedicated community of gamers who followed their videos, Matt and Dave were now in a position to explore their passion of miniature war gaming further by developing their own war game and models. Since the beginning of Mini War Gaming, the co-founders had an ever-present desire to establish their own games, but it was never a real possibility, as their company in early stages of development never had the funds to invest in NPD. Matt had previously posted his proposal to the Mini War Gaming community though their blog posts and other gaming forums, and occasionally would discuss his aspirations to create his own miniature war game with club members' help, but the timing and funding were never quite right for him. Mini War Gaming was already drawing maximum amount they could from a bank so another bank loan was not possible.

However, despite not seeing a clear path for introducing another small company into the market of making war games, Mini War Gaming decided to conduct some primary research on the demand, as well as the logistics of producing miniatures on a large scale. The feedback received was very encouraging. They found many supporters in online communities for hobbyists who liked what Matt had proposed and wanted Mini War Gaming to pursue the project.

FUNDING CHALLENGE

With the positive feedback from the community, Mini War Gaming set out to test the process of getting miniature models sculpted and casted for large-scale production. They had the miniature casted and reproduced in limited quantities. A company located in Guelph, Ontario was able to provide the services necessary to reproduce the model with a high standard of quality approved by Mini War Gaming. Shortly after the test models were also created. Mini War Gaming had done the homework and was finally ready to seriously consider the possibility of creating their very own and new war game. However, funding this innovative process was a serious challenge.

CROWDFUNDING "DARK POTENTIAL"

Considering that the project was already so heavily supported by an online network of individuals, Mini War Gaming decided to test its supporters whether they participated in funding the development process through crowd funding. The project was given a name, Dark Potential, and was introduced to the Mini War Gaming community through several long video blog sessions. Detailed history for this new science fiction table-top miniature war game was developed. Dark Potential would be unique in several ways from other sci-fi games, which were adapted into the rules to allow for a unique game play for hobbyists.

Mini War gaming found that their video blog were heavily viewed and commented on by war game enthusiasts on the Internet. These viewers voiced their opinions, offered suggestions, and linked the video blog series to other online community forums, thus extending the information to new viewers through social media. Already the excitement was buzzing about the new project and a support group of followers appeared to Mini War Gaming to be larger than was first expected. This early excitement encouraged Matt to hire -with his own finances - a concept artist who was able to produce the ideas and initial concepts for the Dark Potential universe into highly detailed art-work. They had the miniature casted and reproduced in limited quantities. A company located in Guelph, Ontario was able to provide the services necessary to reproduce the model with a high standard of quality approved by Mini War Gaming. The miniatures would be made from molded metal, which was less costly for smaller quantities then plastic or resin models. Finally, Mini War Gaming was ready to execute their new project and share the Dark Potential game with hobbyists around the world.

Many competing Crowdfunding portals were available, as the model had already gained a lot of publicity due to a few highly successful campaigns. The heavy support which "Dark Potential" gained online also justified the use crowd support to continue the development process through crowdfunded financing. The other benefit of this approach, it ultimately allowed the "ultimate consumers" to take a stake in the project and decide if this project was going to go forward or not. Mini War Gaming would get a direct feedback which could help it decide whether to abandon the project or proceed. Originally, Mini War Gaming decided to run their campaign through the most popular crowdfunding portal, KickStarter.com. However some legal restrictions and the limitations on donating methods led Mini War Gaming to switch to IndieGoGo. com. Table 1. provides a brief comparison of the two portals. IndieGoGo provided more flexibility as it allowed contributors the option of donating through PayPal as well as through a major credit card.

Table 1: KickStarter.com vs. IndieGoGo (highlighting only the differences)

	KickStarter.com	*IndieGoGo.com*
Startup fee	No	No
Successfully funded projects	5% of funds raised	4% of funds raised
Unsuccessful projects	All or nothing	9% of funds raised or an "all or nothing option"
Payment options	Credit card	Credit card, or Paypal
Third party fees	3-5% Amazon credit card processing fees	3% for credit card processing, $25US wire fee for non-US campaigns, Currency exchange fees may also apply

THE CAMPAIGN

The co-founders conducted a lot of research and analysis of the past crowdfunding data available from analysis other campaigns on both KickStarter's and IndieGoGo's websites. The findings of this analysis was used as a resource for making their own successful campaign. After examining the success patterns of successful campaigns on the two websites it became apparent that successful campaigns offered high perceived value to donors through rewards. These "perks" or "rewards" were used to entice interested patrons of the project into supporting the project through small and sometimes even substantial cash contribution. An analysis of successful campaigns on popular portals (Kickstarter and IndieGoGo websites) revealed that $10 to $25 donation range projects yielded the most donations. The $50 to $100 donation range was next higher contributing level provided the rewards offered were adequate to reflect the donation amount. Putting very nominal donation (less than $5)and higher donation (more than $100) amount choices was also found to be important as there could be some contributors who will want to donate in these levels and should not be ignored as should also appropriately reflect a proper reward (Kickstarter website). See Table 2 for the donation categories and corresponding rewards used by Mini war Gaming.

Table 2: Dark Potential's Perks for contributors

Donation Amount	Name	Detailed Description of the Perk	# of Claims
$5	Great Potential	Acknowledgement on the Mini War Gaming website in a group video, as well as a Dark Potential computer desktop wallpaper.	49
$25	Kinda like a pre-order	Get the $5 level, plus choose one miniature (when completed), and Mini War Gaming will ship it anywhere in the world at no extra cost.	172
$50	Five pre-orders!	Get the $5 level, plus get all five miniatures shipped to you in the world at no extra cost. If Mini War Gaming makes more than five, you get to choose which five you get.	413
$100	Limited Edition Awesomeness	Get the $50 level, plus the miniatures will be packaged in special limited edition packaging available only during the funding campaign, and signed by Mini War Gaming.	90
$150	Get both Starter Sets	Get the $5 level, plus get both starter sets that are first created (each starter set will contain 7 miniatures), shipped anywhere in the world for free, in limited edition packaging signed by Matthew from Mini War Gaming.	98
$250	Lifetime Silver Vault	Get the $100 level, plus a lifetime Silver Mini War Gaming Vault membership (see miniwargaming.com/vaulttrial for vault member details).	29
$350	Lifetime Gold Vault	Get the $100 level, plus a lifetime Gold Mini War Gaming Vault membership (see miniwargaming.com/vaulttrial for vault membership details).	33
$500	All painted up…	Get the $100 level, but have all five miniatures painted by worthypainting.com painting services.	8 out of 10
$500	Dark Potential terrain	Get the $350 level, plus get one of the 10 unique pieces of terrain designed specifically for Dark Potential by our vault painter and terrain maker Austin.	1 out of 10
$500	Package-Quality Painting	Get the $350 level, plus worthypainting.com will paint one miniature on a display level standard. This is the same quality that you will see on the packaging for the miniatures.	3 out of 5
$1,000	You'll be famous!	Get the $350 level, plus have your name put on the packaging of one of the very first miniatures (it will read something like "This miniature made possible by ___"), and your name will be prominently displayed in the alpha, beta, and first creation edition of the rule books. (Note that the $1,500 level will get the rulebook inclusion, but not the product packaging inclusion to do the limited availability).	0 out of 8
$1,500	Get your name in	Get everything from the $1,000 level, plus get a special character from the game (either in the storyline or an actual model) named after you (or your favorite username, or some modification to your name).	10 out of 10

Mini War Gaming carefully considered their findings to work out a range of donation amounts and complementing rewards. The rewards were methodically worked out so that contributors would feel comfortable contributing to the campaign. Sometimes the donation sizes would be similar to the price the donors would have normally had to pay for product once it was released. Matt and Dave also included some fun rewards for their community through comedic YouTube videos. As per Matt these silly perks were offered for two main reasons:

"first, they are inexpensive and second, they helped in contributing to the excitement of the crowdfunding campaign among the online community. These rewards offered a blend of acknowledgement, humor, and by providing actual end product."

Based on the rewards offered and the assessment of the other similar campaigns a realistic goal of $10,000 was set by the co-founders for their crowd funding campaign. However, internally they hoped of raising at least $20,000. The modest $10,000 goal would have only helped them produce a few playable miniatures. However, if they were really successful and reached their stretch goal, they would consider making a complete starter set of miniatures.

WELL TARGETED VIDEO MESSAGE

Once the rewards and a targeted funding amount were established, Matt then made an excellent introductory video introducing the campaign, his goals, and detailing all the perks. The video was done in similar style to their other YouTube videos which was easily recognizable to their fans. The video was recorded on a high definition home video camera with an external lapel microphone to capture better audio. The video was then edited down to contain only the most essential components of the campaign and inter spliced and overlaid with early concept art. Mini War Gaming wanted to provide potential investors with a vivid mental picture of what the Dark Potential universe looks like. Earlier in the preproduction process Matt's concept artist created some images of the Dark Potential landscape as well as some character sketches. It was these early concept sketches which really got the community, and donors excited.

By boosting the production value of the introduction video Mini War Gaming was able to present itself as profession firm capable of fulfilling the campaign. This gave their stakeholders a sense of creditability based on the quality of their video. Mini War Gaming also understood that for many contributors this would be their first impression of the Dark Potential campaign and to Mini War Gaming, and that they needed to be as informative and committed as possible. This they achieved by producing a well put together "sales pitch" to be their first impression to potential donors.

COMMUNITY BUILDING

After every video, Matt would encourage contributors to post links to the campaign on their social networking sites, and to talk about it on internet forums, anything to get their message of their crowdfunding campaign out to as many people as possible. Matt also urged to their supporters to not to spread the word irresponsibly through methods like "spamming", but to use networks and sites that they were already actively engaged in. The word spread through the Internet through many hobby sites was the primary form of communication to their potential customers.

The initial welcome video was not the only video Mini War Gaming produced during the campaign. Many follow up videos on the campaign's progress were also created to help keep the community informed on the campaign's progress. The Dark Potential campaign reached its goal with the first few hours of launch, and many contributors were anxious to know what was going to happen if they continued to surpass their preliminary goal of $10,000. At the beginning of the campaign Matt did comment that he was willing to produce more miniatures if the funding and support were there, which soon became a reality. After only three days into the campaign they already had surpassed their stretched goal of raising $20,000. This excited the community but also made them anxious to know what the company would do with the extra funding.

TRANSPARENCY AND ENGAGEMENT

Mini War Gaming response to crowd inquiries was to get their supporters to tell them what they would like them to do with the added support. The response was an overwhelming plea to create two playable starter sets with seven miniatures in each. This was definitely possible with the kind of support they were getting. Matt and Dave made preparations to add on an additional seven miniatures and the same was communicated to the stakeholders through another campaign video. During the campaign Matt and Dave carefully monitored their perks, and noticed that many of the perks were receiving little to no attention while others were outperforming their original guesses. Six days into the campaign the perks were tweaked and the ones that had previously not been given any attention were revamped to include the above mentioned humorous perks, such as Matt taking a pie to the face and Dave getting shot on the bare chest with paintballs. These modifications to the rewards found new donors who were willing to support the project or caused previous donors to increase their donation amount to reach a new perk level.

With the increase in the donations Matt made another follow up video thanking their supporters repeatedly for their generous contributions but also introduced a new goal of $70,000 along with their revised plans. At this point the campaign had already surpassed both previous goals within the first week. With this new goal Matt also introduced the new outlined details about how the design will unfold. These details included the hiring of two new writers, more concept artists, and the production of a printed rulebook. These would be used to help develop the "lore and history of Dark Potential" which would be used to "help breathe a lot of life into the universe"

It was also around this time that Matt decided to run a contest to determine the name of one of the currently unnamed faction of the Dark Potential game. Up until this point Matt had been referring to this group simply as "the corporation", and did not as of yet have a proper name for "the corporation". He knew that this playable faction would be a large corporation that specialized in the new high-tech weapons development of the game's focal element, dark matter, and wanted to run a contest to see who could name the nameless corporation. The responses he got were great and ultimately "the corporation" was named by the fans. It was important to Matt that the game was as much a part of the community as it was of Mini War Gaming, after all the fans would be the ones playing the game. So he wanted to give the fans as much of a voice as possible. After every video play-test of the rules video the community would comment on the modification of the rules to help with the development and balancing of the game. By acknowledging their suggestions and implanting their feedback into the game's mechanics, Mini War Gaming was able to produce a working prototype very quickly.

DISCUSSION AND CONCLUSION

At the end of the month long campaign Dark Potential had successfully raised $89,849, which was an 898% increase over their desired funding request. Their success was largely due to two key success factors; the careful planning and execution of the Dark Potential universe and by actively engaging a community of supporters in the development of the product. We found that Crowdfunding in this case emerged as a very feasible way for companies worldwide to gain access to capital. This method has a huge potential to change the way small business ventures in new media businesses can gain access to the financial resources.

Going forward small business in new media businesses can use this approach very well to share the risks associated with NPD and innovation with their online supporters. However, the success of the approach may heavily depend on the design and execution of the campaign. Factors such as community support, quality of communication, transparency of linkages with the supporters were also important for Mini War Gaming's success in crowdfunding.

REFERENCES

Agency Group (2011)"The American Jobs Act: Fueling Innovationand Entrepreneurship', FDCH Regulatory Intelligence Database, Issue September 9, 2011

Accessed through Business Source Complete, EBSCOhost, viewed 27 June 2012.

Crowdsourcing, LLC. (2012) "Crowdfunding Industry Report (Abridged Version): Market Trends, Composition and Crowdfunding Platforms", Crowdsourcing.org, viewed 24 July 2012.

Kaplan, R. S. (2012) "The Balanced Scorecard: Comments on Balanced Scorecard Commentaries", Journal of Accounting & Organizational Change, 8(4).

Pratt, A.C. (2000). "New media, the new economy and new spaces", Geoforum, 31, 425-436

Schumpeter, J.A. (1942). Capitalism, socialism and democracy.New York: Harper.

Enterprise Resource Planning vs. Bespoke Software in Public Policy: A Case Study on FCI Kerala Region Project Implementation

Resmi. A. G*, Ar. Icy P.** Choyan and C.T. Sunil Kumar***

ABSTRACT

The share of implementation of ERP software in corporate world is increasing day by day and to compete, government agencies and organizations are also on the path of implementing them. The usage of ERP system in public offices can definitely provide better results, This paper is a comparison of ERP software with bespoke software from a public policy perspective.

Keywords: ERP, Bespoke, Business Process Reengineering, public policy, FCI.

INTRODUCTION

Enterprise Resource Planning is an enterprise solution software system that allows a company to automate and integrate the majority of its business processes, and share common data and practices across the enterprise through integration of various functions in the organization, managers and staff alike can use timely information to make better decisions and to perform activities, which add value to the company. An ERP system may thus provide:

1. A repertoire of standard business process tools to support management initiatives such as activity based costing , business process reengineering and supply chain management;

2. An integrated computer system with a common framework for all corporate processes and data.

*   Resmi. A. G, is Research Scholar, University of Kerala.
**   Ar. Icy P.Choyan is Assistant Professor, Department of Architecture, MES Engineering College, Kuttipuram.
*** C.T. Sunil Kumar is Asst. General Manager (ME), Food Corporation of India, Kerala Region.
E-mail: resmi.agr@gmail.com, ar.icypc@gmil.com, ctsunil@gmail.com

3. Potential real-time analysis of key issues for enterprises, such as material usage, costs, quality, customer satisfaction and profitability.

Enterprise Resource planning is the term used for pre written, off the shelf software designed to support and automate the business process of organizations. The well-known ERP applications are SAP, Oracle, BAAN, Peoplesoft etc. In general, ERP systems are built on generic system rules and each implementation requires a lot of customization based on the processes and practices in the organization.

Success stories of ERP implementation are explained differently "we suggest that the success of ERP implementation and operations depends on the firm's intention to use the ERP system to automate, informate and transform the organization". (Donald Chand,2005).

This paper addresses the issue of ERP implementation in government organizations and its comparison against bespoke software.

COMPARISON

ERP is the solution for the future. If you are able to implement the ERP software as such, it will be a better option, because it has all the best practices in the industry integrated in to it. Once you implement ERP, you should adopt the path of BPR (Business Process Re-engineering) rather than customization because then only it will be able to use the best practices in the industry in a better way. But in the case of bespoke, there is nothing called best practices. It makes use of the computer in functions which were previously done manually.

Table 1: Comparison Between ERP and bespoke

Sl No.	Criterion	ERP	Bespoke
1	Time taken for Implementation	Less, as the enterprise solution is already there and requires only customization	More, will have to start everything from the beginning
2	Management / Organization change required.	More, if Business Process Reengineering is used but will get the benefit of best practices.	Less, will actually change the manual work to computer.
3	Cost Factor	Timeline and obsolesce should be taken into account	Timeline and obsolesce should be taken into account
4	Quality	Use of Standards	May or may not use industry standards
5	Best Practices in Industry	Available	Not Available

6	Expertise of Staff required for customization	Functional Level	Technical Level
7	Integration of Functions	High	Low
8	Proprietary License	No	Yes
9	Availability	Off the shelf	Not Available, have to build from the scratch

When we consider software project management, 90% of the software projects are scrapped. The reasons may be many. The long term retention of employees in a software company is generally not possible. The person who wrote the software code in case of bespoke may not be available for any future reference or change in the package. But in the case of ERP, there is a standard procedure developed over several years. The leading corporate giants of the world use applications like SAP. Companies like Microsoft, Tata Consultancy Service, IBM, Colgate, Steel Authority of India Limited etc use SAP for their functioning. Risk associated with technology obsolescence is greater in bespoke software in comparison to ERP. ERP software is updated frequently and there is no question of ERP going out of business. But bespoke software can be obsolete as early as the time of completion itself. Many reasons can be attributed for this, including modifications required in the later part of development at the stage of testing and modification by trial and error.

CASE STUDY: SOFTWARE PROJECT IMPLEMENTATION IN FCI KERALA REGION

Food Corporation of India is the largest public sector undertaking in India which deals with procurement, storage, preservation, logistics and distribution of food grains. It operates throughout the length and breadth of the country with its strong network of 1820 depots (owned and hired) aggregating to 294.77 lakhs metric tons in capacity. FCI Kerala region is a small region of FCI taking care of the food security of the Kerala state with one regional office, 9 district offices and 22 operating owned depots having a total capacity of 5,08,696 metric tons (Ref. Fig. 1.)

Computerization in FCI was in an infant stage till the year 1996. At that time, computerization was limited up to the district level. The computer cells in regional and district offices were having one SCO Unix server and 2 to 3 UNIX client terminals. The computer was mainly used for running the payroll package developed on Foxplus dbase. Currently FCI is still running the software for its salary calculation and CPF (Contributory provident fund) schedules. In the beginning of 1997, 486 AT &T machines loaded with Windows 95 and Lotus Smart suite reached FCI regional and district offices in Kerala. The operation of the computers was limited to a few of the clerical staff in the organization at that time. The computers were added to the computer cells during the subsequent years mainly at year ending due to the fear of funds allotted to the regions geting lapsed. The main items of purchase were UNIX client machines and dot matrix printers.

IISFM INTEGRATED INFORMATION SYSTEM FOR FOOD GRAIN MANAGEMENT

The IISFM is a web based bespoke software and was made a part of a tripartite agreement between Food Corporation of India, National Informatics Centre and National Informatics Centre Services Incorporation on September 24,2003. The project at Rs 97.66 crores was supposed to be completed in 3 phases commencing from 2003-04 and to be completed in 2005-06 under India's 10th five year plan. It captured the complete workflow of FCI from depot to head office levels and extended a new way of reconciliation of stock figures thereby transforming the current depot set-up into a computerized environment. IISFM is a web–based ASP application with SQL server as database and COM (Component Object Model) compliant. Components are used to cater to the needs of business logic and data

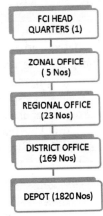

Fig. 1: Organizational Structure

services. Password protection mechanism is also provided for the security over the internet. IISFM in the initial design phase was divided in to five modules to meet FCI hierarchical requirements.

1. Depot Information System for Food grains Management for Food Storage Depot

2. District Information System for Food grains Management for District Office (DISFM)

3. Region Information System for Food grains Management for Regional Office

4. Zonal Information System for Food grains Management for Zonal Office

5. Integrated Information System for Food grains Management for Head Office

The application used component based architecture, and the main characteristic was multi-tier-layering model. Business logic works between the user and data services by implementing business rules which define how the application is working and controlling the data that is being accessed, manipulated and interpreted for making business decisions. With the implementation of the IISFM project, the MIS is strengthened by:

(*a*) the aim of ensuring the correctness of depot stock figures.

(*b*) making available the data pertaining to inventory and availability of stocks in various type of storage such a covered, open and silos.

(*c*) regular availability of unit wise data of day-to-day operations like receipts, storage, issues, transportation details and quality control inspections.

(*d*) maintaining the stack wise receipt and issue details.

The data entry to the software is to be fed through the data entry module of the software, which also takes care of the data validation and data security. The software generates a number of reports that can be used by the depot, district and other higher offices to report the day to day stock position. Data transmission from one level to another i.e. uploading of data can be achieved through dialup/ broadband connections. As part of the IISFM project new hardware was supplied to all the offices including the depot offices. The offices were supplied with one Acer Altos G700 server loaded with Windows 2003 operating system and SQL server and two Celeron based client machines and a printer along with UPS. This was the first time the food storage depots received computers (year 2003).

As part of the project, software training was given to a selected few FCI staff. The existing staff according to the level of knowledge were designated as DEO (Data Entry Operators) and FTS (Functional Technical Supervisors) and were given separate specialized trainings. FTS training was provided by NIIT who were not the developers of the package. Training was organised only on 2003 Server administration. The NIIT trainers were unable to answer the queries of FCI employees relating to IISFM as they were not the developers of the package. The DEO were given training on desktop printing (DTP) rather than hands on experience on the IISFM software.

In a survey (Sunil, 2010) of 34 respondents of FCI in Kerala region, who were in the job of IISFM implementation and data entry, 82.36 % started using computer after 2003 and only 17.63% had ever used computer prior to the implementation of this project. The survey also pointed out that 76% of the persons were trained by FCI, 18% of the employees took training other than FCI training and 6% never underwent any training.

The district offices were connected through VPN of BSNL with the help of Cisco routers, the depot offices were using dial-up connections and some depot offices never had internet connections. The data base transfer of the IISFM software was a tedious process due to the slow connections. In district offices the reconfiguration of the setting for shifting from broadband to VPN and back in case of failed connections was a difficult job for the ordinary users in FCI who were trained only for data entry purposes.

The data transfer model was itself wrong and the data updation was supposed to be done from all depot offices by dial up connection, broadband connection or by VPN connection. All the data transfer technologies failed, the reasons could be attributed to the non-availability of internet connection in remote parts of the country during the year 2003. FCI was having operations in every nook and corner of the nation and the internet connectivity was not up to the expectations of the FCI package. The software designers and developers stationed in Delhi failed to understand the ground realities in the rural areas in India.

The only advantage of the implementation of IISFM project in FCI was that its depot got computerized and the common workforce started using computers. The typewriters were replaced with computers. The FCI in 2003 had not conditioned itself to take up a project of the magnitude of IISFM. The knowledge level of FCI staff in computers was very low and the training provided was inadequate for implementation.

The project being a bespoke one was developed by design based on requirements laid down by higher offices rather than considering the ground realities at depots, was forced to be revised many times and the trial and error went till on the management issued orders to keep the project in abeyance. The FCI operations are vivid and do not have uniform operating procedures throughout the country or even in one region. It was difficult for the developers to have a package developed for the requirements received after the software started its implementation stage. The pilot study conducted for developing the package was wrong or the sample areas selected for the study never represented the actual population. FCI also failed in putting across its requirement for the software.

The reasons for the non-completion of IISFM project are listed below.

1. The computerization in FCI was in an infant stage to take up a project of the magnitude of IISFM in the year 2003.

2. No proper pilot study was conducted before going ahead with the project. The consultants appointed were unable to realize the hardcore field realities of FCI operations.

3. No BPR (Business Process Re-engineering) was done in the organization prior to the implementation of the project and also even after the implementation of the project to suit the requirements

4. Due to the vast difference of operations in different parts of the country and within the regions, the bespoke software developed by studying certain areas was not acceptable/ or viable in the other depots and regions in FCI.

5. The FCI domain experts failed in explaining the requirement at one go to the developers and more number of revisions adversely affected the attitude of the staff in implementing the software.

6. The testing of the package was done by trial and error method. When the staff started using the software, there were real problems and the developers failed in addressing the issues in time. With the depleted work force, the implementation

became a huge task and as the main stream work force was utilized by providing training, the operational efficiency of FCI was badly affected.

7. A proper reporting system was not there in the initial stages and was added n later stages.

8. The initial data transfer design in the software model took a drastic phase shift in the later stages due to problems relating to connectivity in the remote areas in this country.

However, IISFM implementation also had some advantages such as listed below.

1. The level of usage of computers increased in the organization

2. Accessibility to computers was extended to the staff in depots (point of operation)

3. Staff and Officers got access to the world of internet due to this project.

4. FCI came up with a refined web based package "online simplified depot module" called IRRS for daily stock position management.

DISFM WEB BASED MODULE

The web based DISFM was stared in March 2005 as part of the IISFM project and the districts started entering the data from the month of June 2005.In DISFM, the district was entering consolidated data relating to depots under its jurisdiction on a fortnightly basis. The data entered is based on crop year wise and Issuable or Non-issuable criteria. The stock inflow and outflow of grain to the depot is taken in to account by the "stock figure data entry" option. Crop year wise data is entered. The data on crop year basis for inflow is taken through options such as procurement centres, agencies, other depots, state agencies. The storage gain and transit gain are also entered through inflows. In case of out flows, scheme wise issue, transfer out, storage loss, transit loss and tender sales is entered. The various data entry options with the details pertaining to the data to be entered are cited in Table 2.The issue of the foodgrains from the depot is entered through the "scheme wise off take entry". The stock wise off take is entered in commodity wise, rice, wheat or paddy and there is no provision for variety bifurcation such as raw rice or boiled rice and category bifurcations like grade 'A' or common rice. There are 37 different issue scheme options and some of them are non-operating schemes. When new schemes are added, the software is updated to accommodate them.

The data for the days from 1st to 14th is uploaded as first fortnightly data and from 15th to 31st is uploaded as second fortnightly data is entered within 3 days after ascertaining the accuracy of the data by cross checking the same with the commercial section and quality control section figures of respective offices. Once the data is entered by the district office it is the responsibility of the respective regional offices to validate the data. Once data is validated no change is permitted on the data. The regional office will have to collect the CMR (Custom Rice Milling) data from the state civil supplies corporation and enter in the DISFM software. CMR is the rice purchased directly by state government and the account of the same is kept by FCI. The quantity is adjusted against the central pool allotment of the state.

Table 2 Stock Figure Data Entry in DISFM

INFLOW	
Procurement:	Procurement of Food grains from markets
From Agency:	Stock received from Agencies
Conversion of Paddy:	In-flow of stock due to Conversion of Paddy into Rice.
Other depots	Stock Received from other depots
Change of Category	Inflow of stock due to change in category eg. A Category changes to B.
Storage Gain	Inflow of Stock due to Storage Gain.
Transit Gain	Inflow of Stock due to Transit Gain.
Levy Rice	Levy Rice receipt.
Stock accumulation during procurement	Non-Issuable Stock accumulated during Procurement
Stock in as non-issuable	Receipt of Non-Issuable Stock
OUTFLOW	
Scheme-wise Issue	Stock Issued by Depot
Transfer Out/ Despatches	Out-flow of food grains due to despatches to other depots
Transfer-out (Classification of Variety)	Out-flow of stock due to classification of variety. i.e. Classification into A, B, C etc.
Transferred as Non-Issuable	Out-flow of stock declared Non-Issuable
Storage Loss	Out-flow of stock due to Storage Loss
Transit Loss	Out-flow of stock due to Transit Loss
Tender Sale	Out-flow of stock due to Tender Sale
Issued to FCI by Agencies	Stock Issued to FCI Depots by Agencies. (Only applicable for Agencies)
Damaged Issued (Non-Issuable)	Out-flow due to Damaged Stock Issued

The main limitation of DISFM is that it is only having crop year wise variety wise data; but in the case of IRRS there is data pertaining to in all commodity, variety, crop year (year of production), category as well as issuable and non-issuable.

Table 3 : Terminology Explanation

1	2	3	4	5	6
Commodity	Variety in FCI	Category	Crop Year	Classification	Schemes
1. Rice	1. Raw Rice	1. Grade A	1. Year of Production e.g.:- 2009-10, 2010-11	1.Clear	1. Above Poverty Line
2. Wheat	2. Boiled Rice	2. Common		2.Few	2. Below Poverty Line
3. Sugar	3. Indigenous Wheat			3.Heavy	3. Antyodhaya Anna Yojana
4. Paddy	4. Imported Wheat				4. Mid-Day Meal Scheme

IRRS (INTEGRATED INFORMATION SYSTEM FOR FOOD GRAINS MANAGEMENT FOR FOOD CORPORATION OF INDIA RAPID REPORTING SYSTEM)

After an implementation exercise of IISFM project for 6 years, in July 2010, the Project Monitoring Committee (PMC) headed by Chairman and Managing Director of FCI decided to keep the depot module Version 3.1.0 in abeyance and to implement the online simplified depot module and hence the birth of IRRS. The long name of IRRS reveals that it is a continuation of IISFM project and after keeping in abeyance the original IISFM project which was implemented by spending 97.66 crores . The entire design is different in the case of IRRS and it needs only normal computers to connect to the website.

IRRS package started on August 2010 and the data from July 2010 was fed to the system. The IRRS system is having options to enter the data commodity wise, crop year wise, variety wise and category wise. The IRRS is bespoke web based online software which requires daily data entry from depot (point of operation). The data relating to commodities like rice and wheat based on variety, crop year and scheme wise issues and receipts in depots are entered on a daily basis. The storage loss incurred and storage gain obtained due to operational parameters are also adjusted and entered in the IRRS.

Table 4: Comparision Between IRRS And LISFM

IRRS	DISFM
Daily data entry	Fortnightly data entry
Depot wise data available	District wise data only available
Variety wise, Category wise data available	Variety wise , Category wise data not available
Accuracy of data not authenticated at Regional level	Regional level authentication of data by cross checking with commercial figures
Custom Milled Rice (CMR) data not available.	CMR data available and entered at District level

FAP (FINANCIAL AND ACCOUNTING PACKAGE)

FCI follows the double entry book keeping system as the one which is normally followed by the corporates in India. Financial and accounting is based on an ERP package. The package is an Oracle application 11.5.10.2. Tata Consultancy Services(TCS) are the consultants for the project and the customization of the ERP has also been done by TCS. All India rollout of this package was carried out the in Regional office of FCI at Thiruvananthapuram on 15th January 2010. The package aimed at fully computerizing FCI accounts.

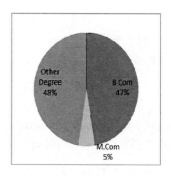

Fig. 2: FCI Kerala Region Qualification of Accounts Cadre Staff

The implementation is at a slow pace and is not likely to be successfully implemented unless drastic measures are taken for bringing in employees with knowledge of accounts and computers.

FCI account is like an ocean. The FCI accounting operations consist of maintenance of 10 major categories;

1. General ledger : comprising of part 1 and II trial balance , cash books, inter office transfers, railway credit notes etc.,

2. Payables; dealing with making payments for food grains purchased and services availed,

3. Receivables; food grains are issued on prepayment basis and in certain cases on credit to government,

4. Assets Management; dealing with the purchase, sales and inter unit transfers of assets,

5. Bank reconciliation; done in all units including headquarters and FCI is having more than 1000 accounts unit offices in various banks,

6. Budgeting and costing: budgeting is based on planned activities and costing to ascertain the average acquisition cost and economic cost,

7. Treasury Management; dealing with verification of accounts and interest charged by banks,

8. MIS and auditing; trial balance, P&L account and balanced sheet,

9. Pay roll accounting; salary payments in IDA and CDA pattern, payments like tax ,GPF, CPF and LIC etc,

10. CPF Trust Accounting at various levels where CPF accounts of employees are maintained.

There are 74 accounts cadre staff in Kerala region of which 35 are Managers and 38 clerical staff and one Asst. General Manager. The qualification of accounts cadre staff is shown in Fig. 2. From the chart it is clear than even the accounts cadre staff is not having the required accountancy knowledge. Other than accounts cadre, there are general cadre and other cadre staff working in accounts cadre, where most of them did schooling either from sports quota admissions or dependent quota.

The reasons for the slow implementation can be attributed to

1. The poor knowledge base of FCI staff. The accounts cadre itself does not have employees with the basic knowledge in accounting principles.

2. Quality of staff is poor in accounts cadre due to more number of non-qualified staff and other general cadre staff.

3. Total number of staff is not sufficient for the functioning as the work load is double as the paper based accounting system is not discontinued fully.

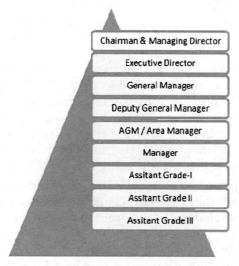

Fig. 3: FCI Hierarchy

OPERATIONAL DIFFICULTIES

The operations in FCI are not uniform throughout the region or even in same district. The labour payments are not uniform and it is difficult to change the existing practices with labour legislation. The FAP is a responsibility based accounting software. The Category 3 assistants will do the data entry and the Manager has to verify the correctness of the data and approve the same. The FCI hierarchy is depicted in Fig. 3. No other person up the ladder is directly associated with the FAP package in real sense or accountable for any of the activities of FAP. Even the head of the unit does not have a direct role in FAP except for preaching for implementation.

The policies made in appiontment and ban in recrutments and delay in promotions are the factors responsible for the present conditions. Another major work force is Class 4 staffs who were promoted as Typist and then as AG II (General). A majority of them carry high school qualification. The recent appiontments in 2010 of Category III with qualification specifying degree and 'O' level computer certificate or degree in computer and entrance test based on aptitude and general knowledge has left the cream of job aspriants out of the competition to enter FCI. The computer qualified persons who where appionted to the accounts cadre are finding it difficult to cope with the accounting procedures. Neither of these, with some exceptions are good at accountancy nor at computers.

PUBLIC POLICY PERSPECTIVE

Implementation of bespoke in operational area and ERP software in accounting system has not brought fruitful results at FCI. There are many private organizations in India which have successfully implemented the same ERP software but when it comes to government organizations (such as FCI) it is a failure. Prior to the implementation of ERP, a bespoke software project IISFM (Integrated information System for Food grain Management) was initiated by the management. The failure of IISFM was one of the reasons for going into an ERP based solution with Oracle financials. The implementation was also entrusted to one of the leading multinational software firms. Measuring of ERP systems implementation can be done (P. Booth et.al, 2000). Non analytical framework exits to examine the successful implementation of ERP (Davenport T.H., 1996) points out different types of benefits such as automate level, informate level and transformate level benefits. But in whatever way we look at the implementation in FCI, the evaluator is going to end up in difficulty.

FCI accounts were perceived to be one of the elite cadres in FCI with high efficiency and many role models. But they have not been able to go ahead with the implementation till now. The operations relating to food grain management are unique in nature and if ERP software is implemented it will require a lot of customization. In a government organization, the operations cannot be changed overnight and resistance to change is very high. When customization is large, we may lose the integrity of the system. Each time a new version of ERP is launched in the market, the ERP company will force the government organizations to upgrade to the new package and each time they will have to customize the upgraded one. Customization is normally included in the 5 year Annual Maintenance Contract (AMC) at the rate of 22 % of the implementation cost per year; this adds to the cost of ERP implementation.

The successful completion of ERP packages is very low. A lot of commitment from top level management is required to change any process in a government organization. One of the advantages of the ERP system is that you have the best practices of industries embedded in the ERP systems. However it is also thought that it will not have the options to take care of the nitty-gritty of food grain management in large organizations like Food Corporation of India where the industry is vertically integrated. In India the material management or inventory function is not fully automated. The government sector requires a great deal of flexibility in operations.

Another advantage projected by ERP is that the ERP software can be customized by functional level persons but for changes to be made in bespoke software, you require technically skilled people. In case of government offices technical as well as functional level people are all equal with no expertise. The desired output is difficult to reach.

Software made to the requirement of the customer is actually computerizing the ongoing manual operations. Because of the lack of knowledge of computer systems expertise the government companies and organizations are being cheated by the implementers by using technical jargons. For any successful implementation of ERP software, the role of a consultant is very important.

In an organization like Food Corporation of India, data must be fed in to the system from 1,820 locations across the length and breadth of the country. Due to the immature telecommunication network and lack of high speed internet in all parts of the country the data entry from remote areas is not effective and the implementation of project with data entry from point of operation is going to be affected. In the case of software implementation in various locations, the operations can vary from state to state and region to region. Another concern is that if a functional level consultant at any of the regions customizes the software, it will lose the uniformity though out the organization and therefore a central location is required to maintain the updating and revisions.

It requires a greater understanding of ERP systems rather than the normal operation of the organization to operate an ERP package. Therefore, the expertise of the employees will come in to picture which is low in government when compared to private organizations in India.

Another aspect is of cost. If we implement bespoke software, we are having option for changing the design itself later to suit the specific requirement. Agreement for purchase or development of software is made with less number of licenses and after the entire software is put in to use and is fully functional, the organization purchases balance of 5000 or 6000 licenses for the implementation in the entire organization.

With ERP marketing in India, people are trying to implement software created based on someone else's requirement and want to implement the same by treating it as best practices in the industry.

CONCLUSION

Since the technology is taking quantum leaps every day,Markus et.al, 2004 suggest that ERP benefits should be measured at different points in time and hope that the ERP implementation in FCI will be a success in years to come. But in the case of software projects, it will be better to have government agencies and establishments concentrate on their core competency and the best technologies doing the job for them. Since operations of similar nature will be there in the other part of the globe in same industry or operation of the same nature in different industry, best practices can be included in ERP. The government organisations can learn from the public policy initiatives of developed nations and can review the merits and demerits and come to a conclusion regarding implementation. It will be better if the government organizations leave the job of assisting development of software and rather leave the job to enterprise solutions like ERP to provide the complete solutions.

ACKNOWLEDGEMENT

The authors wish to thank Zonal Office (NE) of Food Corporation of India for according approval towards presentation and publication of this study at ICMC 2012.

REFERENCES

Davenport T.H., (1996) Mission Critical: Realizing the promise of Enterprise system, Harvard Business Scholl press, Boston, MA

Donald Chand et.al ,(2005), Computers in Industry, A balanced scorecard based framework for assessing the strategic impacts of ERP systems (p 561)

M.L Markus, S AxlineD.Petrie & C,.Tannis, (2000) Learning from adopters experience with ERP; problems encountered and success achieved , Journal of Information Technology 15(4) (2000) 245-266

P. Booth et.al (2000), The impact of enterprise resource planning systems on accounting practices- the Australian experience Accounting Review 10 (3) (2000) 4-18

Sunil kumar C.T. (2010)., Study of ICT Systems in FCI, Dissertation as part of PDGPPM at MDI, Gurgaon, New Delhi

ENDNOTES

1   FCI, IISFM Website, Retrieved August 3, 2011 from http://164.100.17.112/iisfm_ho/Edit_Weekly_Stock.asp

2   Prepared by the author

3   Opinions are based on the survey conducted by the writer among senior officers in FCI and other government agencies

The Influence of Marketing Strategies on Software Firm: A Case Study of Syber Systems and Solutions Pvt. Ltd.

Surabhi Singh*

ABSTRACT

Marketing of software firm is a challenging task. This requires constant analysis of customer needs and technology up gradation. The paper identifies the marketing challenges small software firms face during the growth process. It starts with the analysis of small software firm and the influence of marketing strategies on the growth of same. Marketing strategy is more important for software companies now than it has ever been. The strategy of a software firm determines the phases it will undergo. The computer software industry is undergoing some major changes which are making an impact on software vendor business models, as well as marketing and sales tactics. A successful marketing strategy can change the present and future of any software firm. In such a competitive scenario where every software company is competing with each other, strong strategy enables them to have a competitive advantage over others. This case illustrates the determinants of successful marketing strategy for the software firm and how it impacts the future of the firm.

Keywords: Knowledge, competitive advantage, strategy, business models, software, technology.

INTRODUCTION

SSSL BELIEFS

Syber Systems and Solutions P Ltd (SSSL) is a growing software company that specializes in software packages for manufacturers, distributors, government/semi-government and other small and mid-sized firms. Additionally, the company provides custom database applications and customized features for software packages. SSSL believes

* Surabhi Singh, Lecturer, IMS Noida, India.
E-mail: surbhi777@gmail.com

in forming personal relationships with their customers. They serve their customers after analyzing their operations. Their full product line and their commitment to service are the primary reasons that their business has been successful since many years. Providing excellent software service by a software company requires more than just dedication. The personnel servicing the customer must meet high standards, and the product must be capable of being serviced quickly without the risk of damaging or losing customers' sensitive data. As most software companies grow, the quality of support declines. Employee satisfaction is significant for SSSL. From an operational standpoint, SSSL has several mechanisms in place to maintain their level service. SSSL set up temporary backup procedures for their customers and train them to use them on a scheduled basis. SSSL maintains a library of corrective software utilities to reset activity in the system in case of operator error or system failures, and they utilize a highly reliable telecommunications package for remote support. SSSL support options allow it to serve customers from a centralized support location or at their business site, whichever is needed. Customer satisfaction is an important factor in SSSL. It is its goal to provide their clients with the most cost effective solution available. SSSL provides it all, including on-site installation and training of their personnel only after they have conducted an in-depth analysis of their operation. In this way their personnel are trained how to use the software as a tool to enhance their productivity. Updated technology is another important factor. SSSL dedication to same day response to support issues minimizes the loss of personnel productivity. It is its belief that when it looks at the total cost of ownership, their solution is easily the most cost effective available.

SSSL SERVICES

SSSL complete service offerings include, Business Process Re-Engineering, Business Consulting, Project Management, System Implementation, Custom Enhancements and Customer Support Services. The marketing strategies currently executed by SSSL are Inter product marketing, Creative Social Network Marketing, Viral Marketing etc. Apart from consulting and training SSSL have developed implementation models like Syber eXpresso, Syber Cappuccino and Syber Latte. Customized offering is a significant factor for its growth (Source: www.syber.in)

SSSL is a Microsoft certified partner in Uttar Pradesh (Source: www.syber.in). Businesses are under continuous pressure to improve customer service, while reducing operating costs and increasing bottom-line margins. This dynamic environment requires relentless efficiency throughout every process of any organization. SSSL has a huge client base, these include RPG Cables Ltd. Rae Bareli. (RPG group Company, DSM Sugar Mansurpur, Mansurpur, Muzaffarnagar (DSM Group Company), J.K. Sugar Ltd. Mirganj, Bareli. (J.K. Group Co.) and so on. (www.syber.in).

One direct marketing strategy, used by SSSL marketing staff, is searching the internet for potential partners which can be used to piggy-back the products of SSSL Solutions. Data on all the potential partners are stored in a database and when necessary potential partners are contacted by phone or e-mail. Native employees are employed in marketing. This direct marketing provided by native workers is an effective marketing strategy. Potential partners prefer to communicate in their own language and it creates more trust when someone from their own origin contacts them. By offering new partners a pilot project SSSL tries to convince them and contacts them for a longer period. SSSL also tries to contact potential distributors via indirect marketing. SSSL has created profiles on popular social network sites like Linked-in. These network sites are used in the same time to search for potential distributors. Software firms like Microsoft uses promotion packs like SAAS (Software as a service) and seat pack pricing.

LITERATURE REVIEW

Marketing strategy is more important for software companies now than it has ever been. The computer software industry is undergoing some major changes which are impacting software vendor business models, as well as marketing and sales tactics. The fact is that current software industry trends such as SaaS (software-as-a-service), mobile and cloud computing are having a major impact not only on the business of software but on the entire computing industry. (Source: *www.software-marketing-advisor.com*). Implementation of holistic marketing would ascertain higher customer satisfaction, increasing profits, expanding revenue base, lowering of product cost and increasing the reliability of software products. (Prem Vrat et.al, 1998). Implementation of holistic marketing in software products processes considers four components which the traditional marketing has not given the due importance. (Kotler et.al 2006). The software product firms needs to be competent in offering services with ever changing demands of the dynamic marketing environment. To overcome these barriers, the firms should deploy holistic marketing strategies based on the established niche markets for specialized software products (Nigam, 2011). India is one of the strongest countries on the field of software development in the world. India is a fast developing country (Niosi and Tschang, 2009). Holistic marketing focuses on high degree of correlation and interrelationship with firms marketing plan, customer service and Internet advertising with core customer orientation. (Nigam, 2011).Many Indian software companies decide to export to the United States because of their large and lucrative markets. According to Niosi and Tschang (2009), these larger developed markets are also the most mature and most ready to outsource services.

A single case study is applied that analyzes the global marketing strategy of a small software firm with five employees, that globalized instantly and that serves global business-to-business markets by using an Internet-based sales channel strategy (Fuerst, 2010). In terms of finding suitable partners, the main challenge for the managers of a software company will be to balance the allocation of resources between the expansion of the network through the current relationships and a focus on establishing new relationships and customers independent of existing networks. These two activities are not mutually exclusive, however, due to the limited resources experienced by many small software companies, a balance must be found (Moen et.al, 2004). Marketing of software products is different from the traditional product due to uniqueness inherent in the product. The marketing mix of the software product is very flexible, as it is neither a pure service nor a pure product. The marketing of the software product has to be dealt sensitively otherwise the firms would lose its brand equity in the market (Nigam, 2011).

OBJECTIVES

In this case, a model is developed about the characteristics of a successful marketing strategy for Indian software companies to enter the market and factors which influence the marketing strategies of the software firm. Data modeling techniques and tools capture and translate complex system designs into easily understood representations of the data flows and processes, creating a blueprint for construction and/or re-engineering. These characteristics are based on what is found during the visit and interview with Director, SSSL, Mr Sanjeev Singh. The characteristics from the model are; Effective customer service, Updated knowledge of the market, Updated technology, Employee satisfaction, Customer satisfaction, Customized offerings. (Source: Syber Systems and solutions P Ltd). In this study we will try to find out which characteristics are important and how Indian software companies have to handle these characteristics to develop a successful marketing strategy.

The case highlights the issues and effect of marketing strategies on Software firm by taking a research case of Syber Systems & Solutions P Ltd.

1. To develop the conceptual model of marketing strategies used in Syber Systems and Solutions P Ltd and its determinants.

2. To explore the association between marketing strategies and its factors.

3. To analyze the contribution of significant factors for Successful marketing strategy and its impact on the growth of SSSL.

RESEARCH DESIGN

To test our model an in-depth case study at Syber Systems & Solutions P Ltd, a medium sized Indian software company, is used. The in-depth case study tests our model in practice by taking a look into a single company. The study follows a time period of 3 months. During this period we have collected and analyzed data by conversing with the CEO, employees and partners. The questionnaire was also distributed to know the impact of determinants (as derived from the model) of marketing strategies on SSSL. Further, all the results are reported in our study and matched with our model.

The characteristics from the model are: Effective customer service, Updated knowledge of the market, Updated technology, Employee satisfaction, Customer satisfaction, Customized offerings (Refer Fig. 1).

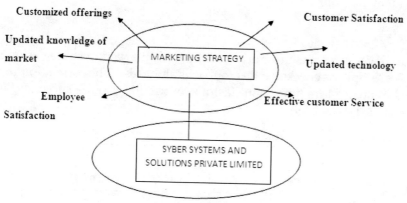

Fig. 1: The Model

Hypothesis Considered

H0 - There is no association between marketing strategies of SSSL and its determinants.

H1 - There is an association between marketing strategies of SSSL and its determinants.

Sampling

A sample of 50 was collected from customers of SSSL and employees of SSSL in Lucknow,* for knowing the impact of marketing strategies on success of SSSL and for knowing the significance of factors for marketing strategy and effectiveness of the same for success of SSSL. Convenience sampling was adopted as the methodology of sample collection.

Research Methodology

SPSS 20 was used as the statistical tool for analyzing the tabulated data. Cronbach alpha test was applied to check the reliability of data. Correlation analysis is meant for knowing the association between marketing strategy and its factors. Regression analysis is performed to know the significant impact of marketing strategies on SSSL.

* an up country town and a state capital with population of over 3.0 million

The questionnaire for customers was developed on six factors i.e Updated technology, Updated knowledge of market, Customer satisfaction, Customized offering, Employee satisfaction and Effective customer service to be drawn on five points Likert scale. Employees response on marketing strategies as used in SSSL was also obtained on five point Likert scale. Marketing Strategy is an independent variable and six factors are dependent variables.

Data Analysis

The research was conducted to study the impact of marketing strategies on SSSL. The reliability of samples is checked with cronbachs alpha test. The correlation analysis was conducted to analyze the important factors contributing to the successful marketing strategies. (Ref. Tables 1-19)

Table 1: Case Processing Summary

		N	%
	Valid	50	100.0
Cases	Excluded[a]	0	.0
	Total	50	100.0

a. Listwise deletion based on all variables in the procedure.

Table 2: Reliability Statistics

Cronbach's Alpha	N of Items
.334	7

After continuously deleting items with which the cronbach's alpha becomes higher.

Table 3: Item-Total Statistics

	Scale Mean if Item Deleted	Scale Variance if Item Deleted	Corrected Item-Total Correlation	Cronbach's Alpha if Item Deleted
Marketing Strategy	23.3000	6.622	.027	.347
Customized Offering	24.9800	5.979	.087	.332
Customer Satisfaction	23.9800	5.979	.039	.364
Employee Satisfaction	24.0600	5.609	.070	.354
Updated Technology	24.2200	4.175	.428	.068
Updated Knowledge	23.8600	5.184	.362	.181
Effective Customer Service	23.9600	5.958	.029	.373

Table 4: Scale Statistics

Mean	Variance	Std. Deviation	N of Items
28.0600	6.915	2.62958	7

After continuously deleting items with which the cronbach's alpha becomes higher.

Table 5: Case Processing Summary

Cases	N	%
Valid	50	100.0
Excluded[a]	0	.0
Total	50	100.0

a. Listwise deletion based on all variables in the procedure.

Table 6: Item Statistics

	Mean	Std. Deviation
Employee Satisfaction	4.0000	.98974
Updated Technology	3.8400	.99714

Table 7: Item-Total Statistics

	Scale Mean if Item Deleted	Scale Variance if Item Deleted	Corrected Item-Total Correlation	Cronbach's Alpha if Item Deleted
Employee Satisfaction	3.8400	.994	.579	.
Updated Technology	4.0000	.980	.579	.

Table 8: Scale Statistics

Mean	Variance	Std. Deviation	N of Items
7.8400	3.117	1.76543	2

We have got significant cronbach alpha value and correlation analysis is used for knowing the association between marketing strategy and factors viz employee satisfaction and updated technology.

Table 9: Correlations

	Corelation	Marketing Strategy	Employee Satisfaction	Updated Technology
Marketing Strategy	Pearson Correlation	1	.087	.261
	Sig. (2-tailed)		.550	.067
	N	50	50	50
Employee Satisfaction	Pearson Correlation	.087	1	.579**
	Sig. (2-tailed)	.550		.000
	N	50	50	50
Updated Technology	Pearson Correlation	.261	.579**	1
	Sig. (2-tailed)	.067	.000	
	N	50	50	50

**. Correlation is significant at the 0.01 level (2-tailed).

Table 10: Variables Entered/Removed[a]

Model	Variables Entered	Variables Removed	Method
1	Updated Knowledge, Employee Satisfaction, Customized Offering, Effective Customer Service, Customer Satisfaction, Updated Technology[b]	.	Enter

a. Dependent Variable: Marketing Strategy

b. All requested variables entered.

Table 11: ANOVA

Model		Sum of Squares	Df	Mean Square	F	Sig.
1	Regression	2.800	6	.467	2.411	
	Residual	8.320	43	.193		.043b
	Total	11.120	49			

a. Dependent Variable: Marketing Strategy

b. Predictors: (Constant), Updated Knowledge, Employee Satisfaction, Customized Offering, Effective Customer Service, Customer Satisfaction, Updated Technology

Table 12: Coefficients[a]

Model		Unstandardized Coefficients		Standardized Coefficients	t	Sig.
		B	Std. Error	Beta		
1	(Constant)	5.111	.615		8.313	.000
	Customized Offering	-.034	.084	-.055	-.400	.691
	Customer Satisfaction	-.221	.077	-.406	-2.851	.007
	Employee Satisfaction	-.046	.084	-.095	-.540	.592
	Updated Technology	.129	.083	.269	1.548	.129
	Effective Customer Service	-.113	.073	-.216	-1.543	.130
	Updated Knowledge	.191	.104	.292	1.832	.074

a. Dependent Variable: Marketing Strategy

Table 13: Variables Entered/Removed[a]

Model	Variables Entered	Variables Removed	Method
1	Updated Knowledge, Employee Satisfaction, Customized Offering, Effective Customer Service, Customer Satisfaction, Updated Technology[b]	.	Enter
2	.	Customized Offering	Backward (criterion: Probability of F-to-remove >= .100).
3	.	Employee Satisfaction	Backward (criterion: Probability of F-to-remove >= .100).
4	.	Effective Customer Service	Backward (criterion: Probability of F-to-remove >= .100).
5	.	Updated Knowledge	Backward (criterion: Probability of F-to-remove >= .100).

a. Dependent Variable: Marketing Strategy

b. All requested variables entered.

Table 14: ANOVA[a]

	Model	Sum of Squares	Df	Mean Square	F	Sig.
1	Regression	2.800	6	.467	2.411	.043[b]
	Residual	8.320	43	.193		
	Total	11.120	49			
2	Regression	2.769	5	.554	2.917	.023[c]
	Residual	8.351	44	.190		
	Total	11.120	49			
3	Regression	2.721	4	.680	3.645	.012[d]
	Residual	8.399	45	.187		
	Total	11.120	49			
4	Regression	2.277	3	.759	3.948	.014[e]
	Residual	8.843	46	.192		
	Total	11.120	49			
5	Regression	1.753	2	.876	4.398	.018[f]
	Residual	9.367	47	.199		
	Total	11.120	49			

a. Dependent Variable: Marketing Strategy

b. Predictors: (Constant), Updated Knowledge, Employee Satisfaction, Customized Offering, Effective Customer Service, Customer Satisfaction, Updated Technology

c. Predictors: (Constant), Updated Knowledge, Employee Satisfaction, Effective Customer Service, Customer Satisfaction, Updated Technology

d. Predictors: (Constant), Updated Knowledge, Effective Customer Service, Customer Satisfaction, Updated Technology

e. Predictors: (Constant), Updated Knowledge, Customer Satisfaction, Updated Technology

f. Predictors: (Constant), Customer Satisfaction, Updated Technology

Table 15: Coefficients[a]

Model		Unstandardized Coefficients		Standardized Coefficients	t	Sig.
		B	Std. Error	Beta		
1	(Constant)	5.111	.615		8.313	.000
	Customized Offering	-.034	.084	-.055	-.400	.691
	Customer Satisfaction	-.221	.077	-.406	-2.851	.007
	Employee Satisfaction	-.046	.084	-.095	-.540	.592
	Updated Technology	.129	.083	.269	1.548	.129
	Effective Customer Service	-.113	.073	-.216	-1.543	.130
	Updated Knowledge	.191	.104	.292	1.832	.074
2	(Constant)	5.029	.574		8.763	.000
	Customer Satisfaction	-.219	.077	-.403	-2.860	.006
	Employee Satisfaction	-.042	.083	-.086	-.501	.619
	Updated Technology	.126	.082	.264	1.537	.132
	Effective Customer Service	-.115	.072	-.219	-1.582	.121
	Updated Knowledge	.185	.102	.282	1.809	.077
3	(Constant)	4.883	.490		9.957	.000
	Customer Satisfaction	-.220	.076	-.404	-2.894	.006
	Updated Technology	.100	.063	.210	1.585	.120
	Effective Customer Service	-.110	.071	-.209	-1.543	.130
	Updated Knowledge	.199	.097	.305	2.059	.045
4	(Constant)	4.549	.447		10.185	.000
	Customer Satisfaction	-.208	.077	-.383	-2.717	.009
	Updated Technology	.107	.064	.223	1.664	.103
	Updated Knowledge	.155	.094	.237	1.651	.106
5	(Constant)	4.935	.388		12.734	.000
	Customer Satisfaction	-.162	.073	-.299	-2.233	.030
	Updated Technology	.127	.064	.266	1.984	.053

a. Dependent Variable: Marketing Strategy

Table 16: Variables Entered/Removed[a]

Model	Variables Entered	Variables Removed	Method			
1	Customer Satisfaction	.	Forward (Criterion: Probability-of-F-to-enter <= .050)			

a. Dependent Variable: Marketing Strategy

Table 17: ANOVA[a]

Model		Sum of Squares	Df	Mean Square	F	Sig.
1	Regression	.968	1	.968	4.578	.038[b]
	Residual	10.152	48	.211		
	Total	11.120	49			

a. Dependent Variable: Marketing Strategy

b. Predictors: (Constant), Customer Satisfaction

Table 18: Coefficients[a]

Model		Unstandardized Coefficients		Standardized Coefficients	t	Sig.
		B	Std. Error	Beta		
1	(Constant)	5.414	.313		17.324	.000
	Customer Satisfaction	-.160	.075	-.295	-2.140	.038

a. Dependent Variable: Marketing Strategy

Table 19: Excluded Variables[a]

Model		Beta In	T	Sig.	Partial Correlation	Collinearity Statistics
						Tolerance
1	Customized Offering	.004b	.027	.978	.004	1.000
	Employee Satisfaction	.066b	.474	.638	.069	.995
	Updated Technology	.266b	1.984	.053	.278	1.000
	Effective Customer Service	-.127b	-.923	.361	-.133	1.000
	Updated Knowledge	.283b	1.973	.054	.277	.872

a. Dependent Variable: Marketing Strategy

b. Predictors in the Model: (Constant), Customer Satisfaction

RESULTS

Correlation is drawn on the reliable sample. By using correlation analysis, we conclude that the two significant factors viz Employee satisfaction and updated technology which was successful with the cronbach's alpha test also, is positively associated with dependent variable i.e successful marketing strategies.

The regression analysis proves that the association between marketing strategies with customer satisfaction is strong. Hence the marketing strategies of SSSL are effective and customer satisfaction is enhanced in SSSL.

CONCLUSION AND IMPLICATIONS

This study of the effectiveness of marketing strategies on SSSL throws light on the significance of marketing strategies for the software firm. Updated technology, Employee satisfactions are significant for the internal growth of company and customer satisfaction is important for the external growth of company. The software firm must focus on the employee satisfaction and updated technology. Marketing strategies are effective if advanced technology is used. The impact of marketing strategy is successful if customer of software firm is satisfied. There are three generic strategies for being successful in business, cost leadership, market leadership and niche focus. Most strategies employed by successful software firms fall into one of these three categories. The software companies must improve SaaS customer's experience which includes the speed of deployment, ease of configuration, access to support, and the simplicity of the purchase process. It is essential to market all these features and benefits of the entire "service", and not just the product functionality.

LIMITATIONS

The sample size is restricted to 50 only. Due to lack of time, large samples could not be collected. The six limited factors were taken for the study undertaken although additional factors are also possible.

ACKNOWLEDGEMENT

The author would like to express her sincere thanks to Mr. Sanjeev Singh, Director, Syber Systems & Solutions P Ltd for the support in developing the case as well as consent to present and publish the same at ICMC2012.

REFERENCES

Fuerst Sascha(2010), "Global marketing strategy: the case of a born global software firm in Colombia", Revista Ciencias Estratégicas, vol. 18, núm. 24, julio-diciembre, 2010, pp. 271-286

Kotler Philip and Keller Lane Kelvin (2006), "Marketing Management", Prentice Hall of India, 12th edition.

Nigam, Dr. Ashutosh (2011), "Holistic Marketing of Software Products: The New Paradigm", IJCSMS International Journal of Computer Science & Management Studies, Vol. 11, Issue 01

Niosi, J. and Tschang, F.T. (2009), "The strategies of Chinese and Indian software multinationals: implications for internationalization theory", Industrial and Corporate Change, Vol. 18 No.2, pp. 269-294.

Øystein Moen ; Gavlen Morten; Endreson Iver, "Internationalization of small, computer software firms Entry forms and market selection", European Journal of Marketing Vol. 38 No. 9/10, 2004 pp. 1236-1251

Prem Vrat, Sardana G.D and Sahay B.S. (1998), "Productivity Mangement: A system approach", Narosa Publication House, New Delhi.

Svensson GoÈran (2001), "Re-evaluating the marketing Concept" European Business Review, Volume 13. Number 2. 2001. pp. 95±100.

www.software-marketing-advisor.com (accessed on 20-07-12)

www.syber.in (official website of Syber Systems & Solutions P Ltd)

Excerpts of interviews from Director, Syber Systems & Solutions P Ltd

Delivering Sustainable Innovations by P&G Through LCA

Raveesh Agarwal* and Monica Thiel**

ABSTRACT

P&G is committed to improving people's everyday life by making products more environmentally sustainable. To understand how a company such as P & G can make products more environmentally sustainable, the present case focuses on the scientific approach called Life Cycle Assessment (LCA) adopted by P & G to deliver sustainable innovations without tradeoffs in performance or value of the products.

Keywords: Environmentally sustainable, Life Cycle Assessment P & G, Strategy, social responsibility, Conservation.

INTRODUCTION

P&G – Brief Profile

P&G was founded in 1837 at Cincinnati, Ohio, U.S. by two entrepreneurs named William Procter, a candle maker emigrating from England, and James Gamble, a soap maker originally from Ireland. They met each other by chance. Mr. William Procter married Olivia Norris who was the daughter of Mr. Alexander Norris, a prominent candle maker in Cincinnati. Mr. James Gamble married Elizabeth Ann Norris who was the sister of Olivia, and second daughter of Mr. Alexander Norris. Mr. Norris suggested both son-in-laws create a joint venture. Finally on October 31, 1837, Mr. William Procter and Mr. James Gamble signed the partnership agreement that founded the Procter & Gamble Company, which began as a small family-run candle and soap business, and has now become a multi-national giant and the largest consumer goods

* Raveesh Agarwal is with CCS University, Meerut.
** Monica Thiel is with Tilburg University, the Netherlands.
E-mail: drravish15@gmail.com, mt2652@gmail.com

company in the world. Grounded by core responsible business values with a long history of excellence in business decisions, P&G is now at the forefront and turning its attention toward sustainability, conservation, and social responsibility on a global level.

P&G's world headquarters is located in the founding company's city of Cincinnati, Ohio, U.S. P&G sells its products in more than eighty countries to serve more than one and half billion consumers around the world. P&G has over 130 manufacturing facilities in over forty countries. Roughly 10-15 percent of the company's manufacturing volume is completed by contract manufacturing. However, the percentage of P&G production supplied by contract manufacturers varies according to the needs of the business. P&G has a number of products in its portfolio of quality brands. Some of the most popular selling brands around the globe include Pampers, Tide, Ariel, Always, Whisper, Pantene, Mach3, Bounty, Dawn, Fairy, Gain, Pringles, Charmin, Downy, Lenor, Lams, Crest, Oral-B, Duracell, Olay, Head & Shoulders, Wella, Gillette, Braun, Fusion, Ace, Febreze, and Ambi Pur, etc.

Innovation is the fundamental driver to develop these brands as leading brands in the global market. P&G has a global network of external innovation partners, which leads to an effective investment in innovation and research. The company is committed to making socially responsible products that are better for the environment, thereby improving the environment and safety of the world's consumers (P&G Connect, 2012).

P&G SUSTAINABILITY STRATEGY

P&G has a long history of envisioning sustainability as a responsibility to do the right things for the environment and for human safety. P&G encountered issues in the 1950s related to surfactants. Surfactants were used in laundry detergent at that time, and were not fully biodegradable. These surfactants were partially biodegradable resulting in suds forming in the rivers. As a consequence, P&G established an environmental science department.This resulted in evaluating biodegradability and developing methods for evaluating environmental safety and environmental toxicology with the invention of a "Sturm Test" by a P&G employee named Bob Sturm. The Sturm Test allowed P&G to change some of its ingredients in the manufacturing of the products that were not environmentally friendly and further opened ways to create more new technologies to provide assurance that products developed by P&G will be safe for the environment and safe for people to use the products. Today, the environmental science department continues to develop and improve methods for evaluating environmental safety and environmental toxicology for product sustainability.

P&G strives to ensure that consumers need not make a choice between sustainability, performance, and value. Hence, it is very important to find out what kinds of technology and innovation P&G is exploring in order to meet these criteria.

At the same time, sustainability could be more than just responsibility, it could also be an opportunity to build the business. Therefore, P&G developed its programs to include not only responsibility, but also opportunity. For P&G, that opportunity came to improve the environmental footprint of its products, its operations, and to deliver the products that enabled them to be more environmentally sustainable in a meaningful way for consumers and to the bottom line. P&G conducted research to better understand how consumers thought about "green products". This research demonstrated that the vast majority of consumers, which they refer to as the "sustainable mainstream", are not willing to accept any trade-offs in performance or price in order to purchase green products. Consequently, P&G focused on this "sustainable mainstream" and developed new products, which enabled consumers to be environmentally sustainable, but for which there were no tradeoffs, and this is where this idea of Sustainable Innovation Products (SIPs) originated. The invention and development of SIPs resulted in reduced environmental footprints for which there are no trade-offs to the consumer. P&G uses the following criteria for defining SIPs (Sauers & White, 2008):

- A reduction in environmental footprint achieved through technical or commercial product innovation impacting one or more of the following: energy, water, transportation, packaging, and substitution of non-renewable energy or materials with renewable sources.

- A significant reduction of more than 10% in at least one indicator, or a reduction equivalent to the footprint of at least 10,000 people for one or more of the indicators.

- The reduction is not offset by a meaningful increase in other indicators and does not negatively impact the overall sustainability profile of the product.

- Reductions are supported by sound and transparent assumptions, scientific methodologies substantiated by data, and pass existing approval systems at P&G.

P&G believes that the environmental benefits of SIPs should be significant, obvious, and easy to communicate. P&G has been able to reduce the amount of materials, which they use to manufacture a product along with the energy it takes to produce them and the waste at the end of consumer usage. SIPs have significantly contributed in terms of environmental protection while minimizing negative product impacts. In 2011, some of the products which were reinvented by P&G through analyzing the footprint of the products throughout its entire life cycle arePowder Laundry Detergents (Cheer, Dreft, Era, Gain Ivory Snow, Tide), Pantene Nature Fusion, Gillette Fusion ProGlide Razors, Pampers Cruisers, Pampers Baby Dry, Swaddlers, Baby, Active Fit, Active Baby, Juegos Latin and Cruisers with Dry Max, and Pampers Wipes Sensitive. All of these products are available in different countries of the world and these products strive to benefit the environment with no consumer trade-offs.

P&G PRODUCTS WITHOUT TRADEOFFS

Compaction of Powder Laundry Detergents

P&G created a winning formula for customers, retailers, and for the environment of the world in terms of compaction of powder laundry detergents. P&G focused on the compaction the entire portfolio of Canadian and U.S. carton powder laundry detergents (Tide, Gain, Cheer, Dreft, Ivory Snow, etc) by 33%, which provides different benefits to consumers as well as the environment. The compacted powder formulas of laundry detergent use a higher proportion of dense active cleaning agent which provides better cleaning and shine with use of lesser product, the product being lighter to carry and easier to store, resulting in greater consumer benefits. The retailers also benefited with compaction because now 33% lesser inventory space is required. At the same time, fewer trucks, fewer pallets are required which provides more efficient supply chain. This compaction step taken by P&G results in less wasteas a smaller carton size, less use of diesel in transportation as fewer trucks required, which ultimately provides environmental benefits (Saouter & White, 2002). This initiative taken by P&G shows that sustainability can create more benefits to the consumer as well as to the environment. Similarly changes in Pampers Cruisers' packaging increased the number of units that could be placed on a truck, delivering an overall reduction in transportation and energy.In total, there are significant savings in CO_2 emissions and transportation fuel (Muller, 1992).

Gillette Fusion Proglide Razor Tray:

P&G focused on reduction of packaging material and the result was Gillette's Fusion ProGlide razor, which was introduced in Western Europe in 2011. In the packaging of the razor, a plant fiber-based razor tray and recycled 100% recycled polyethylene terephthalate (rPET) was used which was the replacement of plastic clamshell plastic. It uses 57% less plastic and weighs 20% less than the original Fusion outer pack and razor tray. The molded pulp tray, which is made from bamboo, sugarcane, and bulrush fibers, was designed collaboratively by the Gillette unit of P&G and "BeGreen Packaging". The razor is smaller than the previous razor contributing to an overall lighter pack and reduction in total packaging material. The new design significantly reduces materials by minimizing the internal tray and simplifying the design. The new packaging structure stays strong under compression, sealing and opening forces, and distribution and transportation stresses, while also maintaining a strong visual presence on the shelf. This packaging is 100% free of Polyvinyl Chloride (PVC).

Pampers Swaddlers, and Cruisers Diapers with DRY MAX Technology

P&G introduced DRY MAX technology in diapers, which is one of the biggest innovations in Pampers Swaddlers and Cruisers diapers. It allows for the removal of the air felt ("paper pulp") found in the diapers resulting in a thinner and less bulky core. The thinner core is enabled by the new Absorbent Gelling Material (AGM), removing the need for air felt. The AGM is more permeable, meaning it locks wetness in faster than previous AGM. With this DRY MAX technology, Pampers Swaddlers and Cruisers Diapers became leak-proof diapers, in which wetness is locked in for up to twelve hours. These diapers are able to withstand large quantities of moisture. The new dry max technology pulls the moisture away from the skin keeping the baby's bottom dry, and helping to prevent diaper rash. The new technology allows these diapers to be 20% thinner than before and provide flexibility and comfort to babies. Changes to product formulation and package design delivered reductions in material usage as the new design also contains 10% less material weight, which helps families to reduce their impact on the environment. "Despite such improvements, P&G surveysand on-line blogs show that some parents feel confused or guilty about how diapers fit with sustainable living approaches, as they try to balance diaper cost, convenience,hygienic containment, baby's skin health, and uninterrupted sleep, with potential environmental impacts"(Weisbrod &Hoof, 2011).

Pantene Pro-V Nature Fusion

P&G produced shampoo and conditioner bottles made primarily from plant-based plastic. This material is made from sugar cane and used for the packaging of shampoo and conditioner under the brand Pantene Pro-V Nature Fusion. The new bottles initially launched in Western Europe in 2011. The packaging contains plastic derived from sugar cane, a natural and renewable resource, as opposed to traditional plastic, which is made from petroleum, a non renewable material. The process starts with harvesting of sugarcane, which is crushed mechanically, and sugar juice is obtained. This sugar juice is converted to ethanol through fermentation with yeast. The ethanol is chemically converted to ethylene, which is then combined to make polyethylene. The resultant product is known as Bio-Polyethylene (Bio-PE). This plastic is chemically identical to polyethylene plastic made from petroleum. Sugar cane-derived plastic consumes more than 70% less fossil fuels and releases more than 170% less greenhouse gases per ton than traditional petroleum-based plastic. As a result of these efforts, the sugarcane being used is definitely sustainable sourced and the plastic itself provides tangible sustainability benefits. The use of sugar cane-based plastic in Nature Fusion packaging allows P&G to offer the same performance, which consumers expect, from Pantene but in a more sustainable way. By using renewable resources, such as sugar cane-based plastic, Pantene is supporting P&G's goal of replacing 25% of petroleum-based materials with sustainably sourced renewable materials by 2020. P&G's long-term vision is to use 100% renewable or recycled materials on all of its products. (P&G Sustainability Overview, 2011).

Tide Cold Water

Consumers can save on their energy bills with Tide Cold Water. P&G introduced Tide Cold Water detergent liquid, powder and soap, which required no hot water.

It has a substantial impact on the environment resulting in energy saving, and these savings would translate into million tons of carbon dioxide per year not released into the environment.

DELIVERING SUSTAINABLE PRODUCTS THROUGH LIFE CYCLE ASSESSMENT (LCA)

Through years of rigorous study, P&G has learned that in order to truly embrace sustainable practices, the company must employ a three-legged approach. The three-legged approach includes environmental protection, economic development and social responsibility that play a key role in developing sustainable innovation products and processes. A tool called Life Cycle Assessment (LCA) was used by the company to help P&G understand where the company can make the most meaningful improvements in a product's environmental footprint. LCA is an important product-oriented method for environmental sustainability impacts. In 2007, P&G commissioned an independent LCA of liquid laundry products designed to identify and quantify the environmental changes related to compaction, with the following goals:

- Provide internal decision support on the possibilities to promote compaction on environmental grounds.
- Quantify the environmental impacts per wash of a liquid laundry detergent compaction /concentration.
- Quantify the environmental impacts per wash related to detergent formulation and production, packaging, distribution and end-of-life stages.

By using a scientific method and approach such as the LCA, P&G has adopted a systematic way to understand and assess the environmental impact of consumer products. The company developed an ISO-compliant database for LCA evaluation of laundry detergents. The product life cycle is evaluated using 11 environmental indicators that are considered relevant for the product category. The LCA analyzed 11 different parameters including: Total primary energy; Total water consumption; Total solid waste generated; Climate change; Photochemical oxygen formation; Eutrophication; Ozone depletion; Human toxicity; Acidification; Aquatic Eco-toxicity (CML); Freshwater toxicity. The LCA approach is shown in Figure 1.

This approach is also known as "Cradle to Grave Approach" and looks at the product from its infancy state, which means "cradle" or "beginning", to its disposal or end of life, which represents "grave" or closed loop. Open loop recycling (OLR) is another LCA method for potential recovery of the end of the product life, providing waste management for one product system that provides material for another in the end of the product life cycle (Nicholson, et al., 2010). The different stages of Life Cycle Assessment within laundry detergents are shown in Figure 1. These stages consider raw material production, transport, manufacturing and packaging the way in which the detergent is used by the consumer, the disposal of the detergent and the packaging after use (Saouter & Hoof, 2002). LCA allows scientists to take a "snapshot" of the entire life cycle of a product to systematically assess the impact of each step. It is a tool to examine environmental impacts of technologies and products through the entire product life cycle. Furthermore, LCA is an analytical computer-modeling tool that allows scientists to account for many variables, spanning from the time a product is created until the moment the empty container is discarded. The analysis begins as early as the mining and harvest of raw materials and takes into account manufacturing methods, delivery of the product and final disposal of the packaging (The Sustainable Approach, 2006).

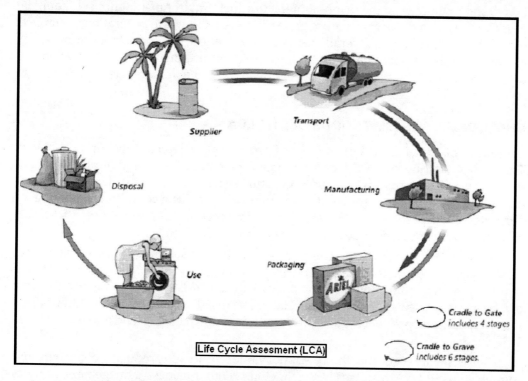

Fig. 1: Life Cycle Assessment (LCA) - A Case of Laundry Detergent

Source: Erwan Saouter (2003), Cutting Environmental Effect by half: Compact detergents can do it! P&G External Relations, Geneva (www.scienceinthebox.com)

LCA is a systematic framework with various methods for comprehensive qualitative and quantitative environmental assessment of goods and services (Christiansen, 1997).

The primary objective of carrying out a LCA is to provide a complete picture as possible of the interactions of human activity within the environment. The other objectives are to understand the overall and interdependent nature of the environmental consequences of human activities and to provide decision-makers with information to identify opportunities for environmental improvements (Pant, 2007). Business leaders should recognize that different product systems might require distinct LCA methods because environmental values are not clearly integrated in market pricing (Christiansen, 1997). Furthermore, critical and comparatative LCA review processes are vital for potential environmental impacts and differential significance. Consumers can quantify the footprint and impact, across a product's entire life cycle, from the creation of raw materials that are used in the product, to manufacturing, to logistics, to use in the home, and to ultimately the disposal of the product. Environmental impacts could be described as energy use, greenhouse gas emissions, solid waste generation, water use, etc. (Saouter, et. al., 2002). Overall, designing more effective products and influencing behaviors in the supply chain are the most impactful things that a corporation can do to achieve sustainable product development and enablemore sustainable living" (Weisbrod & Hoof, 2011).

CHALLENGES AND LIMITATIONS OF THE LCA

There are four phases within the LCA framework as depicted in Figure 2 below. The phases describe how LCA product data can be interpreted and applied in many different ways. LCA primarily focuses on natural science. "LCA considers all attributes or aspects of natural environment, human health and resources. By considering all attributes and aspects within one study in a cross-media perspective, potential trade-offs can be identified and assessed" (Finkbeiner, et. al, 2006).

LCA product systems from companies' site-specific data have disadvantages and advantages for business management. The advantage for companies such as P&G is that the product data is not based on a mean score and is specific to the product line of the company (Lewandowski, et. al., 2004). The disadvantage is that the LCA cannot easily capture one product system for the entire supply chain (Hendrickson, C., et al., 1998).

Many scholars argue that the LCA is not value free, thereby reducing objectivity and completeness of LCA results (Hertwich, et al., 2000). Business management analysts should understand the "need to clearly identify and state value-based choices" in LCA (Ibid). Furthermore, value-based choices are a snapshot of the present without "taking the future into account" (Stevels, et. al., 1999).

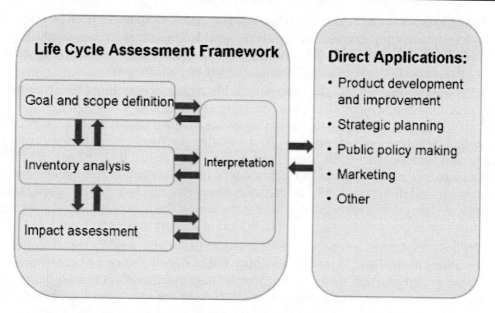

Fig. 2: Phases and applications of an LCA (based on ISO 14040, 1997).

Most if not all-human activities have some environmental impact. Differing human needs, preferences and incomes may limit the capacity of LCA due to consumer choices and preferences. For this reason, economic and social impacts are not currently assessed within the LCA. Therefore, corporate strategy should consider combining LCA with other tools for social and economic assessments of products and services. Furthermore, management should not solely rely on the LCA tool for environmental impacts. Including other methods and approaches will increase data reliability, decision-making and corporate strategy (European Environment Agency, 1997). P&G recognizes more tools and methods are necessary to meet the company's long-term environmental sustainability vision. For example, P&G recently signed a Cooperative Research and Development Agreement (CRADA) with the Environmental Protection Agency (EPA) National Risk Management Research Laboratory (NRMRL) to develop tools and methods for optimization and improvement of sustainability metrics and indicators within products, manufacturing and supply chain contexts (Business Wire Press Release, July 24, 2012).

P&G GLOBAL SUSTAINABILITY INITIATIVES

P&G strives to change the perceptions of consumers through education. P&G launched a series of programs to educate consumers with ties of several Non-Governmental Organizations (NGOs) in different countries. Advertising and partnering with different utilities such as the electrical utilities, etc. are other initiatives taken by P&G to educate consumers throughout the world. The company launched "Future Friendly" – a consumer education campaign in U.K. that helps consumers to reduce their impacts on the environment through the use of P&G brands.

P&G established a P&G Global Sustainability department in July 1999. The Global Sustainability department focuses on defining the company's overall sustainability policy, identifying emerging sustainability issues, managing corporate sustainability reporting, building external relations, and assisting the business units to incorporate sustainable development into their businesses. To further their efforts, they also established Single Points of Contact (SPOCs) who lead sustainability for their respective businesses and functions. The advantages the company received by establishing SPOCs are integrating sustainability in the rhythm of the business, having programs across all of its business sectors, and goals around its operations and products.

In 2009, P&G was added to the Global 100 list of the world's mostsustainable corporations in the Dow Jones Sustainability Index (DJSI). Today, P&G continues the company's DJSI position as a global leader in sustainability. This is an independent recognition of the company's strong performance in the area of sustainability. P&G also has been a member of the FTSE4Good index since its inception and won the 2008 European Business Award for Corporate Sustainability, recognizing its new strategy and goals. These types of indicators have a global scope and will continue to be an important measure of the company's performance in sustainability (Sauers & White, 2008). P&G is producing an annual global sustainability report. The company prepared its first sustainability report in October 1999 based on the format developed by the Global Reporting Initiative (GRI). The GRI provides a common format for sustainability reporting that assists both the organization providing the report and those using the report as a key source of data. The GRI consists of multinational corporations, NGOs, international associations, universities, and other stakeholders from around the world. P&G has embedded sustainability into its purpose, values, and principles as a company. For example, the purpose of P&G is as follows:

"We provide branded products and services of superior quality and value that improve the lives of the world's consumers, now and for generations to come."

(Source: Company Website 2012)

P&G also added a new principle that states:

"We incorporate sustainability into our products, packaging, and operations."

(Source: Company Website 2012)

This means that sustainability is built into the rhythm of its business through employees taking responsibility by taking a next step or action to integrate sustainability into the home and workplace. Employees are guided by P&G's purpose, values and principles. This is important. For sustainability to be "sustainable," it needs to be embraced by employees and consumers. P&G follows the definition of Sustainability that is defined by the U.K. government. This definition describes better quality of life for every human being in the developed and developing world. According to this definition, sustainability is about ensuring a better quality of life for everyone, now and for generations to come. It integrates economic development, environmental protection, and social responsibility.

P&G sustainability includes both environmental sustainability and social responsibility by making products and services in an environmentally responsible manner, and through its social responsibility investment and employee volunteer programs to help needy peoples throughout the world. The long term environmental sustainable vision of P&G includes powering the plants with 100% renewable energy, using 100% renewable or recycled materials for all products and packaging, having zero consumer and manufacturing waste go to landfills, designing products that delight consumers while maximizing the conservation of resources, etc. P&G's social responsibility programs helps children in need around the world to receive a healthy start, access to education and to build skills for life, etc. These goals were originally set by P&G in 2007 across different areas of products, operations and social responsibilities (Franke, 2007). Overall, P&G strives to understand consumers' financial, social and environmental needs and concerns to develop environmentally and socially responsible products. P&G equips all employees and stakeholders to build sustainability thinking and practices into their routine work with a focus on integrity, leadership, ownership, passion for winning and trust between employees, P&G brands and consumers. Reducing consumer waste in landfills and maximizing the conservation of resources are examples of shared social and environmental sustainability where the consumer and P&G benefit. However, it is not easy to achieve 100% results immediately. Therefore, P&G set two strategies in products and operations to achieve its vision for 2012 and 2020 within products and operations for making its employees and stakeholders accountable.

CONCLUSION

Finally, it can be said that success is based on the approach of getting the final results by making meaningful efforts. With a growing emphasis on sustainability these products appear to be well positioned to take advantage of the trend. So by creating a consumer product that targets mainstream consumers with meaningful improvements and with no trade-offs, P&G makes positive impacts in environmental sustainability and social responsibility. Over the years sustainability continues to be a top priority at P&G and as P&G already has implemented several successful sustainable initiatives, the company continues to strive for further improvement.

ACKNOWLEDGEMENT

The authors would like to thank Mcaneny, Jack, P&G for his support in developing this case and permission to use information derived from the interviews in the case study.

REFERENCES

Business Wire. P&G and U.S. EPA Sign Research Agreement to Help Company Attain Sustainability Goals. Press Release July 24, 2012. Retrieved at http://www.marketwatch.com.

Christiansen, K., (1997). Simplifying LCA: Just a cut? SETAC Europe LCA; Screening and streamlining working group; Final report.

European Environment Agency. (1997). Life Cycle Assessment (LCA): A Guide to Approaches, Experiences and Information Sources, Environment Issue Series no. 6, August 1997.

Finkbeiner, Matthias, et al. (2006). The New International Standards for Life Cycle Assessment: ISO 14040 and ISO 14044. International Journal LCA, 11 (2) 80-85.

Franke, Marina (2007). Sustainable Manufacturing @ P&G. Sustainable Manufacturing and Competitiveness, OECD Conference, DK Copenhagen. Retrieved at: www.oecd.org/dataoecd/12/47/38876439.pdf.

Hendrickson, C., et al. (1998). Economic Input-Output Models for Environmental Life-Cycle Assessment. Environmental Sciences and Technology, April 1; p. 184A-191A.

Hertwich, EG, et al. (2000). A Theoretical Foundation for Life-Cycle Assessment. Journal of Industrial Ecology, v.4, Muller, E.J. (1992) The Quest for a Quality Environment, Distribution, Logistics & theEnvironment, 32-36. Pant, Rana (2007). Life Cycle Assessment in a consumer goods company, LCA group, Product Safety & Regulatory Affairs, Central Product Safety (CPS), Procter & Gamble Eurocor NV/SA Strombeek-Bever.

Lewandowsky, A., et. al. (2004). New Directions of Development in Environmental Life Cycle Assessment. Polish Journal of Environmental Studies, Vol. 13, No. 5, 46-466.

Nicholson, Anna, et al. (2010). LCA Allocation Methods in Open-Loop Recycling: Incentivizing Recycled Material Sourcing and Creation of Recyclable Products.

Retrieved at: www.lcacenter.org/LCAX/presentations-final/212.pdf

Saouter E, White P (2002). Laundry detergents: cleaner clothes and a cleaner environment. Corporate Environmental Strategy. 9: 40-50.

Sauers Len, and White, Peter (2008). Global Sustainability Communications, One Voice. Retrieved at: http://onevoice.pg.com/pa/word/default.htm.

Saouter E, Van Hoof G (2002). A database for the life cycle evaluation of Procter & Gamble laundry detergent. International Journal of Life Cycle Assessment. 7: 15-28.

Saouter E, Van Hoof G, Feijtel T C J, Owens J W (2002). The effects of compact formulations on the environmental profile of north European granular laundry detergents. Part II: Life Cycle Assessment. International Journal of Life Cycle Assessment. 7: 27-38.

Stevels, A., et al. (1999). Application of LCA in Eco-Design: A Critical Review. The Journal of Sustainable Product Design, April: 20-26.

The Sustainable Approach to Sustainability (2006). Breakthroughs Science News from P&G Beauty & Grooming, vol. XIX, pp1-4. Retrieved at www.pgbeautyscience.com.

Weisbrod, Anne V. & Hoof, Gert Van (2011). LCA-measured environmental improvements in Pampers diapers, Sustainable Development, International Journal of Life Cycle Assess, DOI 10.1007/s11367-011-0343-1.

RETRIEVED INFORMATION FROM THE FOLLOWING WEBSITES

http://www.globalreporting.org.

http://www.pg.com.

www.pgconnectdevelop.com

PART III: Focus on Operational Competencies

Since the advent of globalization and free access to trade all over the world economies the customer now has a number of alternative choices to choose from and uses his criteria to select a product or service. The text books refer to these performance criteria in the domain of price payable, quality, flexibility, delivery and the service. Together as a package these are supposed to deliver value or generate satisfaction to the customer. These performance criteria find origin in use of resources and their application in various management processes. Efficient application of the resources results from operational competencies. Location of right resources, in right quantity at right price are the first considerations to aim at operational competencies. Thus an enterprise locates a resource in one part of the world, finds another somewhere else, achieves transformation at a third location whereas the market for consumption could be at a different place. In another dimension, an entrepreneur might try to achieve competencies by reengineering the processes. The cases in this PART are grouped around this common theme. A total of seven cases are included. These are drawn from diverse areas and cover diverse locations. Both tangible products and services are covered.

In Japan, automobiles with very small engines are called light cars. Two major K-car companies are 'Daihatsu' and 'Suzuki'. These small cars were developed in Japan to meet local requirements of narrow roads. Iijima Masaki and Itoh in the Chapter 12, aim to discuss the difference in foreign business development of these companies for their success and failure.

Networks of informal entrepreneurs or rag-pickers operate within large cities of the developing world. Rag-pickers' networks and waste streams hold not only economic, but also environmental and social value. In this research Sameer Prasad et al. in Chapter 13, use qualitative methodology and archival data to develop a model connecting supply chain linkages to the three value streams.

All India Warehousing Private Limited provides a complete range of services related to warehousing, handling and storage services, to manufacturers, exporters, clearing agents, transporters and distributors. Saroj Koul and Ankush Guha in Chapter 14 trace the growth and the tribulations the company met on its its journey to ocuupy its present status.

Improper material flow can result in increase in overhead costs , increased waste, increased expenses, loss of potential profit, inaccuracies in monitoring and documenting materials flow. Shettiger and Sudhamsavalli in Chapter 15 seek to analyze the material flow in medium duty vehicle assembly line of Ashok Leyland.

The cargo mix of major ports of India suggests that one to two types of cargo constitute the major share. Natural resources are depleting in nature. Ashutosh Kar and Deepankar Sinha in Chapter 16 identify the constraints in deciding on the cargo mix that a port would support and plausible course of action in this regard.

Collaboration between Subcontractors and RERI (university-affiliated Regional Economic Research Institutions) in the technological field has produced satisfactory synergistic results. Hiro Mitsuyama in Chapter 17 discusses on need of SMEs' managers to improve their theoretical management capabilities

Standardization of quality in services is not an easy task, especially in a multi-service organization, if there are too many service variants. Arvind Chaturvedi et al. in Chapter 18 study the working of an Indian restaurant in Lithuania. The restaurant suffers from substantial variability in service quality. The case analyzes the process of providing service to the customer.

Co-Creation of Value in Stakeholder Relationships

Hanna Lehtimäki*, Päivi Myllykangas** and Johanna Kujala***

ABSTRACT

The purpose of this case is to deepen understanding of co-creation of value. The paper presents a case study on a medium-sized company providing industrial services. Stakeholder relationships are studied in a process where the company transformed from a division of a large industrial corporation into an independent service company. As an outcome, students will learn to identify stakeholders and understand the role of stakeholder relationships in co-creation of value. The case is targeted to Master's students in business and MBA students.

Keywords: Stakeholder relationships, co-creation of value.

INTRODUCTION

The purpose of this case is to develop understanding about value co-creation and different stakeholder perspectives in determining what is perceived as valuable in business operations. World Watch Institute (2010) claims that in order for the business to sustain its' value in the eyes of customers, the owners and other stakeholders, the business and the logic behind it have to change. The global economy is closely interconnected through open financial markets and information and communication technology, and thus, a new narrative for creating value in business is called for (Parmar et al., 2010). Responsible management literature provides a strong argument that business organizations can no longer create sustainable strategies by merely satisfying the needs of owners or stockholders, instead, strategies for management of relationships and interest negotiations with and between various actors has become

---

*   Hanna Lehtimäki is Professor, Department of Businss, University of Eastern Finland, Kuopio Campus, Kuopio, Finland.
** Päivi Myllykangas is Managing Director, Tredea, Finland.
*** Johanna Kujala is Professor, University of Tamp ere, Finland.
E-mail: hanna.lehtimaki@uef.fi, Paivi.Myllykangas@tredea.fi, Johanna.Kujala@uta.fi.

vital for ensuring sustainable long term success (Crane et al., 2008, Freeman et al., 2007; Argandoña 1998; Wheeler & Sillanpää, 1997). Marketing literature, in turn, makes a strong argument that in the service oriented economy of 2010's, value is created not for the customer but with the customer (Prahalad & Ramaswamy, 2004; Vargo & Luch, 2004). In this new logic of value creation, value is perceived and understood as value in-use and the role of companies as providing value propositions with the goods and services they supply (Vargo & Luch, 2004, p. 7).

The traditional, industrial view treats value creation as a question of linear value production i.e., value chain thinking. It is thought that the actors continuously increase value by working in the assemblage of sequential operations until the products or services reach the customers. (Porter, 1985.) Theory of value co-production, in turn, highlights value creation as a synchronic and interactive instead of a linear and transitive process. It, thus, calls for reconsidering the roles, actions, and interactions among economic actors (Normann & Ramirez, 1993; Ramirez, 1999). Sveiby (2001) argues that value co-production and capability co-creation emerge through interactions between organization's external relationships, internal relationships, and individual knowledge/competence. Individual actors use their competence to create value by transferring and converting knowledge externally and internally to the organization they belong to. The external relationships comprise the ongoing and dynamic interactions between the members and non-members of an organization. Correspondingly, the internal relationships refer to the internal actions the members take, the way they work and communicate with each other, and the beliefs, values, and stories they share with each other.

In this case study, joining the responsible management studies, we examine the role of different stakeholders in the value creation process. Advocates of stakeholder theory are pushing the idea of a stakeholder organization where the interests of different parties are incorporated by the process of value creation (Freeman et al., 2010) and focus on how value is created in business and, in particular, how companies make different stakeholders better off (Freeman et al., 2006). Drawing on stakeholder theory, we will present a study of a company that has changed from being a division of a large industrial corporation to becoming an independent service company. Stakeholder theory directs attention to examining relationships between a business and groups and individuals who can affect or are affected by it (Freeman, 1984). With this stance, we are better equipped to understand how value is created not only for stakeholders but with stakeholders (cf. Freeman et al., 2007).

The data for the study was collected by personal interviews with managers and reading company documentation. The interview sessions were organized as open dialogue with a few broad questions to allow for hearing the interviewees viewpoints and interpretations of the situation, thus, the main question asked was: 'How would you describe these past three years?' The interview data consisted of 11 interviews, each of which lasted one and a half hours. Eight of the interviewees represented the case company's management and personnel, and three of them external stakeholders (customers, industrial area, and local authorities). The analyzed data comprised of 350 pages of transcribed interviews, close to 100 strategy related documents, a large body of intranet documents, 120 personnel related documents, six customer-related documents and seven documents related to the industrial area. The documentation was collected for a period of three years between 2004–2007. The data has been analyzed using qualitative content analysis method (Eriksson & Kovalainen, 2008; Yin, 2003). The data analyzes has followed the advice of Denzin and Lincoln (2000) who recommend qualitative methods when a researcher aims at capturing an individual's own experiences and point of view and wishes to secure a rich description of the social world explored.

In the following, the story of OnePoint will be told, based on the extensive data collected on the company and in-depth analysis on data collected (Myllykangas 2009). The quotes in the text are excerpts from the interview data.

THE CASE ONEPOINT: FROM A CORPORATE SUB-DIVISION TO AN INDEPENDENT SERVICE COMPANY

The case company, OnePoint Ltd, started its operations in 2004 and it was officially founded in 2005. The company employs 250 people and its turnover is close to EUR 11 Million. The company is under a strategic change from a division of a large industrial corporation to an independent service company. The transition began when the parent corporation, Kemira Plc, made the decision of redefining its strategic business areas, and the service function did not belong to the newly defined core businesses. Thus, One Point Ltd, a company offering all services for production was established (Figure 1.)

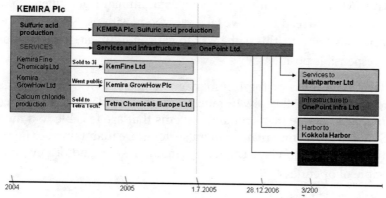

Fig. 1: The Service Company OnePoint Ltd.

The mission of the company is 'to improve the competitiveness of companies inside Industrial Park.' The vision is to enable clients to focus on their core businesses and to be successful by providing and developing infrastructure and industrial services. Three types of services are provided: technical services (e.g. mechanical and automation maintenance), infrastructure services (e.g. electricity distribution), and support services (e.g. environmental, health and safety services and HR services).

OnePoint is situated in an industrial area called Industrial Park. It provides industrial services for other companies in the area from 'OnePoint'. The company seeks to build its' competitive advantage on a broad service offering, co-partner network and long term customer relationships. OnePoint is not only developing its' own business but also very active in developing the infrastructure of the industrial area and the region.

TRANSFORMATION FROM DIFFERENT STAKEHOLDER PERSPECTIVES

Management

The management of OnePoint are excited about the transformation. They see it as a great business opportunity. Close to ten people were selected into the new management team. The team comprises the CEO, four managers of business units, three shop stewards, an industrial safety delegate and a personnel representative. A broad management team was set to build a broadly based commitment to the new company. The top management team meets weekly to carefully administer the process of transformation.

> 'There is a whole load of people in it, what have we got, over ten. Is there any sense in having such a big steering group? It's now been planned and assembled. That's how it ought to be. That's why we always have a powwow at a certain time on Fridays. What it is, is that first we get a commitment from different people in different divisions to lead it and we take everybody with us. Never mind whether good or not, just join in. This is the way to get commitment, the commitment of those in responsible positions.'

One of the main tasks of the top management team is to set new management systems and processes for the new organization. As an independent service provider, the company has to create management systems that are feasible to a medium sized company. Some of the former management systems are maintained to help in keeping the big companies as customers. The management system and organization are built on the principle of openness.

'That serves to prove that we are looking for as many contacts as possible so that we don't need to do it ourselves, so we keep the ball rolling and see to it that no balls roll in the wrong direction...'

As a locally established company, OnePoint has more independence in decision making and more freedom of action. The viewpoint has now changed from operating as a part of a big conglomerate to an SME perspective with a requirement of entrepreneurial competence. An understanding about finance and accounting and their principles have had to be built anew, and this is experienced as particularly challenging. Competence of the top management team is put under a test, as only a few members of the top management team have a background in the duties of financial management. Learning new ways of doing is not only difficult but also exciting.

'We have been working really hard; we have learned, for example, about the financial matters. An engineer does not need to know too much about the financial matters, so we have really put effort on them. So it has been a real learning experience, this starting path.'

'We have some kind of a drive in doing things, so we have really wanted to put things forward. We have not had too much time for routines, but we have been forced to do new stuff all the time.'

Ways of achieving profitability in a service company have become one of the main interests of the top management. During the Kemira times, the main subject in the management meetings was in the fluency of actions, not on profitability. In the OnePoint management meetings, the discussions typically start self evidently from profitability numbers and the target is to root profitability into the minds of every OnePoint employee. In relation to profitability, calculating efficiency has become important. The invoicing degree needs to be high, as salary costs are almost 80% of all costs in service business.

'For example, during the Kemira times, an investment of five thousand euro was seen as peanuts, whereas we soon learned that even small investments need to be considered in terms of profitability.'

The management of OnePoint is committed to advance co-operation and development in the industrial area. They see collaboration as a possibility in the long run in enlarging OnePoint's business activities.

Owners

In planning the future of the service unit, the co-operation of Kemira is essential. Before establishing OnePoint, Kemira as the owner, first, demanded that all potential alternatives were explored, and then, gave approval to set up an independent service company.

'Of course, we also compared that if each service business were sold separately, who would be the candidates for buying them and what would be the solution to the service unit. In the end, we came to the conclusion that the best option was to set up an independent service company.'

'And then Kemira made a solution that a professional service company could be suitable for this area. But, maybe, we were a little bit too early, in my opinion.'

Kemira has committed itself as the owner of OnePoint for the time being and it is a trustworthy participant in the strategic planning of OnePoint. Kemira keeps a low profile and adopts a supportive and patient role, even though service business is not one of its' strategic focus areas. Kemira believes there is great potential in the innovative service concept of OnePoint.

Other companies within the industrial area have shown interest in becoming owners of OnePoint. There is a common practice in industrial areas across Europe to have co-ownership in the 'a real service provider'. Delegations are sent to benchmark the other industrial areas. The local business managers are interested in establishing co-ownership in the area, but they face difficulties in getting support from their headquarters located abroad. The idea of local co-ownership does not appear as attractive from the head office perspective as it does from the perspective of the local management.

'And we want to find an owner, who will take care of the whole package, so that our customers would be able to become owners.'

'When the local management from the industrial area presented the potential of co-ownership of OnePoint to their headquarters, the answer came quickly; they could not be involved in OnePoint.'

All companies operating in the industrial area have a keen focus in competitiveness and cost saving. The companies are in constant negotiations in seeking ways to integrate the overlapping functions to either achieve savings or better enable innovations. For example, there are four laboratories in the area and each of them has own automation departments. Yet, only some of them are ready to expand the co-operation.

'When the lunch meetings are over, it becomes to that wretched matter, that you are supposed to start investing in something new and to disassemble some of your own structure and to buy new company's services, then they put on the brakes.'

OnePoint has started to look for a new owner outside the industrial area. Several different bids have been made to buy OnePoint but the company wants to keep its business concept 'all services from one point' and develop it further. The portfolio of services that OnePoint provides is typically the business of several different companies acting in different industries. As of now, a plausible large scale buyer interested in the full-scale business concept has not yet turned up. The interested companies tend to see the business concept of OnePoint as too broad and think that owning the company as such is more of a burden than a business with earnings potential. Kemira is unhappy about the lengthened process of finding a new owner to OnePoint.

At the end of 2006, a local power and energy company, Kokkolan Voima, owned by a regional power company, Pohjolan Voima, expresses its interest in buying OnePoint after long negotiations. The negotiations proceed successfully, and at the beginning of 2007 it is agreed that the ownership of OnePoint is transferred to Kokkolan Voima. Immediately after the transfer of ownership, Kokkolan Voima passes a large part of ownership to Maintpartner Ltd, a company with established experience in maintenance business and a former competitor of OnePoint.

Personnel

The personnel view the change and find it as positive. They are content with the solution of putting all services into one profit unit, an independent company. The personnel are enthusiastic and proactively involved in making the change and sharing ideas for development.

'Well, the personnel have joined in surprisingly well. No strikes or walkouts...'

Management is putting efforts on keeping the personnel informed of the process. Monthly information sessions are held, personnel representatives are invited to the management team, and continuous exchange of viewpoints and reporting of news using many different channels are performed. The personnel are listened to and they are encouraged to use all potential channels in communicating with the top management. Top management and personnel share the aspiration of creating something new and the importance of sharing information. Personnel have a trusting relationship with the top management.

'When you sit in the meetings of the managerial group you are right up with what's going on, you know a lot more and...'

Selling services require novel abilities of the personnel. The mindset from being an employee of a company selling industrial goods to being an employee of a services solutions provider is significant. It takes time and effort to adjust to the new business logic and adapt to the entrepreneurial way of thinking. What is particularly new is the requirement to define and asses the value of their competence from the customer perspective.

'Then, when OnePoint is established, so then, of course, we begin to think that now we really are the seller, and we need to serve, so we are not just one part of a large company. So, yes, we have to change our way of thinking, that we are the service provider and not just another employee.'

'...people are not used to the idea that they should charge something for their own work.'

Also, the systems of management accounting and financial reporting have to be put in place and new service processes have to be implemented. Despite the profound transformation, the personnel are quick in adapting to the service and customer orientation and in building the competencies for servicing the customers.

Since the beginning, the personnel were well aware of the fact that a new owner was being searched for. Only when the process of finding the new owner was prolonged, uneasiness increased and while all the duties were accomplished, excitement and motivation towards developing the new business diminished.

Customers

Most customers operate in the local industrial area. The biggest customers, in terms of sales volumes, are GrowHow (37% of the sales), Tetra (23% of the sales), Kemira Oyj (21% of the sales), and KemFarine (12% of the sales). The rest of the customers accounts for 7% of the sales. Technical services form the most significant part of the sales, approx. 60%, while the infrastructure services account for around 30 %, and the support service approx. 10 %.

The customers have a long standing partnership with the company and each customer has an established way of working. The customers appreciate the long term knowledge and competence of OnePoint in the customers' processes. Due to the shared history and relationship of trust, it is thought that the transition of the business will go very easily with customers.

In the initial discussions, customers have expressed their interest in the new business model as an attractive opportunity. However, when seeking to determine how to put the model in practice, most customers appear hesitant to adapt to the new business model. From a customer perspective, the risk is not high in the new model but the change from an hourly based pricing to comprehensive service solutions does not appear as lucrative. The former hourly based pricing has enabled and made it easy for the customer to do price comparisons between the different suppliers. Compared with other service providers, OnePoint has a deeper understanding and experience with customers' processes, but this is not apparent to most customers.

'This is the problem if we talk from the customer's point of view, they don't know all that they buy and all that they need. Many of them, they knew more because we had been integrated in the past. And now, as one integration element has been pulled out, we have to sell the service. In our people, it's like that we've always bought this and well they should know what this is…'

The customers react to the new business model very differently. While one customer wants to set rigid rules and roles, the other is flexible in adapting to the new business situation. After the structural changes in the pricing and the pricing models, contract negotiations are often described as 'hard bargaining'. Closing the deal requires now more time in the negotiations to make sure that everyone understands the principles of pricing and that distrust is relieved between the two parties. Also, considerable attention to detail is paid by the customers, and even the smallest billing errors are enthusiastically brought up. Despite the complicated negotiations, the customers value the respect between the customer and the seller even in the most difficult situations.

'So, of course, going forward by small steps, maybe, a firmer basis is built. People learn to know each other and trust each other. Then it's that matter of trust again that… that, well they're the good guys, they can do…'

As the boundaries of business operations change, former colleagues within one company are now representatives of companies in business partnerships. Both parties have to learn to do business differently with each other. This includes learning a new way of talking and negotiating with each other.

'We used to work in the same company and now we are in two different companies. One must buy and the other must sell. Is it easier to one of us, I don't know…'

CONCLUSIONS

The purpose of this case is to develop an understanding about co-creating value and allow for questioning different stakeholder perspectives in determining what is perceived as valuable in business operations. Drawing on stakeholder theory, we have presented a study of a company that has changed from being a division of a large industrial corporation to becoming an independent service company. The case company is under a strategic change from a division of a large industrial corporation to an independent service company.

In this case study, we join the responsible management literature and invite readers to examine the role of different stakeholders in the value creation process. Following the ideas of stakeholder theory, attention is called for examining the relationships between the focal company and the stakeholders whom can affect or are affected by its' business operations.

Both responsible management and stakeholder literature claim that not only stockholders but also other actors with interests in the company's operations are vital for ensuring the sustainable long term success. Also, it is important to consider what is valuable to different parties and how they join the process of value creation. From the stakeholder perspective, the question of how companies make different stakeholders better off, becomes apparent. It is a question of how value is created not only for stakeholders but with stakeholders.

LEARNING QUESTIONS

What creates value for each stakeholder?

How could the stakeholders co-create value in the next steps of business development?

REFERENCES

Argandoña, A. (1998). The Stakeholder Theory and the Common Good. *Journal of Business Ethics*, 17 (9–10), 1093–1102.

Crane, A., Matten, D. & Spence, L. J. (2008). *Corporate Social Responsibility. Readings and cases in a global context.* London and New York: Routledge.

Denzin, N. K. & Lincoln, Y. S. (2000). Introduction: The Discipline and Practice of Qualitative Research. In Denzin, N. K. & Lincoln, Y. S. (eds.) *Handbook of Qualitative Research*, 2nd edition (pp. 1–28). Thousand Oaks, CA: SAGE.

Eriksson, P. & Kovalainen, A. (2008). *Qualitative Methods in Business Research.* London: SAGE.

Freeman, R. E. (1984). *Strategic Management. A Stakeholder Approach.* Boston: Pitman.

Freeman, R. E., Velamuri, S. R. & Moriarty, B. 2006. *Company Stakeholder Responsibility: A New Approach to CSR.* Business Roundtable Institute for Corporate Ethics.

Freeman, R. E., Harrison, J. & Wicks, A. (2007). *Managing for Stakeholders. Survival, Reputation, and Success.* London: Yale University Press.

Freeman, R. E., Harrison, J. S., Wicks, A. C., Parmar, B. & de Colle, S. (2010). *Stakeholder Theory. The State of the Art.* Cambridge: Cambridge University Press.

Myllykangas, P. (2009). *Value creation in stakeholder relationships. From a corporate sub-division to an independent service company.* (In Finnish). Acta Universitatis Tamperensis 1387. Tampere: Tampere University Press.

Normann, R. & Ramirez, R. (1993). Designing interactive strategy: From value chain to value constellation" *Harvard Business Review,* 71 (4), 65–77.

Parmar, B. L., Freeman, R. E., Harrison, J. S., Wicks, A. C., Purnell, L. & de Colle, S. (2010). Stakeholder Theory: The State of the Art. The Academy of Management Annals, 4 (1), 403–445.

Porter, M. E. (1985). *Competitive Advantage: Creating and Sustaining Superior Performance.* New York: Free Press.

Prahalad, C. K. & Ramaswamy, V. (2004). Co-creation experiences: The next practice in value creation. *Journal of Interactive Marketing,* 18 (3), 5–14.

Ramirez, R. (1999). Value Co-Production: Intellectual origins and implications for practice and research. *Strategic Management Journal,* 20 (1), 49–65.

Sveiby,K. E. (2001). A Knowledge-Based Theory of the Firm to Guide in Strategy Formulation. *Journal of Intellectual Capital,* 2 (4), 344–358.

Vargo, S. & Lusch, R. F. (2004). Evolving to a New Dominant Logic for Marketing. *Journal of Marketing,* 68 (January), 1–17.

Wheeler, D. & Sillanpää, M. (1997). *The Stakeholder Corporation.* London: Pitman.

World Watch Institute (2010). State of the World 2010: Transforming Cultures. Massachusetts.

Yin, R. K. (2003). Case Study Research. Design and Methods. 3rd edition. London: Sage.

Development in Foreign Countries of Japanese Small Car Firms

Masaki Iijima* and Kazunori Itoh**

ABSTRACT

In Japan, automobiles with very small engines are called light cars, or "K-cars," and they sell very well. Two major K-car companies are 'Daihatsu' and 'Suzuki'. This paper aims to discuss the difference in foreign business development of these companies for their success and failure as part of the story of the company's history.

Keywords: Japanese small cars, foreign business, competition, Suzuki, Daihatsu.

INTRODUCTION

In recent years, India has been improving economic development and moving toward free trade. Many automobile companies have planned to make and sell full-dressed systems in India. Intensive competition has expanded. As shown in Figure 1, vehicle production share in India, is occupied largely by Maruti Udyog and Tata Motors. In 2010, total production was 280 M vehicles for passengers and commercials, about 76 M three wheel cars, and 1,280 M motorcycles. In the long-term, Maruti has swept passenger car market, Mahindra & Mahindra has dominated the Jeep market, and Tata and Ashok Leyland the commercial car market.

According to Bartlett & Ghoshal (1989), there are four kinds of strategies for industries expanding in foreign countries. The first strategy is the international type in which the parent company in advanced countries has a very high technological power, and they sell their products in the world. The second is the global strategy in which the requirements of the products are similar in different countries, and companies assemble and sell global standard products. The third is the multinational strategy

---
* Masak i Iijima is Professor Supply Chain with with Aichi Gakuin University, Aichi, Japan.
** Kazunori Itoh is with Sensyu University, Japan.
E-mail: iijima@dpc.agu.ac.jp, itoh@isc.senshu-u.ac.jp

in which the requirements of the products are different compared to as in the parent country and local regions, and they produce appropriate products for local markets. The fourth plan is the transnational strategy in which industries share processing on the products.

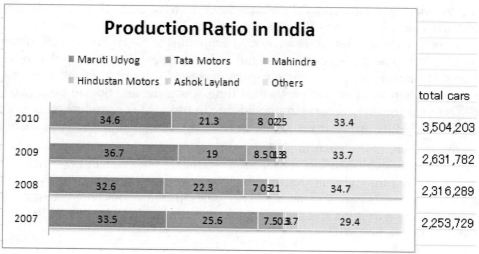

Fig. 1: Company's Production ratio in India
Source: Automotive Yearbook 2011-2012, p.513.

From 1973 to 1983, the sales level of cars stood at around 40,000 nos. The Government of India started to select foreign partners beginning in 1981. At that time, their candidate was thought to be Renault's sedan car ('Renault18' in France). Indian government planned to produce large passenger cars suitable to carry over 6 persons because of the large families. On the contrary, management of Maruti supported a counterproposal from their results of market research that more than 90 percent of owner used for carrying less than four persons, and customers wanted to have fuel-efficient cars. Furthermore, if the company could attain the government sales plan of 100,000 cars, they were required to select car models adjusted to customers' requirements and to possess production technology. Though the production lines in Maruti lowered their automated level, the company introduced existing Japanese technology (Masaki. Iijima, K. Ito, 2001).

On October 1982, Suzuki made a joint-venture contract with the Indian state-run business 'Maruti Udyog', and started local joint production for the four wheel car 'Maruti 800' from 1983. The Maruti 800 was the multinational strategic car with a new engine adapted from Japanese light car. In 1993, the license system for the automotive industry was abolished, and it became possible to invest 100 percent foreign-owned capital. In the latter half of the 1990s, the automotive market grew bigger. GM started local production in 1994, Honda in 1995, Hyundai in '96, Fiat and Ford in 1997, while

Maruti got off to a bad start expanding production. As a result, Maruti dropped its majority share. In 1997 and 1998, a contentious matter occurred related to the top management of personnel affairs, but in May 2002, Suzuki acquired a majority of stock of 'Maruti Udyog' to become a subsidiary of Suzuki and changed the company's name to 'Maruti Suzuki India' in March 2007. In May 2005, Suzuki launched the world strategic car 'new Swift' by the upper rank B instead of smallest level A, and they recorded good sales (Nikkan Kogyo Shinbunsha 2011). From 2008, onwards new car development has been carried out in Indian subsidiary to reap the customer requirement in India. In 2010, the company recorded sales of 1,066,000 cars. It thus crossed 1 million cars per year for the first time. it was the first time to clear 1,000,000 cars. Overseas four-wheel cars strongholds are in India. Major production is made in Hungary and India. Another stronghold is Pakistan, along with Canada, and China.

While looking at Daihatsu, in 1993, the company participated in the second national car project, and established a joint concern 'Perodua' in Malaysia. In 1994, they started to make and sell the light car 'Kancil'. In 1998, Toyota acquired a majority Daihatsu stock and became its parent company. Their sales in China could not get established, so the company left China and the company concentrated in Indonesia and Malaysia(Masaki. Iijima, K. Ito, 2001).

ON JAPANESE LIGHT VEHICLES

As the public roads in Japan are narrow, in 1949, the light cars' regulation was first introduced in Japan. Light cars are much smaller than compact car. Afterwards, several revisions were made, and in 1998, current standards were provided below 660cc for light cars and length below 3.40m in 2010 as shown in Figure 2. This light vehicle length is the same size as mini segment in India.

In the mountainous regions, the elderly citizens are increasing and under populated area are expanding, so light cars ratio is high, from 40 to 50%. In the urban area, the ratio is low. According to the statistics from 2011, the lowest ratio is minimum in Tokyo at 17.7%, followed by Kanagawa, Osaka, and Aichi in 20% level(T. Yamada, 2012)'

When we purchase light vehicles in Japan, we can get some privileges not offered to drivers of standard or larger vehicles.

1. Price is inexpensive.
2. Taxes are also cheap when purchasing.
3. It is very economical on gas.
4. Maintenance cost is inexpensive.
5. It can easily turn in a small radius.
6. It is much easier for parking.
7. It is easier for driving.

8. It is comfortable.
9. It is versatile for use.
10. It is much cheaper for driving toll roads.

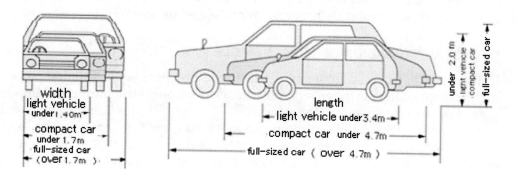

Fig. 2: Vehicle's standard in Japan

Source: http://www.keikenkyo.or.jp/about/standard.html

Fig. 3: Example of Suzuki and Daihatsu new light cars

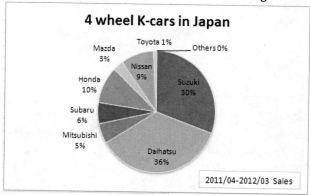

Fig. 4: Sales share of four wheel cars

Source: http://www.zenkeijikyo.or.jp/statistics/ (Japan Mini Vehicles Association)

In 2002, Nissan took the OEM (original equipment manufacturing) from Suzuki. Also Fuji Heavy Industry withdrew from producing light cars and decided to take the OEM from Daihatsu in 2008. In 2011, Toyota joined light car market by 'PIXIS' from Daihatsu' OEM. Figure 3 shows a picture of light cars. Figure 4 shows share of light cars' in Japan. Suzuki and Daihatsu are competing at the same level.

OVERSEAS EXPANSION OF LIGHT VEHICLE INDUSTRY

Until the 1970s, Japanese automobile industries didn't have equal technical power to match other countries. In those days, most car sales were only for domestic consumption, a few for overseas. Because of the oil crisis in 1973 and 1978, fuel efficient and popular cars started to sell not only in the domestic market, but overseas as well. Toyota, Nissan, Honda, etc. expanded through a global strategy until 1990. After the 1990s, the Japanese auto industries took a severe shock in cost competitiveness because low wages in China. These were the limits of globalization, and auto companies changed to transnational strategies by 2000, They moved to divide into optimal functions.

Up to 2007, as their economic growth had been flattened in the advanced countries, emerging markets had expanded. Only developing uniform and public cars for advanced countries formed industrial development. Developing countries had big potential markets, but in these regions, consumers' requirement was an innovative low cost vehicle. It meant that as long as the company adopted a multinational strategy, it was very difficult to grow in the industry.

Figure 5 depicts rapid growth in India.

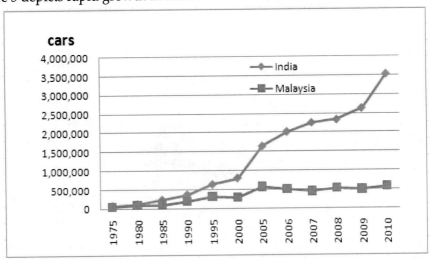

Fig. 5: Annual car sales in India and Malaysia
Automotive Yearbook 2011-2012, p.473.

SUZUKI AND INDIA

Suzuki was set up as 'Suzuki Loom Works' in 1909 by Michio Suzuki in Hamamatsu. In 1937, the motorcycle business, and in 1939, automobile business were started. In 1952, sales of motorcycles were very good. For these reasons, the company changed its name to 'Suzuki Motors' in 1954. In October 1955, the first four-wheel light car, named 'Suzuki Suzulight', was launched, and the company advanced toward automobiles in good earnest.

In the 1980s, Suzuki launched a business alliance to enter overseas market. Suzuki agreed to a joint production with Mazda for four wheel light vehicles in 1987. For foreign business, Suzuki aimed to enter Pakistan in 1982, India in 1983, Spain and Canada in 1985. In 2000, Suzuki started a new sales channel of Arena shops specialized in small cars, and restructured the domestic sales network. In 2001, basic contracts of OEM supplements were signed through agreements with Nissan and Mazda. In 2002, Suzuki and Fuji Heavy Industry, agreed that parts were to be common in both company's light cars , and strengthened their alliance.

In 2004, joint concern subsidiary with 'Maruti Udyog' was established as 'Maruti Szuki India'. In 2009, Maruti Udyog implemented M&A with the four wheel manufacturer 'Maruti Suzuki Automobile India', and started to produce the 'Swift' with Diesel Engine. Suzuki started developing reinforcement of production systems and reorganization, investments in R&D and facilities in Asia, in order to demonstrate counter measures of cost reduction and quality improvement(Masaki. Iijima, K. Ito, 2001). Suzuki is localized just like Indian domestic company. New car development in India proceeds in a different way from Japan. This can be expressed as a multinational strategy.

Daihatsu Motor and Malaysia

In order to promote industrialization in the policy of national cars in Malaysia, in 1983 the first national car company, 'Proton', was established, and in 1993 the second national car 'Perodua' was established. Daihatsu were selected as partners for making a popular small car in Japan.

Total demands of vehicles in Malaysia grow smoothly except during the Asian Financial Crisis in 1997, the Lehman Shock in 2008, and reached 600,000 cars in 2011. The share of these two national car makers is 57% (Perodua 30%, Proton 27%), and next comes Toyota, 15%. Stock holding company POSB is the parent company of Perodua Sales Company PSSB, a 100% Malaysian Capital. The PCSB is the 51% stock share of Manufacturing Company PMSB/PEMSB by Daihatsu and Mitsui Trading. The current car has three types being produced since 2005. These cars have a multinational strategy with taking the Malaysian taste in design.

One hundred and fifteen parts suppliers of the total of 130 part suppliers are based in Malaysia, 14 are in ASEAN countries, and one in China. The ratio of local procurement attained is over 85% by Malaysian standards.[3)]

SUZUKI'S STRATEGY AND COST MANAGEMENT IN INDIA

In May 2009, Maruti Suzuki India introduced world class car 'Splash' (Ritz in India) refer Figure 6. Indian Maruti Ritz has variants of petrol and diesel engine. These engines have excellent performance and fuel efficiency to match the demands of eco orientation.

This compact car matches with low fuel consumption and environment oriented 1300cc diesel engine. Maruti Suzuki took in the following requirements of vehicles after trial and error practice in India. (Bhargava and Shimada 2006)

1. In India, price difference between gas and diesel is wide enough. The general user prefers a Diesel car. The success of Maruti 800 is dependent on fuel efficiency.

2. In India, durable consumer goods such as automobiles, tend to be used as long as possible. The reason is that a sales tax for new cars is high. Besides, maintenance cost of parts replacement is relatively cheap.

3. Some of the Japanese light car specifications do not suit the Indian style. Indian people are tall, and have many family members; therefore residential space and trunk space should be large enough.

Fig. 6: Indian Maruti Ritz

This way, differences of country influence the car sales. The car maker should reflect consumer feedback. We understand that these are multinational strategies taken by Suzuki. Furthermore, Suzuki discusses introduction of new models positioned between light cars and Swift made in India or Indonesia, because of 'severe global competition' and 'continuing strong yen', and intend to re-import to Japan.

Under the multinational strategy, local subsidiary companies are asked to complete on cost management. These initiatives are centered to reduce materials and labor costs, effective use of R&D cost, control of capital expenditure, and so on.

In current models, the reduction of purchased parts price, improvement of yield rate, or use of alternative materials is encouraged. Value creation is claimed through VE (value engineering). On the other hand, pushing ahead on labor cost reduction, results in confrontation with employees.

Development of new models should satisfy local customer expectations of price, functions, and quality. Until now, new models for advanced countries have been developed to attach importance both on quality and cost, but for developing countries, cost reduction is more important than adjusting to requested quality and functions.

Control of investment in plant and equipment does not mean stopping all investment, but to invest new facilities suiting customer needs, or machinery for rationalization of Investment restraint is essential for investment on machinery for rationalization of production.

SUMMARY

In this study, we discussed the strategic differences of overseas advancement between Japanese two light car makers, Suzuki and Daihatsu. Both companies take in the multinational strategy.

1. Suzuki has aimed at overseas markets, and in the past few years, the company has launched the world strategic cars. Suzuki's advancement suits the needs of the developing countries of India and China. In contrast, Daihatsu is careful to advanced countries that request small cars, and has withdrawn from China because of unprofitability.

2. From the global context, Suzuki aims to advance in developing countries by collaborating with competing companies , such as eco Diesel engines and shared platform and so on. Daihatsu develops new cars with a focus on original production technology.

3. After selling a car, Suzuki implements model changes to harvest consumer feedback. Their efforts attach high priority to cost reduction of interior . In India, good mileage has an impact on sales. Daihatsu takes in Malaysian preferred design from market research.

In the Japanese light car market, Suzuki and Daihatsu are well matched, but in the global competition, some of the approaches are different. In these past few years, car deregulations have been implemented in India, therefore major automobile companies have come to India. .

ACKNOWLEDGEMENT

Authors wish to thank staffs of Perodua Pvt Ltd. for offering data, and Professor Gregory Rohe of Aichi-Gakuin University for revising our paper.

NOTES

1. At the end of Mar. 2011, the 3 and 4 wheel light car holders and their share （Japan Mini Vehicle Association）
2. Ryoko Yuasa, 2012/03/19, Suzuki threw world strategic cars, Weekly Diamond No. 614, http://diamond.jp/articles/-/16650.

REFERENCES

Bartlett, Christopher A. and Sumantra Ghoshal (1989), *Managing Across Borders: The Transnational Solution*, Harvard Business Press. (H. Yoshiwara eds., (1990), Nihon keizai shinbunsha)

Bhargava, R.C , T. Shimada, eds., 2006, *Suzuki's strategy in India* (in Japanese). Tyukei Shuppan, pp.32-44.

Masaki. Iijima, K. Ito, 2001, Malaysian National Car Project, Proceedings of EurOMA International Annual Conference, Vol.2, pp. 883-94.

Nikkan Kogyo Shinbunsha & Chamber of Japanese Car eds(2011).: Cars almanac in 2011-2012, Nikkan-Kogyo Shinbunsha, 2011.

http://www.zenkeijikyo.or.jp/introduction/index.html

Solid Waste and the Informal Sector:
A Supply Chain Perspective

Sameer Prasad*, Ashish Jain**, Jasmine Tata*** and Shantha Parthan****

ABSTRACT

Networks of informal entrepreneurs or rag-pickers operate within large cities of the developing world; these rag-pickers collect, sort, process, and dispose of solid waste. Rag-pickers' networks and waste streams hold not only economic, but also environmental and social value. In this research we use qualitative methodology and archival data to develop a model connecting supply chain linkages to the three value streams within this informal solid waste network. Specifically, we find that the tight supply chain links between the rag-pickers and their upstream and downstream network agents yield superior economic, social, and environmental returns.

Keywords: Solid waste, entrepreneurship, NGO, supply chain, multi-value stream, Indian Pollution Control Association .

ORGANIZATION, PROBLEMS, ISSUES, NEED FOR STUDY

Issues

In many cities of the developing world, the municipal solid waste management system does not have the capacity to collect, sort, process and dispose of the various forms of waste from millions of households which can result in piles of garbage accumulating. Not only do these un-official "dump" sites become eye sores but they can be harbingers of pests and diseases. Given unplanned urban growth it is approximated that only

*   Sameer Prasad, is associated with Management Department, University of Wisconsin. Whitewater.
**   Ashish Jain is with Indian Pollution Control Association.
*** Jasmine Tata is with Management Department, Loyola University – Chicago.
**** Shantha Parthan is with University of Canterbury.
E-mail: prasads@uww.edu, ashish_ipca@yahoo.co.in, jtata@luc.edu, shantha.parthan@pg.canterbury.ac.nz

about 30 per cent of the waste is handled by the formal sector (Scheinberg, Spies, Simpson, & Mol, 2011).

To fill this niche in the solid waste disposal market, the 'informal sector' consisting of rag-picker individuals, families, groups or small enterprises carries out unregistered and unregulated waste management activities (Schübeler, Wehrle, & Christen, 1996).

Problems

The rag-pickers working in the informal unorganized sector of waste management suffer from low incomes, poor social conditions, and are able to recover only a small proportion of the waste.

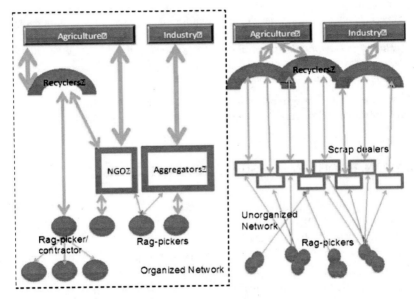

Fig. 1: Organized and Unorganized Network

Large metropolitan areas in India have thousands of rag-pickers competing against each other while supplying waste to scrap dealers who are themselves in competition with each other. Transactions are based on on-site negotiations between rag-pickers and scrap dealers. The scrap dealers in turn negotiate with recyclers who then provide supplies to industry or agricultural customers (Figure 1). This network is adversarial in nature, is only able to recycle approximately 15 per cent of the waste generated, and all entities in the network earn very little due to inefficiencies. For example, rag-pickers earn about Rs. 4000 or $USD 80 per month. In addition, the rag-pickers and their families are in dire shape in terms of social and health conditions. Given the environment in which the rag-pickers operate and lack of proper safety procedures, most of these individuals suffer from water- and air-borne diseases such as asthma, diarrhoea, jaundice, and severe skin and eye allergies, many have no rights and lack residency in the city in which they work, their children often work instead of going to school, and given their level in society, they are often harassed by public official and at best ignored by the citizenry.

Need for Study

Ironically, solid waste has both an economic and environmental value. Given the inability of the municipality or the formal sector to tap into this waste, the informal sector has taken advantage of this opportunity. Non Governmental Organizations (NGOs) and other interested entities would like to see how the informal solid waste network could yield higher economic, environmental and social returns for the rag-picker micro-entrepreneurs.

In this research we will examine the influence of such organisational efforts on supply chain integration. In turn we explore their impact on the three value streams: economic, environmental and social.

Researchers have adopted a life cycle approach in mapping the flow of waste material through a network (Finnveden, 1999). However, this life-cycle approach does not build in the flow of information/money within the network nodes or the linkages between these nodes. In this research we will borrow terminology, constructs and measures from supply chain management in order to assess the effectiveness of the organized networks relative to the unorganized ones for the informal solid waste sector. To understand the organized informal sector we will examine the case of the Indian Pollution Control Association.

ORGANIZATION

The Indian Pollution Control Association (IPCA) is a not-for-profit NGO based in the National Capital Region of India. Its primary objective is to create awareness of Integrated Solid Waste Management (ISWM) and on the ground level manage a decentralized system of solid waste.

IPCA was formally established in 2001. Today, it draws upon the experiences and capacities of a range of individuals including those from the business, legal, engineering, and the energy and environmental sectors. IPCA has tried to organize approximately 700 rag-pickers in the informal sector, and provide them with a permanent source of income through solid waste management. IPCA provides these entrepreneurs with allocated territories in residential areas, corporate offices, educational institutes, and industries for collection of Municipal Solid Waste (MSW), as well as space for segregation and connects them directly to recyclers or aggregators to enable them to obtain higher prices for their segregated waste. In addition, IPCA provides them with identity cards and uniforms to protect them from social and public harassment.

The informal system for solid waste management is coordinated by IPCA sources waste from some 300,000 individuals living in a 10 sq. km. area of the National Capital Region of New Delhi. This decentralized system is supported by a network of rag-picker families. These families are indeed micro-entrepreneurs as the richness of the solid waste they are able to tap provides them with their livelihood. These families primarily belong to two disenfranchised communities: migrant *Bihari* and *Bengali*.

OBJECTIVES

In this research we hope to get a better understanding of the networks within which rag-pickers operate. We will model the network as a supply chain and examine this network in terms of the three outcomes: economic, environmental and social. Through this broad research endeavour we hope to achieve the following objectives:

- Understanding the role of supply chain linkages in the informal solid waste management network.
- Examining the yield of the three multi-value streams (economic, environmental and social) within this informal network for the organized and unorganized sectors.
- Exploring the role of NGOs in augmenting supply chain linkages within these informal networks to augment the yield of the three multi-value streams.

RESEARCH METHODOLOGY

In our study, the unit of analysis is at the level of the micro-entrepreneur. We examine three categories of outcomes that relate to sustainability: economic, environmental, and social.

Our methodology consists of a number of research tools: a literature review to frame our research and identify relevant constructs, a qualitative case study, and archival data analyses to develop a model. The model is prescriptive and provides guidance to NGOs and other entities in organising the informal sector and helping deliver superior economic, environmental, and social returns to the network of micro-entrepreneurs.

DIAGNOSIS AND ANALYSIS

In this research we propose that rag-pickers' outcomes are a function of the underlying supply chain linkages.

SUPPLY CHAIN LINKAGES

As part of our model development, we rely upon three variables of supply chain linkages: long-term orientation, supply chain integration (coordination), and supply chain interaction and communication

Long-term Orientation

The initiatives undertaken by NGOs to encourage long-term relationships with solid waste network partners are crucial for the development of supply chain linkages. Long-term relationships refer to the intention of the parties that the arrangement between them is not temporary(Chen & Paulraj, 2004). In the unorganized sector there are usually no long-term partnerships between the rag-pickers and their suppliers/customers. Being small, rag-pickers are often perceived as having less power than their larger supply chain partners. A dominant buyer (e.g. scrap dealer) might make demands not only about the delivery and quality of products, but may also force entrepreneurs to supply materials at a loss.

We hypothesize that long-term relationships with direct and indirect supply chain partners can be influenced by NGOs who can help in the selection of those partners as well as by ties of family or kinship. Although the literature largely focuses on long-term relationships with suppliers, similar relationships with customers (aggregators & recyclers) and other organizations in the supply chain are also important in developing strong linkages. Trustworthiness and integrity as indicated by a willingness to share information on costs, quality, and volumes should be considered in the selection of suppliers(Dyer, 1997).

We employ the following properties to measure long-term orientation (Table 1) based on the mainstream literature: relationships with key suppliers last a long time, suppliers see relationship as a long-term alliance, relationships with key customers last a long time, and customers see relationship as a long-term alliance. Based upon the qualitative observations for the various properties, we assign scores of 1 = low to 3 = high to both the organized and unorganized sectors, and obtain aggregate scores for long-term relationship of 1 (low) for the unorganized sector and 2.5 (medium/high) for the organized sector.

Table 1: Properties of long-term orientation.

Properties	Organized (O) vs. Unorganized (U) informal sector.	Low Medium High
Long-term orientation	U = Low (1) O = Medium/High (2.5)	
Relationships with key suppliers last a long time.	Organized sector develops a long-term relationship with residential homeowners and businesses. This relationship develops over a time period of 4-5 years The unorganized sector cannot even connect with suppliers.	U = Low (1) O = High (3)

Suppliers see relationship as long-term alliance	The organized sector provides the rag-pickers with identity cards and uniforms. In addition, they provide a way to track waste in case valuables are inadvertently discarded such as architectural drawings, phones and even laptops. The suppliers (residential and commercial entities) provide care to the rag-pickers and bonuses in times of holidays. The unorganized sector has no relationship with suppliers.	U = Low (1) O = High (3)
Relationships with key customers last a long time.	The relationship with customers depends on the entity. For the organized sector dealing with aggregators is a long term proposition, whereas with the scrap dealers it is a relative short-term proposition. The unorganized sector consists of mainly short-term relationships with scrap dealers in competition with each other.	U = Low (1) O = Medium (2)
Customers see relationship as long-term alliance	Within the unorganized sector rag-pickers are not viewed as part of any alliance. For the organized sector only a few recyclers recognize that they are part of the network with the aggregators and rag-pickers.	U = Low (1) O = Medium (2)

Supply Chain Integration (Coordination)

Supply chain integration refers to the degree of coordination among supply chain partners. The wider the range of coordinated and interdependent activities between a rag-picker and his or her direct (scrap dealer) and indirect (recyclers/industry) supply chain partners, the greater the level of integration. This integration can be downstream in orientation (coordination of information and logistical flows through the supply chain from the rag-picker to scrap dealer) or upstream (coordination of information flows from the residents to rag-pickers to customers to aggregators) (Cousins & Menguc, 2006).

Supply chain integration can be influenced by the degree to which a micro-enterprise develops and involves supply chain partners in important activities. Supplier development can be any activity initiated by an organization to improve the performance of its suppliers (Krause, Handfield, & Tyler, 2007).

We employ the following properties to measure this supply chain integration (Table 2) based on the main stream literature: key suppliers involved in the product design and development stage, suppliers have major influence on the design of products, key customers involved in the product design and development stage, customers have major influence on the design of products, and key customers included in business and strategic planning. Based upon the qualitative observations for the various properties, we assign scores of 1 = low to 3 = high to both the organized and unorganized sectors, and obtain aggregate scores for supply chain integration of 1 (low) for the unorganized sector and 2 (medium) for the organized sector.

Table 2: Properties of integration

Properties	Organized (O) vs. Unorganized (U) informal sector.	Low Medium High
Integration	**U = Low (1)** **O = Medium (2)**	
Key suppliers involved in the product design and development stage Suppliers have major influence on the design of products.	Depending on the nature of the micro-enterprise operation, the level of involvement varies. Generally the suppliers are not involved in any design and development stage.	U = Low (1) O = Low (1)
Key customers involved in the product design and development stage. Customers have major influence on the design of products.	Large customers such as Reliance petrochemical, Tetra Pak, and Moser Bare work with the organized sector as part of a way to ensure quality material, reliable delivery times and sufficient quantities. In addition, Reliance being the largest consumer of plastic bottles provides balers to aggregators so as to ensure sufficient volume and compactness for transportation. Corporations generallydo not invest in the unorganized sector.	U = Low (1) O = High (3)
Key customers included in business and strategy planning	The organized sector meets frequently and works together to make policy and decisions about strengthening the network, spreading information, exploring new opportunities, and bringing scrap dealers into the network.	U = Low (1) O = Medium (2)

Interaction and Communication

The literature notes the importance of effective interaction and communication within a supply chain network(Krause, 1999). Chen & Paulraj(2004b)define effective inter-organizational communication as frequent, genuine, and involving personal contacts with the parties willing to share sensitive information. Micro-enterprises operating within the unorganized informal solid waste sector are at a disadvantage in trying to obtain information and cooperation from larger supply chain partners (scrap dealers/recyclers). However, careful development of interaction mechanisms by NGOs can result in the formation of strong ties with both direct and indirect supply chain partners, resulting in a flow of information and resources to micro-enterprises.

We employ the following properties to measure interaction and communication (Table 3) based upon the mainstream literature: frequent face-to-face communication with key suppliers, sensitive information shared with key suppliers, key suppliers keep rag-pickers informed about any changes that might affect them, frequent face-to-face communicationwithkeycustomers,sensitiveinformationsharedwithkeycustomers,and

Table 3: Properties of interaction and communication.

Properties	Organized (O) vs. Unorganized (U) informal sector.	Low Medium High
Interaction and communication	**U = Low (1)** **O = Medium/High (2.6)**	
Frequent face-to-face communication with key suppliers	Rag-pickers in the organized sector interact with customer several times a week, especially customers living in houses as opposed to apartments.There is no regular contact between rag-pickers and customers in the unorganized sector.	U = Low (1) O = High (3)
Sensitive information (e.g., financial, design, research, and/or competition) shared with key suppliers. Key suppliers keep rag-pickers informed about any changes that might affect them.	Household and residential suppliers inform rag-pickers when they have additional material and the types of material. At times they aggregate the materials for the rag-pickers or give them information about other households that might have supplies for them.	
Frequent face-to-face communication with key customers.	For the organized sector there are meetings with recyclers on a yearly basis. Most of the recyclers (owners) are based in other states. For the unorganized sectorthere is very minimal contact (transaction information) with customers.	U = Low (1) O = Medium (2)
Sensitive information (e.g., financial, design, research, and/or competition) shared with key customers	The organized sector shares information about the market value of waste, best practices to increase volume, how to segregate, and how to store waste properly to minimize losses of 20 to 30 per cent. The unorganized sector has no such access to information.	U = Low (1) O = Medium (2)
Key customers keep rag-pickers informed about any changes that might affect them	The organized sector shares information on the benefits to up stream operations in storing material compactly is transmitted throughout the network. This is communicated via the aggregators or the NGO. In the unorganized sector it is a competitive relationship though the network and no information shared.	

key customers keep rag-pickers informed about any changes that might affect them. Based upon the qualitative observations for the various properties, we assign scores of 1 = low to 3 = high to both the organized and unorganized sectors, and obtain aggregate scores for interaction and communication of 1 (low) for the unorganized sector and 2.6 (medium/high) for the organized sector.

RAG-PICKERS' OUTCOMES

The outcomes of the solid waste network can be viewed in terms the degree of supply chain linkages. The entire unorganized sector is relatively inefficient in terms of income and recovery rates. On an annual basis the rag-pickers within the organized sector earn approximately twice that earned by rag-pickers in the unorganized sector. In addition the recovery rate of the organized sector is almost nine times that of the unorganized sector. As such, we score network income and recovery rates as low for the unorganized sector and high for the organized sector.

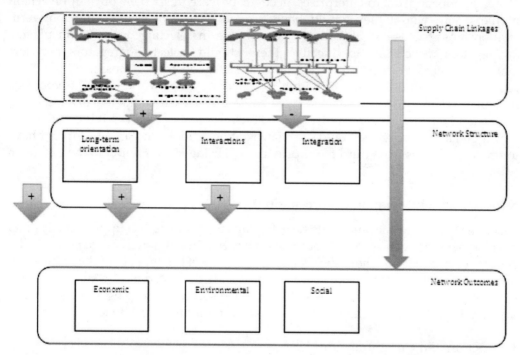

Fig. 2: Supply Chain Model of the Informal Sector

Social outcomes are based on the level of empowerment, health and education. Within these dimensions, the unorganized sector was rated low and the organized sector was rated moderate. Thus the combined score for rag-pickers' outcomes was high/moderate for the organized sector and low for the unorganized sector.

Thus, the model and data suggest that supply chain linkages positively influence the level of network outcomes (Figure 2), with high levels of supply chain linkages (integration, interaction, long term orientation) likely to yield better outcomes (economic, environmental, social).

RECOMMENDATIONS

Based upon the scores it seems that the influence of an NGO and its ability to organize the solid waste network is quite significant. However, there are a few additional steps an NGO can take to ensure tighter linkages for enhanced yields. Next, are some of the recommendations derived from literature and from Tables 1-3.

Long-term Orientation

NGOs supporting micro-enterprises need to be careful to seek out supply chain partners with whom they would have a good chance of establishing long-term relationships. NGOs can also play a critical role in selecting downstream players (aggregators/recyclers). Specifically, they should select aggregators/recyclers that have well-developed strategic plans, are in good market positions and have relationships with other entities within the solid waste network. Also, it would be helpful if the downstream players have some managerial competence/experience, understand the underlying realities and use business tools. However, it is possible that few aggregators/recyclers would have such sophistication, and an NGO might have to procure services from third party providers to bring such training to the upstream players.

Supply Chain Integration (Coordination)

It is unlikely that rag-pickers would have the capacity to engage in supplier or customer development. As such, an NGO could take a key role in this issue. For example, NGOs could inform residential households and corporate waste suppliers of the importance of segregating waste at the source and even provide dedicated bins. Similarly, NGOs can help recyclers and aggregators with improved sorting, packaging and distribution methodology through training/educational programs and access to technology.

Interaction and Communication

NGOs can invest in both formal and informal processes to communicate expectations and share information between supply chain partners. Information that could be shared includes sorting preferences, quality specifications, reliability, lead times, pricing/cost, volumes and even logistics. Formal processes could include regular meetings, teams, site visits and creating publications/brochures for residential households and corporate suppliers of waste. Informal interaction mechanisms often move outside the workplace with a greater focus on informal, expressive aspects of the relationship; examples of informal mechanisms include social events (e.g. weddings) and casual meetings (e.g., sharing a cup of tea).

CONCLUSIONS

Large metropolises in developing countries are overwhelmed by population growth, and do not have the capability to carry away all the waste being generated. Correspondingly, an informal sector has grown with rag-pickers tapping into the piles of waste.

Our case study demonstrates that by organizing this sector, solid waste can be a very rich stream yielding income, improving the environment and laying the foundation for the development of entire disenfranchised communities. This transition, however, requires an attentive NGO willing to help tighten supply chain links throughout the entire network . Only then can properly managed solid waste provide the necessary economic, environmental and social returns.

ACKNOWLEDGEMENT

Prasad would like to acknowledge the support of UWW CoBE Social, Economic and Environmental R sponsibility and Sustainability Research Grant Spring 2012.

REFERENCES

Chen, I. J., & Paulraj, A. (2004). Towards a theory of supply chain management: the constructs and measurements. Journal of Operations Management, 22(2), 119. doi: 10.1016/j.jom.2003.12.007

Cousins, P. D., & Menguc, B. (2006). The implications of socialization and integration in supply chain management. Journal of Operations Management, 24(5), 604-620. doi: 10.1016/j.jom.2005.09.001

Dyer, J. H. (1997). Effective interfirm collaboration: how firms minimize transaction costs and maximize transaction value. Strategic Management Journal, 18(7), 535-556.

Finnveden, G. (1999). Methodological aspects of life cycle assessment of integrated solid waste management systems. Resources, Conservation & Recycling, 26(3/4), 173.

Krause, D. R. (1999). The antecedents of buying firms' efforts to improve suppliers. Journal of operations management, 17(2), 205-224.

Krause, D. R., Handfield, R. B., & Tyler, Beverly B. (2007). The relationships between supplier development, commitment, social capital accumulation and performance improvement. Journal of Operations Management, 25(2), 528-545. doi: 10.1016/j. jom.2006.05.007

Scheinberg, A., Spies, S., Simpson, M. H., & Mol, A. P. J. (2011). Assessing urban recycling in low-and middle-income countries: Building on modernised mixtures. Habitat International, 35(2), 188-198.

Schübeler, Peter, Wehrle, Karl, & Christen, Jürg. (1996). Conceptual Framework for Municipal Solid Waste Management in Low-Income Countries. In S. S. C. f. D. C. i. T. a. Management) (Ed.). Switzerland: UNDP/UNCHS/WORLD BANK-UMP.

Oasis in a Desert: The Triumph of All India Warehousing Private Ltd.

Saroj Koul* and Ankush Guha**

ABSTRACT

Joy Banerjee and Gaurav Tripathi have recently joined as Managers in the Planning Department at All India Warehousing Private Limited (AIWPL). Their on-job training is completed. They have met almost all the officials at the warehouse and even interacted with labour to understand the company and the functions and now set to meet Kamlesh Patel, the Managing Director next week to discuss the upcoming challenges and opportunities and to suggest strategies. Will they be able to make a satisfactory presentation to Kamlesh Patel on the company performance and the parameters that are going to be crucial to AIWPL's continued success and survival in the industry? This case study may prove useful to practicing managers and management students on understanding the working of a family run private warehouse, business environment in the warehousing sector, use of technology and organizational capability to manage multi-product, multi-location warehouses.

Keywords: Logistics, Warehouse, Materials-handling, Record Management, Profitability, Performance, India.

INTRODUCTION

All India Warehousing Private Limited, a family owned concern had been in business for over 25 years, with full service warehousing and distribution experience behind them. The company provided a complete range of services related to warehousing, handling and storage services, to manufacturers, exporters, clearing agents, transporters and distributors with merchandise ranging from raw materials, industrial goods - including office equipment, machine parts, light bulbs, and heavy equipment to promotional toys, ceramics, food and paper products. It came into existence with a 1000 square feet rental space in Kalamboli, in Maharashtra, India. Those were the days

* Saroj Koul is Professor with Jindal Global Business School, NCR, India.
** Ankush Guha is Assistant Professor with ITM Business School, Navi Mumbai, India.
E-mails: koul@jgu.edu.in, ankushg@itm.edu

when the upcoming distribution centre owners manned the cargo themselves and relied upon third party go-downs to give them their full load. Work was hard to come by and Kamlesh Patel made many a visit in person to market his 1000 square feet plot to prospective customers. With changing times and diversified business prospects the company made acquisitions in cotton green (near Mumbai port) in 1998 and later one year at Bhiwandi (near Kalyan), but it was in year 2000 when the entire operation were regrouped and christened All India Warehousing Private Limited (AIWPL).

Banerjee and Tripathi could sense that AIWPL was within 5 km area of all Container Freight Stations (CFSs), a premium location. They also learnt that the warehouse offered a wide range of value-added services such as inventory control, packaging, product re-work and inspection and fulfilment operations. As a part of the specialized offering, AIWPL had in its repertoire; stuffing, de-stuffing facilities, import-export container loading/unloading, roll paper handling. All India Roadlines (AIR) its subsidiary trucking company handled local, regional and interstate deliveries for its customers. More details on the company that they gathered are as follows.

ORIGINS: EARLY DAYS

Kamlesh Patel came from a farming background, with his father and elder brother being practicing agriculturists. A tryst with destiny saw him take a cue from his peers who had left for Mumbai, and made him make the journey from Gujarat to the city of dreams. It was not all easy, on reaching Mumbai, Kamlesh had to work in a warehouse from 1988-90. These were important years, as this is where he learnt his trade and what culminated finally into laying of the plinth for AIWPL.

The warehouse predominantly handled grains, food products and engineering goods. Kamlesh had a vision beyond merely waiting for overflowing cargo from nearby and already established warehouses. Customers were king and he went the distance, to get their business and attention. It was not easy; many had expressed grave reservations about utilizing the company's services, for even in those days a measly 1000 square feet could barely substantiate your position in the market place. As a vendor of repute, AIWPL was no exception, its owners were subjected to carping comments such as 'how do we know you will last, how do we know you are not a fly by night operator'. Amidst all this grinding opposition and very demanding set of circumstances Kamlesh followed an equally rigorous marketing strategy. He went door to door, marketing to all the importers and exporters who were listed in the yellow pages. During those early days shortlisting clearing agents and exporters, from the yellow pages he would make 5-10 daily visits, simply to build a relationship with the dispensing officer, who might one day consider him worth the while, for an order. Not enticed by greed since inception, AIWPL had as its policy the non-handling of hazardous cargo even though the margins were high.

FIRST BLOOD

Back in the early 90's Russia had a problem with food supplies, medicines and drugs; being a party to 'The Indo Soviet Treaty of Peace, Friendship & Co-operation' (signed in 1971), led to the steep rise in exports from India to Russia in the 1990's and coupled with it the extensive marketing of Kamlesh Patel, bore fruit when one of the contacted clearing agents, Usha Shipping deployed their services for an export order of edible oil to Russia. The oil was manufactured in Kota, Rajasthan in India and was kept at AIWPL's warehouse before being exported to Russia. The oil was brought from Kota to the warehouse in Kalamboli by an independent transporter and the liability and responsibility of the product, belonged to the manufacturing or the clearing agent, i.e. the inbound logistics was not part of the responsibilities of the warehouse. The outbound logistics did form an important function and responsibility that the warehouse performed for their client, a chart that Banerjee and Tripathi primed had been given at Fig.1regarding the process and movement of cargo that took place for the oil company.

KOTA	INBOUND →→→	Warehouse at KALAMBOLI	Responsibilities under the Warehouse
Taken care by a different transporter not the warehouse		↓ ↓ ↓ ↓ ↓ ↓ OUTBOUND	➢ Goods were offloaded ➢ Condition of the goods were checked ➢ Report to the clearing agent sent stating the condition and quality of the goods received ➢ Goods were then stored ➢ On authorization the goods were transferred to the customs warehouse (cost incurred by the warehouse), for custom clearance and container stuffing
		KALAMBOLI Customs Warehouse	

Fig. 1: Cargo Movement for the First Client of the Warehouse

The second major client that made a mark in the history of AIWPL was 'Modern Terri Towels'. It was one of the biggest exporters of finished towels to Europe, shipping containers to the tune of 100 – 150 containers a month. The model followed a similar pattern like that of the oil exports, the only difference being the origin of the cargo (Ahmedabad). Handling finished goods was where the relationship started for AIWPL and Modern Terri Towels, but with the changing strategy of the client, to export raw materials resulted in the evolution and scaling-up of the operations and relations.

After opening up of the economy in 1991 and during 1997-1998 the government's duty drawback policy resulted in scams. Empty containers were being shipped with proper shipping bills, custom clearances etc. to avail the drawback duty. The government realized this when the amount of currency flowing in did not match the trade that was being shown on paper, i.e. even though the drawback flowing out was on the rise. This resulted in a raid by the customs and the CBI (Central Bureau of Investigation) department and most of the exporters had to shut shop in the area of Kalamboli. As result of this crisis in the industry, AIWPL had made the following observations and changes:

(a) **The JNPT Shift**: This crisis in the industry led to the drop in business. The businesses then were said to have moved to Bangladesh, Philippines and similar countries and this resulted in the reduction in the number of warehouses then operated by AIWPL also, i.e. from ten warehouses that were then in operation, they came down to five. This also led to the rise of JNPT as a new hub for the export related activities and also its proximity to the port was another feature that attracted AIWPL to such a location.

(b) **Risks faced at JNPT**: In 1997, the local authorities (CIDCO) marked the JNPT area for logistics purposes, including warehouses. Tenders were given which AIWPL failed to grab back then and this resulted in the scarcity of availability of land. The only option left was to acquire an agricultural land and convert it for private use. The background of the family as farmers came in handy at this point of time in the process of land acquisition; it helped them in bypassing government restrictions on buying agricultural land for private use. After much struggle about 4.5 acres were purchased. Also, due to insufficient infrastructure, like availability of communication links, law and order in the neighbourhood, it took some time for the warehouse to commence full operations at that time. However, the vision and endeavour of Kamlesh Patel had led the warehouse group to what it achieved 20 years down the line; a highly technologically advance warehouse with all the modern communication and facilities, that may be required.

(c) **The Scope observed by AIWPL in JNPT**: Already existing empty container yards in the JNPT area had prompted AIWPL to take the decision of diversification and enter the container business in the initial years of JNPT. They operated in both reefer and non-reefer containers. OOCL (Orient Overseas Container Line) and ZIM line formed the core of their clientele. The container yard management was leased out to M/s Ocean Container Terminal (OCT). Responsibilities related to containers that were undertaken by them included: Storage, Handling, Survey, Repairs and Depot Reporting on Client Specified formats (Systems). Further, AIWPL with an expertise in handling LCL cargo had realized that JNPT port, which had the largest LCL cargo movement in India (relative to Gujarat, Chennai and Kolkata which tend to concentrate on bulk cargo), should be their obvious choice. Inability of AIWPL to handle bulk cargo due to the lack of capital had restricted them to LCL and thus optimization of their resources had led them to JNPT.

GOVERNMENT REGULATIONS & OTHER CHALLENGES

With regulatory changes, where cargo could be stuffed at the factories, there was a lot of clientele loss for AIWPL. Organizations constantly began looking into reduction of cost, particularly with the advent of ICDs (Inland Container Depots) and factory stuffing which had resulted in the elimination of warehouses from the supply chain model of many of AIWPL's clients. Constant competition from pre-established and capitally well off competitors forced them into price wars that were unsustainable, leading to a closure of the arrangement with OCT (Ocean Container Terminal) and a loss of business in terms of the empty container depot operations.

1999-2000 ERA: THE BIRTH AND CHRISTENING OF AIWPL

To counter and answer some of the trust deficit issues raised by their prospective clients, AIWPL, in the year 2000, for the first time became a private limited company (not listed). For better administration and purposes of centralization of command an office was purchased in the suburb of Masjid Bunder in the heart of Mumbai's transportation district. The office handled all the billing, staffing, technical, accounting and marketing activities of the entire group. Heavy investment in technology was also made around this time, namely in developing an integrated warehouse management system. The labour force quadrupled with AIWPL appointing twenty permanent and 50 contractual staff under its banner. To cater to their customers' logistics requirements AIWPL invested in 10 trucks around this time. Land was also acquired around Bhiwandi (Mumbai outskirts) for future prospects and expansion of the group. The Bhiwandi warehouse initially concentrated on imported cargo, while JNPT focused on the exports. While Figure.2 provides the organization structure of AIWPL, Figure.3 provides the turnover and the profit & loss at AIWPL during the past 15 years.

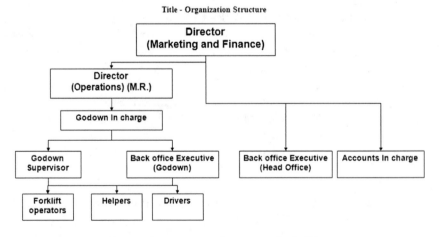

Fig. 2: Organization Structure of AIWPL

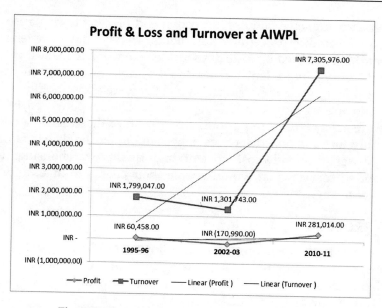

Fig. 3: Profit & Loss and Turnover Trend at AIWPL

THE ORGANIZATION AND SERVICES

AIWPL used their small company stature to minimize bureaucracy and cut through red tape to handle special projects and provide a more personalized service. Banerjee, the Planning Manager recalled the words of Patel 'We handled the cargo as a client would handle it, if they themselves only had the time'. Their company developed and planned the processes needed for service realization. Planning of service realization was consistent with the related procedures of the Process Management System and included the following:

1. Quality objectives and requirements of the system
2. Need to establish processes, documents, and provide resources specific to the service
3. Required verification, monitoring, inspection specific to the service and the criteria for service acceptance, and
4. Records needed to provide evidence that the realization processes and resulting service fulfill requirements.

The output of this planning was the continuous improvement planning process as articulated in procedure for go-down operations. To best meet the diversified needs of the complex market environment, AIWPL had developed a full range of special and custom services. Some of the services included a computerized inventory management with perpetual maintenance of inventory records; outgoing order assembly; stock rotation; re-packaging; merchandise inspection and product testing; case stencilling; assistance with insurance procedures for clients; 15-days payment terms,(however AIWPL clients have received up to 20 days further extension to make their payments); 'No Discount Policy', (precedents of discounts during special conditions however, existed); allocation to specific organizations which were excise notified; distribution services; and no direct selling; and 12.3% service tax. Their experienced, highly trained personnel were always ready to perform any and all of these tasks as needed, but a client paid only for customized services depending upon the demands of the client. Their mission was to provide cost efficient, high quality warehousing, distribution, and value added services that would enable their clients to meet and exceed the expectations of their customers.

BUSINESS PROCESS

Banerjee found that the company officials followed the loop of gauging customer requirements, addressing complaints, ensuring customer service levels or satisfaction and provided feedback to the clients. The interactions with the customer happened essentially at three levels:

(a) Marketing, which concluded with the signing of the storage contract by the Head office with the client

(b) Distribution, which involved delivery of the goods as per instructions from the client and

(c) Training included a loop of competency and skill requirements, effectiveness and feedback. Basic and advanced level training in warehousing operations was provided to contractual and in house personnel respectively.

The feedback loop (Figure.4) ensured that at the head office, invoices were prepared, as per instructions received from the go-down. Head office was also kept informed about the delivery of cargo.

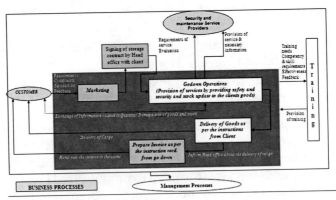

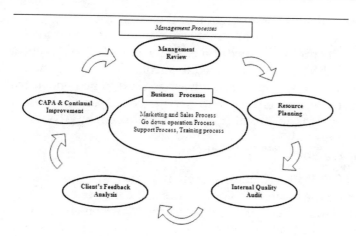

Fig. 4: The business process (developed after discussions with the company officials)

THE WAREHOUSE

The warehouse buildings were constructed of pre-cast concrete and steel, enough to meet both expanding and peak storage requirements. Public warehousing at AlWPL enhanced the flexibility of a client in respect to the space to accommodate seasonal and cyclical inventory build-up, as well as emergency or unexpected inventory surges, while eliminating the capital costs associated with building and owning a warehouse space and helped avoid long-term commitments. The whole warehouse space was completely protected by fire and security systems. Fire systems hydrants were automatically operated with power back facility, giving the client the lowest possible insurance rates and an unlimited insurable valuation for warehoused goods. With their clear ceiling heights from twenty to thirty feet, their storage facilities were designed to maximize usable storage space and permit ready access to stored goods. AIWPL had in-house equipment to facilitate time bound, safe and easy loading and unloading of many types of product packages. It had the state-of-the-art warehouse management system that allowed the customers to view and pick orders online.

During one of the meeting rounds Banerjee and Tripathi could sense that something which was of concern to Kamlesh Patel and the senior management at the warehouse was the fact that if contraband substances were found in the warehouse they could be held liable for possession of such substances. They found that the management took cognizance of the matter as they made it necessary to take from the client (on receiving cargo), a document that gave a written description of the cargo contained inside the packaging: specifically the quantity and description of the cargo. This ensured that as a matter of regulation, there was proof of ownership of the cargo, so that after the tenure of warehouse booking space was over, the client could not refuse to accept the cargo, as theirs.

If there was a dispute or a rejection of the cargo, due to which the client had not collected his material, the costing/rent levied would go up for the first three months and would double up for the next three. At the end of nine months if the cargo was still unclaimed, AIWPL was authorized to auction the cargo in the market place. The proceeds would then be retained in a trust account to be handed over to the client, after the costs and consequences due to AIWPL were refunded to them. Thus, as far as claims went, there was an ethical & legal code followed, by AIWPL.

Record Management

The owners of AIWPL, Kamlesh Patel in particulars, had a vision of strategic diversification for the future. He saw a future in the field of records management. This was long before the advent of Crown Records Management of Australia and other such pioneering organizations, into the country. He launched in 2010 a subsidiary company namely 'Storage Solutions India Pvt. Ltd.' (SSIPL). would look to provide secure storage and indexing of paper records, digital media and other business-critical information, including computer disks and tapes, optical disks, micro film, audio and video tapes and medical records. Further SSIPL would look to provide customized document management services, including Records Retention Schedules, data conversion and OCR, Records Relocation and web-based access to records information. SSIPL would also look to provide, specifically designed media storage boxes that simplified document management. The services that SSIPL would provide included Box and File Storage, Strong Storage Boxes, Document Management, Archival Services, Cataloguing Service, Document Scanning & Data Entry, Reporting Service, Box and File Retrieval, Document Collection & Delivery and Box destruction review date/ Secure Document Destruction. While providing these services it was essential to monitor the personnel at AIWPL and in doing so the management looked to develop certain key performance indicators (Figure.5) for the warehouse:

Key Performance Indicator /Measure to Follow	This Would Lead To
Increased yard management capability	Better control & visibility into workloads
Optimized usage of space	Improved employee productivity, minimized physical inventory
Reduced errors in handling (picking)/Shipping	More accurate inventory counts
Fewer damaged goods reduced paperwork	Increased ability to onboard technologies
Increased ability to meet complex fulfilment requirements	Prioritize warehouse activities for maximum customer service
Optimize reporting abilities	Better labour management capability
Improved EDI Support	More efficient reporting systems

Fig. 5: Key Performance Indicator Affecting the Warehouse

Joy Banerjee could sense that the above processes and systems would help AIWPL to integrate and develop all their processes and systems, reducing their operational costs, shipping costs and increasing the satisfaction level of their customers.

While Joy Banerjee and Gaurav Tripathi now part of the planning team at AIWPL were giving finishing touches to their presentations that included details on the company performance and sensing that the company was already in the process of doubling their capacities, some queries kept aside for Kamlesh Patel were:

- What specific steps need to be implemented for AIWPL to stay one step ahead of the competition?

- What expansion plans have been identified for AIWPL in the next 5 years?

- What new technologies are proposed for adoption in the next 5-10 years?

What does Kamlesh Patel recommend to them and why? Will the answers be visionary for AIWPL's continued success and survival in the industry?

ACKNOWLEDGEMENT

The authors would like express their sincere thanks to All India Warehousing Pvt. Ltd. for a total support provided to access data and information in developing this case. The authors express their thanks for permission to submit and present this paper at ICMC 2012.

SUGGESTED FURTHER READING

Coyle, J.J., Langley, C.R., Gibson, B.J. & Bardi, E.J., (2009). A Logistics Approach to Supply Chain Management (3rd Indian Reprint) Cengage Learning: New Delhi.

Report by India Infrastructure, Logistics in India 2012, 4th Edition, 258 pgs, India Infrastructure Publishing: New Delhi.

Material Flow Streamlining in MDV Assembly line: A Case Study of Ashok Leyland

J. Shettiger* and Sudhamsavalli Ravichander**

ABSTRACT

This paper seeks to analyze the material flow in medium duty vehicle assembly line of Ashok Leyland located in Hosur. The purpose of the paper is to find the reason behind the accumulated stocks of parts and improper flow of materials and to provide suggestions to address these issues.

Keywords: Pulse, two-bin, display matrix, Just–In-Time, time, lean production.

INTRODUCTION

Materials flow in the assembly line is the movement of materials through a defined process or a value stream for the purpose of producing an end product. Controlled and well-monitored materials flow will allow robust and accurate understanding of the usage and waste of materials within a process and the cost to run the process, etc. This information is crucial when understanding and evaluating the value the organisation's process provides. Improper material flow can result in increase in overhead costs (time, labour, etc), increased waste, increased expenses, loss of potential profit, inaccuracies in monitoring and documenting materials flow (Enterprise Resource Planning (ERP) system) etc. while streamlining of material flow will result in reduced overhead costs, minimized machinery usage, increased accuracy in monitoring materials flow, smoother processing of materials, increased profits, reduced waste and a culture of continuous improvement.

* Professor, Birla Institute of Management Technology, Greater Noida, India.
**PGDM Scholar, Birla Institute of Management Technology, Greater Noida, India.
E-mail: j.shetigar@bimtech.ac.in, sudhamasavlli.ravichander13@bimtech.ac.in

Company is working on increasing its quality and efficiency and aims at achieving Deming's Award. But there are number of bottlenecks. This case analyses the bottlenecks concerned with the material flow in MDV assembly line.The objective of the paper is to:

- Understand the causes behind the improper material flow in medium duty vehicle assembly line at Ashok Leyland.

- Suggest ways of improving the material flow and thereby efficiency.

LITERATURE REVIEW

Studies on material flow as a part of supply chain management has been a favourite subject of study by many researchers. Many consider that the heart core of supply chain essentially is an uninterrupted flow of materials to keep the assembly line in continuous operation. To these requirements are added compulsions of keeping low costs, quick response to customers, flexibility of operations and maintaining the delivery schedules. In a complex situation involving many suppliers, diverse needs of supplies with origins in different geographical locations, transportation, warehousing at intermediate stations, the exercise to keep the material flow calls for development of supplier relationships based on trust, reliability and dependability. It is in these environmental situations that the subject assumes wider perspectives and a multi-dimensional approach to seek solutions. Some of the intense studies are worth mentioning.

Ken Altenburg et al.(2003) observes the conditions that prevailed before, present and future prospectus of JIT including transportation, supplier relationships, and purchasing methods,and the period of change known as the "Japanese Revolution," including how quality has affected JIT's role . Ayman Bahjat Abdallah (2007) analyses the relationship between JIT production and manufacturing strategy and their impact on JIT performance. Florian Klug (2006) explains the optimal mix of pull and push principles in automotive supply networks. Rosario Domingo et al. (2007) analyse the internal materials flow in lean manufacturing in an assembly line of the Bosch factory, located in Spain.

ASHOK LEYLAND – COMPANY BACKGROUND

From a humble origin as a 'horseless carriage' manufacturing industry dating back to 1890s, the global automobile industry has come a long way emerging as a market leader in manufacturing activity, providing employment to approx. one in seven people, either directly or indirectly. Hailed as the 'industry of industries' by Peter Drucker, the automobile industry (US) set standards in manufacturing activity by contributing mass production techniques during early 1910s. The first industrial revolution indeed refers to the techniques advanced by Fredrick Taylor and perfected by Henry Ford I in the first of the automobile plants at global level. The Japanese changed them later and introduced lean production techniques in the 1970s, ushering the second revolution.

Indian automobile and auto-components industry came into existence in late 40's. Protected by the state policy both from foreign and domestic competition it survived but could not flourish because of that missing factor of competition. In real terms it got impetus with opening of the economy in 1990's. It was propelled on a growth trajectory, helped by robust economic activity and infrastructure development, growing middle-class population with higher disposable income; and growing consumer demand. The industry witnessed high sales turnover, in the last few years. The industry has also undertaken exports over the years. The industry has also started establishing manufacturing and marketing bases outside the country. However, the recession in world market and financial sector meltdown has affected the growth trend of the industry during 2008-09.

Ashok Leyland is a commercial vehicle manufacturing company based in Chennai, India. It was founded in 1948, and is one of India's leading manufacturers of commercial vehicles, such as buses and trucks, as well as emergency and military vehicles. Ashok Leyland also makes spare parts and engines for industrial and marine applications. It has six operating plants. Ashok Leyland believes that its historical success and future prospects are directly related to combination of several strengths. The company is doing well in both local and global markets. In India, after the Tata's it is the second largest manufacturer of commercial vehicles.

However, to sustain in the market, the company is working on increasing its quality and efficiency and aims at achieving Deming's Award. Company has started Lean Six Sigma implementation throughout the organization and working hard to raise their sigma level. It is implementing cost-reduction methods and building a culture of high quality production through their 'GEMBA' mission. Lean philosophies are being adopted everywhere. The company intends to build strong long-term supplier relationship.

NOTABLE INFORMATION ABOUT THE COMPANY

- Second largest commercial vehicle company in India in the medium and heavy commercial vehicle (M&HCV) segment.
- Market leader in the bus segment.
- Has one of most comprehensive range of tippers and tractor-trailers in the country
- 25% of Mobile Towers are backed by AL (Ashok Leyland) Gensets
- First to introduce multi-axle trucks, full air brakes and a host of innovations like the rear engine and articulated buses in India.

- Has generated a revenue of around 1.6 billion USD in the financial year 2009-10
- Has a market capitalisation of about 1.65 billion USD (as of 31st March 2012 data)
- In 1997, the company launched the country's first CNG bus and in 2002, developed the first Hybrid Electric Vehicle.
- In the populous Indian metros, four out of the five State Transport Undertaking (STU) buses come from Ashok Leyland. Some of them like the double-decker and vestibule buses are unique models from Ashok Leyland, tailor-made for high-density routes.
- In 1993 Ashok Leyland became the first in India's automobile company to win the ISO 9002 certification.
- In July 2006, Ashok Leyland became the first Indian auto company to receive the ISO/TS 16949 Corporate Certification, specific to the auto industry.
- The company vehicles carry over 70 million passengers a day, more people than the entire Indian rail network.
- Ashok Leyland has supplied over 60,000 of its Stallion vehicles which form the Army's logistics backbone.
- Over 7,00,000 AL Vehicles run on road
- The company has a near 85% market share in the Marine Diesel engine markets in India.

CURRENT SEQUENCE OF PLANNING AT ASHOK LEYLAND

The corporate office develops a master production schedule at the start of every month. This plan is a rolling plan for 12 weeks (6 weeks frozen + 6 weeks tentative) and takes into account inputs from marketing, unit capacity, and production plan of all units.. This plan is common for all units. The performance is assessed every fortnight in a formal meeting held at Chennai on 10th and 23rd of every month. The gaps in performance are analyzed. Communication and interactions such as the constraints, and issues are provided as input to MPS. Two plans result.

Material plan is provided to to all related departments such as Purchase, Planning and Production control (PPC) etc. BOM of materials is exploded to last stage following parent-child relationship.Schedules for the month are communicated to suppliers and IUT through a weekly format . Daily production plan is confirmed along with a production plan for the next two days. PPC converts weekly format to a daily plan .This forms the basis for sequencing the production of vehicles based on various issues and inputs. Daily day sequence can be changed within the date with the approval . These inputs are fed to SAP (systems) which issues 'daily issue list' to stores.

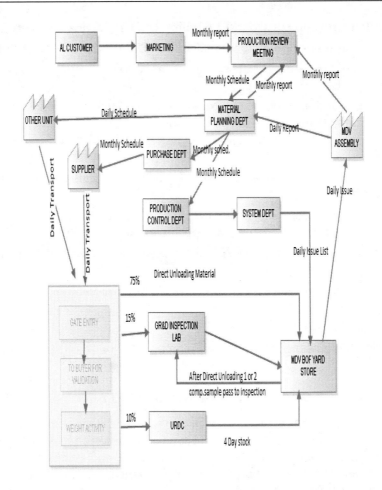

Fig. 1: Process Plan

Hosur H1 plant produces engines and vehicles (truck). The daily capacity of plant is fifty. There are 9 unloading points. For vehicles alone there are six unloading points depending on whether it is supplier certified or not . If it is supplier certified then it is directly unloaded at the demand point such as Bought out fabricated (BOF)/ bought out rough(BOR),axle(in house), engine (in house), yard. If it is not self certified then the materials are transferred from the gate to Goods and Receipts (Vehicle) where it is inspected and sent to main store. In addition to these, unit to unit material flow is taken care by URDC (Units Receipt and Dispatch Control). Suppliers are mainly located in Chennai (70-80%), Hosur, and Bangalore.

Product layout is employed in chassis assembly and engine assembly where the facilities are tare arranged in a line as per the process sequence of the component manufactured. The major characteristics of plant layout are mechanized material handling, less work- in- progress, and usage of special purpose machines.

There are 19 stages in chassis assembly followed by mounting of cockpit on the body of the truck correctly. It is sent, thereafter for a drive or to the storage area. For every 16 minutes a truck rolls out. 50 chassis are assembled per day as per agreement. Both these sections have a conveyor belt on which each process is carried on.

PROBLEMS AT MDV ASSEMBLY LINE

Some of the major concerns are discussed in the following sections:

Space is one of the major concerns in assembly line. On an average a vehicle contains 900-1000 parts. Each day nearly 50 vehicles of variety are produced. The production is sequenced. To accommodate all these items in assembly area at right location at right quantity at right time is an area of major problems . The SAP system has been implemented eight months ago. There is a mismatch between SAP list location area and the actual issue area. Certain items in the list have become non moving items. Some items are assigned to wrong vehicle model or V part number. This has resulted in unwanted or non moveable item in the stores. This also gives rise to the following wrong picking of materials, and supply to wrong supply area.

TVS is the service provider for logistics. Varieties of vehicles are assembled per day in different sequence due to conveyor capacity. The materials should be available at the assemble point as per the models. 95% of items are binned in their respective assembly points during previous night. If the sequence is changed due to some issues like material non availability then this causes confusion and duplication of work for TVS as the material has to be changed and new parts are to be binned as per new model. Sometimes these sequence changing causes assembling of wrong modeled parts besides delays in processing. The constraint of space does not allow the concept of 'kit assembly' to be used. The plant will need space for a kit for every vehicle to be assembled

Another concern is about the non moving items. The daily sequencing plan is based on material availability and conveyor capacity. Most of the voluminous materials arrive on Just in time basis whereas the small parts and imported items are safety stocked. When a particular model fails to be assembled, it results in a large stock of non moving item . Then there are items difficult to differentiate as these look alike except for some small difference in dimensions. This also results in wrong picking up of items and wrong misuse.

In case of in-house manufacturing there is a separate GRD for engine and vehicle sections. Engines are supplied to MDV assembly. Even to obtain this on an instant demand needs a lot of formalities which invariably are time consuming and result in delay in materials reaching the demand points . The materials based on ASN number is given a gate number and transferred to GRD and then to the store. Based on gate number the accounts department initiates the transfer of ownership. A vehicle contains both engine parts as well as the vehicle parts. Even if there is a critical requirement for vehicle assembly it can be addressed only if the materials are unloaded in engine section.

APPROACH TO THE PROBLEMS

Some of the problems discussed in preceding sections are addressed and certain measures are proposed to avoid or minimize it.

Two-bin items are those items which are smaller in size and lighter in weight. Bulk materials are those materials which cost less than forty rupees each. Most of these bulk materials come under the two-bin system, but some of these cannot be accommodated in two-bin system because of the size and weight e.g. thin metal plates. Similarly, there can be pulse items which should come under two-bin system. To address this issue first of all data of twenty one runner models of vehicles BOM, ABC is collected from SAP. From this data, bulk material data for each vehicle model is obtained location wise. With this data and the data from PEP each sub location is visited and the materials are assessed to determine if the same will come under two-bin system. Besides, appropriate locations are identified from the angle of interaction and convenience of pickers. Among the non bulk item also the two-bin items are identified and their locations are recommended. This way a total of 778 two-bin items and their locations are recommended.

For the pulse material the optimum quantity at which the pulse and sequence materials can be stored at location is found and from this information the pulse rate at which it can be issued is estimated. For example, if only four items can be stored then it comes under one hour pulse issue. In future the issue list is to be changed to pulse base. This way 1078 pulse items and their locations, optimum quantity along with their pulse rate are recommended.

From SAP list of location area mismatch, non-moving or absurd items, wrong assigning of V part numbers and materials were analyzed and 146 items were found to be redundant or non-moving for which corrections or recommendations were made.

In order to address the difficulty of differentiating look alike, parts display matrix is prepared so that the pickers and assemblers can easily differentiate and assemble the parts.

SOLUTIONS SUGGESTED

SAP data has to be updated as a large number of items with location mismatch, Vehicle model – material mismatch, non- moving or redundant materials exist. These occupy costly store space.

Sometimes even though a particular material e.g. clamp is mapped to vehicle model it is not used as the absence of clamp at present scenario does not harm the vehicle but on a longer time span it could prove be the cause for the reduced performance or life of that vehicle. Hence the vehicle – material mapping has to checked and unwanted material has to be removed. Similarly, if SAP data has correct material-vehicle mapping then that material has to be used even though its absence in shorter run does not affect the performance of the vehicle.

At present two-bin is present only in fame assembly area; it has to be introduced to rest of the assembly line to avoid wastages and to achieve optimum use of assembly area.

In the present system two-bin boxes are filled up to capacity level which gives rise to spilling of material during picking ,assembling . These materials can be issued to supply area with zipped or closed pouches. Optimum quantity has to be decided for each material keeping the demand, bin capacity, material dimensions etc. in mind and then issued. In any case three-fourth of the bin capacity must be the threshold level to avoid spillage and wastage.

Valve, spring bracket, wiring harness, modular hose, pipes, power steering hoses, cables which are issued presently in sequence can be issued on a pulse bases.

Negative cable, battery cable, engineering wiring cable, metallic earth cable can be issued as a kit to the sub assembly area.

ACKNOWLEDGEMENT

The authors wish to record their sincere thanks to S. Ravichandran, AGM – HR, Ashok Leyland Ltd Plant 1, Hosur for his kind support in development of this management case and permission to use the developed case at ICMC2012.

REFERENCES

http://www.ashokleyland.com/ (accessed on 17 July 2012) .

Ayman Bahjat Abdallah et al.(2007),"The relationship between JIT production and Manufacturing strategy and their impact on JIT performance", POMS 18th annual conference, Dallas, Texas, U.S.A.

Florian Klung (2006), "Synchronised automotive logistics: an optimal mix of pull and push principles in automotive supply networks." available at http://www.zalnet.de/images/Hauptseiten/Synchronised%20Automotive%20Logistics.pdf (accessed on 22 September 2012).

Ken Alternburg et al. (2003), "Just-in-time logistics support for the automobile industry", Bloomfield State College, Bloomfield.

Rosario Domingo et al. (2007), "Materials flow improvement in a lean assembly line: a case study", assembly automation, Vol. 27 iss: 2, pp.141 – 147.

Cargo Mix Strategy for Ports:
A Case of Major Ports of India

Ashutosh Kar* and Deepankar Sinha**

ABSTRACT

Cargo mix at the Indian ports is witnessing a major change. New Managlore port has been an exclusive port to export iron ore. The natural deposits getting depleted gave a warning bell to the state to create restrictions. Demand for the iron also came down from major exporters as China for economic reasons. On the other hand there has been a major increase in demand of imports of coking coal. Petroleum products continue to be a major cargo flow. The study concludes that the cargo mix is likely to undergo a major change in mix in coming years and this will need planning of appropriate infrastructure replacing the present infrastructure which is no longer needed at some at some of the ports.

Keywords: Ports, cargo, infrastructure, Haldia port, New Mangalore Port, exports, imports.

INTRODUCTION AND OBJECTIVES

The sea ports across the world are cargo specific, that is, the ports are designed to handle specific type of cargo. For example port of Singapore is a container-handling port and does not handle any other type of cargo such as dry or liquid bulk. The growth of a port is dependent on the type of the cargo and it's potential to flow through the port. Major ports of India handled more than 70% of the cargo. The cargo mix of these ports suggests that one to two types of cargo constitute the major share. Some of these ports have been primarily based on handling single type of natural resource such as iron ore through New Mangalore port. At this port iron ore constituted the major cargo. Natural resources are depleting in nature and hence may not be viable for the port in

---

* Ashutosh Kar is with NSHM College of Management Technology, Kolkata.
** Deepankar Sinha is with IIFT, Kolkata.
E-mail: ashukar1@gmail.com, dsinha2000@gmail.com

long run. Such ports are at present struggling to keep their operations viable. Hence if iron ore stops flowing through New Mangalore port, it has to look for other types of cargo to remain viable. This would mean that the existing facilities for handling iron ore should be used for other cargoes. This paper identifies the constraints in deciding on the cargo mix that the port would support and plausible course of action in this regard. Two ports, namely New Mangalore port and Haldia Dock Complex have been considered as case studies to identify their cargo mix, the shift in such mix and future course of action to offset the loss arising out of stoppage of flow of cargo for which the port was originally designed to handle. This paper aims at studying strategic and operational issues related to cargo mix of these two ports of India. This paper aims at identifying the major cargo handled by the ports

SEA PORTS

Ports are the interface between land and sea. The primary function of a port is to provide efficient low cost inter and intra- modal transfer, storage, form change and control of cargo. A port is essentially an economic concept, and economic infrastructure that serves coastal and overseas traffic. It is a subsystem of total transport network and a meeting place of other modes of transport. It provides necessary infrastructure for effective handling of vessels. The type of infrastructure varies with respect to the cargo and the vessels carrying cargo. The common infrastructures for respective cargoes include the following (Table 1):

Table 1. Common Infrastructures for Respective cargoes

Sl. No.	Cargo	Infrastructure
1.	Dry Bulk	Tipplers, Conveyors Stacker-cum-reclaimers, grab and similar equipment..
2.	Liquid Bulk	Unloading and loading arms comprising pumps and pipelines; and storage tanks and similar equipment.
3.	Containers	Mobile harbor cranes, quay cranes, Rubber Tyred Gantry cranes, Rail Mounted Gantry cranes, Reach stackers, Straddle carriers, fork lifts and similar equipment.
4.	General cargo	Quay and yard cranes, fork lifts and similar equipment.

The storage requirement varies with type of cargo. Table 2 below provides a general view of such storage requirement at ports.

Table 2: Storage Requirements at Ports

Sl. No.	Cargo	Storage Infrastructure	Space Requirement
1.	Dry Bulk	Open yards or top Closed ware-houses	High to moderate depending on stackability. For example coking coal can be stacked to greater heights compared to thermal coal

2.	Liquid Bulk	Tanks	Moderate
3.	Containers	Concrete yards	Low to Moderate depending stacking heights
4.	General cargo	Warehouses of different types, Closed, semi-closed, temperature controlled, and similar types. Open yards for cargo such as logs, steel and project	Low to Moderate

Besides, the size of ships varies with the type of cargo. The general cargo carriers are the smallest ones and are never as big as container carrier. Container carriers are smaller than dry bulk carriers and dry bulk carriers are not bigger than crude carriers.

Bruun (1989) established the relationship between the size of the vessel with fixed and variable cost associated with carriage of cargo and time at sea and port.

$$D_{opt} = \sqrt{[(A/V)*\{(U+S)/T_2\}+U]*(1/R)} \qquad \qquad ... (1)$$

where

$\qquad\qquad\qquad$ D = The ship's deadweight

$\qquad\qquad$ U + WD = Ship's fixed cost per day (U AND W are two constants)

$\qquad\qquad$ S + GD = Ship's variable costs, excluding port expenses (S and G are constants)

$\qquad\qquad\quad$ RD^2 = Ship's running cost per day in port (R=constant)

$\qquad\qquad\qquad$ T_1 = Number of days at sea

$\qquad\qquad\qquad$ T_2 = Number of days in port

$\qquad\qquad\qquad$ T_1 = A/V, where

$\qquad\qquad\qquad$ A = Distance covered in miles

$\qquad\qquad\qquad$ V = Speed in knots

Equation 1 reveals:

1. Less time the ship lies in port (t_2 is small), larger will the optimum ship's size.

2. If port turn rounds in a certain trade are slow, then the smaller the optimum ship will be.

3. If the cargo, a ship will carry in a certain trade is difficult and time consuming to handle in port (e.g. timber), the optimum size of the ship will be less than for the carrying of other easily handled cargoes

4. But in as much as the cargo is easy to load on board and to land and in as much as there are no narrow limits on the handling capacity of the shippers and the receivers (e.g. oil, ore), the most economic size of ship for the relevant steaming distance will be considerably greater.

5. Wherever port expenses are steeply progressive with the ship's size, the smaller the optimum ship's size will be.

6. The longer the steaming distance is, the larger the optimum ship will be – other things remaining unchanged

7. But in as much as the cargo is time consuming to handle in port, port turn rounds are slow, it may be that on long steaming distance one uses a smaller ship than on a shorter distance, where the time in port is short.

8. Wherever the steaming distance is 'a', and the time spent in port t_2 are given, a raised (high) speed for the ship (v knots) make a smaller dimension of ship (in dead weight) more economic.

MAJOR PORTS OF INDIA

India's long coastline of over 7500 km is home to the country's 13 major ports and around 200 non-major ports located along the western and eastern corridors. While the number of non-major ports is large, only about one-third of them undertake regular commercial operations. (Ghosh, Ravichandran, and Joshi (2011)) Since the last decade, the Indian port sector has been witnessing certain structural changes, with state monopoly gradually giving way to greater private sector participation in port investment activity. Seaports act as an interface between land and sea or other waterways. It is a part of the transportation network through which cargoes are routed to different destinations. The strengthening of the supply chain and optimum utilization of the resources are the key factors for any port to succeed in the modern competitive environment.

The cargo handled in these ports increase from 56 million tones in the year 1970-1971 to around 570 million tones in the year 2010-11, (IPA, 2011). The increase is shown in the figure-1 below.

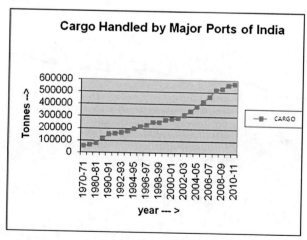

Fig. 1: Cargo growth in Major ports of India

The shares of the tonnage handled by the major ports decreased from 90% in 1990s to less than 70% of the total sea-borne cargo throughput in the year 2009-10 (IPA, 2010). Initially when the number of ports was less and other modes of transportation especially of bulk cargo were not so developed, the major ports of the country had specified cargo movement from the neighbouring states that served as their hinterland. But with the setting up of Inland Container Depots, construction of National Highways, lying of pipelines and development of other ports (also under state Governments, called minor ports) the hinterland was no more captive. Thus ports had to compete with other ports and other modes of transport. The increase in growth of traffic in minor ports is shown in Figure 2.

The major ports experienced only around 1.6% increase in 2010-2011, reaching 569.9 million tons. The annual growth of cargo traffic at major ports varied between 2% to 12% as against 1% to 35.5% growth experience by minor ports during this duration.

Thus, the significant rise of these minor ports has adversely affected the growth rate of major ports as cargoes. In addition, minor ports are mushrooming in many coastal states. As regards competition with other modes of transportation, the transportation of petroleum cargo from port of Paradeep to Haldia by pipeline is an example of shift in mode of transportation from sea to pipeline. This has led to redundancy in oil jetties at Haldia Dock Complex.

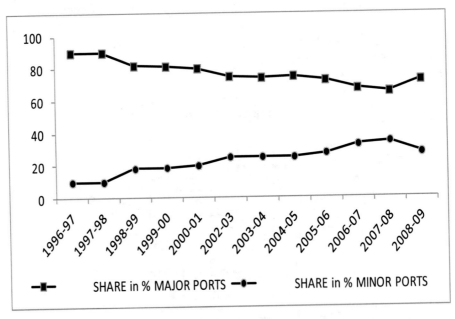

Fig. 2: Share of Cargo Handled at Minor Ports

FACTORS AFFECTING THE GROWTH OF PORTS

Since the ports are cargo specific, the growth is dependent on the type of cargo and the potential to flow through the port. However, given the type of cargo the growth varies with effectiveness of ports with respect to its competitors, effectiveness of supply chain in which port is a part of the network and the total cost of handling cargo at the port.

Ghosh, Ravichandran,and Joshi (2011), suggested that in terms of cargo composition, India's basket over the years has diversified from the traditional crude oil and iron ore to other cargo categories including coal, petroleum, oil and lubricants (POL) and containers. In 2009-2010, of the total traffic handled at major ports, POL accounted for the maximum at (31%) followed by containers (18%), iron ore (18%) and coal (13%). ICRA expects cargo growth to continue on an upward trajectory over the medium to long term. (Table 3) However, this does not assure flow of cargo through a particular port. This projection is made at national level and the cargo may be handled at any port, of the country, that appears to be viable in terms of volume and interest of the trader to route the cargo through the port. For example export of iron ore seems to increase over the years, but may not flow in future through the New Mangalore port or Haldia Dock Complex, as prevalent at present.

Table 3: Key Cargo Categories and Projected Growth

Cargo Volumes all Ports (MMT)	2009-10 Actual	2011-12 Projected	2016-17 Projected	2019-20 Projected	7 Year CAGR (FY 10-17)	10 Year CAGR (FY 10-20)
Coal	113	187	476	570	23%	18%
POL	320	333	528	660	7%	7%
Iron –ore	149	156	228	259	6%	6%
Containers	116	148	384	486	19%	15%
Others	151	208	403	520	15%	13%
Total Cargo	849	1032	2019	2495	13%	11%

Source: Maritime Agenda 2010-20

NEW MANGALORE PORT

The minor port of Mangalore was one among the 19 ports in the state of Karnataka. It had long maritime history. A number of committees were appointed to suggest ways and means for the development of the minor port into a major one. The important ones among them are the Ports technical committee in 1946, the West coast major ports development committee in 1948 and the Intermediate Ports development Committee in 1958.The last Committee, after a detailed study of the economic, engineering, navigation and traffic aspects relating to the Karnataka ports recommended Mangalore for development as a deep sea all-weather port. The reasons for its recommendations for Mangalore were the availability of infrastructural facilities, existence of rich mineral deposits and other resources in the hinterland and long maritime tradition. (Ray, 1993)

In 1979-1980, before constitution of the port trust board in 1980 showed traffic at 9.02 lakh tones. Comparative traffic for the years 1981-82 and 1991-92 shows five time increase from 16.43 lakh tones to 82.74 lakh tones. In 2001-02, it rose to 175.01 lakh tones and touched the figure of 329.41 lakh tones in 2011-12.

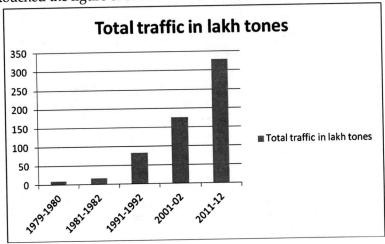

Fig. 3: Total Traffic Handled in Mangalore Port over the Years

New Mangalore is basically a bulk commodity port. Bulk cargoes like iron ore, crude, POL products, and coal constitute 90% of the total traffic projected in the Master Plan, which was prepared by the Indian Port Association and was ready by 1985. The share of the other cargo is only 10%.

Iron ore is the main traffic of the Mangalore port. Rich iron ore mines are situated in the hinterland of Mangalore. In Chickmagalur district there are mines at Gangamala-Aroli-Gangrical range; 65 km away from Mangalore and Kudremukh mines with reserve over 600 million tones, at a distance of 110 km from Mangalore. Iron ore concentrates and pellets are exported through Mangalore Port by a single agency which is the Kudremukh Iron Ore Company Limited (KIOCL). The Kudremukh Project was implemented at cost of Rs. 630 crores. It envisaged export of 7.5 MT of iron ore concentrates annually. The first shipment of iron ore concentrates through the port was made on June 12, 1981 to Romania. Thereafter concentrates were exported to Romania, Bahrain, Japan, Turkey and other countries. However, there was slothful development in export of iron ore concentrates. KIOCL decided to export iron ore in the form of pellets also. The pelletisation plant of KIOCL came up in Mangalore in 1986. The pellets are being exported to Japan, Czechoslovakia and other countries. (Ray, 1993)

Volume of iron ore which is one of the major export items at present in the Mangalore port would continue to be a function of policy and any restriction or ban on iron ore fines or lumps (like the recent one instituted by the state government of Karnataka), could impact ports and terminals, where the share of iron ore cargo is high in the overall cargo mix.

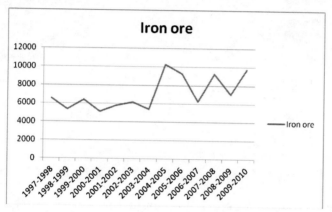

Fig. 4: Share of Iron ore Handled by the Mangalore port

The cargo share of POL over the years is given below. In 1990-1991 oil traffic was just 0.6 MT (POL products) against the projection of 4.5 MT. This was because the refinery did not come up and there was no import of crude or export of POL products. Import of POL products continued.

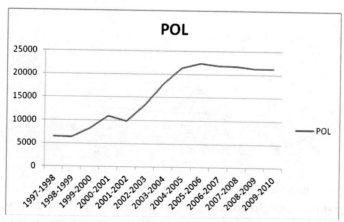

Fig. 5: Share of POL Handled by the Mangalore Port

Coal also consttitutes the major part of the cargo mix. For the import of coal a separate jetty was constructed at the west of the ore berth. As the import of thermal coal, was very good, a coal berth with mechanical handling facilities should be developed, after viable linkage with coal fields and thermal plants.

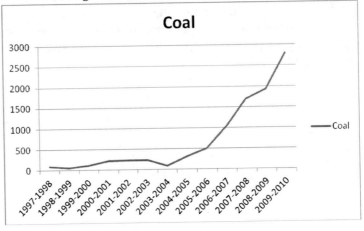

Fig. 6: Share of coal handled by the Mangalore Port

In 1990 four additional berths were built for handling dry bulk and break bulk excluding iron ore. Two additional berths were introduced in 1995 and 2000 respectively. Berth number 4 was used as container berth. (Ray, 1993)

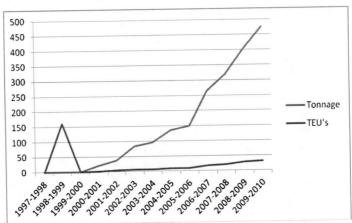

Fig. 7: Share of Container Handled by the Mangalore port

As the Karnataka state government was putting a ban on the iron ore, diversification of cargo profile with emphasis on general cargo and agricultural and forest products should be attempted by the port authorities under the aegis of the Union Government.

Facilities for handling containers should be developed in the Port. Linkage with ICDs will boost up general traffic of the port. There should be linkage with other ports through costal shipping. Coastal traffic through New Mangalore Port will be economic and convenient

HALDIA PORT

During the 1950s, the search was on for a suitable location of a port down the river Hooghly near the estuary which would not have the problem of navigability and would provide adequate draft for big vessels. Haldia is situated 104 km, from Calcutta and is near to the sea. Due to the increase in oil import through large oil carriers, a modern and deep drafted oil jetty was necessitated. Haldia was recognized as outlet providing facilities for large oil and ore carriers. It became operational in the year 1968, under the Kolkata Port Trust. Kolkata Port Trust, thus, had two dock systems, namely, the Kolkata Dock System (KDS) at Kolkata and Haldia Dock System (HDC) at Haldia. The facilities at Haldia evolved over a period of time and the capacity of the HDC for different cargo is given below (Table 4).

Table 4: Cargo handling in Haldia Dock System

Sl.No.	Cargo	Capacity in MMT (Million Metric Ton)	Cargo handled in 2009-10in MMT
1.	POL	17.00 (3+2 BJ)	9.38
2.	Iron ore	6.00 (2)	7.684
3.	Coal	7.00 (2)	7.525
4.	Container	4.00(2)	2.010
5.	General cargo	12.7 (8)	6.399

Figures in the brackets denote number of berths. BJ=Barge Jetty

The bulk of cargo composition was crude and POL (petroleum, oil, liquid) till few years back. This accounted for 45% of the total cargo. Haldia Dock Complex has four river side oil jetties which handle crude, POL products and liquid ammonia. Jetty No. 1 has connecting pipelines to Haldia refinery, Barauni refinery, and fertilizer plants of Hindustan Fertilizer Corporation and Hindustan Lever Limited. However the share of POL declined over the period of time. (Ray 1993). The share of POL handled by the Haldia Port over the years is given below.

The Indian Oil Corporation Ltd. is a major client of Haldia Port. Although there was strong opposition, from the Kolkata Port Trust and the West Bengal government, but IOC decided to go ahead with the Paradeep-Haldia pipeline project to carry crude. This had affected both Haldia and Kolkata, docks. That resulted in the decline of the share of POL from 2005-2006.

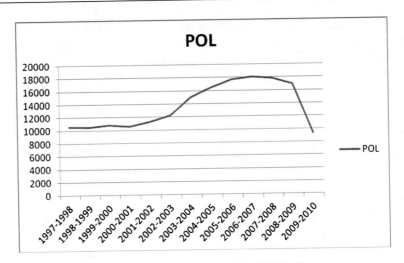

Fig. 8: Share of POL Handled by Haldia Port

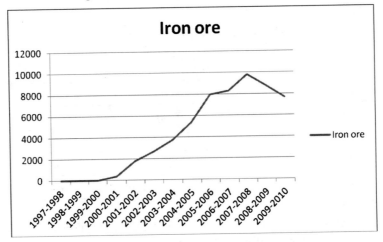

Fig 9: Share of Iron ore Handled by Haldia Port

Iron ore handled by the ports over the years are shown in the above figure. This cargo started flowing only after 2000 and started declining since 2008-2009. This decline is owing to reduction in imports of iron ore by steel makers of China. The demand for steel from Chinese manufacturers decreased due to economic slowdown.

Coal forms an integral part of the cargo mix. Thermal coal is exported to Tamil Nadu. TISCO and SAIL are mainly importing coking coal in increasing quantity through their captive berths. Fig 10 shows the handling of coal over the years.

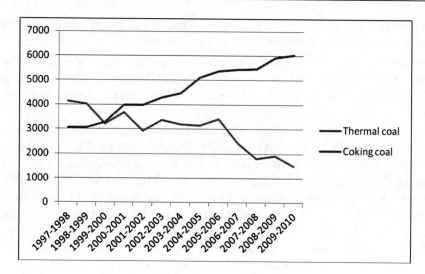

Fig. 10: Share of Coal Handled by Haldia Port

The share of container handled by Haldia port is shown in the following table:

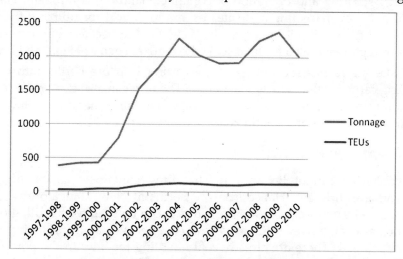

Fig 11: Share of Container Handled by Haldia Port

CONCLUSION

The above analysis leads to the following conclusions:

i. Ports need to earmark their cargo mix as different types of cargo require different infrastructure. Shift in cargo may lead to either complete or partial redundancy of assets. For example, oil jetties are not suitable for handling of dry bulk cargo, while conversion of dry bulk berth to container berth or vice versa, would require higher investments and significant restructuring; else efficiency would suffer.

ii. Demand of a cargo in a region is not the demand for the mode of transport. This can be observed from the case of POL transport from Paradeep to Haldia, which once moved by ships now being transported through pipelines. The port should draw up long term strategy to effectively utilize the oil jetties. Conversion of oil jetties to other category of cargo is a distant possibility. The future of iron ore also does not seem to be bright and as such the focus should shift to coal as the country is poised to increase its power generation from coal fired plants. The port should enhance its productivity and reduce turn round time to remain attractive to coal carriers. Or else inspite of demand for coal in that region or in the hinterland the cargo may not move by the port, instead make take alternate routes as in case of POL. Though the growth of containers are promising in the region, Kolkata port is already specializing in containers and being sister organization of Haldia may not allow Haldia Dock Complex to venture fully into container handling. In addition conversion of bulk handling berths to container berths would be a difficult proposition. Port also needs to construct concrete yards to sustain the container stacking and operation of container handling equipment. Haldia port should enhance marketing and sales promotion effort for utilizing the berth for handling chemical, liquidified gas such as LNG. It can act as a hub for eastern and northern region and also for land-locked countries such as Nepal and Bhutan.

iii. New Mangalore has the option of converting iron ore berths into other bulk handling cargo berths such as coal berths. The port can also explore the possibility of setting up container terminal to enhance container handling effectively. The viability of such recommendations can be assessed from the following perspectives.

OPERATIONAL PERSPECTIVE

Bulk cargo berths cannot be used for handling containers as its infrastructure requirements are different. Hence iron ore berths at New Mangalore would stand redundant once its exports from the port stop. It can be used for handling other bulk cargoes such as coal, however linkages with coal fields or appropriate infrastructure needs to developed. There are already coal handling facilities in the port and hence utilization of the iron ore berths for coal can only be partial. A long term strategy should be drawn up to ensure adequate return on assets (ROA).

New Mangalore port has draft of thirteen (13) meters i.e. allowing bulk vessels to be handled at the port. New Mangalore port can accommodate ship of DWT up to 1 lakh tons. This would enable the port to accommodate coal carriers along with container vessel of Suezmax category.The existing equipment such as reclaimer and ship loader meant for iron ore handling can be used for coal handling.

ECONOMIC PERSPECTIVE

The demand of electricity is increasing over the years in India. Figure 12 shows the demand for power over the years.

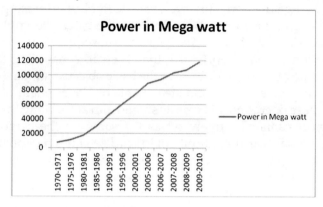

Fig. 12: Demand of Thermal Power over the Years

As coal is one of the ingredients for the thermal power plant, so the import of coal has to be increased to meet the demand. Figure 13 shows the demand for coal over the years.

The demand for coal and demand for power has a strong correlation of 0.99713.

Container is one of the important item of the cargo mix of the above two ports. The GDP (gross domestic product) reflecting country's economy bears an association with container handling in the ports. They have a strong corelation of 0.976628. GDP of India has been increasing over the years justifying the expected growth in container handling. Hence, the ports may consider enhancement of their container handling facility.

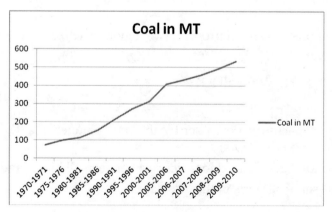

Fig 13: Demand of Coal Over the Years

ADMINISTRATIVE PERSPECTIVE

New Mangalore operates under the aegis of Ministry of shipping, Government of India. Government of India can initiate action for creating coal and container handling facilities at New Mangalore port. However, Private Public Partnership can be explored for creating facility for cargo handling. In both the cases the entities will have to operate under the Major Port Trust Act 1963 and subsequent laws enacted regarding private participation in major ports of India. The cargo handling facility by either Government, private or jointly would have the basic objective of maximizing the stake holders wealth. The power plants and steel plants of Government of India are major stake holders of these operations. The ports should aim at fulfilling their requirements. However, the tariff cannot be freely set as the same on the cargo and vessel are regulated by the TAMP (Tariff Authority of Major Ports).It is a regulatory body under The Ministry of Shipping, Government of India, whose major objective is to ensure that monopoly of port services leading to excessive tariff at one end and inadequate return on operation of port facilities causing losses to authority are avoided i.e. it looks for rationalization of port charges. Hence, the private or government agencies or joint operations by them will have to operate under the constraints of Major Port Trust Act (1963) and subsequent amendments and major regulations of TAMP.

In major ports all major decisions are taken under 5 year plans under the aegis of Planning Commission of India and the respective ministries. Once approved in principle in regard to plan outlay, the project planning and the phasing of expenditure are done on the basis of annual plan.

THE VIABILITY MODEL

A detailed feasibility study on conversion of an existing iron ore berth to a coal berth or creating a container handling facility has to be carried out before zeroing down into the firm decisions. The following optimization model can be used to determine such feasibility.

The formulation of the main problem (we denote as (P)) is as follows:

$$\text{Min } Z = \sum_{i \in K} \sum_{j \in L} C_{i,j} (Q_i, j \in L \ X_{i,j} (Q)/Q_i) \times X_{i,j} (Q) \qquad \ldots (2)$$

Sub to: $0 \le Q_i \le W_i$ for all $i \in K$ ... (3)

Where

- Q_i –   The capacity of Port i set by the port planner, $i \in K$; Q is the vector composed of all Q_i's;
- Z   –   The total generalized logistics cost between all hinterlands and ports;
- K   –   The set of all ports in this problem;

L   –   The set of all hinterlands in this problem; (For simplicity, from here on, "hinterland" means to all shippers within a hinterland region.)

$X_{i,j}$ –   the quantity of freight that is transported between Port i and Hinterland j, where i€K and j€L;

$C_{i,j}$ –   the logistics cost per unit freight between Port i (i€K) and Hinterland j (j€L), which is a function of Qi and ▯, j€L $X_{i,j}$ (Q)/Q_i

W_i –   the maximum capacity constraint of Port i (i ∈ K), which is usually determined by the physical and geographical restrictions; (Feng, Wang,Zhang,Jiang, 2011).

Global Perspective

Ports being interface for international trade, its activities are significantly determined by the global economy. In case of economic slowdown at national and global level, import and export of goods are affected.

Scope for Further Work

A further study on these ports using optimization models similar to the one described above may be carried out that will reveal the right cargo mix.

REFERENCES

Bruun P, (1989), Port Engineering, Vol I, Gulf Publishing Company.

Feng.X,Wang.W, Zhang.Y and Jiang.L (2011) "Optimization of Capacity of Ports within a Regional Port System", pp.1-14, presented in TRB Annual Meeting

Ghosh.A, Ravichndran.K, Joshi.N (2011) "Indian port sector: Growth plans ambitious but uncertainty hangs over implementation', published in ICRA Rating Services.

IPA (Indian Port Association), (2010), Major Ports of India - A profile: 2009 – 2010, New Delhi.

IPA (Indian Port Association), (2011), www.ipa.nic.in, 01.08.2011

Ray.A (1993) "Maritime India: Ports and Shipping", pp.364-384, published by Pearl Publishers, Kolkata.

Necessity of the Development of SMEs Manager's Capability and Strategic Management Level

*Hiro Mitsuyama**

ABSTRACT

Collaboration between Subcontractors and RERI (university-affiliated Regional Economic Research Institutions) in the technological field has produced satisfactory synergistic results. On the other hand, successful collaboration on the strategic management level is still unprecedented. Long term business experience, as well as manufacturing high quality products, used to be very important elements for SMEs to establish sustainability. However, it is indispensable to not only depend on the conventional empirical approach, but for SMEs managers to also improve their knowledge and comprehension of theories of strategic management. The purpose of this study is three-fold:
To find out how important it is for SMEs' managers to improve their theoretical management capabilities,
As well as to verify what comprises successful collaboration on a strategic management level,
And, finally, to propose an effective collaboration model.

Keywords: Technology push, market pull, global competition, synergy effect, autonomous management, competitive strength, academic theory, long term commitment.

INTRODUCTION

Definition of the Subcontractors

This study deals specifically with small to medium sized subcontractors with 300 or less employees with low autonomy. These subcontractors are supplied with specifications and drawings for parts and are only responsible for manufacturing. The parts are typically not vertically integrated products specific to one industry, such as the automotive industry, but rather horizontally specialized products with cross-industrial applications. Hereafter, these subcontractors will be referred to as SPM.

---

* Hero Mitsuyama is associated with Research Institute of East Asian Economies of Fukui Prefectural University, Fukui. Hiro Mitsuyama is also pursuing doctoral programe in Management of Technology, at Ritsumeikan University, Kyoto Japan.
  E-mail: j-mitsuyama@fpu.ac.jp

Most of SPM products are "custom made products" which are designed by the clients, and the SPM receives drawings and specifications from the clients. This clearly distinguishes these subcontractors from "standardized mass production" manufacturers. The SPM in this study do not have integrated relationships with their clients, so their performance is their only differentiating element.

When the provided parts manufacturers produce products, clients are in charge of R&D and provide drawings and specifications for the SPM. All the SPM is required to do is provide reliable high quality, as well as punctual delivery. Furthermore, as certain products are expected to be manufactured for about 5 to 10 years, it is very important to have the technical capabilities to implement value analysis and value engineering to reduce the cost every year in order to keep the client's business for a long time. Since there is no integrated relationship with the client cost is a major factor, with clients demanding simultaneous cost reduction without any reduction in quality or punctuality. The ability to deliver high quality products punctually at a low cost is a critical factor when clients evaluate trial products.

A critical determinant of these SPMs' ability to respond to market crises in the past, such as the oil crisis, the Plaza Accord, etc., has been employees' skills and experience, and bottom-up innovation via *kaizen* activities. This employee-driven innovative production engineering has been a successful model since the 1950's; and in SPMs with relatively few employees the importance of retaining and developing employee capacity is a critical long-term determinant of success.

Research Question

Many SPM owners and managers (hereafter described simply as manager) are operation managers, as well as engineers, in most of the cases. Many engineers are product-oriented, and so managers tend to focus on hard work and depend excessively on employee's endurance and patience to get through crises. However, ever since the IT revolution, managers have found it very difficult to deal with the new economic phase, such as diversification, and shorter product life cycles. These changes are incompatible with past knowledgeable and experience, and hard work by employees cannot fully compensate for deficits in strategic planning. Also many SPM managers are aging, reaching 60+ years, and might find it difficult to understand and embrace the new manufacturing paradigm, and analyse the detailed global diversification of market needs. SPM managers believe that reliable and high quality products automatically bring stability and competitiveness, as in technological push theory, especially with economic growth; and that repeat business from clients guaranteed made a certain amount of sales automatically. Before long, a philosophy of "obtaining client inquiries without effort" was established behind this economic growth. Many managers felt certain that all that needed to be done was to manufacturing reliable products on time. This philosophy treated academic knowledge, such as strategic management theories and marketing, as unnecessary, and so knowledge in these areas gradually devolved and led to a loss of competitive strength in the global market. In addition Japanese companies tended to focus on the value at sales instead of profit. The problem with a sales volume orientation is that a lot of Japanese SPM are involved in competitive production engineering but, because the savings from this are normally translated into customer discounts for large volumes or long-term contracts, it does not transform into profit improvement. Lack of marketing strategy causes high quality products with higher price even in emerging markets where the economy is still developing and growing. Managers need to break away from this technology push strategy; a strategy based on a pre-IT revolution market, where mass production and mass consumption were the norm. It is time to realize that SPMs should recognize the importance of strategic management in order to efficiently enhance their competitive strength and improve profit margins in order to manage autonomously.

It's essential to change the manufacturing paradigm within SPM from the technical push strategy to a market pull strategy, where customers needs are the first priority. To achieve this innovation, they need to change their marketing strategy fundamentally, from routine sales activities to marketing actively. In order to seek out customers and find out what they need, SPM managers need to learn about the market by improving their knowledge of marketing and management skill academically. Without learning, it would be very difficult to compete with global rivals under complex market conditions.

Of course developing this knowledge of marketing and strategic management independently would be extremely difficult, so it would be better to collaborate with external academics to acquire these skills and improve SPM competitiveness.

Circumstances of Collaboration in Japan

There has been a long history of collaboration between business and academia on the R&D level ever since late 1800s in Japan and this collaboration has expanded to joint research, contracted research, and HR development. As shown in Figure 1, the sales of SPM which are involved in industry-university collaborations show about 3~5 times more sales than non-collaborating SPM. Thus, if one views sales as a measure of success, then collaborating SPM are more successful than non-collaborating ones.

US$ million

However, there are not many SPM efficiently improving sales or profits by collaborating on new technology or products. This tendency shows that even big Japanese companies, as well as SPM, don't recognize the importance of strategies. Even though small, SPM frequently command world leading production engineering and technology capabilities, there is the matter of recognising importance of academic theories of management as well as HR development improvement. SPM should realize the importance of theories that would be able to utilize the competitive strength which they have cultivated over a long period. What Japanese SPM need to do is to collaborate with professionals who could improve the SPMs' profit structure by efficiently utilizing their competitive strength and possibly could support them from a long-term point of view.

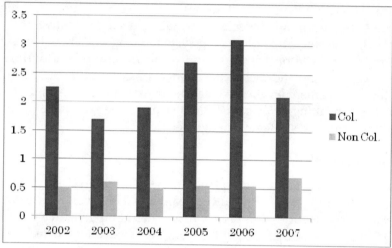

Fig. 1: Sales Comparison between Collaborative SPM and Non Collaborative SPM
Source: Ministry of Internal Affairs and Communications Survey of Scientific and Technological Research 2010

HISTORY OF SPM AND CONSULTING FIRM'S COLLABORATION IN STRATEGIC MANAGEMENT FIELD

Not only SPM, but also most of the Japanese manufacturing industry, faced a severe crisis, known as bubble economy, in the early 1990s. To get through this, many SPM tried to collaborate with major consulting firms, but usually consulting firms needed to accomplish the best result with limited team resources and time, so consulting firms tended to rely on data analysis or trends to propose solutions, without figuring out what was really going on or having an in-depth knowledge of the nature of the company. Thus proposals from consulting firms tend to be unfocused, and also far from what SPM really expect, because the latest theories usually follow a macro-economic paradigm focused on larger companies. There has been big gap between what SPM expected and what consulting firms proposed. Important factors for consulting firms to consider were, the business structure of SPM, such as limited human resources, so that most employees needed to be cross-trained and multi-skilled, as well as given authority over their section in order to make necessary decisions and changes. Bottom up *kaizen* activities, continuously utilizing perception and tacit knowledge, to improve production engineering are the norm in SPM. However, depending on, and competing with, technical advantage or tacit knowledge alone is no longer advantageous anymore, because, as a result of the improvement of production machinery, it is much easier to manufacture high quality products. However, each type of production machinery still has to be maintained and managed correctly, so production engineering and techniques are still dependent on individuals' skills to ensure consistent high quality. Thus engineers are often more powerful than managers (and in many SPM they are the same person). Consulting firms proposing systematic organizational change without an understanding of SPM organization will result in only partial optimization and make, not only employees and each department confused and chaotic, but also spread distrust to the management level, as well as being extremely expensive. As a result of this experience, consulting firms gave SPM a strong negative image of collaboration with consulting firms at a strategic management level.

LITERATURE REVIEW

The necessity of industry-university collaboration in the social science field has already been recognized by university and RERI researchers. However, most SPM managers believe that academic theories don't really help when competing in a real market, and also the Japanese domestic market is still big enough, even after the decline in strategic management (Porter and Takeuchi,2000). Industry-university collaboration in the R&D field has progressed comparatively smoothly because it doesn't really need SPM to disclose or discuss management issues, especially financial information. As former studies indicate that collaboration on the strategic management level can be difficult, the following are recommended: *"Establish a project team to tackle important subjects for regional society"*, *"Establish a cooperative system and substantial organization support"* and *"Publishing research outcomes positively to local society"* (Toda and Hirao, 1998). Thus, the only close relationships in the literature have been with administrative organizations, and it is difficult to propose how to construct close strategic management relationships with individual companies.

Generally, most SPM are experiencing difficulty in diversifying their business strategically due to limited management resources, so they tend to concentrate on a few competitive products to sustain their business. However, the auto industry constructed a vertical integration system and this self-integration might possibly be holding back the progress of industry-university collaboration in this industry (Motohashi, 2001). Being in a vertical integration chain, especially in the auto industry, SPM are automatically able to receive inquiries from regular clients, as long as auto makers manufacture cars. Therefore, it could be imagined that SPM don't need to establish strategies and this lead to a decline in autonomous management capability.

There used to be a certain amount of economic growth in domestic market but, now the market circumstances have changed drastically so that each SPM needs to analyze what would be really destructive to their own growth, or to them sustaining their abilities. However, a lot of managers still believe that technology push is the only strategy to maintain competitive strength, rather than academic theories or strategic management.

STUDY FRAMEWORK

To survive in a diversified global market, is necessary to change the way that we deal with the market where technology push model used to have competitive strength, and to accomplish this change, it is necessary to select for and concentrate on management resources. Most SPMs' managers are not familiar with academic theories, such as strategic management, so it is necessary to collaborate with external professional organizations, such as RERI, in order to achieve objectives such as the development of the regional economy. Both SPM and RERI operate in different domains, but they are both professionals, so this interactive collaboration could be expected to yield a synergistic effect, not only providing successful collaboration on a strategic management level, but also improving SPMs' managers' theoretical capabilities. To overcome these challenges, we need to consider four bottlenecks, as shown in Fig 2, to assign independent variables, focus, and evaluate each objective.

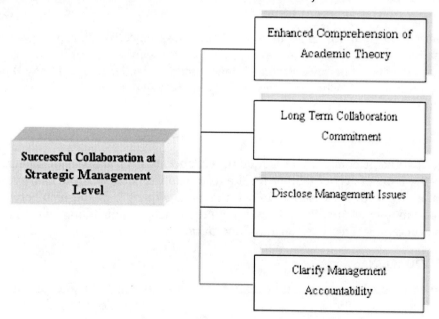

Fig. 2: Challenges for Successful Strategic Collaboration Field

Enhancement of Academic Theory Comprehension

Most SPMs' managers and engineers believe in the philosophy that, "high quality products result in stability". Engineering processes and high quality products always come first, rather than theory or strategy. There is a mistrust of researchers and intellectuals who don't know what is going on at the factory-floor level. The key factor in breaking through this barrier is to better educate the managers of the company on the latest theories relating to technology, otherwise lack of comprehension will usually lead to them disregarding these theories as irrelevant or worthless.

Long Term Collaboration Commitment

In order to limit the time and cost, as well as to provide the best advice to management, it is necessary to establish a system that extends the understanding of the importance of theories not only to managers, but also to the entire workforce. To accomplish this innovative change, it will take a lot of time for employees to realize the importance of theories, and to learn these theories. The key objective is to take a long view of the collaboration, especially in PDCA processes, because the continuous modification of such processes could be the only way to establish competitive strategies.

Disclosure of Management Issues

It is very important for SPM to disclose business objectives, even very sensitive information such as financial issues or earnings to researchers in order to accomplish successful collaboration on a strategic management level. However, this will depend entirely on how seriously the SPMs' management views the collaboration and how committed they are to innovation.

Clarify Management Accountability

The most difficult challenge in achieving collaboration on a strategic management level is the issue of accountability for the results of the collaboration. Clarifying joint accountability would be essential in helping management to distinguish between this being just another academic study taking place in their organization, versus this being a serious and integrated long-term collaboration.

METHODOLOGY

Key to accomplishing successful collaboration on a strategic management level is to establish the expectations of both parties in advance, in order to establish from the outset whether collaboration is possible and to try and evaluate in advance whether these expectations are achievable and compatible.

Concerns About Collaboration from the Point of View of Both SPM and RERI

Table 1 shows that there are anxieties about collaboration on a strategic management level from both SPM and RERI.

Table 1: Issues of Concern with Collaboration

Concerned by SPM	Concerned by RERI (multiple answers allowed) (n = 77)
• Too much paper work	• Require results quickly
• Anxiety over the collaboration cost	• Under budgeted
• Taking too long to get results	• Agenda is not clear
• Hard to find reliable researchers property	• Unfamiliar with a contracts and intellectual
• Ineffective in collaboration	• Leave all the decision to SPM
• Unclear each responsibility researchers	• Lack of understanding of researching and
• Lack of operating resources	• Lack of knowledge about global markets

Source: Chamber of Commerce of Tokyo Survey for Collaboration 2005 *Kansai Bureau of Economy Survey 2007, Feb*

Points of concern for SPM are, "lack of clarity about responsibility", and "too much paper work", however there is no specific concern about, or dislike towards, the universities themselves. In essence the SPM aren't worried about the universities, but rather the concerns are focused on their own organizational environment.

RERI likewise have concerns, such as "require results quickly", "Leave all the decision to the SPM". These concerns indicate that RERI and SPM possibly had differing expectations in terms of collaboration on a technological level.

There is also a mismatch in terms of the evaluation of outcomes. The stated outcome of RERI is to stimulate and contribute to the regional economy, however the output of RERI is evaluated at conferences, in journals and as authors, and the primary evaluation criteria are academic, rather than economic.

However, according to a survey by the Kansai Bureau Economics in February 2007, 32% of RERI researchers responded that prioritised collaborations with SPM, rather than major companies, and 43% of RERI responded that collaborations with SPM were the most important advantageous to regional economic development, as SPM had significant advantages when compared with major companies, such as "decision are made quickly", "easy to form good relationships with business owners" and "flexibility". This indicates that important elements in collaborations are not only the size of the company, but also the potential to utilize synergies in order to create regional and national economic development.

COMPARISON OF RERI ACTIVITIES BETWEEN JAPAN AND OVERSEAS

Table 2 shows a comparison of activities of RERI in Japan and overseas, in order to consider what kind of activities RERI should be engaging in.

Table 2: Survey of Contribution and Social Role of RERI

Organizational Activities	% of Respondents	
(multiple answers allowed)	Japan	Overseas (n = 147)
Research papers	98%	76%
Open seminars or Symposia	85%	64%
Sending instructors on training courses	53%	31%
Research projects with local think tanks	50%	60%
Lifelong programs	20%	33%
Publish local economic data on the Internet	20%	55%
Consulting work for public administration and companies	15%	81%
Supporting business ventures	13%	17%

Source: Ministry of Education 1999 (Overseas=North America 23, EU 16, Others 3)

What is immediately apparent is that overseas RERI tend to engage in consulting activities with local companies and public organizations more often than in Japan as Table 2 indicates, Japanese RERI mostly publish "Research papers", or "Open seminars or Symposia", however the flow of information and learning is one-way, back into the academic community, when compared with the more interactive consulting role of overseas RERI. Moreover, publishing research papers has a short-term focus as the paper needs to be tied up before the publication date, and as such longer-term goals such as regional economic development are relegated to a lower priority. Seminars and symposia measure success in terms of volume of delegates, and in order to be viewed as a success they sometimes need to call on some celebrities, whether they like it or not. Consequently, the contents of seminars or symposia tend not to focus on issues of long-term importance to SPM and the economy. However, seminars and symposia are not all negative. In order to survive RERI need to justify their existence, and it is important for RERI to disclose information to the public about what they do.

CIRCUMSTANCE OF SPM'S HR DEVELOPMENT

Figure 3 shows the reasons why SPM have some difficulties in developing their own employees. As indicated below, "shortage of trainees", and "lack of time" are the major issues. These reasons are not very difficult or complicated, and thus it can be assumed that SPM managers don't take the necessity for innovative change in a diversified market environment very seriously. This needs to change. SPM managers need to be educated about the new skill set required in order to be competitive in the global market.

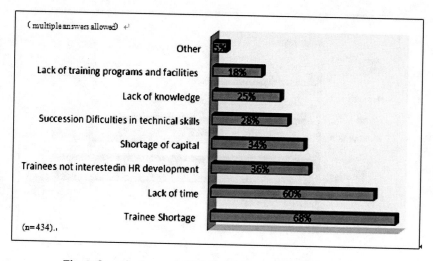

Fig. 3: Specific Issues in Human Resource Development
Source: Keidanren Policy proposal 2010 July

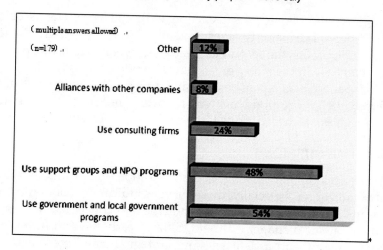

Fig. 4: Classification of Specialized Agencies in Use
Source: Keidanren Policy proposal 2010 July

Figure 4 is a summary of the types of collaborations which SPM used to engage in the past. It indicates that SPM often tried to collaborate with central or local government organization to improve their organization, as well as to reduce expenses during difficult times. The types of past collaborations bear out that SPM managers do not see the value in spending time and money in learning academic theory.

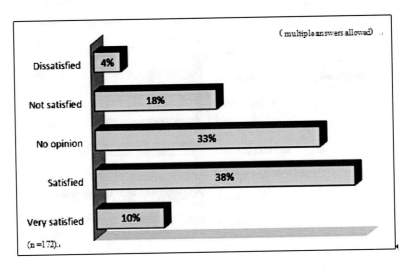

Fig. 5: Degree of Satisfaction with Specialized Agencies
Source: Keidanren Policy proposal 2010 July

Figure 5 shows the degree of satisfaction with collaborations as evidenced by several organizations. The majority of respondents (38%) reported satisfaction. Thirty-three (33%) of respondents, the second largest category, reported "no opinion", which is a fairly obvious flaw in the study given central tendency bias in Likert-type scales, and given the Japanese bias against expressing a negative opinion this may indicate that the eighteen (18%) of respondents who reported "not satisfied" might, if the "no opinion" responses are included, be as large as fifty-one percent (51%).

ANALYSIS AND DISCUSSIONS

Many SPM are seeking networking or collaboration opportunities with external professional organization, especially, these surveys indicate, collaboration with public organizations instead of consulting firms. Thus the best collaboration partners would be RERI in the strategic management field. SPM already have sufficient expertise in the field of technology, and a deficiency in strategic management expertise. It has been suggested that SPM managers should participate in MOT (management of technology) courses in under graduate school, however, given managers' workloads and responsibilities, attending regular classes is not realistic. Moreover, MOT classes are aimed at graduate students or project leaders in companies. SPM managers require tailored coursework that caters to their schedules, as well as focusing on immediately applicable and practical material that they can implement as they learn.

The next section will deal with four major potential challenges to collaboration on a strategic management level.

ENHANCEMENT OF THE ACADEMIC THEORY COMPREHENSION

Based on their experiences of collaboration with consulting firms in the past, SPM felt strongly that it was not necessary to depend on academic knowledge and theories in order to enhance their competitiveness. This experience reinforced their belief that technology push management and production engineering is the best way to promote and maintain competitive advantage in the market. To make SPM realize the importance of using the latest information and theories to enhance competitiveness efficiently, it is important to establish a place where SPM could meet with RERI researchers to talk frankly. Talking frankly doesn't sound really important, but it is very difficult to do because of past misunderstandings between these parties. Seen from the outside it is obvious that improving the SPM managers' management skills is critical. Establishing Advanced Personnel Development Programs (APDP) to enhance the theoretical knowledge of SPM managers is important. Figure 7 proposed a SPM and RERI collaboration model focused on areas of shared interest, in order to improve the capability and comprehension of academic theories to keep an advantageous position in the global market.

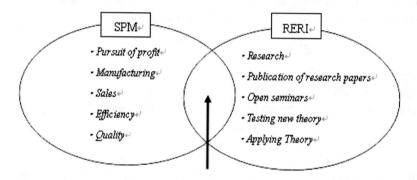

Fig. 7: Image of the Advanced Personnel Development Programs

One of the goals in collaborating with SPM thorough APDP is to learn how to approach improving their own company, including human resource development, in reference to the theories. On the other hand, to face the practical issues and objectives in companies RERI researchers might have a great opportunity to learn as well, and it is realistic to expect some sort of a synergistic effect. This project always has to encourage SPM managers to engage with initiative and to be fully motivated to participate in the long term to construct trusting relationships as well as making them understand the importance of learning theories. On top of that, APDP program should be supportive, as managers will have to attend after work.

To understand the increasingly diversifying global market, it is essential for SPM to catch up with strategic management, which includes analysis tools, financial strategy and corporate governance to maintain competitive superiority, and to have a detailed knowledge of many theories could be grant immeasurable benefits, such as enabling SPM managers to lead cross industrial networks to harness synergistic effects.

LONG TERM COLLABORATION COMMITMENT

By directly linking learning theories in APDP to practical advantages would be easy for SPM managers to recognizing that short-term collaborations with consulting firms are ultimately self-defeating as the PDCA process limits the scope of innovation, and without in-house expertise it just places the SPM in a position of an endless, expensive, series of single-innovation collaborations with consultants. However with RERI collaborations the focus would be on capacity-building, with a lower long-term cost, and with the increased awareness of the utility of academic theory the project would become self-reinforcing as managers saw the value of the program and incorporated it into the organization's training regime. Moreover, since 2002 National and Public Universities have been encouraged to collaborate with private companies, so the arrangement would be mutually beneficial. Collaboration between SPM and RERI possibly improve and expand in the future because of improvement in the law and the possibility of earning additional income for faculties.

DISCLOSE MANAGEMENT ISSUES

The most severe risk for collaboration would be information leakage. Particularly management issues, including financial objectives, have tended to be revealed by employees. However, disclosure to RERI about real issues in the company is essential, otherwise misunderstandings by RERI over essential issues could result in the RERI recommending strategies take the company in unwanted directions, or entirely the wrong direction. Another thing which needs to be discussed and prepared is a system of confidentiality, especially where researchers are associated with several SPM, which might include rival companies. Any system needs to take into account the need for RERI to publish, while simultaneously respecting the confidentiality of SPM.

CLARIFY MANAGEMENT ACCOUNTABILITY

Clarification of management accountability could be the most difficult challenge for collaboration on a strategic management level. On top of that, industry and academia have different backgrounds, as well as many elements that might trigger conflicts, such as history, culture, social responsibilities and stake holders. Thus, it is essential to draw up contracts, and letters of consent which are absolute and respected by the both parties in order to avoid serious trouble and reinforce a cooperative and positive relationship. The ultimate objective is that PDCA would produce beneficial results that would create strong bonds of trust and respect between the parties, and ensure collaboration into the future, and that ultimately these contracts would become formalities as trust deepens.

CONCLUSIONS AND LIMITATIONS FOR FUTURE RESEARCH

Twenty years have passed since the Japanese economic downturn. The Japanese economy has become increasingly decentralised during this time. It is time to energise the regional economies in Japan, as well as develop global human relations.

SPM owners have been dominated by traditional and conventional way of managing such as technology push model. Whether they believe it or not, they need to adopt to the market pull model to keep pace in the changing global market. By the same token, RERI should not a single theoretical model, but also educate SPM about a variety of market pull and other models in order to provide genuine development. To learn and comprehend academic theories should not only for managers' self-development but also for development of all employees, because it is efficient to develop as many employees as possible in critical thinking skills, in order to maintain competitive strength. Collaboration with RERI is expected to create new knowledge by which competitive advantage will be achieved, as well as developing the regional economy.

The first important step for collaboration on a strategic management level is to change the level of collaboration from organization-to-organization to person-to-person in order to build trust and bonds of friendship, so, "it is easy to picture the face of the person helping you", or "it's easy to call and talk frankly" so this could be the ideal relationship between SPM and RERI.

This study found that most SPM strongly believe that the technology push management model is the best way to save their companies, as well as depending on traditional and conventional ways of thinking from their successful past experiences. However, to maintain competitive strength in the global market, SPM need to improve their comprehension of academic theories to take advantage of their technological strength effectively and to overcome this challenge, it is necessary to collaborate with RERI on a strategic management level. In future studies, it will be necessary to clearly propose practical and detailed collaboration model on a strategic management level.

ACKNOWLEDGEMENT

The author would like to thank Mr. William MacDonald at Fukui Prefectural University, for revising English in this article.

REFERENCES

Baba.Y & Goto.N(2007) Experimental study for business-academia collaboration. *University of Tokyo publications*

Collinson, Elaine; Quinn, Leonie.(2002) The Impact of Collaboration Between Industry and Academia on SME Growth *Journal of Marketing Management,Apr2002, Vol. 18 Issue 3/4, p415-434, 20p, 3 Charts*

Cusho kigyokinyukoko (2006) HR of SME and MOT, *cyushokouko report No.2005.6*

Motohashi, K, (2003) Implication of Japanese innovation system RIETI Discussion Papers Series 03-J-015

Motohashi. K, (2005) SME-Academia collaboration and R&D Network *RIETI Discussion Papers Series* 05-J-002

Nishio,K, (2000) Verification for mechanism of practical collaboration study in U.S. *Fuji economic research institution FRI research report No 94 2000.10*

OECD, (2005) The response of higher education institutions to regional needs. University of Tamagawa

Toda, T & Hirao, M, (1999) Survey of regional economic research institutions of Universities / Colleges in Japan, *Ministry of education Grant-in-Aid for Exploratory Research paper 10873006*

Toda, T & Hirao, M,(2001) Survey and Research on the philanthropy of Universities. ~ It focus on the social role of the regional research institutions of universities in Japan~, *Ministry of education Grant-in-Aid for Exploratory Research paper 12430010*

Toda, T & Hirao, M, (2002) Survey of regional economic research institutions of Universities / Colleges in Japan and U.S., *Ministry of education Grant-in-Aid for Exploratory Research paper 10873006 plus touch up report*

Toyoda.S, Kondo.J & Yoshikawa.H (2007) Make from business-academia

Collaboration to develop human resources, *Toyokeizai shinposya*

Yoshida, S (2002) The time of education of executive, *UFJ Institute report 2002.6 Vol.7 No.3*

ONLINE REFERENCE

Land mark for business-academia collaboration, http://sangakukan.jp/

Kyoritsu research institute, http://www.okb-kri.jp/cyousa/kako.html

Improve Food Quality and Service at the Restaurant "Indian Maharaja"in Lithuania

Arvind Chaturvedi*, Siddharth Varma*, Dalius Liaugminas**
and Tran thi Thanh Van***

ABSTRACT

Standardization of quality in services is not an easy task, especially in a multi-service organization. If there are too many service variants, like in an eatery, the services can be highly customized. On the other side, some sort of standardization in quality of services needs to be provided to keep customers happy, leading to repeat buys and develop loyalty. This case attempts to study the working of an Indian restaurant in Lithuania. The restaurant suffers from substantial variability in service quality. This case analyzes the process of providing service to the customer in detail. A project management approach (PERT) has also been used for this analysis. The perspective of the customer regarding quality of service at a restaurant has also been studied. Based on this analysis some recommendations have been made which would help in reducing variability in quality of service provided at the restaurant.

Keywords: Service operations, hospitality sector, customer satisfaction, project management, customer survey, quality of service.

THE BACKGROUND

Lukas was driving to his new venture "Indian Maharaja" restaurant and was hoping it would all be fine when he reached the restaurant. He was still ten minutes away when he received a buzz on his mobile phone. He guessed it might be from Maharus,

---

*   Professors at International Management Institute, New Delhi, India.
**   Department of Law and Personnel, Ministry of Environment, Vilnius, Lithuania
     (PG Student at IMI, New Delhi).
*** Liksin Industry Printing-Packaging Corporation, Ho Chi Minh City, Vietnam
     (PG Student at IMI, New Delhi)
E-mail: achaturvedi@imi.edu, svarma@imi.edu

the chief manager of the restaurant. He was right. It was Maharus who informed in his anxious tone that the meat supply had been delayed yet again and the existing stock might not be sufficient for the day's lunch. It was enough to upset Lukas as he was experiencing a new problem everyday and trying to fix the problems on a daily basis.

It was only seventh day of this dream project. For Lukas, 20 years old young boy it was a big challenge. His parents, both serving officers in Lithuanian Government, were a bit reluctant initially but allowed Lukas to experiment this venture.

The restaurant was situated in Trakai Street of the old town. This street had a lot of other restaurants and several offices. It was a tourist attraction. Restaurant of the Town Hall Square was barely five minutes' walk, from the popular German street, just about two miles away from the bus station and about 2 minutes walk, from the railway station. The restaurant was located on the second floor, while the first floor had a cake bakery and an Indian souvenir shop, with a nightclub in the basement. In the neighborhood there were pizzeria, Brandy Bar, Turkish kebab restaurants. The other side of the street was a cosmetic shop and one more night club. It was a convenient location as there were 8 free parking places for cars. Across the street there were other free car parking lots.

Lukas developed the liking for Indian food during his visit to India last year with his parents and since then was considering to enter this business. This restaurant was targeted to middle-income clients with a promise of high level service, quality food, at reasonable prices.

After reaching the restaurant Lukas looked at the 'Customers Book' .he was once again disturbed to see a customer's complaint about quality of food. When he was discussing with Maharus about the days plans and how the customers satisfaction could be increased, he overheard the conversation in the restaurant between a client and the waitress and this time it was about delay in service.

Lukas fixed a review meeting same day and also invited his friend Marita ,a management student and Yohanas Diamangs ,her father who was a known management consultant. The primary purpose of this meeting was to deploy known techniques to run the outfit smoothly and without facing a new problem every day. He realized that the success of this project depended on planned actions to accurately carry out the recommendations or proposed changes, which would ensure better control..

The business objectives were clearly defined . Lukas ,the director of the "Indian Maharaja" knew that food and service quality had to be top priority as it would generate prestige and popularity, and thus the number of visitors. By maintaining a high level of service and food, one could expect more regular visitors. Visitors who received high-quality delicious food, carried a good experience of visiting the restaurant would certainly come again and again. Word of mouth publicity was the best advertisement for a restaurant.

THE TASK

Lukas sat down the same evening to prepare a note for the meeting with Mahrus, Marita and Yohanas . It was clear to the team that the following should be paid due attention.

The production process: The sequence of actions by the different teams engaged in production (preparation of dishes) once the raw material had been procured in the desired quantity.

The procurement process: This covered the assessment of requirements and ordering items in right quantity at right time at most appropriate prices.

The service process: This included a sequence of actions after the customers arrived. It covered serving cold drinks, soup, main course etc in a given order.

Improving service at the restaurant: Steps which would enhance overall satisfaction by improving quality, quantity and also the service time.

He identified the issues experienced by him so far. Other than the inconsistency in the quality due to non standardization, the service delay was the main issue. He felt that the service time for the same order for two customers also varied at times. Variation in making dishes existed, often in the same dish taste was different. Service quality was poor. Waitresses did not know the composition of dishes, manufacturing technology. The tables were set incorrectly . Customer service time was unstable. Sometimes the dishes were produced very quickly; at other times it took longer. Some dishes were made at the same time by varying the temperature . Visitors' expectations were not known.

The serving process for business lunch had following activities: waitress presents menu, waitress takes order, waitress brings the order to cash machine, kitchen produces the main dishes, waitress serves drinks, waitress serves soup, snacks, customers take snacks, soups , waitress serves main dishes, customers have their food, customers are presented bill, settlement of bill.

ANALYZING DATA

Next day onwards Lukas and his team led by manager Maharus followed the advice of duo his father and daughter . First thing was to assess the perceived service quality through a survey of visitors and checking the feedback from the waiters including the customer book. The restaurant's management needed to determine as precisely as possible the expectations of visitors. The dimensions identified were: Quality of dishes, Variety of dishes, quality of service, Quantity of dishes, price, time (duration), Environment.

In order to find out visitor's expectations the team prepared a questionnaire (Exhibit 'A' appended)

This questionnaire was handed over to restaurant for administering to the visitors. Twenty two visitors completed the questionnaire in business lunch time, 17 at other than lunch time. This was enough input to evaluate the customers priorities and also to find out if the difference existed between lunch time customers and customers arriving at other timings. The data collected through these questionnaires was tabulated.

Lukas and his team also prepared a chart depicting the time taken on daily basis by various activities just after opening of the restaurant. The sequence of events needed to be checked not only to ensure smooth functioning but also to detect any problems such as running out of stock etc. This was followed by yet another chart for sequence of cooking related activities and the expected time taken for each of them. This was to ensure that the activities which were likely to delay the service to the customers were handled on priority. Based on the past experience of the team various activities and estimated times for the same were arrived. These are presented in Exhbit 'B'.

The norms were set to ensure that the customers got the service within reasonable length of time .These were as follows:

1. The probability that business lunch time was 35 minutes should be not less than 95 percent. This means that there should be 95 percent probability that lunch will be completed in 35 minutes.
2. Dishes can taste differently for up to 5 percent of the visitors. This means that 5 percent of visitors may feel that the same dish tastes differently, that is there is variability in preparation of dishes.
3. Business Lunch time can exceed for not more than 5 percent of the visitors. This means that business lunch time should not exceed 35 minutes for more than 5 percent of visitors.
4. Meal size may vary up to 5 percent. This means that variability in size of serving may vary upto 5 percent.

After using appropriate techniques and preparing a strict activity chart based on the analysis, the situation has dramatically improved. Every morning the food supplies are organized by the director Lukas. Every morning, chef tells how much and what foods they need. The restaurant's chief manager Maharus orders the quantity of the products needed.

Cook no more under estimates the delivery time for products ordered .There is a rare case of the restaurant running out of crucial stock due to flawless planning .The expiry date of the products is recorded in writing to ensure freshness of the ingredients.

Chef's Routine is Defined

-Inspection of stock, record shelf life, -Start cooking rice, Cook rice, prepare meat, Start making soup, make soup, preparing vegetables, Start heating sauce, Heat sauce, preparing vegetables. Since rice, soup and sauce must be prepared exactly before opening the restaurant, the calculation has to be done based on backward scheduling.

As it takes longer to cook the rice, chef needs to start much earlier before the restaurant opened for customers . Soup needs to start production at few minutes before opening the restaurant for customers. Soups production takes some time so it should also be planned in advance so that it is delivered at the right time to the customers. Another dish that must be made exactly before opening the restaurant is sauces. Sauces are made one day before and warmed up in the morning only. Waiters usually spend a minute to pour the sauces into the pot, and then another 9 minutes to heat.

According to the calculations, we find that the minimum processing time is of 43 min. However, there is no planned time for errors.

Given the data and useful information in the attachments , the case analysis requires strategic solutions, identifying critical activities, using appropriate project management tools to provide a guideline to the director of the restaurant. This includes product ordering system and other recommendations related to the quality of production.

Specifically ,the following questions emerge from the above case:

Q 1. What should be the competitive priorities for the Indian Maharaja restaurant?

Q 2. Prepare a flow chart for the following processes: a) activities to be carried out before opening restaurant b) serving customer at the table.

Q 3. a) Carry out a network analysis based on PERT for the business lunch.

b) Determine the time taken to complete business lunch.

c) Find out the probability of completing the business lunch in 40 minutes.

Q 4. What are your recommendations for improving quality of service at the restaurant.

Exhibit 'A'

QUESTIONNAIRE QUALITY SETTING

DEAR VISITOR OF THE RESTAURANT

We are very happy that you are dining in our restaurant. We make every effort to ensure that your time spent at the restaurant would meet your expectations of the food and service to relax and have fun with us.

If you have never eaten Indian food, we believe that you will become Indian cuisine lovers.In order to better understand your wishes and that needs satisfy all of your expectations, we are constantly analyzing our work, looking for ways to provide excellent service and food quality.

Each of your comments are important to us. Please rate the quality of our restaurant. Only you can evaluate our work!

	No	Average	Yes
Does the meal is always delicious?	◯	◯	◯
Is the price corresponds to quality?	◯	◯	◯
Does the service satisfy the time?	◯	◯	◯
Or satisfy a portion size?	◯	◯	◯
Are the communications of waiters pleasant?	◯	◯	◯
Do the waitress provide detailed information about the dishes?	◯	◯	◯
Do you like the restaurant environment?	◯	◯	◯

Exhibit ' B' : Time taken for different activities related to Business Lunch

		Process Time		
		Optimistic	Real	Pesimistic
A	Waitress lodges Menu	0.4	0.5	0.6
B	Wait	0	1	2
C	Waitress takes order	1	2	3
D	Waitress brings the order to cash machine	0.5	1	1.2
E	Kitchen producing the main dishes	5	6	9
F	Waitress lodges drinks	2	3	4
G	Kitchen Producing snacks	2	3	4
H	Waitress lodges soup, snacks,	1.2	1.5	2
I	Visitors are eating	4	5	8
J	Waitress lodges main dishes	1	2	3
K	Visitors are eating	8	13	16
L	Waitress lodges bill	0.5	1	1.3
M	Wait	0	1	3
N	Settlement	0.5	1	1.3
		26.1	41	58.4

PART IV: Marketing Strategies

Acid test of success of any economic venture is said to be the acceptance of its products or services in the market. Success demands that the products or services should able to compete and win the customers on sustainable basis. The competition may come from within or from outside. I t is presumed of course that there would be level playing field. The competitive environment provides a challenge to the managers . He is called upon to carry out analysis of the external and the internal environment, discover the core competencies and exploit the same to maximum advantage. The young manager takes recourse to different concepts he has picked up in management studies to gain competitive advantage. Creation of brands, marketing a product suited to a specific customer segment, focus on customer preference, niche marketing , customization, setting appropriate distribution channels to meet the demand, customer service are some strategies adopted to a great advantage.

This section comprises of four cases each unique and demonstrating the application of a strategy in diverse situation.

Poonam Sharma et al. in Chapter 19 present a case study on Aakash Android-based tablet computer with a low price that opens up a world of new technology to millions of individuals. The objective of the this case is to outline ways in which organizations can develop strategic partnerships, expand strategy to consider a market that has largely been untouched.

International trade occupies a significant place in Indian economy. Anuj Sharma and Sudeep Mehrotra in Chapter 20 focus on international trade operations of HHEC North for its major client FABTECH a German apparel retail brand. The case aims at finding the shortcomings of the entire operations and ways to overcome them.

The purpose of this research study from Gagan Katiyar and Shubhneet Kaur in Chapter 21 is to analyse the customer perception and indentify the key attributes affecting the brand image in ceramic industry. The study concludes that major factors influencing the brand image are Design, Durability, Availability, Quality, Price and Product Range.

In a competitive world, SMEs are not just selling products or services but a mass of branded products, services and people to sustain in the business. Mukund Deshpande and Neeta Boparikar in Chapter 22 reveal significant marketing policies helping Pune SMEs become competitive.

Aakash Tablet - Steps Towards Becoming a Marketing Superstar

Poonam Sharma*, Victor Coburn** and Marcy Engle***

ABSTRACT

The Aakash Android-based tablet computer opens up a world of new technology to millions of individuals in India and other emerging markets around the world. With a low price product and the support of the Ministry of Human Resource Development in India, many bottom of the pyramid (those living on less than $2 USD per day) gain the potential to purchase a tablet. The tablet provides for educational applications for students and adults and an outlet for young professionals to experience the excitement of interacting with a broader community. Using the Aakash tablet allows individuals to grow and prosper within a challenging economic situation. A business model that delivers self-sustaining products, such as the Aakash tablet, establishes the first step towards economic sustainability. In addition, an organisation that focuses on producing goods and services for households at the Bottom of the Pyramid (BOP) and Bottom of the Urban Pyramid (BOUP) should create a successful business model that creates real value for themselves and consumers.

Keywords: Bottom of the Pyramid, technology, blue ocean strategy, value innovation, aakash.

INTRODUCTION

The concept of Bottom of the Pyramid (BOP) markets has been emerging since 2005 . Prahalad(2005). Prahalad's premise that "If we stop thinking of the poor as victims or as a burden and start recognizing them as resilient and creative entrepreneurs and value-conscious consumers, a whole new world of opportunity will open up." (Prahalad,

*   Poonam Sharma is faculty with Jaipuria Institute of Management, Noida, India.
**   Victor Coburn is with Eastern Mennonite University,Virginia, USA.
*** Marcy Engle is with Eastern Mennonite University Virginia, USA.

E-mail: poonam.sharma103@gmail.com, poonam.sharma@jaipuria.ac.in, vcobum30@gmail.com, marcy. engle@emu.edu

2005, p. 1) The objective of the this case is to outline ways in which organizations can develop strategic partnerships, expand strategy to consider a market that has largely been untouched, and to produce a product that empowers individuals at the Bottom of the Pyramid.

LITERATURE REVIEW

The BOP markets encompass households which live on less than $2 USD per day. While individual household income remains low, the power of the market comes from sheer number of households. It is estimated that 4 billion households exist in the BOP markets (Prahalad, FT Press, 2006). These numbers include a growing urban population at the bottom of the pyramid, which are called the "bottom of the urban pyramid" (BOUP). "By virtue of their numbers, the poor represent significant latent purchasing power that must be unlocked" (Prahalad, 2005, p. 11). Traditionally due to lack of matching between producers and sellers, as well the high cost of transactions, consumers at the BOP have found it difficult to access essential goods and high product variety (Karnani, 2007).Traditionally organisations focus on the supply side of economics and tend to take a defensible position against the competition in existing market space (Kotler & Keller, 2009). Kim and Mauborgne(2005), on the other hand, employ a reconstructionist view or "blue ocean" marketing strategy. Instead of viewing competition in a defined structure or defensive position, the reconstructionist view understands that companies expand and change the rules of the game. Organisations achieve success through value innovation and finding ways to expand market boundaries currently unknown to competitors. Through value innovation, organisations eliminate and reduce costs while simultaneously raising and creating value, opening up a new world of untapped markets (Kim & Mauborgne, 2005). For organisations seeking substantial profits, creating a core business plan that targets BOP households opens a world of "blue ocean" marketing where organisations tap into markets unoccupied or unknown by other competitors. Blue ocean strategists consider new products and services by creating demand by increasing value to customers or value chain.

Considering the volume of households in the BOP market and the potential for value innovation marketing, three principal problems exist. The markets experience restriction in physical access, suffer from limited availability of affordable products, and experience challenges from lack of regulations and enforcementof contracts. (Anekal & Tarafdar, 2011). Value innovation by employing the power of Information and Communication Technology (ICT) assists markets in growing communities both socially and economically. ICT assists in matching buyers and sellers, facilitates transactions, and provides institutional infrastructure. Communities, therefore, reap rewards by having access to products and services, access to credit, employment generation, and social inclusion. According to Anekal&Tarafdar, "ICT-enabled market development is a mediating mechanism for ICT-enabled social and economic benefits at the BOP" (Anekal & Tarafdar, 2011, p. 9). Technology provides an avenue for BOP markets to experience economic growth.

ICT provides a means for value innovation. However, the establishment of partnerships brings financial success for organisations that target their products to BOP markets. Gulati, Nohria, and Zaheer state that "strategic networks potentially provide a firm with access to information, resources, markets, and technologies; with advantages from learning, scale, and scope economies; and allow firms to achieve strategic objectives, such as sharing risks and outsourcing value-chain stages and organizational functions". While traditional partnerships with governments and public administration may be necessary to manage the political environment, alliances with non-traditional partners (local micro entrepreneurs, non-government organisations (NGOs), microfinance institutions) provide local understanding, access to resources, along with legitimacy and trust. Marketing networks build their capacity by engaging organisations close to BOP communities and establish BOP entrepreneurs as brokers. By developing BOP entrepreneurs, doors open for these individuals and communities to increase their income opportunities (Hietapuro, 2011). "In particular, a call has been made for companies to build new kinds of partnerships with actors such as citizen sector organisations and local microentrepreneurs, which are familiar with the BOP, but less familiar as cooperation partners to companies." (Hietapuro, 2011, p. 1) Partnerships, therefore, allow for value innovation to flow to the BOP markets.

No matter how strong the partnerships, technology, and marketing strategy in order to pursue the Bottom of the Pyramid markets, the manufacturer of goods or services must tackle customer perception. According to C.K. Prahalad, BOP Markets are brand-conscious. "An aspiration to a new and different quality of life is the dream of everyone, including those at the BOP" (Prahalad, 2005, p. 14). According to Furai, "Customers make decisions in order to reach their goals, which include making the best choice among alternative policies...." (Furai86, 2011) The process of consumerdecision making is largely influenced by perceived quality and value, as well as perceived risk of outcomes (Furai86, 2011).

CASE STUDY

DataWind officially launched the Aakash tablet in October, 2011. The product was created in partnership with the Indian Ministry of Human Resource Development (HRD) to promote and make available to students a low-cost tablet (approximately $50 USD). The Indian government promoted the purchase of this product for students by subsidizing the cost. The subsidy ranged from $25-$50 USD.

DataWind's introduction of the tablet has been fraught with quality, customer service, and marketing challenges. Some of the key complaints center around the sluggish processor, short battery life, need for GPRS technology, and speed to market. (Raina, 2012)

DataWind originally offered the Aakash tablet for the educational system, and the Ubislate7 to the general consumer. Following the initial concerns, DataWind developed and introduced the Ubislate7+ in December, 2011 with improved technology and a higher purchase price. Evidence for high demand for this low-cost tablet exists with sold out pre-orders through April, 2012 at 1.4 million units.(Chopra, 2012)

However, with the quality issues surrounding the Aakash tablet, the Indian government discontinued their partnership with DataWind in February, 2012.(CMN Correspondent, 2012) The Ministry of Human Resource Development is now seeking another organisation in which to partner to produce the low cost Aakash ("sky" in Hindi) tablet.

COMPETITION

Positioning: The Aakash tablet is the lowest priced tablet in the market, but on par for quality with other tablets that sell for less than $150 USD. High end tablets like the iPad, Playbook, and Galaxy sell for ten times the price of the Aakash and are completely out of the purchasing reach of 80 to 90 percent of the Indian people. Figure 1 shows the Aakash as having good quality at the lowest price.

There are two important aspects of the Aakash that help separate it from other lower priced tablets. The Aakash is made in India so there is pride in ownership that appeals to emotions. Most Indians carry USB travel drives for transporting files and the Aakash is the only tablet with two USB ports.

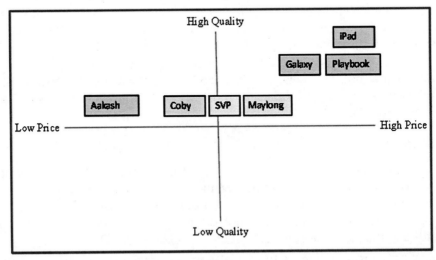

Fig. 1: Tablet Market Positioning

MARKETING STRATEGY FOR BECOMING A SUPERSTAR

Market Size

As companies consider changing their marketing focus to bottom of the pyramid households, a new market opens up. With India's population continuing to rise, the country faces ongoing economic challenges. According to Alison Granito with the Wall Street Journal, 80% of Indians, or roughly 960,000,000 people, live on less than $2 USD a day (Granito, 2007). With the significant financial issues for many of India's nationals, financial constraints exist for purchasing products and services. The economic challenges not only exist for India, but many other neighboring and other emerging market countries.

The base of the pyramid (BoP) or bottom of the pyramid economic group includes those who spend less than $75 USD on goods and services per month. Approximately 76% of households in rural India fit this category. With bottom of the pyramid marketing concepts, organisations view a large population as having buying potential instead of being poor or a victim to their circumstances. The bottom of the pyramid group desires to change their circumstances and these individuals are open to advanced technology (Prahalad, 2012). Even with tight finances, many individuals in India own a cell phone. Analysts predict that by 2015, India nationals will connect over 1 billion cell phones with internet service providers (Sharma, 2010).

With the Aakash tablet, the manufacturer's current marketing focus centers on students in India, they miss the market potential beyond the education system. In order to expand their marketing base, the emphasis must be placed on the low to low-middle income households in India and other emerging markets. Demographic segments support selling more than 1 million Aakash tablets outside of the educational systems.

Key factors: population growth (300 million in 20 years), number of children and young aspiring professionals (500 million), and increase of buying power for the bottom of the pyramid (less than $75 per month) economic group (100 million).

The core to successful marketing of the Aakash tablet must align itself with the following target markets.

Target Markets – Bottom of the Pyramid (low to lower/middle income households)
- Adolescents & Young Adults
- Small Businesses
- Women in Rural Areas (skilled trades)

BLUE OCEAN STRATEGY FOR AAKASH

By pursuing a "blue ocean" strategy, organisations identify markets in terms of "noncustomer" (those without current product or brand loyalty) allowing the manufacturers to pursue markets with the greatest economic rewards. In considering the areas of education, small business, women in rural areas, the following description provides a basis for strategic marketing.

Noncustomers – Waiting to Jump Ship to Another Industry with a Better Product to Meet Their needs

First tier of noncustomers consists of individuals who express disappointment in the failure of the products performance. They have no commitment to the product – just looking for a tablet or other product that meets their technology needs that performs better and costs less. *Young Professionals* in BOP or BOUP markets desire success and look for personal and professional growth and do not necessarily remain loyal to the product.

Noncustomers – Refuse to use your Industry's Offering

Individuals like the possibility of owning a tablet. Unfortunately they believe that the purchase is unattainable or fear that the tablet may change how they personally or professionally interact. The changes to a way of doing business appear overwhelming and frightening. By educating the market on the product's value and function, fears of current noncustomer subside. *Small business owners*

Noncustomers – Never Thought of Using the Market's Offerings

This group of noncustomers lacks exposure to the internet. They are unfamiliar with the product or the potential for its use. Fear or lack of interest could keep these individuals from using a tablet. This may particularly be an issue with the rural areas of emerging markets where women in rural areas lack awareness of capability to expand their market for their goods or services. While many households own cell phones, exposure to internet remains limited. *Women in rural households* (Kim & Mauborgne, 2005, pp. 101-115)

In manufacturing and marketing the Aakash tablet, while appealing to the desires of the various customers and noncustomers, the following chart provides the outline for designing the products to meet the needs of the target market.

Fig. 2: Designing Products Outline

Young Professionals	Small business owners	Women (rural)	
Educational resources	Systems that support sales presentations	Educational tools: children or self-help	Programming customization
Social Media outlets	Easy business applications	Simple – easy marketing applications	

Internet capability & strength	Strong connectivity to the internet	Internet capacity	Functional customi-zation
Strong battery life	Strong battery life	Ease of Use	
Good memory	Good memory	Good memory	
Fun	Color screen Prosperity	Potential	Design orappear-ance customization

While this matrix provides a simple comparison, the organisation must explore commonalities and differences among the three tiers. As far as commonalities, all of the noncustomers need applications, programming and internet capabilities. Possible strategies would be to partner with application developing organisations to add these applications to the tablet or an option to choose from a market of applications. For the internet capacity, need for GPRS technology to utilize existing cell phone technology. The infrastructure in India (particularly in the rural areas) does not currently support 3G or 4G technology and Wi-Fi may be limited to certain areas.

Both the young professionals and the small business user must have a highly functional tablet. However, not all customers need the same features. For value innovation, a potential strategy consists of a basic model with various add on features. The company may sell "add on" functionality with an incremental price increase (i.e. stronger battery, additional memory, etc.) By offering different features, purchasers select the necessary components. In all cases, the quality and performance of the tablet is essential since many individuals strive to achieve success through limited resources. The use and expectations of the tablet among customers may change over time. Continual surveying of customer desires and experiences for the Aakash tablet will provide the springboard for new developments and applications.

The price point of $50 or less and specifications such as a capacitive touch screen and GPRS communication are aspects of creating a blue ocean and value innovation. Focusing on value innovation for buyers of the Aakash tablet unlocks new demand beyond the initial goal of only supplying tablets to students. The manufacturer of the Aakash tablet could tap into non customer markets by co-branding to open the market to young professionals and the bottom of the pyramid economic groups (especially rural women), who desire to increase their disposable income create a new market for the low cost tablet. Tata Group, a multinational conglomerate, which is a highly respected organisation in Indian would provide one avenue to partner. Tata Group consists of key businesses in the areas of telecommunications, electronics, and finances. Tata Group's recent collaboration with Starbucks Coffee opens up a social connection to young professionals.

The potential for sales to explode centers around the Indian government creating a partnership with an organisation that exudes quality, reputation, and a commitment to increasing quality of life to bottom of the pyramid households. Tata Sons (Tata) encompasses the type of organisation that the Indian Ministry of Human Resource Development must collaborate with in order to be successful. Tata, through its experience in manufacturing, ownership of retail stores in technology and telecommunications, collaboration with microenterprise organizations, as well as a strong reputation allow for a low cost tablet to meet the needs of the BOP markets.

Forming the alliance of Tata Sons (Tata), Starbucks, the Government of India (GOI) is the first priority. There are several reasons for believing in this concept. Tata and Starbucks entered in a contractual alliance recently that allows a win-win for both companies. Starbucks reduces requirements for capital investment in retail space for coffee shops by leveraging real estate owned by Tata. Tata's revenue stream increases with Starbucks leasing store space and purchasing coffee beans from Tata. Tata owns almost all of the coffee related agriculture in India. Tata's reputation and expertise will assist in mitigating technology issues and fixing the marketing challenges. In addition, Tata's intimate knowledge of the Indian culture, geography, infrastructure, and government systems provides the basis for success. Other companies like Kellogg spend millions in capital in India unsuccessfully due to poor marketing research and lack of understanding of the culture. Pepsi struggled for years with little success in marketing beverages until forming a partnership with Tata Beverages. Tata's knowledge of how to package and distribute products in the country is huge in synergistic upside.

While Aakash is commercially advertised as a tablet for education, the target market is much wider and will not directly compete with the higher priced products. Differentiation exists in price, communication ports, data transfer with GPRS technology, and the focus on BOP markets create a blue ocean for Aakash.

Promotion and Advertising

The marketing strategy must create consumer awareness about the tablet and communicate through various methods the importance of acquiring one.

Reaching a minimum of one million customers beyond the Government of India's program of distributing the tablet to students at subsidized pricing requires an investment in advertising. Since the target market is primarily students, pursuing a "blue ocean" strategy of targeting young professionals, small businesses, and female artisans in rural areas, communicating the utility and professional aspects of the tablet along with great customer service before and after the sale is primarily the responsibility of Tata. Tata owns retail chains, telecommunication companies, e-learning products and services, hotels, business to business supply and service companies, IT companies, and a direct-to-home television broadcasting enterprise. (Tata Leadership with Trust, 2012).

Because Aakash is a technology product, marketing must focus on the Internet. Aakash's website should be easy to read and navigate. The website should also list a toll free number to access a person. To take promotion a step further, Aakash could organize and/or sponsor events. An educational event is an excellent opportunity for Aakash to be featured through a sponsorship. It could be focused on children and families – to provide opportunities for parents and other siblings to see Aakash as a value added product. The event should appear to be for individuals who desire prosperity and social status. Two objectives to consider: identify with a particular target market or lifestyle or creating an experience.

Cricket is the most popular sport in India followed by soccer. A marketing campaign including regional and national cricket and soccer games with sponsorship by a sports association, popular team, or individual athlete has potential for reaching millions of young people. (World's Most Popular Sports, 2012)

Promotion and finding ways to increase visibility of this value added product to the bottom of the pyramid economic group, as well as other young professionals or small business owners is critical to the marketing success.

CONCLUSION

The Aakash tablet's marketing strategy targeting the bottom of the pyramid economic group with its focus on rural artisans (including women), small business owners, as well as young professionals allows for the organisation to swim in a blue ocean. The low sales price, along with common technology to rural India and other emerging markets, allows the manufacturer of Aakash to bypass the goal of 1 million tablets sold. With the strength of branding and corporate infrastructure that Tata Sons provides, citizens of India obtain the confidence to purchase the product to experience their own fun and prosperity.

REFERENCES

Anekal, P., & Tarafdar, M. (2011). Markets At The Bottom Of The Pyramid: Examining The Role Of Information And Communication Techniques. AMCIS 2011 Proceedings - All Submissions, Paper 140, 1-10.

Chopra, K. (2012). India's $35 Aakash Is Loosing Life, Government Is Seeking Parnters To Build The Tablet Again. Retrieved March 9, 2012, from Internet & Design Inspiration Magazine: http://i2mag.com/indias-35-aakash-is-loosing-life-government-is-seeking-partners-to-build-the-tablet-again/

CMN Correspondent. (2012, February 21). Indian govt dumps Aakash-marker DataWind. Retrieved March 9, 2012, from CyberMedia: http://www.ciol.com/News/News-Reports/Indian-govt-dumps-Aakash-maker-DataWind/160426/0/

Furai86. (2011, September 28). Consumer Behaviour Models: A Theoretical and Practical Approach. Retrieved July 4, 2012, from The Lost Ring Web site: http://www.thelostring.com/2011/09/28/consumer-behaviour-models-a-theoretical-and-practical-approach/

Granito, A. (2007, October 16). liveMint.com The Wall Street Journal. Retrieved March 9, 2012, from liveMint.com: http://www.livemint.com/articles/2007/10/16235421/80-of-Indians-live-on-less-th.html

Gulati, R., Nohria, N., & Zaheer, A. (2000). Strategic Networks. Strategic Management Journal, 203-215.

Hietapuro, M. (2011). Partnerships in BOP business. Helsinki: Aalto University School of Economics, 1-20, 43-69.

Karnani, A. (2007). The Mirage of Marketing to the Bottom of the Pyramid. California Management Review Vol. 49, No. 4

Kim, W. C., & Mauborgne, R. (2005). Blue Ocean Strategy. Boston: Harvard Business School Publishing Corporation, 12-18, 101-115, 209-212.

Kotler, P., & Keller, K. L. (2009). Marketing Management. Upper Saddle River: Pearson Education, Inc., 294-314.

Prahalad, C. (2005). The Fortune At The Bottom Of The Pyramid: Eradicating Poverty Through Profits. Upper Saddle River: Wharton School Publishing, 1-22.

Prahalad, C. (2006, March 24). FT Press. Retrieved April 17, 2012, from The Market at the Bottom of the Pyramid: http://www.ftpress.com/articles/article.aspx?p=442978

Prahalad, C. (2012). 12 Manage The Executive Fast Track. Retrieved April 16, 2012, from What Is The Bottom Of The Pyramid: http://www.12manage.com/methods_prahalad_bottom_of_the_pyramid.html

Raina, P. (2012, January 5). Aakash Tablet: Oversold, underperforming. Retrieved April 9, 2012, from NDTV: http://www.ndtv.com/article/india/aakash-tablet-oversold-underperforming-163986

Sharma, B. (2010, April 15). Rediff Business. Retrieved April 15, 2012, from More cell phones in India than toilets: UN report: http://business.rediff.com/report/2010/apr/15/more-cell-phones-in-india-than-toilets-says-united-nations-report.htm

Tata Leadership with Trust. (2012). Retrieved April 17, 2012, from Tata: http://www.tata.com/company/profile.aspx?sectid=f4fpW5pl8MY=

World's Most Popular Sports. (2012). World's Most Popular Sports. Retrieved April 17, 2012, from Most Popular Sports in India: http://www.mostpopularsports.net/in-india.

International Trade Operation of Handicrafts and Handloom Export Corporation of India

Anuj Sharma* and Sudeep Mehrotra**

ABSTRACT

The case focuses on international trade operations of HHEC North for its major client FABTECH a German apparel retail brand. The case traces the entire process of international trade operations beginning from receiving of export order to the final shipment. The case aims at finding the shortcomings of the entire operations and ways to overcome them. The case has formal objectives of understanding briefly India's International Trade; to understand India's Handloom and Handicraft Sector and recent export performance; and to understand and critically analyze International Trade Operations of HHEC and suggest measures for improvement.

Keywords: HHEC, CECIL, handicrafts and handlooms, international trade, income, employment, domestic economy.

INDIA'S INTERNATIONAL TRADE: HIGHLIGHTS

International trade occupies a significant place in Indian Economy. Since the time of economic reforms that were initiated in 1991 in India the results produced are remarkable. India's trade to GDP ratio has increased from 15 percent to 35 percent of GDP between 1990 and 2005, and the economy is now among the fastest growing in the world. The merchandise trade was recorded at 31.68 percent of GDP in 2010 (World Bank, 2011). In 2010 international trade around the world stood 19 trillion US dollars which is around 30% of world GDP. Thus we can say that about one third of all goods and services which are produced are exchanged internationally. According to "Global

---

* Anuj Sharma is Associate Professor with Birla Institute of Management Technology, Greater Noida.

**Sudeep Mehrotra is with Birla Institute of Management Technology, Greater Noida India.

E-mail: anuj.sharma@bimtech.ac.in, sudeep.mehrotra@bimtech.ac.in

Policy Forum", by 2030, 60% of the world economy will be exchanged internationally i.e. the share of the rest of the world in each national economy will be more than the share of domestic economy. Many current evidences are in line with this prediction. For example, either country in the world is now a member of at least, one international trade agreement. In such circumstances, domestic economy will be affected more and more by the world economy. The level of income, employment, wages, growth, and development in a country is not only a result of its domestic policies, but is also determined by its position in the world economy. Table 1, 2 provided basic information on export from India.

Table 1: Exports 2006-2012

(Value In billion US dollars)

Year	2006	2007	2008	2009	2010	2011	2012
Exports	103	126	163	185	179	251	304
Imports	149	186	252	304	288	370	489
Total trade	252	312	415	489	467	621	792

Source: Ministry of commerce and industry

- India's total merchandise trade has increased three fold from financial year 2006 to 2012.
- Exports –GDP ratio has increased from 12.3% in 2006 to 16.3% in 2012.
- Share of India in worlds merchandise exports was recorded 1.63% in year 2011 and is ranked 19th in the world.

Table 2: Major Export Markets of India (2012)

Markets	Value in billion dollars
UAE	26
USA	25
China	13
Singapore	13
Hong Kong	9

INDIAN HANDICRAFTS AND HANDLOOM

Handicrafts sector occupies an important place in the Indian economy as it contributes significantly to employment generation and export earnings. To a foreign buyer it offers an opportunity to get associated with India and feel the diversity in ethnic cultures. The economic importance of the sector is also emphasized by its high employment potential, low capital investment, high value addition and continuously increasing demand both in the domestic and overseas markets. The sector is highly labour intensive and decentralized, being spread all over the country in rural and urban areas. Jaipur, Jodhpur, Moradabad, Narsapur and Saharanpur are the main handicraft centres of India that cater to international markets, and employ around one million workers.

The handloom sector also one of the oldest in India accounts for about 16 per cent of the total cloth produced in the country (excluding hosiery, wool, silk and khadi). The fundamental strength of handloom industry flows from its strong production base of wide range of fibres/yarns from natural fibre like cotton, jute, silk and wool to synthetic/man-made fibres like polyester, viscose, nylon and acrylic. India has edge in the production of cotton, silk, wool and jute yarns due to availability of raw material in abundance. Handloom accounts for 22% of total textile production in the country. 95% of world's hand woven fabric is produced in India. There are 12.5 million weavers in India out of whom 60% are women.

HISTORY

History of Indian handicraft is very old. The first reference to Indian handicraft can be found in Indus Valley Civilization which is about 5,000 years old. The Indus Valley Civilization had a rich craft tradition and high degree of technical excellence in the field of pottery making, sculpture (metal, stone and terracotta), jewellery, weaving, etc. The craftsmen not only catered to all the local needs but surplus items were sent to Arabian countries via ancient sea routes. Craft history shows that Indian crafts flourished during Mauryan Empire in third century BC. During this time period around 85,000 stupas were built including the world famous Sanchi Stupa, which has beautiful stone carving. Several sculptures in many Indian cities like Mathura, Vaishali, Sanchi depicting women with jewellery are excellent pieces of Indian craft. Rock cut temples of Ellora and Ajanta caves were constructed in the Gupta Age in third century AD. Craftsmen of this period excelled in jewellery making, woodcarving, sculpture, stone carving and weaving.

The Indian textile trade with other countries began as early as the second century BC. A hoard of block printed and resist-dyed fabrics, mainly from the state of Gujarat, situated on the western coast of India were found in the tombs of Egypt. This shows that export of cotton textiles took place even in the medieval ages. During thirteenth century, Indian silk was traded with western countries in exchange of spices. However, towards the end of the seventeenth century, the British East India Company started exports of Indian silks and various other cotton fabrics to other countries. These included the famous fine muslin cloth of Bengal, Bihar and Orissa. Painted and printed cottons were extensively traded between India, China, Java and the Philippines, long before the arrival of the Europeans.

HANDICRAFTS AND HANDLOOMS EXPORTS FROM INDIA

Handicrafts

India's handicraft exports were at its high in 2006-2007 when export of Rs 172,880 million was registered. But due to global slowdown subsequently there has been a significant decrease in year 2007-2008 and 2008-2009. However, since then there has been improvement in situation with India's handicraft exports during 2010-2011 being Rs 105, 339.96 million, registering a growth of around 26 per cent, in comparison to the previous year.

Exporters expect the positive trend to continue, mainly driven by the rise in demand from new markets like Latin America and Africa. Currently around 60 per cent of country's overall handicraft exports are directed towards the USA and Europe . With an aim to lower their reliance on these areas, the exporters have started surveying new markets in Africa, Latin America and Asia. Moreover, the government has also come up with incentives for exporters to help them diversify and enhance their trade with budding markets.

HANDLOOMS

Exports of handlooms from India reached Rs 12,528 million during 2009-2010. The government of India has fixed a target of Rs 13,500 million for the year 2010-2011. Among the importing countries, the USA is the leading importer of handloom products contributing nearly 42 per cent of our exports. EU as a group contributes nearly 33 per cent of exports from India. After USA, Germany, UK, France, Italy are the leading importers in EU. Other major importers include Australia, UAE and Japan.

INTERNATIONAL TRADE OPERATIONS

In order to be successful in international trade a company will have to integrate all elements of trade operations. It involves all activities from the time of receiving an export order till the goods are shipped and payment received. Following are some of the important activities:

Receiving an export order, Sample development, Placing Order for production, Production or out sourcing, Inspection, Packing, Documentation, Shipping

ABOUT HHEC

Handicraft and Handloom Export Corp. of India Ltd. (HHEC) basically deals in export of Handicraft and Handloom products. It provides a very good opportunity to artisans to showcase their creativity out of India and creates demand of handicraft & handloom products. Indian Handicrafts Development Corporation Ltd, predecessor of HHEC was established in 1958. In 1962, it was incorporated as a private limited company as subsidiary of State Trading Corporation (STC), a public sector undertaking of the government of India to carry out trading on behalf of the government for all its needs of imports and exports of general merchandise. Later in 1991 during the phase of liberalization, it was de-linked from STC and made an independent PSU under the Ministry of Textiles as a Schedule "C" Company under the present name of HHEC. The corporation was upgraded to Schedule "B" Company from Schedule "C" Company in 2001.

HHEC deals in export of handicraft and handlooms products. It creates demands for Indian products in markets abroad and tries to fulfill those demands by showcasing the creativity of Indian artisans, weavers and craftsmen. It has been in existence since five decades. HHEC, a Government of India, Ministry of Textile company has an exotic range of handicrafts, handlooms, decorative items, gifts, antiques, leather, gems and jewellery , wrought iron handicrafts.

OBJECTIVES OF HHEC

1. To undertake export of handicrafts, handlooms products, khadi and products of village industries from India.
2. Export promotion and trade development of handicrafts and handlooms products (including hand-knotted woollen carpets and readymade garments) and also to undertake export of gold and silver jewellery/articles and import of bullion, timber and other raw materials.

Vision

"To develop, promote and aggressively market the products of Indian crafts and skills abroad thereby providing a marketing channel for craftsmen and artisans".

Mission

- To make available Indian handicrafts and handlooms products traditionally produced in the remote parts of the country to all parts of globe.

- To achieve qualitative improvement in goods produced by the artisans, weavers and crafts persons in order to augment the credibility of India handlooms and handicrafts products in the export markets.
- To improve the productivity of the artisans, weavers and crafts persons through developmental activities in order to improve and sustain their quality of life.

Values

- Buyers' satisfaction.
- Transparency and courtesy.
- Prompt and professional service.
- Compassion and better business sense.

HHEC Promise

- Prompt responses.
- Quality consciousness.

HHEC Offices: HHEC offices are located in different parts of India. Registered office is located in New Delhi. Corporate office is located at Noida, Uttar Pradesh. HHEC has three regional offices which are located at Kolkata, Mumbai and Chennai.

Main activities: HHEC deals with a large range of products in different categories. These are briefly listed in the Exhibit. The main areas of functioning are:

Export. HHEC generates demand and builds confidence of foreign buyers through participation in international trade fairs and buyer-seller meets. It also organizes stand alone exhibitions abroad as well as in India such as – Textiles and Clothing Exhibition, Argentina and Brazil; Buyer-Seller Meet, Chile and Uruguay; Heim Textiles – Frankfurt; International Handicrafts and Garments Fair – Greater Noida and Tex Trends – India. HHEC has many foreign buyers in the USA, Europe, Canada, Japan, South Africa, South America and Middle East to whom it is supplying the merchandise for their onwards sale in those markets.

Bullion. HHEC is one of the nominated agencies by the Government of India to import bullion. In Delhi HHEC has retail outlets at the locations: National Museum, Craft Museum, Dilli Haat, INA Market, Rajeev Chowk Metro Station.

Products of HHEC: These are classified in categorised as Handicrafts, Handlooms , Ready to wear, Carpets.

Financial Performance: Tables 3 and 4 provided brief details.

Table 3: Financial Performance of HHEC

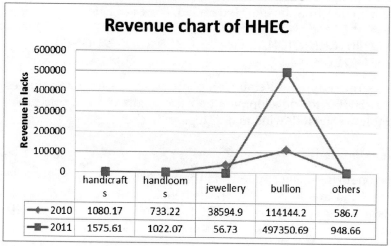

Revenue chart of HHEC

	handicrafts	handlooms	jewellery	bullion	others
2010	1080.17	733.22	38594.9	114144.2	586.7
2011	1575.61	1022.07	56.73	497350.69	948.66

The major segment that constitutes HHEC's Revenue is Bullion that is trading of gold and silver. But share of handicrafts and handlooms exports is also growing year by year.

Table 4: Country Wise Segmentation of HHEC's Revenue

(Rs in lacs)

Outside India	2010	2011 #
Middle east	132.12	2.30
USA	216.91	381.32
Japan	230.60	219.18
EU	1,031.12	1,673.56
Others	390.06	474,49
TOTAL	2,000.82	2,750.85
Sale inside India	153,205.23	497,911.76
Grand TOTAL	155,106.05	5,00,662.61

Unaudited Results

EU is the largest market of HHEC's products followed by US and Japan.

Demand in India for handicrafts and handlooms is also increasing hence revenue from India has jumped 3 times and due to this HHEC is planning to open some retail outlets in major cities in India like Hyderabad, Bangalore etc.

PROCESS OF INTERNATIONAL TRADE OPERATIONS DONE BY HHEC FOR FABTECH

FABTECH, German apparel Retail Company, develops its own samples which are forwarded to HHEC for development and production. The whole process is buyer driven and follows the following major steps.

Sample Development

FABTECH is one of the major apparel retail brands in the Europe. FABTECH depending on the demand and trends in the Europe develops its own sample designs of the scarfs and stoles which it has to procure from HHEC. Mainly these are floral and tribal prints with the use of bright colours like blue, orange, red and yellow.

When FABTECH finalises the samples for a collection, it gives the sample sheets to the sourcing agent which are buying houses located in different countries. 'Interconcepts' is the export buying house of FABTECH situated in Delhi. After these sample sheets reach the buying house, they are forwarded to HHEC for sample piece development. Sample sheet carries the information about the design of scarfs and stoles. It also carries other information like colour combination, smoothness of colour, length, breath and height of the piece, it has the sample picture of the design and instruction of the shape of the product. Sometimes there are special accessories which buyer instructs to accommodate in the product. This information on these things is also included. These sample sheets are taken into account by people responsible for FABTECH's shipment at HHEC. There are 6 to 8 sample sheets for different designs which are given to the different vendors or suppliers for development.

Suppliers

Following are the various categories of suppliers which are contacted by HHEC to complete the export order: Suppliers of all types of fabrics, Fabric printers, Suppliers of scarf and stole décor accessories, Suppliers of hang tags and barcode accessories.

The most important supplier are fabric suppliers and fabric printers. HHEC has selected vendors which have high technology fabric printing technology and vendors that can print high quantity of fabric . Prominent clusters in fabric printing are positioned in Bombay,Nagpur , Farukkhabad, Jodhpur, and Ahmedabad. HHEC has its vendors in most of these places. The expertise varies in printing cotton fabric to viscose fabric. (Refer Table 5)

Table 5: HHEC's Vendors for Fabric Supply and Fabric Printing

Vendor location	Vendor name
Nagpur	ABC Textile
Jodhpur	Noorani Kumar
Farukkhabad	XYZ Printers

Based on the information given on the sample sheet the vendor develops the samples and sends it to HHEC. The sample is developed in two parts

• Sample development at vendors end
• Sample development at HHEC

Sample Development at Vendors

According to the information given in the sample sheet, vendors do the following process:

Fabric procurement, Fabric dying, Fabric printing

Sample Development at HHEC

After the printed fabric reaches HHEC factory, several processes are carried out:

cutting of the fabric according to the specification and shape given by FABTECH, stitching of the pieces, pressing, labelling, tagging

After the samples are developed they are sent to FABTECH and its buying house. The time for sample development given by the buyer is 25 days. The buyer selects the samples and the information is passed on to HHEC and buying house.

Sample Selection

Samples are finally selected by FABTECH out of lot of samples sent HHEC on the basis of quality of printing, quality of finishing, design and quality of fabric used. If certain design is important to the buyer and the sample developed is not according to the standards, it asks HHEC to re- develop the sample on different fabric or get the printing done from somewhere else. If this process is not needed, it selects some samples and places production order for 40 - 90 pieces of each design.

Forecasting of Selected Samples by FABTECH

After the samples are selected, FABTECH gives order to produce these small quantities. The quantity of these samples is small as initially they are displayed in major outlets of FABTECH in Europe and then the feedback is collected on those samples. After monitoring the feedback FABTECH forecasts the sale of these designs. The actual order is then placed on HHEC.

Order Placement

FABTECH places an average order of 35000 pieces. The order is placed in the form of order sheet. This information sheet carries following information:

Article number, number of pieces to be produced, quantity to be sent to each warehouse, country wise order of different designs.

Order sheet is an important document. The packing is carried out and packing list prepared based on information contained in the order sheet.

PRODUCTION

FABTECH places order for scarfs and stoles when sampling and forecasting is over. The order is large at an average of 35000 pieces in different sizes, shapes, colours and designs to be produced. Vendors are authorised to procure fabric and print the fabric.

STEPS IN PRODUCTION

- Fabric procurement by printer
- Dying of fabric: It takes about one week.
- Printing of fabric: After the process of dying is over it goes to the printer for the design printing. Printing of the fabric takes 15 to 20 days. After which it is delivered to HHEC.

The whole process from fabric procurement to printing takes 35 to 40 days. HHEC also has the condition for its suppliers that the cost of the fabric will include fabric cost, dying cost, printing cost and also the rejection cost. Rejection includes any discrepancy in the print design which will happen due to colours and chemical variations. Sometime rejection also includes wear and tear in fabric which happens due to packing and transportation.

PROCESS AFTER THE PRINTED FABRIC REACHES HHEC

Inspection on Arrival

After the fabric reaches HHEC it is inspected to tally the fabric received and fabric ordered and also to check the quality of consignment. A document of record is prepared which contains the information about the fabric received, fabric ordered and rejections. This sheet is also used for further processes.

Fabric Transferred to Cutting Section

On the basis of the inspection report the fabric is sent to the cutting section. In the cutting section there are two tables which are used for cutting the fabric. In the cutting section the master tailor arranges the fabric as per the specifications. After which the fabric is cut as per the dimensions mentioned in the sample sheet.

Stitching

After cutting, the cut pieces go to the stitching section. Every tailor is given 50 pieces for stitching. (Refer Table 6)

Table 6: Stitching infrastructure at HHEC

Stitching machines	60
Pressing machines	5
Tailors	60
Master Tailors	5

These tailors employed for stitching are not the regular employees of the company. Their number varies as per the demand and quantity to be stitched. Generally one tailor can stitch 150 to 200 pieces in a day and if 30 tailors are employed for this work they can stitch 4500 to 6000 pieces per day. Hence it takes maximum 10 days to stitch 35000 pieces. Stitching time also depends upon the type of scarf as some scarfs may have fringes and other decorative items to put on.

Final Inspection

After stitching is done the product goes to the inspection section and every piece is inspected before it goes to pressing section where each and every piece is pressed to provoide the final touch.

PACKING

In packing section hang tags are attached to the stitched scarfs. These hang tags carry logo of the company and other information about the article and the bar code which is printed in India on the format and specification given by the buyer. A-tex, based in Gurgaon is HHEC vendor for FABTECH's hangtags, barcodes, and labels. After these activities are over the product is ready for packing and is then packed as per the packing instructions prepared by the manager.

PROFIT MARGINS

HHEC does not keep any fixed profit margins because prices quoted by HHEC and FABTECH are negotiable. Margins are not fixed but vary from buyer to buyer. Duty drawback, an incentive given to neutralize the duty impact on import of raw material exported by Government of India, ranges between 8 to 10 % ,depending upon the product.

EXPORT SHIPMENT

As the demand of the products is seasonal and changes very rapidly with fashion, therefore shipment is done every month .FOB is the incoterm used for shipment.

EXPORT DOCUMENTATION

FABTECH has dedicated logistics partner, Hellmann Logistics, which takes care of preparation of export documents, custom clearance and shipment from HHEC. Two documents viz, Commercial invoice and Packing List are prepared by HHEC three days before the date of shipment. Both the documents along with instruction sheet are sent to Hellmann Logistics. Instruction sheet carries instructions for shipment from HHEC. After the desired documents reach the CHA it files the documents to the custom department at the airport. It takes one day to clear the documents and then the custom inspection is done by custom officials which give the 'let export' order. Thereafter the consignment is shipped to its desired destination.

Every order of FABTECH is divided into two parts North dispatch and South dispatch. Hence there are two different consignments which are sent to two different cities of Germany. Hence for every shipment two copies of different documents are prepared.

PAYMENT

Payment to HHEC is made by FABTECH through telephonic transfer 'TT' within 15 when shipment reaches FABTECH.

Shortcomings in International Trade Operations

Process of sampling takes much time because of vendor location. Each sample is developed by vendor and sent to HHEC before it sends these items to buying house and FABTECH.

HHEC presently has only one major client i.e. FABTECH. It has to make efforts to increase the client list in existing product line of scarfs and stoles. In doing so it will not take extra resources as HHEC has infrastructure to serve more clients and also has expertise knowledge about the product with varied and large vendor network.

The space in the garment factory is not fully utilized because of which it cannot handle very large orders and major problem can come in future if big orders come from FABTECH or any other buyer.

The in-house inspection by the buying house inspector for the quality is done on the same day when consignment is required to be sent to the logistics partner. There is too much pressure on the employees involved in the process, it results in delays in case some problems occur.

HHEC has its vendors located in many parts of India like Nagpur, Farukkhabad, Mumbai, Ahmedabad and these places are located very far from the Noida office which results in more time for order development. Also the coordination with the suppliers becomes difficult.

There is a shortage of skilled manpower at HHEC like marketing professionals, production managers, designers, merchandisers.

RECOMMENDATIONS

HHEC should increase its vendor network in nearby areas which will give HHEC the advantage of timely delivery and also help in saving cost which will ultimately increase margins and service to buyer.

HHEC's present in-house stitching capacity is 6000 pcs per day but if it uses the available resources efficiently by installing new machines, the production will increase to 7500 pieces. This will not only reduce time for completing existing orders but will also allow HHEC to serve more client with big orders.

HHEC should increase its buyer network specifically in scarfs and stoles by tapping new international buyers. This could be done through

- More participation in international fairs.
- Developing samples and sending them it to big buying houses.
- Developing good quality product catalogue and sending directly to international buyers.
- HHEC should think of developing tie-ups with some national retail chains for selling scarfs and stoles.
- Scarfs and stoles are low value items hence they give low return when order size is low so HHEC should develop the range of high value items like blazers , jackets and leather accessories. These items have high margins. As FABTECH

also buys all these items hence it should develop samples and send to FABTECH as well as to other big retailers.

- HHEC lacks skilled management professionals to look after the operations and marketing of HHEC's products. Hence it should hire some qualified professionals in the area of marketing, operations, retailing and designing.
- HHEC has not been able to retain young management graduates because of low pay packages. Therefore in order to attract and retain good talent HHEC should revise its pay scales.

ACKNOWLEDGEMENT

The authors wish to thank Mr. Arun Vir Singh of HHEC for support provided in developing this case and for permission to present and publish the same at ICMC 2012.

Branding the Business Marketing Offer: Exploring Brand Attributes in Ceramic Business Market in India

Gagan Katiyar* and Shubhneet Kaur**

ABSTRACT

The purpose of this research will be to study the customer perception and indentify the key attributes affecting the brand image in ceramic industry. Boom in the construction industry has lead to high scale sales in ceramic industry. In this highly competitive environment, brand attributes need to be mapped so that competitors can identify important brand aspects and customize their offerings. Information is collected through one to one interaction with respondents and using a structured questionnaire..

Keywords: Brand image, customer perceptions, product attributes, ceramic business.

INTRODUCTION

Different types of ceramic tiles today are in great demand as they help to glorify home interiors in many ways. Indian manufactured tiles also have great competition from imported large variety of tiles and they also have a large export potential as observed from recent statistics available from the ceramic industry. This industry exists in both organised and unorganised sectors.

Ceramic industry has been modernising and improving continuously through newer innovations in design, quality and durability of product. The industry has great potential across segments like housing, retail, IT & BPO. The ceramic industry has experienced an enormous growth of 12-15% as observed in the recent past (ICCTAS).

---

*   Gagan Katiyar is faculty at Birla Institute of Management Technology, Greater Noida, India.
** Shubhneet Kaur is pursuing PGDM at Birla Institute of Management Technology , Greater Noida, India.
E-mail: gagan.katiyar@bimtech.ac.in, shubhneet.kaur13@bimtech.ac.in

The Indian Ceramic Industry is ranked 8th in the world and produces about 2.5% of global output. The industry provides employment to around 550,000 people. Gujarat reports for about 70 of total ceramic production.

The industry is energy demanding. Petroleum and raw material products collectively form the most significant part in the production. Fuel costs have increased, leading to an increase of around 30 per cent cost for raw materials. Gas price and hike in fuel price have also affected manufacturing cost. (Business Standard, October 2011)

These are indications that the Indian ceramic tile industry is becoming more competitive with more of imported brands, designer brands and local labels coming in along with the existing unorganised sector. The options for the customer have multiplied tremendously.

The present study focuses to identify key attributes affecting the brand image which impact the market share of industry players.

LITERATURE REVIEW

The idea of branding presents one of the crucial beliefs of marketing. Kotler (1988) defines a brand as "a name, term, sign, symbol or design or combination of them, which is intended to identify the goods of one seller or group of sellers and to differentiate them from those of competitors" Brands have a crucial role in decision-making process of both B2B and B2C customers (Bendixen et al., 2004; Michell et al., 2001). Brands are also considered as presenting an essential point of demarcation and a sustainable type of competitive benefit for business-to-business marketers. (Michael, et al. 2007). Brand image is mostly defined as "the set of beliefs about a particular brand" (Kotler, 1988) or "a set of relations, usually organized in some meaningful way" (Aaker, 1992). Brand image is normally considered as consumers' observation of a brand (Keller, 1993). This perception also impacts the brand's positioning in the market. A superior brand image improves the brand's position as well as the brand's market performance (Shocker and Srinivasan, 1979).

Severe competition forces companies to adopt appropriate strategies so as to generate sustaining competitive advantage. A firm's status and its sustaining strategies for creation of long term brand image enhances business customers' view of product & service quality. This in turn generates long term value leading to greater customer loyalty (Cretu and Brodie, 2007). To be in competition, companies require to understand the interaction of all existing competitive forces in the markets so that they can position themselves wtih respective to both external and internal factors (Brown et al., 2003; Christmann, 2000; Kleinschmidt et al., 2007). A company with high brand equity creates enhanced perceptions of the company's brand, better customer loyalty, more profit margins, high channel support, efficiency in marketing communications, improved licensing and brand extensions as an option (Keller, 2008). Customer-based brand equity focuses on two components, brand awareness and brand image (Keller, 1993). Customer awareness may be formed through advertising and publicity; brand image can be improved through promotion, use of convincing spokespersons and acceptable product performance (Guiltinian et al., 1997). Also brand image can result from consumers' perceptions of product quality (Kayaman and Arasli, 2007). Attributes form the basis for customer's way of evaluating a product. They also assure advantages to customers during the purchase of the product. Customers also tend to compare attributes with other competitive brands. The significance of analysing attributes is beyond the material characteristics of a product when consumer link attributes to benefits of buying and using products. (Aaker et al., 1992; Belch and Belch, 1995; Kotler, 1991; Mowen, 1993; Peter and Olson, 1993). Aaker (1996) defines brand image as the way brand is recognized by consumers which remains as set of brand associations in consumer memories. The product attributes, the results of using a brand, and brand personality are the three main components of the brand image (Plummer, 1985).

There have been many studies to construct a relationship between brand attributes and brand preference through researchers since the 1960s (Cohen, 1966; Axelrod, 1968). The research shows that encouraging consumers' perceptions of the product attributes of a specific brand lead to better selling of the brand. This study focuses on analysing attributes in terms of customer perception. Various factors like Design, Price and Durability etc. have been considered and their preferences have been analysed.

PROBLEM DEFINITION

Ceramic tiles form an important part of construction business; thus growth in this business has a positive impact on ceramic industry. Ceramic industry is rapidly changing and evolving sector with a large number of retailers, dealers and distributers being an indispensible part of it. The Indian tile industry is divided into organized and unorganized sectors. In such a competitive environment, there is a need of a brand study of major competitors in Indian market.

RESEARCH METHODOLOGY

The research design for the project is descriptive research. Field research has been carried out through a questionnaire to understand the consumer awareness, perception about different competing brands based on certain attributes. Questionnaires were filled by the respondents contacted at various retail outlets and showrooms of ceramic tiles, markets, shopping malls and other public places. The information is collected by directly interacting with the respondents. The printed medium was also used to get the questionnaire filled by respondents. A pilot testing was done on a sample of 25 respondents. Finally, the questionnaire was administered to 150 respondents after the results of the pilot survey.

Five Point Likert scale, a type of itemized scaling technique in non-comparative scaling, was used in the questions. Respondents were asked to provide their perceptions about different brands of ceramic tiles in terms of price, durability, design, availability, product range and value for money. Ratings 1 to 5 were mapped to responses as follows:

> 1 – High
>
> 2 – Somewhat high
>
> 3 – Moderate
>
> 4 – Somewhat low
>
> 5 – Low

Nominal Scale was used in questions when respondents were asked about their exposure to various touch points, satisfaction level and willingness to recommend the brand.

SCOPE OF THE STUDY

The study was conducted in India's NCR region.

Tools & Techniques Used

Microsoft Excel and SPSS are the major tools used. Data-reduction and hypothesis testing was done by using Factor Analysis and single factor ANOVA. Single factor ANOVA was applied to measure the comparison made by the consumers of important players.

Hypothesis

Following were the null hypothesis developed for the major brands.

H01: There is no significant difference among all the brands in terms of Durability.

Similarly, other Hypothesis were formed for all the brands in terms of Price, Design, Availability, Product Range, visibility in the market, Display of Products and level of awareness of brands with respect to the medium of awareness.

Analysis

Unaided recall

Following responses emerged When people were asked to name any three brands:

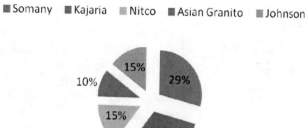

■ Somany ■ Kajaria ■ Nitco ■ Asian Granito ■ Johnson

Graph A: Unaided Recall

Interpretation: 31% people recalled Kajaria among three names asked and 29% people recalled Somany. This means Kajaria is a very close competitor of Somany.

Nitco and Johnson were recalled by 15% people while 10% people recalled Asian Granito.

Assessing the Factors which influence the Brand Image:

The factors influencing the Brand Image of ceramic tile brands are as follows:

Price	Product Range
Design	Value for money
Durability	Availability
Quality	Feel

Factor Analysis was used to get minimum number of composite variables that can influence the Brand Image.

Table I: KMO & Bartlett's test

KMO and Bartlett's Test

Kaiser-Meyer-Olkin Measure of Sampling Adequacy.		.698
Bartlett's Test of Sphericity	Approx. Chi-Square	163.865
	Df	28
	Sig.	.000

KMO and Bartlett's Test: The Kaiser-Meyer-Olkin must be greater than 0.6 to evaluate sampling competence. For the data collected, the value of KMO measure of sampling adequacy is found to be 0.698. Hence, it is concluded that the data is appropriate for Factor Analysis.

Table II: Total Variance Explained

Total Variance Explained

Component	Initial Eigenvalues			Extraction Sums of Squared Loadings			Rotation Sums of Squared Loadings		
	Total	% of Variance	Cumula-tive %	Total	% of Variance	Cumulative %	Total	% of Variance	Cumulative %
1	2.455	30.687	30.687	2.455	30.687	30.687	2.150	26.874	26.874
2	1.108	13.853	44.540	1.108	13.853	44.540	1.351	16.892	43.766
3	1.050	13.122	57.662	1.050	13.122	57.662	1.112	13.896	57.662
4	.949	11.857	69.519						
5	.850	10.631	80.149						
6	.623	7.784	87.933						
7	.576	7.200	95.134						
8	.389	4.866	100.000						

Extraction Method: Principal Component Analysis.

Total Variance Explained: The Table shows 8 factors. However, only the first three factors are taken for analysis in SPSS as the rest have been found to be redundant.

Component and Rotated Component Matrix:

Rotated Component Matrixa

	Component		
	1	2	3
Design	.830		
Availability	.703		
Durability	.675		.319
Quality	.502		.426
Price		.684	
Feel		-.658	
Value for Money	.504	.577	
Product Range			.818

Extraction Method: Principal Component Analysis.

Rotation Method: Varimax with Kaiser Normalization.

a. Rotation converged in 5 iterations.

Table c: Rotated Component Matrix

Rotated Component Matrix shows that there are three main factors which are important in forming Brand Image.

1 Product Functionality-Design, Durability, Availability and Quality

2 Product Value – Price, Value for money

3 Product Range

Comparison of various attributes between five brands of Ceramic Tiles based on consumer perception by ANOVA and Tukey Kramer Tests

Attribute	Ceramic Tile Brand	Mean Values	Calculated value of p	Null Hypo: Reject or Accept (Alpha 0.05)	Tukey Kramer Minimum Significant Difference Test
Durability	Somany	2.016807	4.2E-110	Rejected	Kajaria is considered to be more durable than Somany, Nitco, Johnson and Asian Granito
	Kajaria	1.957983			
	Nitco	2.428571			
	Johnson	4.117647			
	Asian Granito	4.478992			
Price	Somany	1.940397	5.4E-126	Rejected	Nitco is perceived to be high in price; Somany & Kajaria are comparable and low in price. Asian & Johnson have lowest prices.
	Kajaria	1.940397			
	Nitco	1.877564			
	Johnson	4.15894			
	Asian Granito	4.311258			
Design	Somany	1.807947	7.4E-152	Rejected	Somany is considered superior to Kajaria, Nitco, Asian Granito and Johnson in terms of design.
	Kajaria	1.98			
	Nitco	2.629139			
	Johnson	3.9735			
	Asian Granito	4.602649			
Availability	Somany	2.033113	5.1E-157	Rejected	Kajaria is considered superior to Somany, Nitco, Asian Granito and Johnson in terms of availability.
	Kajaria	1.701987			
	Nitco	2.642384			
	Johnson	4.172185			
	Asian Granito	4.450331			
Product Range	Somany	1.827815	4.8E-147	Rejected	Somany & Kajaria are comparable in terms product range and considered superior to Nitco, Asian & Johnson.
	Kajaria	1.823410			
	Nitco	2.735099			
	Johnson	4.02649			
	Asian Granito	4.509934			
Visibility	Somany	2.039735	1.7E-106	Rejected	Kajaria is considered to have better visibility in market as compare to Somany, Nitco, Asian Granito & Johnson.
	Kajaria	1.927152			
	Nitco	2.715232			
	Johnson	4.05298			
	Asian Granito	4.251656			

Display of products	Somany	1.967105	7.3E-120	Rejected	Kajaria is perceived to be superior as compared to Somany, Nitco, Johnson & Asian Granito in terms of display of products
	Kajaria	1.894737			
	Nitco	2.743421			
	Johnson	4.125			
	Asian Granito	4.269737			
Product Display Concept	Somany	1.978203	0.083	Accepted	Tukey Kramer Test is not applicable.
	Kajaria	1.937550			
	Nitco	2.407491			
	Johnson	4.151365			
	Asian Granito	4.013441			
Awareness Level	Somany	1.8133	0.008	Rejected	Kajaria is perceived to have highest awareness level as compare to Somany, Nitco, Asian and Johnsons.
	Kajaria	1.7667			
	Nitco	2.6267			
	Johnson	4.6067			
	Asian Granito	3.9667			

Assessing the Frequency of Customer Visits to Touch Points.

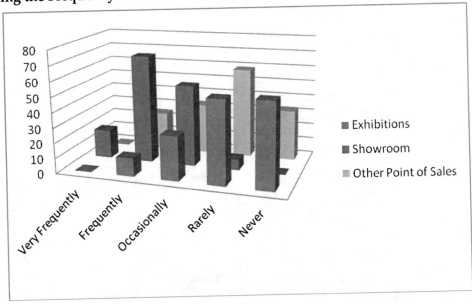

Graph B: Frequency of customer visits to touch points

The responses reveal that most frequently visited touch point is showrooms while other point of sales are rarely visited by the customers. Majority of customers never visit exhibitions.

FINDINGS & INTERPRETATIONS

In case of unaided recall, it is observed that Kajaria is the most recalled brand. Somany stands second, Nitco & Johnsons come next. This means that Kajaria and Somany are very strong competitors. Reference from friends is perceived as most effective medium of awareness for while hoardings and showrooms come next. It has been observed that most frequently visited touch point is showrooms. The customers rarely visit any other point of sale and never visit exhibitions.

Major factors influencing the brand image are Design, Durability, Availability, Quality, Price and Product Range.

Kajaria is considered to be more durable than Somany, Nitco, Johnson and Asian Granito. Nitco tiles are considered to be highly priced, next are Kajaria and Somany and then come Johnson & Asian Granito. Designs of Somany are considered better than its competitors. Kajaria is considered superior to Somany, Nitco, Asian and Johnson in terms of availability of products. It has been observed that Somany and Kajaria are almost comparable in terms of product range and both brands are considered superior to Nitco, Asian and Johnson.

Kajaria is considered to have better visibility in market as compare to Somany, Nitco, Asian Granito & Johnson. Kajaria is considered to have best product display while Somany & Nitco stands second and Asian, Johnson comes afterward. Almost all the brands lack in following proper product display concept.

CONCLUSION

It has been concluded that Somany and Kajaria enjoys the highest awareness among the respondents. Design, Durability, Price, Availability, Product range and Value for money are most important factors influencing the brand image. Significant differences in perceptions of consumers among five different brands based on the six attributes of Price, Design, Durability, Availability and Product range has been studied. Among all brands Somany and Kajaria are close competitors and appear to be better than others in terms of Durability, Product range and visibility in the market. Nitco is perceived to have highest price range. For Design attribute, Somany is the benchmark brand. Kajaria is considered to be good in Product display and Availability.

REFERENCES

Aaker, D.A. (1992), *Managing Brand Equity: Capitalising on the Value of a Brand Name*, The Free Press, New York, NY.

Aaker, D.A., Batra, R. and Myers, J. G. (1992), Advertising Management, 4th ed., Prentice-Hall, Englewood Cliffs, NJ.

Axelrod, J.N. (1968), "Attitude measures that predict purchase", Journal of Advertising Research, Vol. 8 No. 1, pp. 3-17

Belch, G.E. and Belch, M.A. (1995), Introduction to Advertising and Promotion: An Integrated Marketing Communications Perspective, 3rd ed., Irwin, Boston, MA.

Bendixen, M., Bukasa, K.A. and Abratt, R. (2004), "Brand equity in the business-to-business market", Industrial Market Management, Vol. 33 No. 5, pp. 371-80.

Brown, J.R., Dev, C.S. and Zhou, Z. (2003), "Broadening the foreign market entry mode decision: separating ownership and control", Journal of International Business Studies, Vol. 34 No. 5, pp. 473-88.

Business Standard , October 2011

http://www.business-standard.com/india/news/high-raw-material-cost-eats-into-ceramic-industry039s-margins/454022/

Christmann, P. (2000), "Effects of best practices of environmental management on cost advantage: the role of complementary assets", The Academy of Management Journal, Vol. 43 No. 4, pp. 663-80.

Cohen, L. (1966), "The level of consciousness: a dynamic approach to the recall technique", Journal of Marketing Research, Vol. 3 No. 2, May, pp. 142-8.

Cretu, A.E. and Brodie, R.J. (2007), "The influence of brand image and company reputation where manufacturers market to small firms: a customer value perspective", Industrial Marketing Management, Vol. 36 No. 2, pp. 230-40.

Guiltinian, J.P., Paul, G.W. and Maden, T.J. (1997), Marketing Management: Strategies and Programs, 6th ed., McGraw-Hill, Boston, MA.

http://newsletters.cii.in/newsletters/mailer/trade_talk/pdf/Ceramics%20Industry%20in%20India.pdf

ICCTAS ESTD 1990 - http://www.icctas.com/ceramicindustry.htm

Kayaman, R. and Arasli, H. (2007), "Customer-based brand equity: evidence from the hotel industry", Managing Service Quality., Vol. 17 No. 1, pp. 92-109.

Keller, K.L. (1993), "Conceptualizing, measuring, and managing customer-based brand equity", Journal of Marketing, Vol. 57 No. 1, pp. 1-22.

Keller, K.L. (2008), Strategic Brand Management: Building, Measuring and Managing Brand Equity, 3rd ed., Prentice- Hall, Upper Saddle River, NJ.

Kleinschmidt, E.J., de Brentani, U. and Salomo, S. (2007), "Performance of global new product development programs: a resource-based view", Journal of Product Innovation Management, Vol. 24 No. 5, pp. 419-41.

Kotler, P. (1988), Marketing Management: Analysis, Planning and Control, Prentice-Hall, Englewood Cliffs, NJ.

Meenaghan Tony (1995); Journal of Product & Brand Management, Vol. 4 Iss: 4 pp. 23 – 34

Michael Beverland and Julie Napoli, Raisa Yakimova (2007); Journal of Business & Industrial Marketing, Vol. 22 Iss: 6 pp. 394 – 399

Michell, P., King, J. and Reast, J. (2001), "Brand values related to industrial products", Industrial Marketing Management, Vol. 30 No. 5, pp. 415-25

Mowen, J.C. (1993), Consumer Behavior, 3rd ed., Macmillan Publishing Company, New York, NY.

Peter, J.P. and Olson, J.C. (1993), Consumer Behavior and Marketing Strategy, 3rd ed., Irwin, Boston, MA.

Plummer,J.T. (1985), "How personality makes a difference", Journal of Advertising Research, Vol. 24 No. 6, December/January, pp. 27-83.

Shocker, A.D. and Srinivasan, V. (1979), "Multiattribute approaches for product concept evaluation and generation: a critical review", Journal of Marketing Research, Vol. 16.

Emerging Branding Policies in SMEs: Pune Auto-Component Industry

Mukund Deshpande* and Neeta Baporikar**

ABSTRACT

In a competitive world, SMEs have started realizing that they are not just selling products or services but a mass of branded products, services and people to sustain in the business. Therefore movement is captivating in the SMEs to introduce competency through branding for obtaining & enhancing market share. Auto-component is a great feeder industry in the Automobiles Sector that has put India on Global map. Study of branding in this industry brings out a case that reveals significant marketing policies helping Pune SMEs become competitive and gaining highest market share in the world. This research study further exposes growing evidence of core and complimentary branding instruments used to improve effectiveness of marketing in SMEs.

Keywords: Branding, policies, SME, economy, auto-component , Pune, competency.

INTRODUCTION

Commerce is a game of skill, which every one cannot play. Research has however revealed that any great competition could be successfully dealt with innovation. Therefore to deal with this rising global competition a small beginning is necessary. Hard to accept movement to branding has been spreading in the SMEs as a result of enhancing proven payback. Apart from worldwide prominence of SMEs, however, they face challenges in marketing, owing to changing business environment. Insufficient marketing ideas and weak practices in leveraging complex marketing situations form operational blockages in selling the products. As a result, need persistently arises to improve the market setting which make up an excellent branding policy. Close observation of the marketing challenges reveals that they could be conveniently analysed for identifying approaches to address them.

* Mukund Deshpande is Professor & Research Scholar, HNIMRW, Pune.
** Neeta Baporikar is Doctoral Guide, University of Pune, Pune.
E-mail: mvdeshpande49@yahoo.co.in

Innovative marketing strategies are on the anvil of majority of small and medium enterprises (SMEs) and branding has been emerging as an essential instrument to sell products through a convenient mode of messaging that can quickly reach and make appeals to the customer. Branding creates an asset to the firm, which helps to build good reputation. This further assists in changing the company to achieve reputation and motivates the buyer. Branding as well builds an expectation about the company services or products, and encourages the company to maintain that expectation, bringing better products and services to the market place.

Recent decades have shown that the world has grown increasingly inquisitive. Branding policy formulation for messaging the strengths, to the buyers, is an art as it needs to be accepted by the customer at national and international level. Diverse instruments have been proposed by researchers to addressing marketing challenges. Multi-perspective approach has emerged as a forthcoming trend for maintaining competency in the marketing policy.Stuart Whitwell (2005) advocates that brand valuation is a useful process which also helps bridging the differences between marketers and accountants. Since the value of the brand is expressed in monetary terms, all decision-makers have a common point of reference. Brand valuation assigns financial value to the equity created by the name or image of a brand. The expertise spans a myriad of industries and brand issues that get in the way of competitive advantage and profitable growth. It is believed that the brand is reputation and it should be used in helping the SME achieve their strategic and financial goals. There are a few of the problems to be solved that continually frustrate organizations and form the foundation of what best can be done. SME needs a strategy to move forward and find the best way to develop it.

Pune Auto-Component industries have proven their marketing strategy and in that context this study is undertaken to understand their philosophies and policies. Pune industries are highly vibrant owing to presence of large technology workers in the city and Information Technology service providers. Pune is also home for the two very prominent automotive research labs, namely "Automotive Research Association of India" and "Central Institute of Road Transport". Therefore this geographical location of the sample becomes appropriate choice for this case study.

LITERATURE REVIEW

Review of literature has shown diverse opinions on policy making for business. Azhar Kazmi, (2008), states that the business definition is at the core of business strategy. The definition seeks to provide the direction in which action has to be taken. Bala Subrahmanya, (2006), explains that Indian policy makers have been laying emphasis on the promotion of clusters. Debra Percival (1996), examines advantages of multilateral approaches for surviving in business. Deshpande (2011) advocates approach to entrepreneurship should be sustainable. David Shaked (2010) recommends strength based approach to business improvement. Larry Bossidy et al (2004), advocate that a business model should always have the objective to start with and that the model should start with a logical breakdown of the many elements that make up a business. Kaplan & Norton (2004), explain that while designing policies, objectives should be linked in cause and effect relationships. Oscar Iturrioz and Piattini, (1999), stress that business policies have been proposed to bridge the gap between information system professionals and at the same time, for easing system evolution. Pierson, (2005) refer that understanding the sources of policy often requires that we pay attention to processes that play out over considerable periods of time. Sharma (2008), states that, effective performance measurement system for organization is a key factor for successes in today's competitive globalize market.

STUDY PLAN

Following objectives are formulated for the study:

- To study the branding instruments implemented by Pune Auto-Component industries

- To statistically test the hypothesis for consistency of branding instruments.

STUDY DESIGN

The study first aims to initially acquire secondary data, through a literature search that identified the variables for branding policies, in the past decade. This survey used research objectives as the basis for obtaining knowledge on approaches to branding. The study employed observation and logical approach to analyzing the data collected from literature. In order to search primary data, the study used field survey as the instrument. A sample frame of Pune Auto-Component SMEs, obtained from local Chamber of Commerce & Industries Directory was used to get the initial data.

SAMPLE SIZE DECISION

Based on a population of 510 auto-component industries in Pune, and considering a confidence level of 95% and confidence interval of 12% the sample size was computed to 65. However 120 auto component industries samples were actually taken for survey to increase accuracy of the data.

SAMPLE QUESTIONNAIRE

Structured questionnaire was used as an instrument to conduct field survey. Primary Data collected in five point Likert scale served to construe the basis for branding as follows:

Tabulation of Likert Scale Response

Strongly disagree	Disagree	Neutral	Agree	Strongly agree
1	2	3	4	5

Table 1: Questionnaire

	Statement
A)	Ensure to value the requirements of the customer for branding
B)	Prefer internal strength for branding
C)	Consider competitive edge for branding
D)	Promote inducements & customer service for branding
E)	Take advantage of the market Place for Global marketing

DATA COLLECTED OUT OF STUDY

Table 2 is a typical exhibit of the data that was collected by the researcher. Values of mean clearly indicate that majority of them belong to the same sample and further that they agree to prove the hypothesis.

Table 2 : Collected Responses

	1	2	3	4	5	Mean
A	25	30	0	10	55	4.00
B	7	13	12	20	68	4.89
C	0	0	83	10	27	4.24
D	0	76	0	44	0	3.28
E	44	22	30	24	0	2.74

FINDINGS

Branding instruments implemented by Pune Auto-Component industries are briefly discussed as under:

Customer Value Branding Policy

All the Pune entrepreneurs disclosed that the surest foundation of a manufacturing concern is quality. Identification of expressed and latent needs of customers has always been the prominence to offer timely solutions based products & services. Nurturing market sensitivity is often a trouble for manufacturers and that has given rise to a shift in the production policy of the SMEs. These SMEs further revealed that they introduced product application based branding that matches with process or function. For illustration the branding is as follows:

Table 3: Customer Value Brands

1	"Form, Fit & Function"
2	"Art to part "
3	"Domestic Class to World Class "
4	"Self Standards to Customers Standards"
5	"Customers Standards to International Standards"

BRANDING INTERNAL STRENGTH POLICY

In order to branding unique equipment, Pune SMEs identified "World Class Machinery" to be the brand that was unique because of its multi-operational, variable volume and precision quality function that could meet the requirements of the automobiles as per international standards. This being the strength of the SME, it has been branded to quickly render knowledge to the prospective customers.

Table 4: Internal Strength as Brands

Process Brands as	FEA,CAE
Management Brand as	PDM / PLM
Engineering Design Tools Branded as	3D Software
Product Architectural Skills as	Integral
Technology Branding as	Recycling Technology
Strength in Price Branded as	"Sensible Price"
Strength in Cost Branded as	"Low Labour Cost"

Another illustration to be cited is the use of reputation of cluster company in which Pune SMEs have largely been taking benefit. Cluster company has been launched by the state government jointly with two municipal corporations to promote the development of business in the region. This cluster company is a typical example to indicate how the member SME derived benefits of global market and technology to cope up with the diverse needs of the customers. Therefore, the reputation of cluster also became the prime policy to branding.

Competitive Edge Policy

Product quality is followed by cost aspect. SMEs in Pune prefer bringing sustainability by implementing a quality & price policy to gratifying the requirements of their focused clients. Trend has emerged to make the production that is suiting the customers through pursuit of cost savings. The strategy is to look at a cost-benefit analysis job by job and make innovations to discover low cost option is justified. Introducing quality product at competitive price, therefore, remained to be the top priority of these SMEs as the competitive edge over other international suppliers in the business.

Inducements and Customer Service Policy

Raising market share of the products also needed good services to induce the clients in order to obtain repeat business. In view of this requirement Pune Auto-Component industries implemented following branding policies.

1. Capability is branded as "Systems integrators", to organize suppliers capable of designing and integrating components, sub-assemblies and systems into modules.
2. "Global standardizers" brand indicates systems manufacturers capable of setting the standard on a global basis for a component or system – through design, development and manufacturing of complex systems.
3. "Component specialists" brand extends to suppliers capable of designing & manufacturing a specific component or subsystem, for a given car or platform – process specialists or product specialists.
4. Promotional Branding as: "Strong, Efficient and Competitive "Domestic Supply Chain".

Global Marketing Policy

Branding for the worldwide customers happens to be the strength of these SMEs. They found this philosophy advantageous to design the brand and spread the message to the huge buyers spread across the globe. By promoting local products to global markets they created geographical niche to gain competency recognized as global or glocal approach, thus "Local to Glocal" became the brand. Further important revelation is that, the auto-component industries offered products based on the functional variety and applications by continuously pursuing the objective of competency through product variety, price option, market multiplicity and promotional diversity.

STATISTICAL CONSISTENCY OF MULTI PERSPECTIVE MODEL

Mean values in the Table show that Pune Auto-Component industries consistently use high percentage of branding instruments. The exercise of determining consistency of the data was taken to understand if similar instruments are used all over the Auto-

Component Industries in Pune. The hypothesis formulated on this back ground proved the test on the basis of consistency of high mean values.

DISCUSSION

Multi-Perspective Model (MPM) of Branding

Persuasive logic of Pune Auto-Component industries has been that of practicing competent instrument that is inclusive to countenance all the challenges for survival and growth in their business. These SMEs thought that strong brands have a few enormous advantages in the marketplace so that the very best people want to work for them, their brands help their employees focus and make decisions and these brands motivate their employees to do more than they otherwise would have believed they could.

Competency of Branding Instruments

Multi-Perspective Model has introduced competency because it is inclusive or comprehensive instrument. It is able to tackle challenges in marketing the products frequently faced by the SMEs. This instrument extends to diverse factors which enable contribution to the betterment of economy of the enterprise. Inclusive instrument collectively considers the use of individual approaches that have the ability to reach to the routes of internal and external environmental issues of the business.

Branding to Value Customers' Needs

A large number of the Pune Auto-Component manufacturers consistently put into action the "Customer Focused or product centred branding Approach" to stay in business. This approach is predominantly cultured to earn revenue and significantly adopted by Pune enterprises as they have prominently targeted to meet the requirements of domestic automobile giants. As a result, their sale is specifically focused to precise clientele.

LIMITATIONS OF THE STUDY

1. Policy makers may get involved in personalizing things and develop a self sense of priorities rather than the group logic. They may develop some strategies to compete with other members rather than cooperation. These are common limitations particularly while designing policies involving multiple stake holders.

2. Decision-oriented studies need deep knowledge base for making and defending policy decisions.

CONCLUSIONS AND RECOMMENDATIONS

The multierspective approach has a viewpoint which covers financial, customer-related, internal-set-up-related and growth-related perspective that created good impression on the buyers' mind about the strength the SMEs possessed. In essence MPM relies on Products, Processes, Price, Promotion and People's strength

REFERENCES

Azhar Kazmi, (2010), *Strategic Management and Business Policy*, New Delhi, Tata Mcgraw Hill.

Bala Subrahmanya, (2006), Global TNCs and Local SMEs, Chartered Accountant, August 2006, Pages 243-249.

David Shaked(2010). http://www.almond

Debra Percival (1996), "The advantages of a multilateral approach", Full text of an article from The Courier ACP-EU, No. 155, January-February 1996: page 24, Euforic Home Page DG Development.

Deshpande M. (2011). Sustainable approach to SME Development, In *National conference on Sustainable Development-Challenges & Opportunities"*, February 11-12, 2011, Hiraben Nanavati Institute of Management & Research for Women, Karve Nagar, Pune.

Kaplan Robert S. & Norton David P. (2004), *Strategy Maps"*, Boston, Harvard Business School Publishing Corporation.

Larry Bossidy et al (2004). Confronting Reality, Crown Business Publication, New York, page 88.

Oscar Diaz, Jon Iturrioz and Mario G. Piattini, (1997), Promoting business policies in object-oriented methods, Cronos Iberica, S.A. Clara del Rey, 8, 1-4/28002 Madrid, Spain, Received 25 July 1996.

Pierson, Paul, (2005). "The Study of Policy Development, Journal of Policy History" Volume 17, Number 1, 2005, pp. 34-51, Penn State University Press, Volume 17, Number 1, 2005, E-ISSN: 1528-4190 Print ISSN: 0898-0306 , DOI: 10.1353/jph.2005.0006

Sharma Milind Kumar (2008), "Performance Measurement in Small and Medium Enterprises" Int. J. Globalisation and Small Business, Vol. 2, No. 4, pp 359-361.

Stuart Whitwell(2005), Brand Valuation in Brand Management, http://www.intangiblebusiness.com/Brand-services/Marketing-services/News/Brand-valuation-in-brand-management-amp-performance-measurement~465.html

PART V: Creating Excellence through Performance Evaluation

There is an oft repeated maxim in management in literature that measurement of performance is the first step to improvement; what can be measured should be measured and what cannot be measured should be made measureable. Measures lead to identification of gaps to be bridged. These help in finding of weaknesses and help in establishing priorities to allocate resources. In all respects measurement of the performance, its evaluation and monitoring is one of the most important tasks in an organization.   Performance measurement and evaluation can take several forms. The measures can be simply expressed in nominal numbers, scalar quantities, ratios of comparisons, indices or identifications of factors. In some cases it is desired to understand if the practices in the organization follow ethics or the regulations. Compliance to such practices implies that the organization follows the right path and there could be less chances of indifference to the performance or intentional failures. One such area is corporate governance. Much depends on what attributes need to be evaluated.

The section includes six chapters. Two of the cases refer to corporate governance. Another two concern use of DEA. Two of the cases follows a classic mode of measuring performance. One of the studies carries out analysis of factors.

Sardana and Dasanayaka in Chapter 23 identify and analyze factors that affect business to business relationships between telecommunication operators and vendors in Sri Lanka. This study is based on two models developed in telecommunication operator and vendor perspectives, and through in-depth questionnaire surveys .

Pallavi and G.N.Patel in Chapter 24 evaluate the performance of the Rashtriya Swasthaya Bima Yojna (RSBY). The methodology applied includes the Charnes, Cooper and Rhodes (CCR) model of DEA as well as the Tobit regression model to find the key determinants of the efficiency.

An assessment of the sugar mills and setting targets for the relatively inefficient mills to improve their efficiency and productivity is crucial. Harjit Singh et al. in Chapter 25 discuss Saraswati Sugar Mills, Jagadhari(India) to identify areas of improvement and performance evaluation.

Smriti Pande and G.N.Patel in Chapter 26 evaluate the performance of 46 pharmacy retail stores and to analyze the impact of non-discretionary variables on the efficiency of the stores through dividing the Decision Making Units (DMUs) into different categories. Basic Charnes Cooper Rhodes (CCR) and non-discretionary variable models are used to evaluate the efficiency of each store.

Silver Bird Group Bhd, a listed company, fails to issue its 2011 financial reports on time. The aims of the research case as presented by Tengku Akbar Tengku Abdullah in Chapter 27 are to determine whether its board is in a better position to supervise the management, to assess the effectiveness of its audit committee and to determine whether its financial problems could be foreseen.

Dinesh Likhi in Chapter 28 refers that a competent system of governance has to ensure that variables are reported in Corporate Governance/Performance. The objective of the study is to understand the effect of these variables in unlisted companies such as Public Sector Undertakings.

Analysis of Factors Affecting Business to Business Relationship Between Telecommunication Operators and Vendors in Sri Lanka

G.D. Sardana* and S.W.S.B. Dasanayaka* *

ABSTRACT

The main purpose of this paper is to identify and analyze factors that affect business to business relationships between telecommunication operators and vendors in Sri Lanka. This study is based on two models developed in telecommunication operator and vendor perspectives, and through in-depth questionnaire surveys conducted on employees working in telecommunication operator and vendor organizations in Sri Lanka. Analysis shows that relationship strength between telecommunication operators and vendors is determined by trust, commitment, adaptation, communication and satisfaction in the perspective of operators. Satisfaction of operators is determined by product quality, service support, delivery performance, supplier know how and value for money. In the perspective of vendors, relationship strength is determined by trust, commitment and satisfaction. Satisfaction of vendors is determined by economic factors and referencing from personnel networks. The higher management of telecommunication operator and vendor organizations can apply various strategies to improve these identified factors to further strength the business relationships between these parties.

Keywords: Business to Business; B2B, customer relationship management, CRM, telecommunication, operator perspectives, vendor perspectives, Sri Lanka.

INTRODUCTION

Literature on business to business relationship emphasizes that a firm's performance can be improved by focusing on present customers instead of concentrating on

* GD Sardana is Professor in Operations at Birla Institute of Management Technology, Greater Noida, India.
** Dasanayaka is with Dept. of Management of Technology, Faculty of Engineering, University of Moratuwa, Moratuwa, Sri Lanka.
E-mail: gdsardana@gmail.com, sarathd@mot.mrt.ac.lk

attracting new ones (Holmlund and Kock, 1996). Therefore, it is important to build long term relationships with customers in business to business markets (Hutt and Speh, 2004). There is a significant trend over the last few decades towards holding fewer and closer relationships (Ulaga and Eggert, 2006a). Establishing long term relationships not only creates higher value for the supplier, but also the buyer gets advantages; thus it can be mutually beneficial (Leonidou, 2004). Customers need to understand how to build and manage a portfolio of supplier relationships to increase overall return on relationships (Gummesson, 2002). On the other hand, since suppliers are facing a growing trend towards commoditization of products, suppliers need to understand how they can create and deliver value in business-to-business relationships beyond merely selling products (Rangan and Bowman, 1992). Demands for lower prices and an increase in profits, shorter product cycles and global competition are some of the forces affecting suppliers and customers in the industrial market, pressing them to have stronger relationships (Holmlund and Kock, 1995). The strength of bonds affects the strength of the total business relationship. Technical, time, knowledge, economic, legal, social, geographical, cultural, ideological, psychological and strategic bonds exist in a business relationship (Wendelin, 2011). If the relationships between companies are strong, it is usually a sign that the companies will cooperate for a longer time and that may affect the companies' competitive and financial strength positively (Storbacka et al., 1994).

In a theoretical perspective, it is suggested that both relationship marketing concepts and transaction cost concepts can help analyzing business-to-business relationships (Mysen et al., 2011). Transaction cost analysis focuses on the transaction, constituting the economic exchange between buyer and seller, and the reliance of early marketing works on economic theory (Sharma and Pillai, 2003). On the other hand, relationship marketing theory focuses on the importance of developing relationships in the long term (Lui et al., 2009). As Caceres and Paparoidamis (2007) point out that the fundamental principles upon which relationship marketing is based are mutual value creation, trust, and commitment; the greater the level of customer satisfaction with the relationship – not just the product or service – the greater the likelihood that the customer will be loyal to the company providing that service or the product.

The context of business to business relationship has a rich knowledge base. Many researchers and practitioners see the need to create and confirm models of organizational buying behavior as distinct from consumer purchasing behavior (Rossomme, 2003). Different approaches led to development of new interpretation of relationships. Ulaga and Eggert (2006b) refer that there are many ambiguities and contradictory results in studies on business to business relationships.

Telecommunication is an industry gained rapid momentum during the late nineties/early 20's in Sri Lanka mainly due to privatization in 1980s. As of June 2011, there are 64 licenses granted by the Telecommunications Regulatory Commission of Sri Lanka (TRCSL) for providing a wide range of telecommunication services in Sri

Lanka. Among the license holders, there are 4 fixed access telephone service operators and 5 cellular mobile phone operators. As per the TRCSL statistics, the total number of fixed telephones is reported to be 3.60 million and total number of cellular mobile subscribers at 18.18 million in June 2011. The fixed phone tele-density (fixed phones per 100 inhabitants) stood at 17.1 and the mobile penetration (mobile subscription per 100 people) at 86.5; these are higher as compared to other developing countries (TRCSL, 2011).

According to the Central Bank of Sri Lanka (CBSL, 2010), the growth momentum in the telecommunications sector was reflecting the increased demand mainly from the Northern and Eastern provinces in 2010. The growth in mobile telephone connections was 20.9% and the growth in fixed telephone connections was 3.9% in 2010, resulting in an overall growth of 17.6% (CBSL, 2011). The growth was largely fuelled by the expansion and strengthening of network coverage in the Northern and Eastern provinces provided by mobile service providers. Also, the provision of attractive calling charges and value added services at competitive prices in mobile phone connections has stunted the growth in the fixed access telephone connections. According to CBSL (2011), as on end 2010 the telecommunications sector consisted of 33 external gateway operators, and 8 internet service providers, making the industry more competitive. However, the level of internet penetration remains at 2.1%. Existing operators face the challenge of expanding broadband penetration in the country up to at least 10% within the next two years. In 2010 the TRCSL enforced floor prices and interconnection rates for mobile phones. This has helped ensure fair pricing and competition for market players by preventing unnecessary price competition. This facilitates the telecommunications industry to invest in research, development and expansion (CBSL, 2011).There are a number of telecommunication vendors operating in Sri Lanka. Some of them maintain business relationships with telecommunication operators by supplying equipment and services to them. Some vendors do business with other telecommunication vendors who are dealing directly with telecommunication operators. Some others directly supply equipment to the general consumers.

According to the TRCSL web site, telecommunication vendors can be broadly categorized based on the type equipment they supply. These categories include Telecommunication apparatus vendors, Mobile phone vendors, Radio communication vendors, Radio equipment vendors, Satellite receiver vendors, Cordless telephone vendors, Data communication apparatus vendors, Telephone vendors, Toys vendors, and Wireless data communication vendors.

OBJECTIVES AND SIGNIFICANCE OF THE CASE RESEARCH AREA

1. Following are the objectives of this research
2. Identify and analyze the factors affecting business to business relationship between telecommunication operators and vendors in Sri Lanka.

Propose policies and strategies to improve the relationship between telecommunication operators and vendors in Sri Lanka.

Many studies have been made on various business to business relationships. Some examples include insurance industry (Crosby et al., 1990), automobile industry (Kumar et al., 1995a,b), retail sales (Hennig-Thurau, 2000), industrial after sale services (Barry and Terry, 2008), financial services (Chenet et al., 2010), advertising (Chumpitaz and Paparoidamis, 2004; Venetis and Ghauri, 2004), and manufacturing (Gil-Saura et al., 2008; 2009).. However any serious research on business to business relationship between telecommunication operators and vendors is not reported in recent time. A similar kind of research could not be found in the Sri Lankan context for any industry. , Besides, only a few studies have been carried out considering both perspectives of the relationship; the supplier and customer (Terpend et al., 2008). This study analyzes the relationship in both operator perspective and vendor perspective.

METHODOLOGY AND CONCEPTUAL FRAMEWORK OF THE STUDY

Figure. 1 shows the conceptual model in the perspective of telecommunication operators representing the factors affecting business to business relationship between telecommunication operators and vendors in Sri Lanka, which was validated by the industry experts working in telecommunication operator organizations.

Fig. 1: Conceptual model for analyzing factors affecting business to business relationship between telecommu nication operators and vendors in Sri Lanka in the perspective of telecommunication operators

Figure 2 shows the conceptual model in the perspective of telecommunication vendors representing the factors affecting business to business relationship between telecommunication operators and vendors in Sri Lanka, which was validated by the industry experts working in telecommunication vendor organizations.

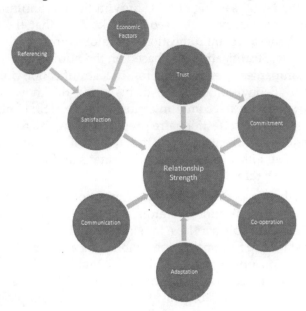

Fig. 2: Conceptual model for analyzing factors affecting business to business relationship between telecommunication operators and vendors in Sri Lanka in the perspective of telecommunication vendors

Sample of the Study

The studies in the two perspectives are conducted independently. The populations considered for the studies in two perspectives are mutually exclusive. For the study in the perspective of telecommunication operators, the population is all the telecommunication network operators operating in Sri Lanka. This definition for the population excludes the external gateway operators and internet service providers. Following fixed line and mobile communication companies were considered as telecommunication operators in Sri Lanka:Sri Lanka Telecom plc (Including Mobitel (Pvt) Ltd.), Dialog Axiataplc, Lanka Bell (Pvt) Ltd., Suntel (Pvt) Ltd., Etisalat Lanka (Pvt) Ltd., Hutchison Telecommunications Lanka (Pvt) Ltd and BhartiAirtel Lanka (Pvt) Ltd.

In any of the telecommunication operator organization, technical professionals (engineers and engineering managers) are the ones who mostly interact with telecommunication equipment and service vendors. Technical professionals are responsible for the planning functions including preparing Request for Proposals (RFPs) for telecommunication vendors, product and vendor evaluations, project implementation functions, and operating functions including maintenance activities. Therefore, technical professionals working in telecommunication operator organizations are the target sample of this study in the telecommunication operator perspective. Stratified sampling was used to make sure that the sample included employees from all the telecommunication operator companies, and no company dominated the sample. Stratification was based on the number of employees working in the operator companies. Percentages for the stratification followed the same percentages used by Senevirathna (2009) in his study on knowledge management practices and strategies of the telecommunication industry of Sri Lanka. Data collection was done via a user friendly questionnaire prepared using Microsoft Word software. A total of 150 questions were sent via email to convenient samples within the stratified samples. An aggressive follow-up via reminder emails and telephone calls was done to improve the response rate.

For the study of the perspective of telecommunication vendors, the population is all the suppliers for telecommunication operators, who sell at least one product (hardware and/or software) and probably services. In telecommunication vendor organizations, sales and presales staffs are responsible for establishing and maintaining relationships with telecommunication operators. They interact highly with the decision making personnel in telecommunication operator organizations. Therefore, sales and presales staff in telecommunication vendor organizations is the target sample of this study in the telecommunication vendor perspective. Unlike the technical staff in telecommunication operator organizations, the sales and presales staff in each telecommunication vendor organization is small in number. Therefore, only convenient sampling was used for the study in vendor perspective. Contacts of vendor organizations were obtained from staff working in telecommunication operator organizations. Data collection was done via a user friendly questionnaire prepared using Microsoft Word software. A total of 100 questions were sent via email to convenient samples in telecommunication vendor organizations. An aggressive follow-up via reminder emails and telephone calls was done to improve the response rate.

Data Collection Instrument

Data collection was done using two questionnaires for telecommunication operators and vendors via emails. Both questionnaires were comprised of four sections.

Section 1 collected some general information about the respondent and his/her company, including the type of the company, the position of the respondent and the respondent's level of experience.

Section 2 gathered some basic information about the other business party with whom the relationship is analyzed.

Section 3 of the questionnaires included statements operationalized through concepts included in each conceptual model. The respondents were given the option to express their level of agreeableness to each statement in a 5-point Likert scale.

Section 4 included some open ended questions on business relationships in the telecommunication industry in Sri Lanka. Respondents could answer these questions based on their general understanding on the telecommunication industry in Sri Lanka.

DATA ANALYSIS, FINDINGS AND POLICY RECOMMENDATION

Data Analysis and Findings

An important aspect of this study included response to question :

"Do you think that improving business to business relationship strength between telecommunication operators and vendors is important? Why?"

This was responded in affirmation by all the respondents irrespective of whether the respondents represented an operator organization or a vendor organization.

The reasons covered a broad spectrum . Following are a few typical aggregated summaries to the above open-ended question.

The stronger the relationship, easier the communication and negotiation will be. If we can build trust upon this relationship, things will be easier. They (the vendors) will not let you down and can get into a win-win situation.

- Operator – vendor relationship should be a win-win deal in practical situations not in agreements.
- It is very important since this synergy can create better value for the customer.
- Vendors depend on the sales to the operators. Operators depend on products from the vendors to keep an edge in the competition. The stronger the relationship better the product development process and shorter the time to market.
- This relationship is important for operators to provide a better service to its customers. It has a cyclic effect where better service will yield more customers and more revenue for the operators, resulting expansions and new deployments, sharing the success with the vendor finally.
- The Telecom environment is changing furiously around the globe. Both operators and vendors are racing to survive in this industry. Technologies change, end-users' likes & dislikes change, etc. Understanding what the operators need and what the vendors can give is the result of a good relationship, hence it's the only way to succeed in meeting the pressing demands of the market.

Another finding of this study is based on the correlation analysis performed between each of the factors assumed in the two models. The results of correlation analysis performed for the operator version model and the vendor version model are depicted in Table 1 and 2 respectively.

Table 1. Relationship characteristics according to correlation analysis (Operator version)

Concept 1	Concept 2	Pearson Correlation Coefficient	Significance	Relationship Characteristics
Trust	Relationship Strength	0.774	0.000	Strong Positive
Trust	Commitment	0.490	0.001	Moderate Positive
Commitment	Relationship Strength	0.538	0.000	Moderate Positive
Co-operation	Relationship Strength	0.566	0.000	Moderate Positive
Adaptation	Relationship Strength	0.411	0.000	Moderate Positive
Communication	Relationship Strength	0.311	0.005	Weak Positive
Satisfaction	Relationship Strength	0.629	0.000	Moderate Positive
Product Quality	Satisfaction	0.661	0.000	Strong Positive
Service Support	Satisfaction	0.729	0.000	Strong Positive
Delivery Performance	Satisfaction	0.349	0.001	Weak Positive
Supplier Know-how	Satisfaction	0.677	0.000	Strong Positive
Value for Money	Satisfaction	0.450	0.000	Moderate Positive

Table 2. Correlation analysis results summary (Vendor perspective)

Concept 1	Concept 2	Pearson Correlation Coefficient	Significance	Relationship Characteristics
Trust	Relationship Strength	0.332	0.026	Weak Positive
Trust	Commitment	0.401	0.006	Moderate Positive
Commitment	Relationship Strength	0.757	0.000	Strong Positive
Co-operation	Relationship Strength	0.389	0.008	Moderate Positive
Adaptation	Relationship Strength	-0.143	0.347	No relationship
Communication	Relationship Strength	0.046	0.762	No relationship
Satisfaction	Relationship Strength	0.687	0.000	Strong Positive
Economic Factors	Satisfaction	0.635	0.000	Moderate Positive
Referencing	Satisfaction	0.338	0.023	Weak Positive

The next finding is based on the regression analysis of the two models. All the factors that showed some kind of relationship in the correlation analysis were included in the regression analysis. Table 3 shows summary results of models using stepwise regression for operator perspective.

Table 3. Summary of models using stepwise regression (Operator perspective)

Model	R	R Square	Adjusted R Square	Std. Error of the Estimate	Change Statistics				
					R Square Change	F Change	df1	df2	Sig. F Change
1	.774a	.600	.595	.41459	.600	116.878	1	78	.000
2	.816b	.666	.657	.38112	.066	15.303	1	77	.000
3	.830c	.689	.676	.37038	.023	5.528	1	76	.021
4	.841d	.707	.691	.36187	.018	4.619	1	75	.035
5	.850e	.723	.704	.35416	.016	4.298	1	74	.042
a. Predictors: (Constant), Trust									
b. Predictors: (Constant), Trust, Adaptation									
c. Predictors: (Constant), Trust, Adaptation, Commitment									
d. Predictors: (Constant), Trust, Adaptation, Commitment, Communication									
e. Predictors: (Constant), Trust, Adaptation, Commitment, Communication, Satisfaction									

In the operator perspective model, Relationship Strength is dependent on Trust, Adaptation, Commitment, Communication and Satisfaction. The foremost factor is Trust with a standardized regression coefficient of 0.606. Satisfaction is dependent on Product Quality, Service Support, Delivery Performance, Supplier Know-how and Value for Money concepts. Co-operation is not a factor that significantly affects Relationship Strength. Adjusted R squared value for the model for Relationship Strength is 0.704. Adjusted R squared value for the part of the model for Satisfaction is 0.702.

Table 4 shows summary results of models using stepwise regression for vendor perspective.

In the vendor perspective model (Table 4), Relationship Strength is dependent on Trust, Commitment and Satisfaction. The foremost factor in the perspective of vendors was found to be Commitment with a standardized regression coefficient of 0.44. Satisfaction is dependent on Economic Factors and Referencing. Co-operation is not a factor that significantly affects Relationship Strength. Adjusted R squared value for the model for Relationship Strength is 0.664. Adjusted R squared value for the part of the model for Satisfaction is 0.431.

Table 4. Summary of models using stepwise regression (Vendor perspective)

Model	R	R Square	Adjusted R Square	Std. Error of the Estimate	Change Statistics				
					R Square Change	F Change	df1	df2	Sig. F Change
1	.757a	.574	.564	.34677	.574	57.831	1	43	.000
2	.807b	.652	.635	.31713	.078	9.415	1	42	.004
3	.829c	.687	.664	.30417	.036	4.654	1	41	.037

a. Predictors: (Constant), Commitment

b. Predictors: (Constant), Commitment, Satisfaction

c. Predictors: (Constant), Commitment, Satisfaction, Trust

CONCLUSIONS

From the first finding, it can be concluded that the employees working in the telecommunication industry are well aware of the importance of business to business relationships. They are in agreement with the suggestion that stronger relationships are advantageous for both telecommunication operators and vendors. From the findings realized by correlation analysis and regression analysis, the factors that affect business to business relationships between telecommunication operators and vendors can be concluded, fulfilling the second objective of this research.

Following factors affect the strength of business to business relationships irrespective of the view point – telecommunication operator or vendor.

Trust

As defined by Morgan and Hunt (1994) trust exists when one party has confidence in an exchange of partner's reliability and integrity. If both parties trust each other, their business relationship becomes stronger. Following attributes can be considered to collectively build Trust between parties.

- Honesty – Openness in all aspects. Being open about each other's strengths, weaknesses, issues, plans, etc.
- Integrity – What is said will be done
- Keeping promises
- Concern about the other party's interests

Trust is the foremost factor affecting the Relationship Strength with a beta value of 0.606 in the perspective of operators. However in the perspective of vendors, it is having a much lesser beta value of 0.261.

Commitment

Morgan and Hunt (1994) define Commitment as an exchange in partner believing that an ongoing relationship with another is so important as to warrant maximum efforts at maintaining it. If one party is having a good level of commitment towards another business party, that party should feel involved with the other party. Following can be considered as indicators of one party being committed towards another party.

- Feeling involved with the other party
- Defending the other party in front of others
- Being proud of having business relations with the other party

Commitment was found to be the foremost factor affecting relationship strength in the perspective of vendors.

Satisfaction

As per the disconfirmation paradigm (Parasuraman et al. 1985; 1994), one's feeling of satisfaction is a result of a comparison process between perceived performance and one or more comparison standards, such as expectations. As expected during developing the conceptual models, the antecedents of Satisfaction differ depending on the perspective; operator or vendor. As per the results of this study, following are the antecedents of Satisfaction in the telecommunication operator perspective, listed in the order of most affecting to least affecting.

- Level of support services – Since telecommunication is a high-tech industry, it is less probable that the operators get all the required technology transferred from the vendors. Therefore it is crucial to have good level of support services from the telecommunication vendors.

- Supplier know-how – It is important for the telecommunication operators to know the product and solution information about the existing and future planned products. Telecommunication operators expect that their vendors will have good knowledge on this aspect.

- Quality of products – In the telecommunication industry, quality of products is something that cannot be compromised. Quality of products is crucial for being competitive in the industry.

- Delivery performance – In order to be competitive in the telecommunication market, all the telecommunication operators are looking for new technologies, and want to implement those new technologies before others do the same. Therefore delivering the software and hardware accurately and in a timely manner is very important.

- Value for money – Telecommunication operators have limited budgets for their capital and operational expenditure. Therefore they want to maximize the value they are getting for what they spend. This depends on the overall pricing, pricing flexibility, terms of payment, etc.

According to this study, in the perspective of telecommunication vendors following are the antecedents of Satisfaction.

- Economic factors – These are the factors such as the level of prices charged for the products and services, level of profit margins gained by selling products and services, and volume of business having with a particular operator
- Referencing – This is communicating good things about the vendor organization by the senior management of operator organization in public forums.
- In this research, following factors were found to be affecting the strength of the business to business relationship between telecommunication operators and vendors only in the perspective of telecommunication operators. In the perspective of telecommunication vendors, they were not found to be significantly affecting the relationship strength.

Adaptation

As defined by Brennan and Turnbull (1998) buyer-seller adaptations are "behavioral or structural modifications, at the individual, group or corporate level, carried out by one organization, which are initially designed to meet specific needs of one other organization". Following items can be considered as contributing the construct of Adaptation in the perspective of telecommunication operators.

- The vendor customizing its products to suit the operator's requirements
- The vendor adjusting its production processes to meet the operator's requirements
- The vendor changing its inventory procedures to match the operator's requirements
- The vendor changing its delivery procedures to meet the operator's requirements
- The vendor investing in tools or equipment to adjust to the operator's procedures better

COMMUNICATION

It can be concluded from this research that Communication is also one of the factors affecting relationship strength between telecommunication operators and vendors in the perspective of telecommunication operators. The level of communication between the two parties is determined based on the following factors.

- Timeliness of communication
- Accuracy of communication
- Completeness of communication

- Adequacy of communication
- Credibility of communication

From the adjusted R squared values, the percentage of variation in Relationship Strength that can be explained by each model can be concluded. In the perspective of telecommunication operators, 70.4% of the variation in Relationship Strength can be explained by Trust, Commitment, Adaptation, Communication and Satisfaction. 70.2% of the variation in Satisfaction can be explained by Product Quality, Service Support, Delivery Performance, Supplier Know-how and Value for Money factors. In the perspective of telecommunication vendors, 66.4% of the variation in Relationship Strength can be explained by Trust, Commitment and Satisfaction. 43.1% of the variation in Satisfaction can be explained by Economic Factors and Referencing such as comparison standards, for example expectations. Another important conclusion that can be reached from this research is that the factors affecting the relationship strength differ depending on from which perspective the relationship is looked at. This conclusion is in line with the previous literature also (Ambrose et al., 2010; Barnes et al., 2007; Forker et al., 1999).

POLICY RECOMMENDATIONS

This section covers recommendations of this research study towards the management of both telecommunication operator and vendor organizations. If the management of both telecommunication operator and vendor organizations pay the due diligence to those factors, the relationship between them would be enhanced for better business opportunities.

All the factors found to be antecedents of Relationship Strength of telecommunication operators are positively affecting it. Therefore in order to enhance the relationship strength, management should take necessary actions to improve those factors. Management of the telecommunication operators should take steps to enhance trust with vendors. By being honest and showing integrity when dealing with vendors, and by being concerned about the other party's (vendor's) interests, trust between the two parties can be enhanced.

Actively showing the commitment towards the vendor organization will also facilitate building strong relationships.

Allowing the vendor organization to earn a reasonable amount of profit by the business transactions between the two parties, and having high business volumes with them will also satisfy the vendor, and in turn it will cause increased relationship strength.

Expressing good references about the vendor in relationship in industrial and public forums will cause satisfying the vendor, and in turn relationship strength will be enhanced.

Factors found to be affecting the relationship strength in the perspective of telecommunication operators were all positively affecting it. Therefore by improving those factors management of telecommunication vendor organizations can enhance the relationship strength with operator organizations.

Management of telecommunication vendors should take steps to improve the trust with the operators, which was found to be foremost factor affecting the relationship strength in the view point of telecommunication operators.

Honesty, integrity and concern in the operator's interests are keys to build trust. Improving the level of trust also improves the commitment, which in turn affects the relationship strength positively. The vendors should actively show its commitment towards its business partner operators, which will help building the relationship.

Being flexible or adaptable to the requirements of the telecommunication operator is also positively affects the business relationship between them. Therefore the vendor should be prepared to customize its products, production processes, inventory processes, and delivery procedures in order to build strong relationships.

The vendor should also be prepared to do specific investments required to do the necessary adaptations. Telecommunication vendors should make sure to maintain very good communication links with the telecommunication operators they do business with. Always the communications with the operators should have the characteristics of timeliness, accuracy, completeness, adequacy and credibility. Good communication links directly affect the business relationship strength positively. Management of telecommunication vendors should keep the telecommunication operators satisfied in order to enhance the relationship strength.

The main factor affecting satisfaction of operators was found to be service support. The vendors should abide to the agreed service levels and if possible should try to improve them. Supplier know-how on the existing and new products was also found to be an important factor affecting satisfaction. Therefore the representatives of the vendor organization who interface with the operator organization employees should be well educated about their products both existing and on the roadmap.

Quality of the products is another factor affecting satisfaction of telecommunication operators. The vendors should make sure that the quality of the products is maintained up to the standards. Quality should not be compromised due to any reason.

Delivery performance also affects the satisfaction. The vendor organizations should make sure that the product and service deliveries to the operators are done accurately and on time. Telecommunication operators are also concerned about the value for money aspects. Therefore the vendor should try its best to offer reasonable overall pricing, flexible pricing and preferable terms of payment for the operators, in order to make them satisfied and thereby to increase the relationship strength.

ACKNOWLEDGEMENTS

Authors highly appreciate research assistance received from W.Weerasena and A.Abeyrathne research students in Department of Management of Technology, University of Moratuwa, Sri Lanka.

REFERENCES

Ambrose, E., Marshall, D. and Lynch, D. (2010) Buyer supplier perspectives on supply chain relationships,*International Journal of Operations & Production Management*,Vol.30, No.12, pp.1269-1290.

Brennan, R., Turnbull, W. and Wilson, T. (2003) Dyadic adaptation in business-to-business markets,*European Journal of Marketing, Vol.*37, No.11 and 12, pp.1636-1665.

Barnes, R., Naude´, P. and Michell, P. (2007) Perceptual gaps and similarities in buyer-seller dyadic relationships,*Industrial Marketing Management, Vol.*36, No.5, pp. 662-675.

Barry, J. and Terry, S. (2008) Empirical study of relationship value in industrial services,*Journal of Business & Industrial Marketing, Vol.*23, No.4, pp.228-241.

Chenet, P., Dagger, S. and O'Sullivan, D. (2010) Service quality, trust, commitment and service differentiation in business relationships, *Journal of Services Marketing, Vol.*24, No.5, pp.336-346.

Chumpitaz, R. and Paparoidamis, G. (2004) Service quality and marketing performance in business-to-business markets: exploring the mediating role of client satisfaction,*Managing Service Quality, Vol.*14,Nos 2 and 3, pp.235-248.

Crosby, A., Evans, R. and Cowles, D. (1990) Relationship quality in services selling: an interpersonal influence perspective,*Journal of Marketing, Vol.*54, July, pp.68-81.

Central Bank of Sri Lanka: CBSL (2011)*Central Bank of Sri Lanka Annual Reports, 2010-11, Various Issues, Colombo.*

Caceres, C. and Paparoidamis, G. (2007) Service quality, relationship satisfaction, trust, commitment, and business-to-business loyalty,*European Journal of Marketing, Vol.*41, No.7 and 8, pp. 836-67.

Forker, B., Ruch, A. and Hershauer,C. (1999) Examining supplier improvement efforts from both sides,*Journal of Supply Chain Management, Vol.*35, No.3, pp.40-50.

Gil, I., Servera, D., Berenguer, G. and Fuentes, M. (2008) Logistics service quality: a new way to loyalty,*Industrial Management & Data Systems, Vol.*108, No.5, pp.650-668.

Gil-Saura, I., Frasquet-Deltoro, M. and Cervera-Taulet, A. (2009)The value of B2B relationships,*Industrial Management & Data Systems, Vol.*109, No.5, pp.593-609.

Gummesson, E. (2002) *Total Relationship Marketing*, 2nd ed., Butterworth-Heinemann, Oxford.

Holmlund, M. and Kock, S. (1995) Buyer perceived service quality in industrial networks,*Industrial Marketing Management, Vol.*24, No.2, pp.109-121.

Holmlund, M. and Kock, S. (1996) Relationship marketing: the importance of customer-perceived service quality in retail banking,*The Service Industries Journal, Vol.*16, No.3: 287-304.

Hutt,D. and Speh, W. (2004)*Business Marketing Management: A Strategic View of Industrial and Organizational Markets*, Hartcourt, Orlando, FL.

Hennig-Thurau, T. (2000) Relationship quality and customer retention through strategic communication of customer skills,*Journal of Marketing Management, Vol.*16, No.1, 2 and 3, pp.55-79.

Kumar, N., Scheer, K. and Steenkamp,B. (1995a)The effects of perceived interdependence on dealer attitudes,*Journal of Marketing Research, Vol.*32, No.3, pp.348-56.

Kumar, N., Scheer, K. and Steenkamp,M. (1995b)The effects of supplier fairness on vulnerable resellers,*Journal of Marketing Research, Vol.*32, February, pp.54-65.

Leonidou, L. (2004) Industrial manufacturer-customer relationships: the discriminant role of the buying situation, Industrial *Marketing Management, Vol.*33, No.1, pp.731-42.

Liu, Y., Luo,D. and Liu, T. (2009)Governing buyer-supplier relationships through transactional and relational mechanisms: evidence from china,*Journal of Operations Management, Vol.* 27, No.4, pp. 294-309.

Mysen, T., Svensson, G. and Payan, M. (2011) Causes and outcomes of satisfaction in business relationships,*Marketing Intelligence & Planning, Vol.* 29, No.2, pp.123-40.

Morgan, M. and Hunt, D. (1994)The commitment-trust theory of relationship marketing,*Journal of Marketing, Vol.*58, No.3, pp.20-38.

Parasuraman, A., Zeithaml, A. and Berry, L. (1985) A conceptual model of service quality and its implications for future research,*Journal of Marketing, No.*49, No. Fall, pp.41-50.

Parasuraman, A., Zeithaml, A. and Berry, L. (1994) Reassessment of expectations as a comparison standard in measuring service quality: implications for further research,*Journal of Marketing, Vol.*58, No.1, pp.111-24.

Rangan, K. and Bowman, T. (1992) Beating the commodity magnet,*Industrial Marketing Management, Vol.*21, No.3, pp. 215-24.

Rossomme, J. (2003) Customer satisfaction measurement in a business-to-business context: a conceptual framework,*Journal of Business & Industrial Marketing, Vol.*18, No.2, pp. 179-95.

Senevirathna,P. (2009) Knowledge management practices and strategies of the telecommunication industry of Sri Lanka. Thesis for the Master of Business Administration in Management of Technology, Department of Management of Technology, University of Moratuwa, Sri Lanka.

Storbacka, K., Strandvik, T. and Gro¨nroos, C. (1994) Managing customer relationships for profit – the dynamics of relationship quality,*International Journal of Service Industry Management, Vol.*5, No.5, pp. 21-38.

Sharma, A. and Pillai, G. (2003)The impact of transactional and relational strategies in business markets: an agenda for inquiry,*Industrial Marketing Management, Vol.* 32, No.1, pp.623-626.

Terpend, R., Tyler, B., Krause, R. and Handfield, B. (2008) Buyer-supplier relationships: derived value over two decades,*Journal of Supply Chain Management, Vol.*44, No.2, pp. 28-55.

Telecommunication Regulatory Commission of Sri Lanka: TRCSL (2011) TRCSL Statistics, http://www.trc.gov.lk/Information/Statistics.html [accessed on August 10th of 2011].

Ulaga, W. and Eggert, A. (2006a) Relationship value and relationship quality: broadening the nomological network of business-to-business relationships,*European Journal of Marketing, Vol.*40, Nos 3 and 4, pp.311-27.

Ulaga, W. and Eggert, A. (2006b) Value-based differentiation in business relationships: gaining and sustaining key supplier status,*Journal of Marketing, Vol.*70, No.1, pp.119-36.

Venetis, A. and Ghauri, N. (2004) Service quality and customer retention: building long term relationships,*European Journal of Marketing, Vol.*38, No.11 and 12, pp.1577-1598.

Wendelin, R. (2011) Bond audit, a method for evaluating business relationships,*Journal of Business & Industrial Marketing, Vol.* 26, No.3, pp. 211-17.

Assessing the Relative Efficiency of Rashtriya Swasthaya Bima Yojna – A Case of Districts of Uttar Pradesh

Pallavi Seth* and G.N.Patel**

ABSTRACT

The purpose of this case study is to evaluate the performance of the Rashtriya Swasthaya Bima Yojna (RSBY) in the districts of Uttar Pradesh. The methodology applied includes the Charnes, Cooper and Rhodes (CCR) model of DEA to find out the relative efficiency of the districts of U.P as well as the Tobit regression model to find the key determinants of the efficiency. The methodology has been applied to all the districts of Uttar Pradesh except one district, Hathras for which data was unavailable. The results show that only a few districts are relatively efficient and the policymakers need to work to make the scheme efficient. The findings of this study provide insights into the efficiency of RSBY in the districts of Uttar Pradesh. This has implications for the efficient management of the scheme.

Keywords: Insurance, health insurance, CCR efficiency, RSBY, India - Uttar Pradesh.

INTRODUCTION

Economic development and national wellbeing are important indicators for the economic growth of a nation. Earlier (1960-2000), growth in labor and capital were considered to be the key determinants of economic growth but empirical evidence have proven that human capital contributes significantly to the economic growth but that human capital is itself dependent on the level of education and health of the people. (Barro and Salai-i-Martin 2004). As per the KPMG report, a 5-year gain in life expectancy is associated with annual average rates of growth of real GDP per capita that is higher by around 0.5 percent. This means- that economic performance may improve if the health of people is improved as shown in the Figure 1. India is at a

---

* Sr. Research Scholar, Birla Institute of Management Technology, Greater Noida.

** Professor, Birla Institute of Management Technology, Greater Noida.

E-mail: pallavi.seth@bimtech.ac.in, gn.patel@bimtech.ac.in

stage where it is undergoing a phase of demographic transition where the proportion of working population is expected to increase in the next quarter of a century. As per the Report of the National Commission on Macroeconomics and Health, Ministry of Health and Family Welfare, Government of India, 2005, this rising young population, if healthy and productive, has the potential of increasing the growth of real income per capita by an annual average of 0.7 percent till 2025. Seeing the implications of healthy and productive human capital on the economic growth of a nation, it becomes very important to set up such a health care system that is inclusive in itself.

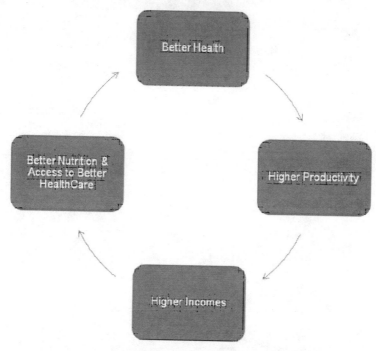

Fig. 1: Importance of Better Health (Source: KPMG Report)

HEALTHCARE FUNDING AND INSURANCE COVERAGE

As per National Health Accounts, World Health Organization, health care expenditure in India in 2009 was 4.2% of GDP, which was quite low as compared to Germany (11.3%), UK (9.3%).Public sector expenditure is 32% which is again quite low as compared to Germany (75.7%) and UK (83.6%).Again, the out-of-pocket expenditure is 50 % for India against Germany (11.4%) and U.K (10.4%), this very high out of pocket expenditure of India is a cause of major concern. It means, people have to pay from their own pocket for health care expenses and they don't have any other support to rely upon.

As per report of GIZ on "Health Insurance for India's Poor" August 2011, less than 6 percent of active workers participate in the organized sector, characterized by higher earnings and job security, whereas more than 94 percent are in the informal sector. Of these, the majority are self-employed and do not earn wages but profit from their own small and marginal agricultural and business enterprises. Most do not have regular jobs and, instead, work on a casual basis, especially in rural areas where 33 percent of all workers depend on casual jobs for income.

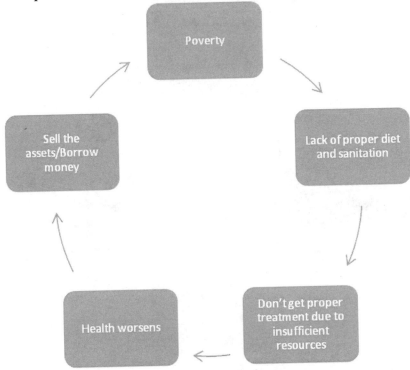

Fig. 2: Vicious Circle of Poverty

When the need to get medical treatment arises for poor people, most of the time they ignore it because of the lack of resources, fear of losing wages and they wait till the time its too late. Even if they decide to get the desired treatment, they don't have the resources to support this and which forces them to sell their assets (if they have any), or borrow the money from the unauthorized money lenders. Ignoring the treatment may lead to unnecessary suffering and death while selling property or taking debts may end a family's hope of ever escaping poverty. This becomes worse for people living below poverty line as an illness not only can cause a big setback to their earning capacity but also could put them into the vicious circle of poverty as shown in the figure above:

As per report of GIZ, August 2011, attempts to provide access to those who could not afford to pay out of their own pockets were few, narrowly-targeted, underfunded and largely ineffective.

This poses serious questions before the government of India:

- How such a health system is to be financed which considers the need of the poor people?
- How can they protect people from the financial consequences of ill-health and paying for health services?
- How can they (govt. or policy-makers) encourage the optimum use of available resources?

To address to the needs of the poor people, Ministry of Labor and Employment, Government of India along with GIZ (a German agency) has launched a health insurance scheme for poor people – Rashtriya Swasthaya Bima Yojna (RSBY).

RASHTRIYA SWASTHAYA BIMA YOJNA

RSBY aims to provide protection to BPL people against the financial consequences of bad-health, sickness, accidental injuries. The BPL families comprising of five members or less are eligible to take the benefits of this scheme by just paying Rs 30 as the membership fees to get the smart card (which is a type of enrollment card having the details of the family members).Whenever any family member falls sick or face any accidental injury, they are entitled to get hospitalization amount worth Rs 30,000 from the listed hospitals (both public and private).Pre-existing diseases are covered from day one of enrollment and there is no age limit. The treatment cost is already fixed with the listed hospitals. Central and State government pays the premium in the ratio of 3:1 respectively (in case of Jammu & Kashmir and North-eastern states, the ratio is 9:1).

Role of Different Stakeholders

Insurers: Central and State Government pays the premium to the insurer selected by the State Government on the basis of a competitive bidding for each household enrolled for RSBY. So, the insurer will collect more premium amount if it enrolls more households, and this is the motivating force for the insurers.

Hospitals: Hospitals are paid for the treatment provided by them to each beneficiary so they have the motivation to provide treatment to large number of beneficiaries. But it has been found in many cases that hospitals have made fraud claims so proper monitoring is very important which is done by insurers.

Intermediaries: NGOs and MFIs facilitate the process of enrollment as well as they help in making people aware about the scheme as they are in direct contact with beneficiaries.

Government: Central & State governments pay the premium amount to the insurers so that the quality health care can be provided to the BPL people.

REVIEW OF LITERATURE

Review of Literature has been completed from three sources:

A. Papers on health insurance/health insurance for poor

B. Papers /reports on RSBY

C. Papers on application of DEA in insurance

The review of literature has been divided into three sections. The first section deals with the research done in the area of health insurance. The second section deals with the review of literature for the studies done on RSBY schemes and the third section reviews the literature in the area of Data Envelopment Analysis i.e., how this tool has been used in different studies to find out the efficiency as well as the inputs and outputs being used by the different researchers.

HEALTH INSURANCE

The research on Health Insurance has been conducted in different contexts.

Bhat et.al, (2006), studied the factors affecting the demand for Health Insurance in a Micro Insurance Scheme. The study concluded that Income and health care expenditure affect significantly the purchase of health insurance and that age, coverage of illnesses and knowledge about insurance also have impact on the purchase of health insurance. Bhat et.al, (2007) studied the factors affecting the renewal of health insurance policy. The study conducted the survey of 301 households in the Anand district of Gujarat policy named as "Krupa", the study showed that those who renewed the insurance scheme had higher annual income than the others

Hamid S.A et al. (2010) evaluated the Health Effects of Micro Health Insurance Placement in Bangladesh, the findings were statistically significant for health awareness and health care utilization but not for health status. Hamid S.A et al. (2010) concluded that there was impact on per capita income and per capita land assets to the users as compared to non-users or recent users of the Micro Health Insurance schemes but there was no impact on any of the indicators of stability of household income. Hyun H. Son (2008) found that Conditional Cash Transfer programs were quite successful in these countries but required ongoing monitoring as well as evaluation. Complementing Conditional Cash Transfer programs with other social programs could be very useful.

Aggarwal A. (2010) studied the impact of the community based health insurance scheme –Yeshasvini on health-care utilization, financial protection, treatment outcomes and economic well-being. The programme had increased utilization of health-care services, reduced out-of-pocket spending, and ensured better health and economic outcomes. Many other papers on health insurance were reviewed and most of the paper's result gave a positive indication of the use of health insurance schemes in terms of decreased health care expenditure, out-of pocket expenditure etc if the schemes are working efficiently.

PAPERS /REPORTS ON RSBY

RSBY has been studied in different states from different perspectives.

Amicus Advisory Private Limited (2010), the study used a blend of quantitative (structured questionnaire) as well as qualitative methods (focus interviews), and showed that there existed lack of awareness about the scheme among the beneficiaries. Around 70% reported decline in their healthcare expenditure & low claim severity as people were unaware of using the scheme. A report on health insurance for India's poor by German Health Practice Collection, August 2011, emphasized the need and importance of health insurance for poor people. The study stressed on the need for further research and evaluation of RSBY was taken as a challenge and the need of the hour. Sheila Rai et al. (2010) studied the various dimensions of RSBY and also emphasized on proper monitoring and evaluation of the scheme. Pilot Post-enrolment Survey of the RSBY Programme in Haryana, March 2011 by Ministry of Labor & Employment, found that there was also a need for measuring the effectiveness of RSBY now that the Phase-I had completed one year. It also stated that the key deliverables should be benchmarked against other successful health insurance schemes of the states. The study itself said that measuring the efficiency of the scheme would not only help bring out qualitative & quantitative findings but would also help incorporate the best practices in RSBY. Amicus Advisory conducted an evaluation study of Shimla & Kangra Districts in Himachal Pradesh, in November 2011, and found that RSBY had done quite well in these districts but more efforts were required from the insurers and TPAs in creating awareness about the scheme. As stated above, many of the studies done on RSBY stated that further research on monitoring the scheme was needed as just implementing the scheme would not serve the purpose but proper monitoring and evaluation was required.

APPLICATION OF DEA IN INSURANCE

Chiang Ku Fan et al, (2009), compared the efficiency of indirect channel with direct marketing channel using DEA, the inputs used were business and administrative expenses and outputs were premiums. Kwadjo Ansah et.al, (2012) found that insurance companies in Ghana might have to invest more inputs to produce the same amount of outputs due to the increasing competition in order to increase or at least maintain their market shares. The major finding from the study was that market share was the key determinant of efficiency among insurance companies in Ghana .Ananth Rao et.al, (2010), analyzed the efficiency and productivity issues of the insurance sector from both the policymakers' and investors' points of view. Xiaoling Hu et.al, (2009), examined the efficiencies of China's foreign and domestic life insurance providers & to explore the relationship between ownership structure and the efficiencies of insurers.

These papers were reviewed to have the understanding of how DEA had been used in the different studies on Insurance companies and the inputs and outputs being used by different researchers. The inputs and outputs used by the different researchers are depicted in Table 1 in the Data and Variables Section. These papers became the basis of identifying the inputs and outputs of this study.

OBJECTIVES OF THE STUDY

RSBY is one of the great initiatives of the Govt. of India to support BPL people in the form of health insurance but every initiative needs proper monitoring and evaluation, otherwise the purpose of the scheme can be lost. This study focuses on the performance evaluation of the RSBY to find out how the scheme is performing and the possible reasons for its success or poor performance.

The objectives of the study are as follows:

- Evaluation of performance of the scheme (RSBY) in different district of Uttar Pradesh
- What are the drivers of efficiency of the scheme (in the districts where it is performing well)?
- What are the constraints for the growth of the scheme

METHODOLOGY

CCR Model

The model allows the Decision Making Unit (DMU) being measured to determine the set of optimal weights for each of its factors (outputs are denoted by y and inputs by x in the following model) so as to determine its relative efficiency. The solution consists of a set of weights (u for outputs and v for inputs) chosen so that the efficiency of any other unit with these weights won't exceed 1, the value at which a unit is relatively efficient.

The general purpose DEA which was developed by Charnes et al. (1978) is called as CCR model. It takes n DMUs into consideration, using m inputs to secure s outputs. The notations which are used in the model are as follows-m : number of inputs $(i=1,2,...m)$

s : number of outputs $(r=1,2,...s)$

n : number of DMUs $(j=1,2,...n)$

x_{ij} : i^{th} input of jth DMU

y_{rj} : r^{th} output of jth DMU

$$X = \begin{pmatrix} x_1 & x_2 & \cdots & x_{1n} \\ x_2 & x_2 & \cdots & x_{2n} \\ \cdot & \cdot & \cdots & \cdot \\ x_{m1} & x_{m2} & \cdots & x_{mn} \end{pmatrix}, Y = \begin{pmatrix} y_1 & y_2 & \cdots & y_{1n} \\ y_2 & y_2 & \cdots & y_{2n} \\ \cdot & \cdot & \cdots & \cdot \\ y_{s1} & y_{s2} & \cdots & y_{sn} \end{pmatrix}$$

The efficiency of each DMU is measured once and hence we need n optimization problem to be solved, one for each DMU_j. Let the DMU_j to be evaluated on any trial be designated as DMU_o, where "o" ranges over $1,2,....,n$. We solve the following LP to obtain values for the input weights $v_1, v2,....v_m$ and output weight $u_1,u_2,....u_s$ as variables.

max $u_1 y_{1o} + u_2 y_{2o} + ... + u_s y_{so}$

s.t. $v_1 x_{1o} + v_2 x_{2o} + ... + v_m x_{mo} = 1$

$u_1 y_{1j} + u_2 y_{2j} + ... + u_s y_{sj} \leq v_1 x_{1j} + v_2 x_{2j} + ... + v_m x_{mj}$ $(j = 1,2,....,n)$

$v_1,v_2,....v_m \geq 0$

$u_1,u_2,....u_s \geq 0$

The dual of LP helps in recognizing the reference set for the inefficient DMUs. These reference sets then help us in identifying the inadequacies existing in the inefficient units. The dual of the above model can be given in the following matrix form-

$\theta^* = \min \theta$

s.t. $Y\lambda \geq y_o$

$X\lambda \leq \theta x_o$ ... (1)

$\lambda \geq 0$

DATA AND VARIABLES

Identification of input and outputs is required while applying CCR model of DEA. In this study, inputs and outputs have been identified on the basis of the literature reviewed as well as the objectives of the study

Inputs and outputs being used by different researchers is shown in Table 1[1]:

Table 1: Inputs & Outputs being used by different researchers

Inputs	Outputs	References
Rehabilitation and compensation costs, Number of full time cases and claims managers in the branch	Right First Time, No. of claimants managed starting this month, No. of claimants starting this month expected to have left in less than 12 months, No. of weekly compensation payments which have met the target timeline	Meimand et al. (2002)
Business administration expenses, commissions, acquisition expenses	Direct written premiums, reinsurance premiums received	Hwang and Kao (2006)
Labor, Capital	Premium, benefits, claim costs	Yao et al.(2007)
Labor expenses, general operating expenses, capital equity, claims incurred	Net premiums written, net income	Wu et al. (2007)
Operating expenses, insurance expenses, direct written premiums, reinsurance premiums	Direct written premiums, reinsurance premiums, underwriting profit, investment profit	Kao and Hwang (2008)
Labor, business services, equity cost, Asset, Underwriting and investment expenses	Benefit payments, Return on Asset	Jeng et al (2007)
Number of sales representatives, Number of branches, Business and administrative expenses, Commission and acquisition Expenses, Agency fee and commissions from insurers, Number of financial specialists Commission and acquisition Expenses, Operation expenses	Premium Income	Chiang Ku Fan et al. (2009)
Administrative and general expenses, Equity +legal reserves	Rate of return on investments (ROI), Liquid assets to total liabilities	Ananth Rao et al.(2010)
Total capital, total operating cost and total investments	Profit or loss, net premium and investment income	Kwadjo Ansah-Adu et al. (2012)
working capital, operating expenses, human capital	net premiums	Xiaoling Hu et al. (2009)

---

[1] Some of the contents of the table have been taken from the paper "An efficiency comparison of direct and indirect channels in Taiwan insurance marketing" by Chiang Ku Fan and Shu Wen Cheng

On the basis of understanding of different inputs and outputs being used by the different researchers, following inputs and outputs are used for this study:

Inputs

- Premiums paid (x1)
- No. of hospitals (x2)

Outputs

- Number of families enrolled (y1)
- No. of Claims (y2)
- Hospitalization Value /Claims amount

Rates of each treatment have been fixed with the hospitals, and insurance companies will pay the treatment cost to the hospitals which is an expense to the insurance companies which the insurance companies want to be genuine and minimum, so hospitals have been taken as an input.

Premiums are being paid by the government to the insurance companies which is a cost to the policy –makers so premiums paid are also taken as an input.

If the no. of claims and hospitalization amounts are high then it means that people are using the scheme and getting benefits of it which in turn means that the scheme is helpful to them so high claim amount and no. of claims is good for the scheme so this is taken as an output, (fraud claims should be monitored by the policy-makers).

No. of families enrolled are also taken as an output because if more families are enrolled for it , it means people are ready to use the scheme and the policy-makers are also able to enroll more and more people which is good indication for the awareness of the scheme.

We had to drop hospitalization amount as an output because of the very high correlation between the outputs,-hospitalization amount and no. of hospitalizations as shown in the Table 2, here y1 represents no. of families enrolled, y2 represents hospitalization amount and y3 represents no. of hospitalizations.

Table 2: Correlation

		y1	y2	y3
y1	Pearson Correlation	1	.213	.262*
	Sig. (2-tailed)		.079	.030
	N	69	69	69
y2	Pearson Correlation	.213	1	.973**
	Sig. (2-tailed)	.079		.000
	N	69	69	69
y3	Pearson Correlation	.262*	.973**	1
	Sig. (2-tailed)	.030	.000	
	N	69	69	69

*. Correlation is significant at the 0.05 level (2-tailed).
**. Correlation is significant at the 0.01 level (2-tailed).

RESULTS AND DISCUSSIONS

The study applied CCR-model of DEA (to find out the relative efficiencies) as well as Tobit regression model (to find the determinants of efficiencies)

After applying the CCR model on the districts of Uttar Pradesh (considered as DMUs), the following scores of efficiencies were obtained:

Table 3: Efficiencies obtained

Uttar Pradesh						
Districts	wts/dmus	(u1)	u2	(v1)	(v2)	Eff.
Agra	1	0.006321	0	0.001664	0.00416	0.15552
Aligarh	2	0.004233	6.24E-05	0.000896	0.02363	0.190342
Allahabad	3	0.00431	1.75E-05	0.001334	0.002851	1
Ambedkar Nagar	4	0.004204	6.2E-05	0.00089	0.023468	0.38949
Auraiya	5	0	0.000149	0	0.071429	0.766912
Azamgarh	6	0.005268	2.14E-05	0.001631	0.003485	0.632497
Baghpat	7	0	0.000261	0	0.125	0.147964
Bahraich	8	0.006495	2.43E-05	0.000487	0.037264	0.840542
Ballia	9	0.004543	6.7E-05	0.000962	0.025362	0.514209
Balrampur	10	0.004556	6.72E-05	0.000965	0.025433	0.475602
Banda	11	0.008788	2.49E-05	0.000403	0.05677	0.371421
Barabanki	12	0.006398	9.37E-07	0.001684	0.004268	0.765273
Bareilly	13	0.005944	2.42E-05	0.00184	0.003933	0.510914
Basti	14	0.006538	9.57E-07	0.00172	0.004361	0.525942
Bijnor	15	0.005365	2.18E-05	0.001661	0.00355	0.395069
Budaun	16	0.006217	2.32E-05	0.000466	0.035666	0.388104
Bulandshahr	17	0.006341	9.28E-07	0.001668	0.00423	0.095919
Chandauli	18	0.003109	4.59E-05	0.000658	0.017358	0.548079
Chitrakoot	19	0.016099	4.56E-05	0.000739	0.104005	0.356993
Deoria	20	0	7.52E-05	0.000272	0.025272	0.588907
Etah	21	0.01055	2.99E-05	0.000484	0.068159	0.21078

Etawah	22	0	0.000138	0.000498	0.046223	0.519573
Faizabad	23	0.006464	9.46E-07	0.001701	0.004312	0.494867
Farrukhabad	24	0	0.000126	0.000456	0.042311	0.534679
Fatehpur	25	0.004136	6.1E-05	0.000876	0.02309	0.313811
Firozabad	26	0.007945	1.16E-06	0.002091	0.0053	0.098618
Gautam Buddha Nagar	27	0.007852	2.22E-05	0.00036	0.050725	0.070681
Ghaziabad	28	0	7.56E-05	0.000273	0.025381	0.082205
Ghazipur	29	0.003616	5.34E-05	0.000766	0.020188	1
Gonda	30	0.011468	0	0.000529	0.072658	0.213881
Gorakhpur	31	0.004925	2E-05	0.001525	0.003258	0.446743
Hamirpur	32	0	0.000139	0.000501	0.046547	0.350429
Hardoi	33	0.005755	2.15E-05	0.000431	0.033016	0.9941
Jalaun	34	0	0.000152	0.000549	0.050931	0.618438
Jaunpur	35	0.004485	2.46E-05	0.001802	0.001288	1
Jhansi	36	0.005708	2.13E-05	0.000428	0.032745	0.285127
Jyotiba Phule Nagar	37	0.003691	5.45E-05	0.000782	0.020604	0.180435
Kannauj	38	0.008452	3.16E-05	0.000634	0.048492	0.339483
Kanpur Dehat	39	0.005737	8.4E-07	0.00151	0.003827	0.473297
Kanpur Nagar	40	0.004194	2.3E-05	0.001685	0.001204	0.48327
Kanshiram Nagar	41	0.013455	3.81E-05	0.000617	0.086925	0.400307
Kaushambi	42	0.007313	2.73E-05	0.000548	0.041955	0.672645
Kheri	43	0.005765	0	0.001517	0.003794	0.519455
Kushinagar	44	0.006625	9.7E-07	0.001743	0.004419	1
Lalitpur	45	0.009984	2.83E-05	0.000458	0.064499	0.371904
Lucknow	46	0.004905	2.69E-05	0.001971	0.001408	0.368189
Maharajganj	47	0.008054	2.28E-05	0.00037	0.052033	0.505083
Mahoba	48	0.007161	8.61E-05	0	0.090909	0.222609
Mainpuri	49	0.010282	2.91E-05	0.000472	0.066423	0.50989

Mathura	50	0.004233	6.24E-05	0.000896	0.02363	0.12796
Mau	51	0.00572	8.44E-05	0.001211	0.03193	0.419924
Meerut	52	0.00606	2.27E-05	0.000454	0.034767	0.066681
Moradabad	53	0.005138	2.09E-05	0.001591	0.003399	0.267243
Muzaffarnagar	54	0.006795	2.54E-05	0.000509	0.038983	0.300789
Pilibhit	55	0.006262	2.34E-05	0.00047	0.035926	0.36964
Pratapgarh	56	0.006951	1.02E-06	0.001829	0.004637	0.615756
Rae Bareli	57	0.006158	9.02E-07	0.00162	0.004108	0.406465
Rampur	58	0.007877	9.47E-05	0	0.1	0.489083
Saharanpur	59	0.006669	9.77E-07	0.001755	0.004449	0.167899
Sant Kabir Nagar	60	0.005493	8.1E-05	0.001163	0.030664	1
Sant Ravidas Nagar	61	0	5.57E-05	0.000201	0.018697	0.701418
Shahjahanpur	62	0.005666	2.12E-05	0.000425	0.032506	0.36811
Shrawasti	63	0.020177	5.72E-05	0.000926	0.13035	1
Siddharthnagar	64	0.009285	2.63E-05	0.000426	0.059982	0.298206
Sitapur	65	0.00676	9.9E-07	0.001779	0.004509	0.819458
Sonbhadra	66	0	0.000152	0.000551	0.0511	0.407975
Sultanpur	67	0.006062	8.88E-07	0.001595	0.004044	0.832317
Unnao	68	0.007661	1.12E-06	0.002016	0.00511	0.720333
Varanasi	69	0.003907	2.14E-05	0.00157	0.001121	1

The results show that Allahabad, Ghazipur, Jaunpur, Kushinagar, Sant Kabir Nagar, Shahjahanpur, Shrawasti and Varanasi are the most efficient districts relatively.

In order to clearly examine the determinants of efficiency, we further applied Tobit Regression model regressing the CCR efficiencies.(as shown in the table 5)

The Tobit regression model is represented as-

$$\theta_i = \alpha_i + \beta_1(\textit{families enrolled}) + \beta_2 \,(\textit{no. of claims}) + \beta_3 \,(\textit{Premiums paid}) + \beta_4$$
$$(\textit{no. of hospitals}) + \varepsilon_i$$

where θ_i is the efficiency score for the districts of Uttar Pradesh computed from the CCR model of DEA.

Descriptive statistics of the efficiencies is shown in the Table 4.

Table 4: Descriptive Statistics of CCR Efficiency

	N	Minimum	Maximum	Mean	Std. Deviation	Skewness	Kurtosis
	Statistic	Statistic	Statistic	Statistic	Statistic	Statistic	Statistic
CCR Eff.	69	.07	1.00	.4829	.26752	.539	-.464

As this is clear from the Table 4 , skewness is 0.539 which means data is right skewed. Also, kurtosis score shows that data is more flat.

The results of Tobit regression model is shown in the Table 5 :

Table 5: Results of Taobit Regression

	Estimate	Std. Error	Z value
Intercept 1	3.7713e-0.1	1.2437e-01	3.0323
Families enrolled*	5.6084e-03	3.7435e-04	14.9816
No. of claims	4.1999e-05	5.8315e-06	7.2021
Premiums paid*	−4.0637e-04	2.3491e-04	−1.7299
No. of hospitals*	−4.7296e-03	7.6677e-04	−6.1682

* Indicates statistically significant

The chi-square test statistics (=1019.7) with 4 degrees of freedom associated with p values >0.0 shows that the model is good fit for the data. Also we find that the value of constant 2 ($e^{-2.271}$) =0.103209 < Sd (Eff.) =0.267521 which again shows that the model appears to fit the data well.

The Tobit model gives the following equation

$$\theta_i = Eff. = 0.377 + 0.005608y_1 + 0.00004199y_2 - 0.00041x_1 - 0.00473x_2$$

which means that no. of families enrolled contributes significantly to the efficiency of the districts; that means more awareness and more usage of the scheme. For an increase in no. of families enrolled, the efficiency of a district will increase by 0.005608. However, the sign of premiums paid and no. of hospitals is negative as expected. This indicates that the efficiency of a district will fall by (-0.00041) and (-0.00473) respectively.

CONCLUSION AND RECOMMENDATIONS

The results of CCR model show that most of the districts are not performing well as the efficiency scores are quite low. Also the average of the efficiencies as shown in the Table 4 is 0.4829 which is again low.

As the Tobit regression model shows that the no. of families enrolled have a significant impact to the efficiency of the districts which implies that more the no. of families enrolled, more will be the efficiency so lesser will be the out of pocket expenditure of the families.

Treatment cost paid to the hospitals should be as minimum as possible as it is having negative impact on the efficiency of the scheme.

Also, the premiums paid to the insurance companies should be as minimum as possible as this is again having negative impact on efficiency of the scheme.

If all these considerations are well taken by the policy makers then it can affect the overall performance of the scheme in U.P

REFERENCES

Amicus Advisory Private Limited. (2010), Rashtriya Swasthaya Bima Yojna: Studying Jaunpur (Uttar Pradesh)

Amicus Advisory Private Limited. (2011). Evaluation Study of Rashtriya Swasthaya Bima Yojana in Shimla & Kangra Districts in Himachal Pradesh.

Aggarwal A. (2010), Impact evaluation of India's 'Yeshasvini' community-based health insurance programme. Health Economics Journal.19 (1) 5-35.

Bhat Ramesh, Jain Nishant (2006). Factoring Affecting the Demand for Health Insurance in Micro Health Insurance. Retrieved May 2012 from IIM Ahmedabad website: http://www.iimahd.ernet.in/publications/data/2006-07-02rbhat.pdf

Barro R, Sala-i-Martin X. Economic growth (2004), 2nd Ed. New Delhi: Prentice-Hall of India

Cummins, D., Tennyson, S. and Weiss, M.A. (1999). Consolidation and efficiency in the US life insurance industry. Journal of Banking & Finance 23. 325-57.

Chiang Ku Fan, Cheng Wen Shu (2009). An efficiency comparison of direct and indirect channels in Taiwan insurance marketing. Direct Marketing: An International Journal. 3 (4). 343-359.

Hamid S.A,Roberts Jennifer, Mosley Paul (2010).Evaluating the Health Effects of Micro Health Insurance Placement: Evidence from Bangladesh. Retrieved from http://eprints.whiterose.ac.uk/10777/1/SERPS2010009.pdf

Hamid S.A, Roberts Jennifer, Mosley Paul (2010).Can Micro Health Insurance

Reduce Poverty? Evidence from Bangladesh. Retrieved from http://www. microfinancegateway.org/gm/document1.9.43777/Can%20Micro%20Health%20 Insurance%20Reduce%20Poverty.pdf

Health Insurance Inc.: The Road Ahead. Report by KPMG and Chambers of Commerce (CII). Retrieved from https://www.kpmg.com/IN/en/IssuesAndInsights/ ArticlesPublications/Documents/Health%20Insurance%20Summit%202008.pdf

Health systems financing: the path to universal coverage. A World Health Organization Report, 2010.Retrieved from http://www.who.int/whr/2010/en/index.html

Hyun H. Son (2008). Conditional Cash Transfer Programs: An Effective Tool for Poverty Alleviation. ECONOMICS AND RESEARCH DEPARTMENT Policy Brief Series No. 51, Asian Development Bank

IRDA website, www.irda.gov.in

Kwadjo Ansah, Andoh Charles, Abor Joshua (2012). Evaluating the Cost Efficiency of Insurance Companies in Ghana. Journal of Risk Finance.1 (3). 61-76.

Meimand, M., Cavana, R.Y. and Laking, R. (2002).Using DEA and survival analysis for measuring performance of branches in New Zealand Accident Compensation Corporation. Journal of the Operational Research Society.53.303-13.

Policy Brief 12, Inter-Regional Inequality Facility sharing ideas and policies across Africa, Asia and Latin America. Health Insurance for the Poor-India.http://www.odi.org. uk/resources/download/3127.pdf

Rao Ananth, Kashani Hossein, Marrie Attiea (2010). Analysis of managerial efficiency in insurance sector in the UAE: an emerging economy. International Journal of Managerial Finance.6.329-343.

Randolph K. Quaye (2007). Health care financing in Uganda: the role of social health insurance. International Journal of Health Care Quality Assurance. 20(3). 232-239.

RSBY website, www.rsby.gov.in

Rai Sheila, Rai Niha. Rashtriya Swasthya Beema Yojna (RSBY): Panacea for the poor. Retrieved from http://www.adbi.org/files/2010.12.11.cpp.sess3.c18.rai.paper.rsby. panacea.poor.pdf

Health insurance for India's poor. (2011), Report by GIZ.A publication in the German Health Practice Collection

Rupalee Ruchismita, Imtiaz Ahmed and Suyash Rai. (2007). Delivering Micro Health Insurance through the National Rural Health Mission. Retrieved from http://www. microfinancegateway.org/gm/document1.9.50818/Delivering%20Micro%20Health. pdf

World Health Statistics 2010 by World Health Organization

Xiaoling Hu, Zhang Cuizhen, Hu Jin-Li, Zhu Nong (2009). Analyzing efficiency in the Chinese life insurance industry. Management Research News.32 (10). 905-920.

Saraswati Private Sugar Mills Ltd:
The Benchmarking Story

Harjit Singh*, Nikunj Aggarwal** and Roma Chauhan***

ABSTRACT

The sugar industry occupies a prestigious place in the predominantly agricultural economy of India. Its contribution to the agricultural development can be gauged from the fact that it offers employment to nearly 25 million small and marginal farmers. An assessment of the sugar mills and setting targets for the relatively inefficient mills to improve their efficiency and productivity is crucial, as the interests of various stakeholders are largely dependent on its performance. This case study discusses the vital role played by Saraswati Sugar Mills, Jagadhari, Haryana in the employment generation and upliftment of the socio-economic status of the district and putting Jagadhari on the Industrial map of the state.

Keywords: Sugar industry, Saraswati Sugar Mill, private sector, effective management practices, performance.

INTRODUCTION

India is one of the largest consumers of sugar in the world and the second largest producer next only to Brazil (GOI 1998). Its contribution to the agricultural development can be gauged from the fact that sugarcane farming constitutes about 1.5 to 2 percent of gross area under cultivation and nearly 25 million small and marginal farmers grow sugarcane on their holdings and hence draw their sustenance from it (Ahuja & Majumdar 1998). With the establishment of a sugar factory, the farmers in the area get about Rs. 1000 to Rs. 1200 crores annually in the form of remunerative cane prices and direct employment to rarely 1000 to 2000 persons. By providing this gainful employment, it puts a strong barrier on the migration of rural people to the

* Faculty, School of Business, Galgotias University, Greater Noida (India).
** Faculty Shaheed Bhagat Singh College, Delhi University.
*** Faculty, IILM, Greater Noida.
E-mail: harjit_mfc@rediffmail.com, aggarwal.nikunj75@gmail.com, roma.chauhan@gmail.com

urban areas. Besides, the farmers also get some fringe benefits from the mills in the form of subsidized inputs such as seeds, fertilizers, liberal loans and expert guidance (Schmidt 1996). In 2010-11, fourty thousand quintals of press mud and 124 quintals of urea were disbursed among the farmers by the sugar industry. The sugar industry is an important source of revenue for the central government which drains an annual income of nearly Rs. 300-800 crores in the form of excise duty. It directly connects agriculture with industry and also acts an important instrument of urbanization. The establishment of a sugar factory in a rural area where there is sufficient sugarcane production accelerates its economic progress (Battese & Coelli 1992). It provides various types of communication channels exposing the rural areas commercial, social and economic progress (Forsund & Sarafoglou 2002). Hence it has a very high potential to stimulate urbanization in the rural areas, which are rich in the natural resources (Charnes, Cooper & Rhodes 1978).

In comparison to an average annual rise of 3.2% in world sugar production during last decade, global sugar consumption has grown by about 2.5% per annum, while in India the consumption has been much higher at about 3.9% per annum. Consequently, Indian sugar industry has become the second largest agro-industry located in the rural India (Singh 2006 a & b). It has a turnover of Rs.700 billion per annum and it contributes almost Rs. 22.5 billion to the central & state exchequer as tax, cess, and excise duty every year. With more than 550 operating sugar mills in different parts of the country, Indian sugar industry has been a focal point for socio-economic development in the rural areas. In order to compete efficiently and prudently, the sugar industry is transforming itself into an integrated chain of value added products which helps in diversifying the business model by eliminating the impact of seasonal volatility in the earnings stream (www.rkfml.com). Mills are converting industrial alcohol into ethanol which is being supplied to refineries for mixing with the fuel and this value addition provides better margins as compared to industrial alcohol (Jones 1989).

This case study was carried out on Saraswati Sugar Mill Ltd (established in 1933), situated on the out skirts of Yamuna Nagar town. Yamuna Nagar is an old city. It is situated just on the U.P. – Haryana border where the Yamuna river flows. It is an important industrial town of Haryana state, situated at about 200 Kms from Delhi and 45 Kms away from main G. T. Road.

OBJECTIVES OF THE STUDY

In broader sense the purpose behind the study is to examine the profitability and performance of the Saraswati Sugar Mill Ltd.

The primary objective of the study is to examine the working efficiency of Saraswati Sugar Mill Ltd and its impact on the society as a whole while the sub-objectives are:

- To study the role of better management and efficient working workmen in the performance of Saraswati Sugar Mill Ltd.

- To discover factors responsible for low performance (if any) and to suggest measures so as to improve the performance and working efficiency of the Saraswati Sugar Mill Ltd.

MATERIALS AND METHODS

- The study is primarily secondary in nature but for the better understanding of the concept, several subject experts and executives of the company were consulted. For the purpose of data collection, first of all the study area was selected and a reconnaissance survey took place. Various financial reports (Annual Reports) were collected and available literature was thoroughly reviewed.
- Ratio analysis and other quantitative techniques have been used in the study as per requirement. To carry out financial appraisal, various financial ratios such as working capital turnover ratio, percentage of net profit to capital employed, percentage of gross profit to capital employed, cost output ratio, value added per man/month were calculated and analyzed thoroughly to understand the financial position of the company.
- The study is based on the secondary sources of data, which have been collected from the various sources, annual reports of the sugar mill and other Government publications.
- The study period is spread form 1995-96 to 2010-11.

RATIO ANALYSIS OF THE SARASWATI SUGAR MILL

i.   Profitability Profile

Profitability of any industry refers to the ability to earn profits i.e., total profit as related to the capital employed i.e. profitability ratio or return on capital. A measure of profitability is quite different from profits, which refers to the absolute quantum. The profitability ratio has been calculated as follows:

Profitability Ratio = (Gross Profit / Total Capital Employed) × 100

ii.   Cost-Output Ratio

Cost output ratio relates to cost per unit of output. It has been calculated as:

Cost Output Ratio = Cost of production / Value of Production

iii.   *Value Added Per Man/Month (₹) :*

Value added per man reflects the contribution made by per man to the total value of production. Employment at Saraswati is shown in Table 2.

(Value of Production / No. of employees) × 12

The concentrations of various parameters are given in following tables.

Table 1: Profit/Loss of the Sugar Mill

(In Rs. Lac)

Year	Profit/losses	Accumulated Profit
1995-96	639.26	639.26
1996-97	495.92	1135.18
1997-98	1062.94	2198.12
1998-99	-356.57	1841.55
1999-00	879.91	2721.46
2000-01	-91.56	2629.90
2001-02	0.55	2630.45
2002-03	356.36	2986.81
2003-04	1127.47	4114.28
2004-05	2688.11	6802.39
2005-06	919.99	7722.38
2006-07	-1299.82	6422.56
2007-08	-268.24	6154.32
2008-09	5319.05	11473.37
2009-10	-218.12	11255.25
2010-11	1318.40	12573.65

Source: Compiled and calculated by author from various annual reports

Table 2: Types of Employees of Mill

Sr. No.	Grade	Number of Employees	Permanent	Seasonal
1.	Unskilled labour	912	57	1025
2.	Skilled labour	1095	301	814
3.	Clerical staff	201	151	56
4.	Supervisory staff	175	99	35
5.	Medical Govt. Grade	14	12	2
	Total	2397	620	1932

Source: Company Website (www.isgec.com)

Table 3: Working Capital Turnover Ratio

Year	Net Sales (₹ Lacs)	Working Capital (₹ Lacs)	Ratio
1995-96	12347.06	6494.65	1.90
1996-97	16085.05	7569.41	2.13
1997-98	16704.75	4924.20	3.39
1998-99	15299.83	5734.19	2.67
1999-00	17023.81	9007.11	1.89
2000-01	24619.26	7033.33	3.50
2001-02	24549.83	13816.05	1.78
2002-03	22458.53	7889.95	2.85
2003-04	37021.20	9224.90	4.01
2004-05	35876.84	7333.18	4.89
2005-06	29760.84	4891.46	6.08
2006-07	33728.47	12762.40	2.64
2007-08	32647.36	21516.77	1.51
2008-09	39855.87	15045.47	2.65
2009-10	33766.78	7795.04	4.33
2010-11	41756.98	10693.28	3.90

Source: Compiled and calculated by author from various annual reports

Table 4: Profitability Profile

Year	Gross Profit (₹ Lacs)	Net profit (₹ Lac)	Capital Employed (₹ Lac)	Percent of net Profit to Capital Employed	Percent of Gross Profit to Capital Employed
1995-96	1019.23	639.26	6043.90	10.58	16.86
1996-97	853.27	495.92	8568.12	5.79	9.96
1997-98	1572.21	1062.94	9991.73	10.64	15.74
1998-99	198.23	-356.57	9836.28	-3.63	2.02
1999-00	1257.29	879.91	13285.06	6.62	9.46
2000-01	379.54	-91.56	14834.49	-0.62	2.56
2001-02	6524.48	0.55	14481.75	.0038	45.05

2002-03	5094.36	356.36	15201.87	2.34	33.51
2003-04	6439.19	1127.47	15593.89	7.23	41.29
2004-05	6767.91	2688.11	17025.36	15.79	39.75
2005-06	13203.46	4159.94	20984.98	4.38	62.92
2006-07	8891.43	2866.12	22375.34	12.81	39.73
2007-08	8423.61	2591.88	24273.65	10.68	34.70
2008-09	19865.39	5717.62	26484.93	21.59	75.06
2009-10	867.86	-218.12	27748.33	-0.77	3.18
2010-11	5685.38	1318.40	29234.68	4.51	19.45

Source: Compiled and calculated by author from various annual reports

Table 5: Cost Output Ratio

Year	Cost of Production (Rs. Lac)	Value of Production (Rs. Lac)	Cost Output Ratio
1995-96	16214.60	16234.34	0.99
1996-97	16410.45	16750.29	0.98
1997-98	13161.44	13161.45	0.99
1998-99	16377.49	16377.59	0.99
1999-00	22781.83	22794.56	0.99
2000-01	26127.12	27134.54	0.96
2001-02	27916.45	26913.23	1.04
2002-03	29823.54	30218.68	0.99
2003-04	31545.67	32517.24	0.97
2004-05	34258.83	35412.53	0.97
2005-06	35598.35	36863.21	0.97
2006-07	36987.27	37233.76	0.99
2007-08	37989.18	38698.34	0.98
2008-09	39786.65	41534.87	0.96
2009-10	42650.87	43874.68	0.97
2010-11	44786.58	46679.68	0.96

Source: Compiled and calculated by author from various annual reports

Table 6: Value per Man/Month

Year	Number of Employees	Value of Production (Rs.Lac)	Value Added Per Man/Month Ratio
1995-96	1832	16234.34	73846.16
1996-97	1842	16750.29	75779.45
1997-98	1508	13161.45	72731.27
1998-99	1519	16377.59	89848.53
1999-00	1323	22794.56	143578.74
2000-01	1252	27134.54	180607.96
2001-02	1235	26913.23	181600.74
2002-03	1878	30218.68	134090.69
2003-04	1962	32517.24	138112.63
2004-05	2052	35412.53	143813.06
2005-06	2278	36863.21	134852.24
2006-07	2154	36985.54	14895.28
2007-08	2016	38541.56	15268.24
2008-09	1856	39625.19	153625.81
2009-10	2154	40658.25	160257.65
2010-11	1958	41358.98	162549.76

Source: Compiled and calculated by author from various annual reports

RESULTS AND DISCUSSION

- Since 1995-96, the mill is showing a mixed trend of profit and losses. In the analysis of last sixteen years, except 1998-99, 2000-01, 2006-08, 2009-10, mill has shown good profits. The reason for the losses was found to be lack of investment in the production capacities and machines. Besides this, increase in wages of workers and employees was one of the main reason to this loss.

- Investment, which plays an important role in the development of an industry, is decreasing continuously from 1995-96 to 2010-11. Annual reports revealed the fact that from 1999 to 2006 there was no investment in the development of the infrastructure. Despite no investment, company has shown profits.

- Overall Net sales has also been showing increasing trend though in some years it showed declining trend. Net sales decreased in the year 1998-99 and 2001-02. Change in net sale was of ₹ 3737.99 lacs in 1996-97, which is of ₹ 125.43 lacs now. This shows that after five to seven years the net sales did not show sufficient increase and consequently the mill had to bear losses.

- Capital employed also showed an increasing trend. From 1995-96 to 2010-11 the capital employed increased by four times. Though this is small change but comparison to its counterparts, the investment is significant.

- Total employment and average emolument per employee has been increasing from 1995-96 to 2010-11. Value of production has been showing a mixed trend of increasing and decreasing.

- The cost output ratio is decreasing. This low cost output ratio shows the efficiency to produce less than the prevalent rate. So there is control in cost of production rather than the high value of production. In this situation when cost of production is controlled, company is gaining competitive advantage over its competitors.

- Capital employed turnover ratio is showing a mixing behavior i.e. sometimes increasing or sometimes decreasing from 1995-96 to 2010-11, so this shows unfavorable trend.

- In nutshell, the financial and operational performance analysis shows the efficiency of the Saraswati Sugar Mill Pvt. Ltd. Because of this efficiency, mill has been making significant profits. Though in 2005-06, mill was not in the condition to pay the cane growers, but the situation has changed and cane growers are getting the amount of their produce well in time.

- The reasons for losses were also studied and the study revealed that losses were not because of poor financial performance but some unavoidable systematic factors :

  - Since the last few years, new recruitment is banned; however, the number of employees is still large and there is a problem of overstaff. As the mill functions only for six months a year and during the remaining period this staff remains unproductive, the mill has to pay salaries to permanent staff throughout the year which puts a big burden on the mill.

  - There is a large difference between the statutory minimum price (SMP) and state advised price (SAP). SMP is fixed by central government and SAP for sugarcane is fixed by the state government over and above the SMP. There is difference of ₹100 per quintals which is causing losses to the sugar mill.

RECOMMENDATIONS

1. The price of sugarcane should be fixed as per recovery and according to the quality of the sugarcane. High price should be paid for the early and better quality and fewer prices be paid for the late varieties. If the pattern is followed it will help in reducing the cost of production.

2. There should be proper price policy. The present sugar policy should be changed. Price of sugarcane should be fixed by taking into account the profits of mills also, and not the profits of growers alone. Due to high price of sugarcane there is profit to the cane growers but also there is a loss to the mill. Therefore, prices of sugarcane should be fixed according to both considerations.

3. Over staffing in the mill should be curbed, emphasis should be given to appoint persons having knowledge of modern techniques. Only efficient, well-qualified persons who have capability to handle the various operations should be recruited.

4. Avoid idle time for men and machines in sugar industry , because of higher incidence of machine breakdowns, labour problems and feeding of cane etc. This has resulted in higher manufacturing, overhead cost per quintal of sugar. It can be controlled through better care of machines, better division of work and labour.

QUESTIONS FOR DISCUSSION

1. What challenges are faced by sugar industry in India?

2. How Saraswati Sugar Mill financial performance has been instrumental in building confidence among rural people and strengthening industrial base in Haryana.

3. Discuss initiatives which are needed to cut down the costs and improve the operations.

4. Do the SWOT analysis of Saraswati Sugar Mill and draw inferences to lay the foundation for road ahead?

ACKNOWLEDGEMENT

The authors would like to express their sincere thanks to Mr. R.K. Verma, Deputy General Manager, Saraswati Sugar Mills Ltd. Yamuna Nagar, Haryana for his wholehearted support in developing this management case and his kind permission to present and publish the same at ICMC2012.

REFERENCES

Ahuja, G and S K Majumdar (1998), "An Assessment of the Performance of Indian State-Owned Enterprises", Journal of Productivity Analysis, Vol. 9(2), pp. 113-132.]

Battese, G E and T J Coelli (1992), "Frontier Production Functions, Technical Efficiency and Panel Data : With Application to Paddy Farmers in India", Journal of Productivity Analysis, Vol. 3 (1/2), pp 153-69.

Charnes, A, W Cooper and E Rhodes (1978), "Measuring the Efficiency of Decision, European Journal of Operational Research 3, pp 338.

Forsund, F R and N Sarafoglou (2002), "On the Origins of Data Envelopment Analysis", Journal of Productivity Analysis, Vol. 17, pp. 23-40.

Garrels, R.M. and MacKenzie, R.T. (1971). " Evolution of Sedimentary Rocks", New York.

Government of India (1998), "Report of the High-Powered Committee on Sugar Industry", (Mahajan Committee), Ministry of Consumer Affairs, Food & Public Distribution, Department of Sugar & Edible Oils, New Delhi.

Jones, C. A., Wegener, M. K., Russel, J. S., McLeod, I. M., and Williams, J. R. 1989. AUSCANE-simulation of Australian sugarcane with EPIC. CSIRO. Div. Tropical Crops and Pastures. Tech. Paper No. 29. Brisbane: CSIRO. Australia: 7—56.

Nadia M A. and Mahmood A K. (2006). "Study on Effluent from Selected Sugar Mill in Pakistan: Potential Environmental, Health, and Economic Consequences of an Excessive Pollution Load", Sustainable Development Policy Institute (SPDI).

Schmidt, P (1996), "On the Statistical Estimation of Parametric Frontier Production Functions", Review of Economics and Statistics, Vol. 58, pp. 238-239.

Singh, S P (2006a), "Technical and Scale Efficiencies in the Indian Sugar Mills : An Interstate Comparison", The Asian Economic Review, Vol. 48 (1), pp. 87-100.

Singh, S P (2006b), "Efficiency Measurement of Sugar Mills in Uttar Pradesh", The ICFAI Journal of Industrial Economics, Vol. 3 (3), August, pp. 22-38.

www.rkfml.com "Industry Report – Sugar" (2008), Accessed on August 26, 2012.

Evaluating Performance of Categorical Decision Making Units using DEA

Smriti Pande* and Gokulananda Patel**

ABSTRACT

The purpose of this study is to evaluate the performance of 46 pharmacy retail stores and to analyze the impact of non-discretionary variables on the efficiency of the stores through dividing the Decision Making Units (DMUs) into different categories. Basic Charnes Cooper Rhodes (CCR) and non-discretionary variable models are used to evaluate the efficiency of each store. First, efficiency is evaluated considering only the discretionary variables using basic CCR model. Second, non-discretionary variable model is used with categorical DMUs taking both discretionary and non-discretionary variables into consideration. Lastly, to analyze the impact of non-discretionary variables on the efficiency scores ANOVA is applied. For situations that are not under the direct control of the management, DEA with categorical DMUs is an appropriate approach for efficiency evaluation because through this approach one can do justice to each store which is a part of the study. This study provides a framework for performance evaluation when both discretionary and non-discretionary variables are to be taken into consideration.

Keywords: Pharmacy, retailing, DEA, performance evaluation, non-discretionary variables, charnes cooper rhodes model.

INTRODUCTION

The Indian pharmaceutical industry has traveled a long way to reach to this stage. Bengal Chemical and Pharmaceutical Works was the first Indian company which was established way back in 1903. However, there was not much achieved in the area of local production till 1947 (Bhati and Shriprakash, 2008). The Indian Design and Patents Act, 1911 favoured the foreign firms. A report on India Pharmaceuticals & Healthcare (Q4, 2010), Business Monitor Intelligence states that by 1960s, about 80% of

* Research Scholar, Birla Institute of Management Technology, Greater Noida, India.
**Professor, Birla Institute of Management Technology, Greater Noida , India.
E-mail: smriti.panda@bimtech.ac.in, gn.patel@bimtech.ac.in

the pharmaceutical market was captured by the foreign firms. It was the establishment of Hindustan Antibiotics Limited in 1954 and Indian Drugs and Pharmaceuticals Ltd. in 1961 which facilitated in achieving self-sufficiency in this industry. But the real turning point came in 1972 by passing of Indian Patent Act, 1970 which recognized patents on processes but not on products. As a result, the Indian firms started to reverse engineer the formulations which were patented by the multinationals in their home countries and sold these generic copies at low prices in India. This further resulted in growth of domestic pharmaceutical industry from a few multinationals to some 20,000 registered pharmaceutical companies today (Rao, 2008). Again in 2005, after a transition period of 10 years, India complied with the TRIPS agreement provisions on the pharmaceutical product patent and it is expected that with this move India's Patent Laws will be updated to the international standards which will encourage more and more R&D in this sector.

Growth of the ageing population and drastically changing lifestyles of the current generation has increased the healthcare expenditure as well as attention to chronic diseases. Increase in medical tourism clubbed with higher investments in the sector is acting as an enticement for the pharmaceutical firms. These factors along with certain growth drivers like increase in domestic population, increased literacy level, conscious spending by consumers on health products, customers' willingness to spend on health and fitness, higher margins etc. are calling for development in pharmacy sector which in turn implies growth and development of organized pharmaceutical retailing sector. With a gradual move of the pharmacy retailing into a service-oriented business there are many aspects to be considered other than just financial performance. The objective of this paper is to evaluate the efficiency of 46 pharmacy retail stores considering both discretionary and non-discretionary variables and also to analyze the impact of non-discretionary variables on efficiency of each store.

PERFORMANCE EVALUATION AND DATA ENVELOPMENT ANALYSIS

Performance evaluation of a retail store is an imperative task in the current Indian retail market scenario because retail is one sector which has suffered through the side effects of recession and therefore remains very cautious for each move planned in its operations. Performance evaluation is important because, consumers also benefit from efficient resource usage and allocation to get lower prices and more professional service (Anderson et al., 1998). Earlier, Input- output ratios were commonly used to measure the performance but these are now being supplanted by enhanced approaches such as data envelopment analysis. Efficiency evaluation and benchmarking have been two most widely used methods so as to improve the performance of any retail store (Mohamed M. Mostafa, 2009).

DEA is applied to varied areas such as banking, financial companies, supplier's selection, schools, hospitals, hotels, airports, insurance industry and nations. Balakrishnan et al. (1994) used DEA to evaluate the relative spatial efficiency of locations of a network of retail outlets and how the imposition of threshold requirements alters their spatial efficiency. Donthu and Yoo (1998) analysed 24 outlets of a fast food restaurant chain for internal benchmarking. The inputs used were store size, store manager experience, store location, promotion/give-away expenses. The outputs used were sales and customer satisfaction. Here, location was considered as an uncontrollable input. Barros and Alves (2003) analyzed the efficiency of individual retail stores belonging to a Portuguese multi-market hypermarket retailing chain using sales and operational results as outputs and full time employees, part time employees, cost of labour, absenteeism, area of outlets, number of point of sales, age of outlet, inventory, and other costs as inputs. Joo et al. (2009) measured and benchmarked the retail operations of eight coffee stores, four being located in an affluent residential area and the other four located in a typical business district area, owned by a specialty coffee company. In this paper again, retail location is being considered as an uncontrollable input.

DEA is a non-parametric method which was first introduced into the operation research by Charnes, Cooper and Rhodes in 1978 which is known as CCR model. This model has an assumption of constant returns to scale. Banker, Charnes and Cooper introduced a new model in 1984, known as BCC model. This model was an extension of the CCR model to accommodate the variable return to scale into consideration while analyzing the efficiency or performance of any DMU. In subsequent years, there is much advancement taken place in this technique.

The general purpose DEA which was developed by Charnes et al. (1978) is called as CCR model. It takes n DMUs into consideration, using m inputs to secure s outputs. The notations which are used in the model are as follows-

m: number of inputs (i=1,2,...m)

s: number of outputs (r=1,2,...s)

n: number of DMUs (j-1,2,...n)

x_{ij} : i^{th} input of jth DMU

y_{rj} : r^{th} output of jth DMU

$$X = \begin{pmatrix} x_1 & x_2 & \cdots & x_{1n} \\ x_2 & x_2 & \cdots & x_{2n} \\ . & . & \cdots & . \\ x_{m1} & x_{m2} & \cdots & x_{mm} \end{pmatrix}, \qquad Y = \begin{pmatrix} y_1 & y_2 & \cdots & y_{1n} \\ y_2 & y_2 & \cdots & y_{2n} \\ . & . & \cdots & . \\ y_{s1} & y_{s2} & \cdots & y_{sn} \end{pmatrix}$$

$$u = (u_1, u_2, \ldots u_s) \qquad v = (v_1, v_2, \ldots v_m)$$

The efficiency of each DMU is measured once and hence we need n optimization problem to be solved, one for each DMU_j.

Let the DMU_j to be evaluated on any trial be designated as DMUo, where "o" ranges over 1,2,....,n. We solve the following LP to obtain values for the input weights $v_1, v_2, ...v_m$ and output weight $u_1, u_2, ...u_s$ as variables.

$$\max u_1 y_{1o} + u_2 y_{2o} + ... + u_s y_{so}$$

s.t. $$v_1 x_{1o} + v_2 x_{2o} + ... + v_m x_{mo} = 1$$

$$u_1 y_{1j} + u_2 y_{2j} + ... + u_s y_{sj} \leq v_1 x_{1j} + v_2 x_{2j} + ... + v_m x_{mj} \quad (j = 1,2,....,n)$$

$$v_1, v_2, ...v_m \geq 0$$

$$u_1, u_2, ...u_s \geq 0$$

In vector matrix the above LP can be written as-

$$\max uy_o$$

s.t. $$vx_o = 1$$

$$uY - vX \leq 0 \qquad\qquad\qquad ... (1)$$

$$u, v \geq 0$$

The dual of LP helps in recognizing the reference set for the inefficient DMUs. These reference sets then help us in identifying the inadequacies existing in the inefficient units. The dual of the above model can be given in the following form-

$$\min \theta$$

s.t. $$Y\lambda \geq y_o$$

$$X\lambda \leq \theta x_o \qquad\qquad\qquad ... (2)$$

$$\lambda \geq 0$$

DEA is a technique which can evaluate the efficiency of a DMU taking both discretionary (D) and non-discretionary (ND) variables into consideration. The non-discretionary variables are usually environmental or competitive factors which are beyond the control of management. Even though these variables are uncontrollable still are important to take into account as inputs so as to estimate the actual measure of efficiency. The model which caters to both discretionary and non-discretionary inputs is known as non-discretionary variable model. The formulation of this model is given as (Cooper et al.1997).

$$\max \sum_{r=1}^{s} u_r y_{ro} - \sum_{i \in ND} v_i x_{io}$$

$$s.t. \sum_{r=1}^{s} u_r y_{rj} - \sum_{i \in ND} v_i x_{ij} - \sum_{i \in D} v_i x_{ij} \le 0, j = 1, 2, ..., n$$

$$\sum_{i \in D} v_i x_{io} = 1$$

$$v_i \ge \varepsilon, i \in D$$

$$v_i \ge 0, i \in ND$$

$$u_r \ge \varepsilon, r = 1, 2...., s$$

... (3)

The dual of the above equation can be in the following form-

$$\min \theta - \left(\sum_{i \in D} s_i^- + \sum_{r=1}^{s} s_r^+ \right)$$

$$s.t. \theta x_{io} = \sum_{j=1}^{n} x_{ij} \lambda_j + s_i^-, i \in D$$

$$x_{io} = \sum_{j=1}^{n} x_{ij} \lambda_j + s_i^-, i \in ND$$

$$y_{ro} = \sum_{j=1}^{n} y_{rj} \lambda_j - s_r^+, r = 1, 2, ..., s$$

... (4)

In the above model it is to be noticed that variable □ is not applied to the non-discretionary inputs because these are the uncontrollable values which are fixed exogenously and therefore it is not possible to vary them at the discretion of the management. Also, these non-discretionary values enter into the objective function; this is because the multiplier values associated with these non-discretionary inputs may be zero as we have $v_i \ge 0$ for $i \in ND$ however, the other values must always be positive. In the dual model s⁻ and s⁺ are the slack variables where s⁻ is defined as input excess and s⁺ is defined as output surplus. For a fruitful DEA study, the input and output should always be chosen very cautiously. In this study also the choice of input and output is dependent upon the firm's objectives, customer expectations and the literature reviewed. The next sections discuss the input-output variables and models used for evaluation.

DATA AND VARIABLES

There are 46 pharmacy retail stores under consideration in this study. Acting as an interface between the company and the customer, store needs to be well maintained for which it needs employees and is either available on rent or is self owned. All these tasks acts as expenses for the organization and therefore, some of the inputs chosen for the study include: store size, rent paid, number of employees, wages given to the employees, maintenance expenditure, marketing expenditure and other day-to-day expenses.

Retailing talks a lot about location. Vyt, 2008 stated that with the tremendous increase in competition and different market conditions, one of the major areas where retailers are focusing is managing the stores at different locations. In this study location is being quantified by number of competitors existing in a kilometers distance from each store and therefore, is categorized as an uncontrollable input in the study. We understand that older the store, greater are the chances of people being aware of it. Thus, another uncontrollable variable considered is age of the store. It is classified as uncontrollable because at the time of efficiency evaluation one cannot deduct or augment the age which the store has already attained.

For any business the ultimate goal is to generate revenue which is the outcome of all efforts put in by the organization. For generating revenue it is essential that customer steps in your store. Thus, footfalls and sales are two output variables under consideration in this study.

The following table shows the descriptive statistics of the variables which are under consideration in this study.

Table 1: Descriptive Statistics

Variables	Maximum	Minimum	Average	S.D	Variable Type
Footfalls {O1}	579.00	70.00	218.24	77.24	Output
Sales {O2}	650.00	40.00	187.28	89.80	Output
Store Size {I1}	600.00	120.00	249.43	99.51	Discretionary Input
Operating Expenses {I2}	229.47	40.77	122.25	28.22	Discretionary Input
Age of the store {I3}	93.00	9.00	80.83	13.65	Non-discretionary Input
Location of the store {I4}	44.00	5.00	20.13	5.58	Non-discretionary Input

RESULTS AND DISCUSSION

First, we applied the basic CCR model (refer equation 1 and 2) where only discretionary variables were under consideration. This model includes two outputs: footfalls and sales and two inputs: store size and operating expenses. Wherein, operating expenses consists of rent, maintenance and marketing expense, wages given to the front end employees including store manager and other sales representative and other expenses. The other expenses include items such as telephone, internet, electricity etc. The result of CCR-I analysis is as shown in Table 2.

Table 2: Efficiency Scores

S. No.	DMU	Category	Categorisation Score	Reference Set	CCR-II Score	Reference Set	CCR-I Score	Reference Set
1	2	1	0.9193	$\lambda 3=0.186$, $\lambda 15=0.842$	0.6656	$\lambda 5=1.24$,	0.6677	$\lambda 5=1.24$
2	3	1	1.0000	$\lambda 3=1$	0.7143	$\lambda 20=.194$, $\lambda 32=0.741$	0.7143	$\lambda 20=0.194$, $\lambda 32=0.741$
3	4	1	0.9587	$\lambda 3=0.114$, $\lambda 15=0.394$	0.5693	$\lambda 12=0.21$, $\lambda 32=0.289$	0.5694	$\lambda 12=0.2096, \lambda 32=0.2891$
4	15	1	1.0000	$\lambda 15=1$	0.9084	$\lambda 5=0.981$, $\lambda 28=0.264$	0.9093	$\lambda 5=0.981$, $\lambda 28=0.264$
5	1	2	1.0000	$\lambda 1=1$	1.0000	$\lambda 1=1$	0.9013	$\lambda 5=1.35, \lambda 32=.387$, $\lambda 34=0.786$
6	6	2	0.5567	$\lambda 7=0.152$, $\lambda 25=0.244$, $\lambda 32=0.277$	0.5400	$\lambda 12=.21$, $\lambda 32=0.289$	0.5400	$\lambda 5=0.079$, $\lambda 28=0.369$, $\lambda 32=0.222$
7	7	2	1.0000	$\lambda 7=1$	0.9550	$\lambda 12=0.22$, $\lambda 28=0.302$, $\lambda 32=0.188$	0.9550	$\lambda 12=0.22, \lambda 28=0.302, \lambda 32=0.188$
8	8	2	0.4553	$\lambda 32=0.253$, $\lambda 34=0.189$	0.4553	$\lambda 32=0.253$, $\lambda 34=0.189$	0.4553	$\lambda 32=0.253$, $\lambda 34=0.189$
9	9	2	0.7270	$\lambda 7=0.566$, $\lambda 32=0.228$	0.6927	$\lambda 12=0.183$, $\lambda 28=0.058$, $\lambda 32=0.374$	0.6927	$\lambda 12=0.183$, $\lambda 28=0.058$, $\lambda 32=0.374$
10	10	2	0.3837	$\lambda 1=0.128$, $\lambda 15=0.149$, $\lambda 25=0.161$	0.3410	$\lambda 5=0.417$, $\lambda 28=0.268$,	0.3410	$\lambda 5=0.417$, $\lambda 28=0.268$,
11	13	2	0.5894	$\lambda 15=0.245$	0.5357	$\lambda 5=0.24$, $\lambda 28=0.064$	0.5360	$\lambda 5=.24, \lambda 28=0.064$,
12	14	2	0.5161	$\lambda 7=0.349$, $\lambda 25=0.275$	0.4913	$\lambda 5=0.065$, $\lambda 28=0.507$	0.4910	$\lambda 5=0.065$, $\lambda 28=0.507$
13	16	2	0.7016	$\lambda 7=0.307$, $\lambda 25=0.413$, $\lambda 32=0.084$	0.6678	$\lambda 5=0.123$, $\lambda 28=0.659$, $\lambda 32=0.005$	0.6678	$\lambda 5=0.123$, $\lambda 28=0.659$, $\lambda 32=0.005$
14	17	2	0.7291	$\lambda 34=0.912$	0.6314	$\lambda 5=0.518$, $\lambda 34=0.415$	0.6319	$\lambda 5=0.518$, $\lambda 34=0.415$
15	18	2	0.7330	$\lambda 1=0.141$, $\lambda 25=0.702$, $\lambda 27=0.043$	0.6786	$\lambda 5=0.530$, $\lambda 28=0.658$	0.6789	$\lambda 5=0.530$, $\lambda 28=0.658$

16	19	2	0.5753	λ7=0.639, λ25=0.214, λ32=0.011	0.5392	λ12=0.014, λ28=0.72	0.5390	λ12=0.014, λ28=0.72
17	20	2	1.0000	λ20=1	1.0000	λ20=1	1.0000	λ20=1
18	21	2	0.5980	λ20=0.068, λ32=0.46	0.5980	λ20=0.068, λ32=0.46	0.5980	λ20=0.068, λ32=0.46
19	22	2	0.7313	λ1=0.0596, λ32=0.467, λ34=0.375	0.7273	λ1=0.024, λ5=0.253, λ32=0.674	0.7186	λ32=0.4, λ34=0.596
20	23	2	0.8637	λ7=0.052, λ25=0.583, λ32=0.207	0.8276	λ5=0.229, λ28=0.669, λ32=0.023	0.8276	λ5=0.229, λ28=0.669, λ32=0.023
21	24	2	0.6437	λ1=0.008, λ25=0.187, λ34=0.562	0.6017	λ5=0.348, λ32=0.327, λ34=0.037	0.6017	λ5=0.348, λ32=0.327, λ34=0.037
22	25	2	1.0000	λ25=1	0.9923	λ1=0.014, λ5=0.435, λ28=0.657	0.9867	λ5=0.457, λ28=0.668,
23	26	2	0.7308	λ1=0.417, λ25=0.006, λ32=0.343, λ34=0.228	0.7018	λ5=0.297, λ32=0.473, λ34=0.176	0.7007	λ5=0.223, λ32=0.403, λ34=0.319
24	27	2	1.0000	λ27=1	0.8247	λ1=0.038, λ5=0.01, λ12=0.384, λ28=0.387, λ32=0.201	0.8128	λ12=0.248, λ28=0.617, λ32=0.225
25	29	2	0.4741	λ7=0.348, λ25=0.357	0.4535	λ5=0.102, λ28=0.563	0.4536	λ5=0.102, λ28=0.563
26	30	2	0.6550	λ7=0.365, λ25=0.484, λ32=0.175	0.6187	λ5=0.133, λ28=0.879	0.6193	λ5=0.133, λ28=0.879
27	31	2	0.6536	λ20=0.148, λ32=0.517	0.6536	λ20=0.148, λ32=0.517	0.6536	λ20=0.148, λ32=0.517
28	32	2	1.0000	λ32=1	1.0000	λ32=1	1.0000	λ32=1
29	33	2	0.6170	λ25=0.163, λ32=0.123, λ34=0.544	0.5860	λ5=0.299, λ32=0.405, λ34=0.078	0.5860	λ5=0.229, λ32=0.405, λ34=0.078
30	34	2	1.0000	λ34=1	1.0000	λ34=1	1.0000	λ34=1
31	35	2	0.8292	λ1=0.003, λ15=0.169, λ25=0.726	0.8058	λ1=0.007, λ5=0.498, λ28=0.521	0.8037	λ5=0.509, λ28=0.528

32	36	2	0.5050	λ1=0.209, λ15=0.063, λ25=0.157	0.4482	λ5=0.475, λ28=0.189, v32=0.01	0.4481	λ5=0.475, λ28=0.189, λ32=0.01
33	37	2	0.7687	λ1=0.098, λ15=0.147, λ25=0.753	0.7326	λ1=0.101, λ5=0.625, λ28=0.411	0.7058	λ5=0.779, λ28=0.509
34	39	2	0.4942	λ1=0.106, λ25=0.283, λ34= 0.166	0.4527	λ5=0.379, λ28=0.212, λ32=0.129	0.4527	λ5=0.379, λ28=0.212, λ32=0.129
35	40	2	0.6965	λ7=0.472, λ25=0.161, λ32=0.307	0.6396	λ12=0.062, λ28=0.799, λ32=0.006	0.6396	λ12=0.062, λ28=0.799, λ32=0.006
36	41	2	0.9495	λ1=0.123, λ25=0.218, λ34=0.498	0.8706	λ5=0.547, λ28=0.009, λ32=0.407	0.8706	λ5=0.547, λ28=0.009, λ32=0.407
37	42	2	0.7332	λ20=0.41, λ32=0.309	0.7332	λ20=0.410, λ32=0.309	0.7332	λ20=0.410, λ32=0.309
38	43	2	0.6601	λ25=0.059, λ32=0.45, λ34=0.225	0.6470	λ5=0.113, λ32=0.551, λ34=0.053	0.6470	λ5=0.113, λ32=0.551, λ34=0.053
39	44	2	0.5348	λ7=0.525, λ25= 0.296	0.5060	λ5=0.046, λ28=0.683	0.5060	λ5=0.046, λ28=0.683
40	45	2	0.9772	λ7=0.036, λ25=0.144, λ27=0.442, λ32=0.27	0.8668	λ12=0.036, λ28=0.582, λ32=0.335	0.8668	λ12=0.036, λ28=0.582, λ32=0.335
41	46	2	0.8599	λ1=0.104, λ15=0.164, λ25=0.72	0.8015	λ1=0.104, λ5=0.73, λ28=0.305	0.7718	λ5=0.884, λ28=0.42
42	5	3	1.0000	λ5=1	1.0000	λ5=1	1.0000	λ5=1
43	11	3	0.9239	λ1=0.015, λ5=0.497, λ12=0.43, λ32=0.2	0.9239	λ1=0.015, λ5=0.497, λ12=0.43, λ32=0.2	0.8965	λ5=0.196, λ28=0.74, λ32=0.267
44	12	3	1.0000	λ12=1	1.0000	λ12=1	1.0000	λ12=1
45	28	3	1.0000	λ28=1	1.0000	λ28=1	1.0000	λ28=1
46	38	3	0.4336	λ5=0.326, λ28=0.464	0.4336	λ5=0.326, λ28=0.464	0.4341	λ5=0.326, λ28=0.464

As there exist an inverse relationship between input and the efficiency of any unit, we have calculated a complementary age for each DMU. For this we have chosen a value (T=100) which is greater than age of each of the DMU. The complementary value is therefore calculated as: ***Complementary Age = T – Actual Age***

Older the store greater are the chances of people being aware of it. However, while calculating the efficiency if we take the age of the store as it is, then higher value of age of the store will have a negative impact on the efficiency. Keeping this in mind, we have considered complementary age of the store rather than using the actual age.

Second, we applied the CCR model for non-discretionary variables (refer equation 3 and 4) which includes the same set of output variables: footfalls and sales and four input variables: store size, operating expenses, age of the store and location where, age and location of the store are non-discretionary variables. Table 2 presents the score of CCR-II analysis where all the DMUs are evaluated together using non-discretionary variables model.

Lastly, we have classified the stores according to their location. We quantified location through the competition existing in a kilometer's range therefore; the classification of DMUs is as follows-

Category I   : Stores facing severe competition

Category II : Stores in normal situation

Category III: Stores in advantageous location with very few numbers of competitors

Then we evaluated the efficiency of stores in Category I only within the group, stores in Category II with reference to stores in Category I and II, and stores in Category III are evaluated with reference to all stores. Table 2 also exhibits, the categorization efficiency scores obtained by applying the categorical DMUs method.

From the table it is clear that DMUs 2, 3, 4 and 15 are the ones which are facing severe competition at their location. Whereas, DMUs 5, 11, 12, 28 and 38 are the advantageous stores with very few competitors around. Rest of all other stores are facing a normal situation at their location.

It can be noticed that the reference set for all DMUs in category I consists of only category I DMUs. In the reference set for DMUs in category II, only DMU 15 is included as a reference set for DMUs 13, 35, 37 and 46 and DMUs 5, 12 and 28 appears only in the reference set of category III. This is in contrast with CCR-II model which is applied to all DMUs altogether, in which DMUs 5, 12 and 28, having full efficiency score frequently appear as reference set for most of the inefficient DMUs. These three units belong to category III which is a group of DMUs that are advantageous in terms of competition.

A descriptive statistics of the efficiencies attained are exhibited in Table 3.

Table 3: Descriptive Statistics of Efficiency Scores

Scores	Maximum	Minimum	Average	S.D
Categorization	1.0000	0.3837	0.7647	0.1983
CCR-II	1.0000	0.3410	0.7137	0.192
CCR-I	1.0000	0.3410	0.7092	0.188

Then, we applied ANOVA to test the following hypothesis-

H_0: There is no significant difference between the means of categorization score and CCR-II score and;

H_1: There exists a significant difference between the means of categorization score and CCR-II score

The result of ANOVA is as shown in Table 4.

Table 4: ANOVA among Categorization Score and CCR-II Score

ANOVA					
	Sum of Squares	df	Mean Square	F	Sig.
Between Groups	.060	1	.060	1.572	.213
Within Groups	3.425	90	.038		
Total	3.485	91			

As the significance comes out to be 0.213 and the F ratio becomes larger than 1, we do not accept the null hypothesis. Thus, there exists a significant difference between the efficiency scores calculated using the same non-discretionary variable model but two different methods.

Further, to analyze the impact of non-discretionary variables we again applied ANOVA on two different sets. First, ANOVA was applied to calculate the variance among the efficiency scores obtained through CCR-I and CCR-II models. In this case the hypothesis to be tested were-

H_0: There is no significant difference between the means of efficiencies obtained through application of CCR-I and CCR-II models.

H_1: There exists a significant difference between the means of efficiencies obtained through application of CCR-I and CCR-II models.

The ANOVA results are as shown in Table 5.

With this high value of significance (0.910) and a low value of F ratio (0.013) we cannot reject the null hypothesis therefore, there is no significant difference between the efficiencies calculated using the two different models. This further implies that non-discretionary variables are not making much of the difference in the efficiency scores calculated. Therefore, the two non-discretionary variables age and location of the store turns out to be ambiguous variables as the efficiency score are not much impacted by them.

Table 5: ANOVA among CCR-I and CCR-II Scores

ANOVA					
	Sum of Squares	*df*	*Mean Square*	*F*	*Sig.*
Between Groups	.000	1	.000	.013	.910
Within Groups	3.243	90	.036		
Total	3.243	91			

Second, ANOVA was applied to calculate the variance among the categorization scores and efficiency score obtained through CCR-I model for testing the following hypothesis-

H_0: There is no significant difference between the means of categorization score and CCR-I score.

H_1: There exists a significant difference between the means of categorization score and CCR-I score.

Table 6: ANOVA among CCR-I and Categorization Score

ANOVA					
	Sum of Squares	*df*	*Mean Square*	*F*	*Sig.*
Between Groups	.071	1	.071	1.900	.171
Within Groups	3.356	90	.037		
Total	3.426	91			

From the above result, it can be clearly seen that, in this case the null hypothesis is rejected because of a low level of significance (0.171) and higher F ratio (1.9). This implies that there exists a significant difference between the two efficiency scores. This further implies that the non-discretionary variables have impacted the efficiency of the stores thus, providing a more realistic measure of the performance of each store.

From this analysis it is clear that in case of non-discretionary variables which are not under the direct control of management it is better to go for DEA with categorical DMUs in order to obtain a more practical approach for the managers of the organization.

CONCLUSION

Looking at the customers' increased willingness to spend, changing trends of the service industry and huge competition existing in pharmaceutical retailing, we decided to measure the efficiency of pharmacy stores using both controllable and uncontrollable factors influencing their performance. An analysis of 46 units was carried out in the complete study. Through this study we have not only evaluated the efficiency of each store but also tried to find the impact of non-discretionary variables using DEA with categorical DMUs. For this, first we calculated CCR-I scores wherein we have calculated the efficiency of each store using the basic CCR model which includes only discretionary input variables. Second, we classified all the DMUs on the basis of competition they are facing at their location, into three categories. Stores facing severe competition were classified as Category I, in a normal situation are classified as Category II and in an advantageous one are classified as Category III. Then we applied the non-discretionary variable model to evaluate the categorization efficiency scores of these categorical DMUs. For this, we evaluated the stores in Category I only within the group, stores in Category II with reference to Stores in Category I and II and lastly, stores in Category III with all the stores in the model. The efficiency score obtained through evaluation of Category III with reference to all stores is termed as CCR-II score in the study. Further, we applied ANOVA to test the following-

(*i*) Is there any significant difference between the categorization efficiency score and CCR-II efficiency score.

(*ii*) Is there any significant difference between CCR-I and CCR-II efficiency scores

(*ii*) Is there any significant difference between CCR-I and categorization efficiency scores.

Through (ii) and (iii), we wished to analyze the impact of non-discretionary variables on the efficiency scores. The result obtained with the application of ANOVA, very clearly portrayed that CCR-II efficiency scores were not significantly different from the CCR-I efficiency scores. Thus, the non-discretionary variables age and location of the store were turning out to be ambiguous. There exists a significant difference between the efficiency scores obtained through categorical DMUs method and through basic CCR model. This indicates that efficiency evaluation through DEA with categorical units is a suitable method of analysis especially, in case of uncontrollable variables which are not under the direct control of the management. This is because with this method one can fairly deal with all the stores that are under consideration in a study. Otherwise, the analysis would be unfair to the stores existing in highly competitive market and would be too indulgent to the stores existing in advantageous environment. Overall, this approach is very useful for analyzing the impact of uncontrollable variables. Inclusion of People factor such as customer satisfaction or employee satisfaction can lead to a better analysis and therefore, to a better practical approach.

REFERENCES

Anderson, R., Fok, R., Zumpano, L. and Elder, H. (1998), "The efficiency of franchising in the residential real estate brokerage market", Journal of Consumer Marketing, Vol. 15, pp. 386-96.

Balakrishnan, P., Desai, A. and Storbeck, J. (1994), "Efficiency evaluation of retail outlet networks", Environment and Planning B, Vol. 21, No. 4, pp. 477-88.

Banker, R. D., Charnes, A. and Cooper, W.W. (1984) "Some Models for Estimating Technical and Scale Inefficiencies in Data Envelopment Analysis," Management Science, No. 30, pp.1078-1092.

Barros, C.P. and Alves, C.A. (2003), "Hypermarket retail store efficiency in Portugal", International Journal of Retail & Distribution Management, Vol. 31, No. 11, pp.549-560.

Bhati, Amita and Shriprakash (2008), "A Comparative Study of Job Satisfaction and its Impact on Employees Performance in Public and Private Sector- A Case of Oil and Pharmaceitical Companies" (Dr. Bhimrao Ambedkar University, Agra).

Charnes, A., Cooper, W.W. and Rhodes, E. (1978), "Measuring the Efficiency of Decision Making Units", European Journal of Operational Research, Vol. 2, pp.429-444.

Cooper, W.W., Seiford, L.M. and Tone, Kaoru (2007). Data Envelopment Analysis: A comprehensive text with models, applications, references and DEA-Solver Software, Springer Science + Business Media, LLC.

Donthu, Naveen and Yoo, Boonghee (1998), "Retail Productivity Assessment Using Data Envelopment Analysis", Journal of Retailing, Vol. 74(1), pp. 89-105.

India Pharmaceuticals & Healthcare (Q4), 2010, Business Monitor Intelligence

Joo, Seong-Jong, Stoeberl, P.A. and Fitzer, Kristin (2009), "Measuring and benchmarking the performance of coffee stores for retail operations", Benchmarking: An International Journal, Vol. 16, No. 6, pp. 741-753.

Mostafa, Mohamed M. (2009), "Benchmarking the US specialty retailers and food consumer stores using data envelopment analysis", International Journal of Retail & Distribution Management, Vol. 37, No. 8, pp. 661-679.

Rao, P.M. (2008), "The emergence of the pharmaceutical industry in the developing world and its implications for multinational enterprise strategies", International Journal of Pharmaceutical and Healthcare Marketing, Vol. 2, No. 2, pp. 103-116.

Vyt, Dany (2008), "Retail network performance evaluation: a DEA approach considering retailers' geomarketing", The International Review of Retail, Distribution and Consumer Research, Vol. 18, No. 2, pp. 235–253

Silver Bird Group Bhd:
A Case of Bad Corporate Governance?

*Tengku Akbar Tengku Abdullah**

ABSTRACT

Silver Bird Group Bhd, a listed company, fails to issue its 2011 financial reports on time. The aims of the paper are to determine whether its board with a majority of independent directors is in a better position to supervise the management, to assess the effectiveness of its audit committee and to determine whether its financial problems could be foreseen. The data for the study is obtained from publicly available information. The data for corporate governance is analyzed using SPSS Version 20. The descriptive statistics used are mean, minimum, maximum, median and standard deviation. The financial information is analyzed using the tools introduced by Hawawini and Viallet (2011) and financial ratios. The study finds that the audit committee is ineffective and the financial problems could have been foreseen. However, the study could not determine whether the independent board is in a better position to monitor the management.

Keywords: Corporate governance, board of directors, audit committee, independent directors, financial performance, managerial financial position.

INTRODUCTION

Silver Bird Group Bhd (Silver Bird), a listed company, is the manufacturer and distributor of frozen and fresh bakery products. It also sells telecommunication and financial related products. Silver Bird was listed on the second board in 2002 and on the Bursa Malaysia Securities Bhd Main Market in 2004.

The trouble at Silver Bird started when it could not meet the February 29, 2012 deadline for the issuance of its 2011 audited financial statements. Oh (2012a) reported

* Tengku Akbar Tengku Abdullah is with Centre for Postgraduate Studies, School of Business Infrastructure, Kuala Lumpur Infrastructure University College, Unipark Suria, Jala Ikram-Uniten, 43000 Kajang, Selangor Malaysia.
E-mail: tengkuakbar56@gmail.com

that '… the reason for failing to issue the outstanding financial statements within the relevant timeframe is due to the company needing more time to resolve audit queries raised by the auditors on Feb 22'.

Ng (2012a) wrote in the Starbiz'… So what went wrong? Did anybody see this coming? Were any transactions red-flagged before the independent auditors raised questions in the financial report?'

The motivation for this study stems from the failure of the company which has an easy access to funding from shareholders and financial institutions every year since 2002 even though it has not been performing. An analyst questioned the amount of that the company needed and where did all the funds go to, as Silver Bird was just a food and beverage company(Ng, 2012a).

OBJECTIVES

The objectives of the study are as follows:

i. To determine whether Silver Bird board with a majority of independent directors is in a better position to supervise and monitor the management;

ii. To assess whether the audit committee has provided an effective oversight that protect shareholders' interest; and

ii. To determine whether the Silver Bird's financial problems could have been foreseen.

CORPORATE GOVERNANCE

Board of Directors

Strong corporate governance is derived from independent directors and committees, the board size, the separation of chairman and CEO roles and the frequency of the board meetings. It has been argued that a board with a majority of independent members is in a better position to monitor the management (Bhagat and Black, 2002). In addition, a high frequency of board meeting enhances supervision and control (Shivdasani and Zenner, 2004).

The effectiveness of board of directors (BOD) depends on its audit committee (AC) (Lary and Taylor, 2012). As AC is an important mechanism to limit problems arising from principal and agent relationships (Fama and Jensen, 1983; Jensen and Meckling, 1976; Abbot and Parker, 2000), its effectiveness is a significant issue in good corporate governance.

Audit Committee (AC)

The effectiveness of AC depends on four variables namely, its coerciveness, its independence, its diligence and its competency. Coerciveness is a function of the legitimate power, influence and responsibility of AC (DeZoort et al, 2002). As AC is often used in organizational politics (Turley and Zaman, 2007), its role may not be effective.

Many researchers highlighted that AC with independent directors can secure integrity of financial reports as they demand a high quality audit work (Vera Munoz, 2005; Abbott et al, 2004; Carcello et al, 2002). Diligence is an important factor to ensure the effectiveness of AC and the literature identifies that the frequency of AC meeting and its size as proxies for diligence (Lary and Taylor, 2012).

Financial competency of AC members is a subject of a widely research area (for example Farber, 2005; Aier et al, 2005; Abbot et al, 2004). To be an effective tool of the board in corporate governance, it is recognized that AC expertise is an important attribute particularly on financial competency (Zhang et al, 2007; Carcello et al 2006; Bedard et al., 2004), industry expertise and a sound business knowledge (Salleh and Steward, 2012; Sun et al., 2012). Farber (2005), Aier et al. (2005) and Abbot et al. (2004) found that companys' with annual financial restatements were due to their ACs with lower financial competency. To avoid a high level of restatement occurrence, the Blue Ribbon Committee formed by the relevant authorities in USA recommended among others that at least one member of AC is a financial expert (see Blue Ribbon Committee, 1999). The restatement of financial reports may be due to a poor management control system and/or ineffective external auditor (Abbot et al, 2004).

RESEARCH METHOD

The data for the case paper is obtained from publicly available information from Internet namely from http://biz.thestar.com.my and http://www.silverbird.com.my/. The information on Silver Bird's board of directors and its committees is taken from the 2002 to 2011 Silver Bird annual reports. The data for corporate governance is analyzed using SPSS Version 20. The descriptive statistics used are mean, minimum, maximum, median and standard deviation. The financial information is obtained from the 2002 to 2011 Silver Bird annual reports. The tools used to analyze financial information are managerial financial position introduced by Hawawini and Viallet (2011) and financial ratios. Managerial financial position tool is used to regroup the financial position variables into invested capital and capital employed. The invested capital variables consist of cash and cash equivalent, working capital requirements (WCR) and net fixed assets. The capital employed variables consist of short-term financing and long-term financing. To measure the liquidity of Silver Bird, net long-term financing and net short-term financing are used. Net long-term financing is the excess of long-term funding after deducting the net fixed assets. On the other hand, net short-term financing is the amount of short-term debt in excess of cash and cash equivalent.

SILVER BIRD

Background

The confectionary business was started in nineteen sixties by Tan Chin Suan. The company was awarded the franchise to make Big Sister Fruit Cakes in 1978 and later in late nineteen eighties, it produced Silver Bird frozen cakes. In 1990, it won a contract to supply moon cakes and fruit cakes to Amway. The factory was later expanded to accommodate a contract to supply bakery products to Malaysia Airline System in 1992. In late nineteen nineties Silver Bird was formed through a scheme of merger and acquisition. The products produced by Silver Bird include frozen cakes and pizzas, fruit cakes, cake mixes, daily-fresh products and shelf-stable products.

Corporate Governance

Board of Directors

The Board of Directors consists of four independent non-executive members, three non-independent non-executive members and two executive members for the year 2011. The Board has a clear and stated responsibility. Among others, the Board is responsible for its strategic business plan, management of risks, succession planning, management control system and investor relation.

Audit Committee

The Audit Committee consists of two independent non-executive members and one non-independent non-executive member. The members of the Committee are Richard George Azlan bin Abas CA (Chairman), Lee KokChuan CA and Lim Hock Chye LLB, CLP.

DIAGNOSIS AND ANALYSIS

Corporate Governance

Table 1 provides the descriptive statistics of corporate governance of Silver Bird. Panel A shows Silver Bird has a Board size of six to ten members of which four are independent non-executive members. Its average size is 8.5 members. The BOD holds an average of 6.2 meetings.

Table 1: Silver Bird Group Bhd Summary Statistics of Governance Variables

	Mean	Minimum	Maximum	Median	SD
Panel A: Board of Directors					
Board size	8.5	6.0	10.0	8.7	1.35

Independent non-executive member	4.0	4.0	4.0		0.00
Non-executive member	2.5	0.0	4.0	2.7	1.35
Executive member	2.0	2.0	2.0		0.00
Meeting	6.2	4.0	12.0	6.0	2.67
Panel B: Audit Committee					
Committee size	3.0	3.0	3.0	3.0	0.00
Independent non-executive member	2.0	2.0	2.0	2.0	0.00
Non-executive member	0.4	0.0	1.0	0.0	0.52
Executive member	0.6	0.0	1.0	1.0	0.52
Financial expertise	2.0	2.0	2.0	2.0	0.00
Meeting	4.6	4.0	6.0	4.5	0.70

Panel B shows Silver Bird's audit committee. The size of the committee is three members. The committee consists of an average of two independent members, 0.4 non-executive members and 0.6 executive members. It means that the committee initially had an executive member and later was replaced by a non-executive member. It holds an average of 4.6 meetings annually with minimum of four and maximum of six meetings. In the period of 2002 to 2011, the financial statements were restated thrice and the financial statements for 2011 were qualified by the independent auditors. The reasons for the qualification were:

i.   Unable to obtain audit evidence and explanations on the validity and recording of certain business transactions,

ii. Unable to receive relevant information and explanations on asset impairment,

iii. Unable to review the recovery of trade receivable, and

iv. Unable to confirm from third parties on the amounts included in the statement of financial position (Silver Bird, 2011).

Financial Performance

Figures1and 2 show the managerial financial positions from 2001 to 2011. During the 11 year period, net fixed assets have grown significantly. WCR have also grown but not as significant as fixed assets. For the same period, short-term loans have grown significantly compared to the growth of equity and long-term loans. Figure 3 shows the liquidity position of Silver Bird. The net short-term financing has increased significantly as shown by the NSF line. In contrast, net long-term financing has experienced a deficit as shown in Figure 3.

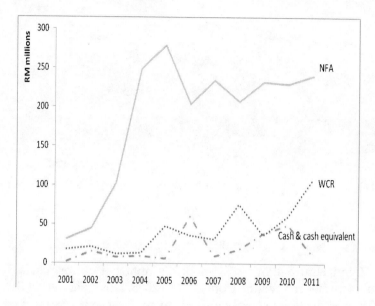

Fig. 1: Silver Bird Group Bhd Managerial Financial Position Invested Capital

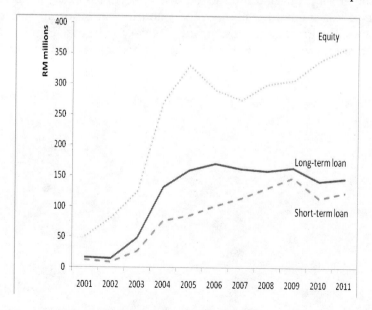

Fig. 2: Silver Bird Group Bhd Managerial Financial Position Capital Employed

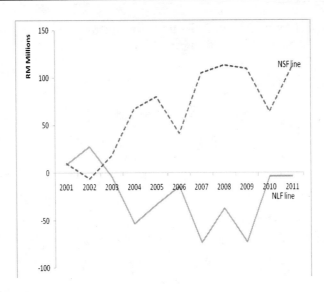

Fig. 3: Silver Bird Group Bhd Liquidity Position

Table 2 and Figure 4 show Silver Bird's financial performance. Figure 4 shows substantial increases in revenue from 2003 to 2005. However, it had flattened out from 2006 to 2010 and declined steeply in 2011. In contrast to the pattern of movement for revenue, the gross profit had not moved drastically. From 2001 to 2003, gross profits were more or less stagnant. Although the amount of gross profit had increased from 2004 onwards, the growth of gross profit was very marginal. Similarly, the earnings after tax did not show any growth. In fact, it suffered losses after tax from 2006 to 2008.

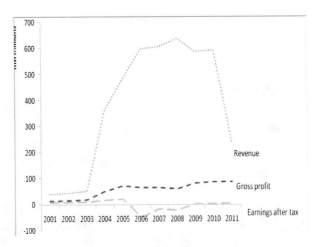

Fig. 4: Silver Bird Group Bhd Financial Performance

Table 2: Silver Bird Group Bhd Financial Performance – Ratio Analysis

	2011	2010	2009	2008	2007	2006	2005	2004	2003	2002	2001
Operating margin (%)	5.2	1.8	1.5	-1.7	-1.0	-6.5	7.0	7.0	21.6	19.9	16.3
Invested capital turnover (times)	0.7	1.8	1.9	2.1	2.2	2.0	1.5	1.3	0.4	0.5	0.8
Return on invested capital (%)	3.3	3.1	2.8	-3.6	-2.3	-13.1	10.2	8.0	9.0	10.8	12.8
Financial cost ratio	0.5	0.4	0.2	2.2	3.0	1.3	0.5	0.8	0.9	1.2	1.2
Financial structure ratio	1.7	1.7	2.2	2.1	2.4	2.5	1.9	1.9	1.6	1.2	1.5
Return on equity (%)	2.3	1.8	1.00	-15.0	-14.2	-40.4	13.0	12.0	13.3	14.1	20.3

Prior to year 2004, it has experienced a growth in operating margin as shown in Table 2. After its main Board listing, the operating margins are marginal and negative (2006 to 2008). The recent returns on invested capital and returns on equity are very discouraging with 3.3% and 2.3% respectively for 2011. The financial cost and financial structure ratios indicated that Silver Bird used more debt financing than from shareholder's equity fund.

Table 3 shows Silver Bird operating cycle management. From 2004 to 2010, its operations are reasonably well managed. However, from 2001 to 2003 and also in 2011 they are not well managed as indicated by Table 3.

Table 3: Silver Bird Group Bhd Operating Cycle Management

	2011	2010	2009	2008	2007	2006	2005	2004	2003	2002	2001
WCR/Sales (%)	46.4	10.2	6.1	11.8	5.1	5.9	9.8	3.7	23.7	48.4	45.3
Inventory turnover (times)	9.7	28.5	40.7	30.8	32.5	35.6	35.9	41.6	7.6	5.4	5.3
Average collection period (days)	201.6	31.5	29.1	26.2	27.2	26.7	41.4	29.4	89.9	167.8	170.9
Average payment period (days)	65.9	13.8	18.8	10.6	18.0	15.4	18.3	20.0	31.9	57.2	53.6

DISCUSSION

BOD is an important mechanism of a company's internal control system (Jensen, 1993) and board size is a relevant issue in the board monitoring and controlling activities. There are arguments that small board sizes are better in monitoring and controlling the activities of the chief executive officer and the management (Andre et al., 2005; Hermalin and Weisbach, 2003; Eisenberg et al., 1998; Yermack, 1996). Hermalin and Weisbach (2003) claimed that larger boards might have free rider and monitoring problems. To avoid these problems, Garg (2007) suggested limiting the board size of six to eight, to six (Jensen, 1993), and eight to nine (Lipton and Lorsch, 1992). Silver Bird adopted Lipton and Lorsch's (1992) suggestion.

Some researchers are of the view that a majority of independent directors are better equipped to monitor the management team (for example Agrawal and Chadha, 2005; Morck and Nakamura, 1994). In contrast, Bhagat and Black (2000) argue that independent directors are not independent enough. This is supported by Harris and Raviv (2006) who claim that outside board control may be value reducing. They state that,

> ... if insiders have important information relative to that of outsiders, giving control to outsiders may result in a loss of information that is more costly than the agency cost associated with inside control (Harris and Raviv, 2006, p 1830).

Based on these arguments and the literature, it is inconclusive to determine whether Silver Bird board with a majority of independent directors is in a better position to monitor the management.

BOD without an effective AC will never be able to monitor the management. Blue Ribbon Committee (1999) noted that AC members should have the commitment to go through the accounting and financial matters. The committee must be able to monitor external financial statements, external auditors, and internal control (see Larry and Taylor, 2012). An effective AC depends on its members' collective traits of being competent, intuitive and decisive (DeZoort and Salterio, 2001).

There are five proxies to measure the effectiveness of AC. First is to maintain the independent of external auditors (Abbott et al. 2003). Second is to protect shareholder interest by employing high quality audit services (Carcello et al., 2002). Third and fourth are the ability to ensure the integrity of financial statements by not having financial restatements (Abbot et al., 2004) and fraud disclosers (Farber, 2005). Last one is to vet the financial statement integrity by adopting abnormal accrual as a proxy for effectiveness (Klien, 2002). Based on these measures, Silver Bird AC has been ineffective as it failed in all the proxies but the first one. This is shown by the number of times that the financial statements have been restated and even qualified. The AC has not been able to secure the integrity of financial reports as financial irregularities in 2011 accounts are reported to be RM 111.5millions.Its external auditors, Crowe Horwath state,

> 'During the course of our audit for FY11, we expressed concerns to the audit committee and the board of directors over the validity and recording of certain transactions for which we were not able to obtain the sufficient and appropriate audit evidence and satisfactory explanations from management (as quoted from Ng, 2012b).'

The implication of poor corporate governance is on the company's financial health. From the analysis of managerial financial position, Silver Bird has been using short-term debts to finance its WCR and acquisitions of fixed assets as indicated by the increase in the amount of its short-term debts. This implies that Silver Bird has used more short-term loans to finance its acquisition of assets and WCR. This is confirmed by Figures1 and 3. Figure 3 shows that from 2003 onwards net short-term financing has extensively been used to finance its WCR and some of the asset acquisitions. Thus, the Silver Bird's financial problems could have been foreseen if AC was more diligence.

RECOMMENDATIONS

BOD plays a very important role in monitoring the work of a company's management. Its effectiveness has been a subject of a debate in the literature. Fich and Sivdasani (2004) confirm that a company with a majority of busy independent board directors who sit on three or more boards performs poorly. They state that '… firms with busy boards display lower operating return on assets, lower asset turnover ratios, as well as lower operating return on sales and that this effect is also economically meaningful' (Fich and Sivdasani, 2004, p. 29).In the case of Silver Bird, all its outside directors either independent or non-independent directors are busy with other work that they do not spend enough time with the BOD work. It has been shown that a firm with busy directors are '… likely to experience a decline in their quality of corporate governance' (Fich and Sivdasani, 2004, p. 29).Based on this argument, it is suggested that Silver Bird only appoints outside directors who are not busy.

BOD will never be effective if it has a poor AC. AC members who are not busy and'… with financial expertise with hands-on experience of preparing financial statements, or industry experience, are better able to monitor the financial reporting than those (sic) have no such experience' (Sun et al., 2012, p. 374).The AC member must also equip themselves with the state of the art knowledge on the tools of accounting and financial management.

Performance review is very important for key contributors in any organization. A survey at Fortune 1,000 companies in 1996 indicated that 69% of the largest companies in USA adopted a formal CEO performance evaluation in contrast to only 10% which assessed their CEO, whole board, and individual directors (Conger et al., 1998). Conger et al. (1998) suggest that the board should be appraised and they put forward the most effective techniques for this purpose.

CONCLUSIONS

When Silver Bird failed to issue its 2011 financial reports on time, many questions were raised. The negative media coverage to Silver Bird motivates this study. Using simple descriptive statistics and financial tools, the study finds that there is poor corporate governance. As appointed independent board members sit in more than three boards, the responsibilities that they are entrusted are not being discharged properly.In addition, AC is very ineffective. If AC had been more diligence, the financial problems that arise could have been prevented.

The study recommends that independent board members should be appointed from those who are not busy and the performance of the board and its members should be assessed annually.

REFERENCES

Abbott, L. J., Peters, G. &Raghunandan, K. (2003).The association between audit committee characteristics and audit fees.Auditing: A Journal of Practice & Theory, 22(2), 1-15.

Abbott, L.J., Parker, S. &Peters, G.F. (2004).Audit committee characteristics and restatements.Auditing: Journal of Practice & Theory, 19(2), 47-66.

Abbott, L.P. &Parker, S. (2000).Auditor selection and audit committeecharacteristics. Auditing: A Journal of Practice & Theory, 19(2), 47-66.

Agrwal, A. &Chadha, S. (2005). Corporate governance and accounting scandals. Journal of Law and Economics, 48, 371-405.

Aier, J.K., Comprix, J., Gunlock, M.T. & Lee, D. (2005).The financial expertise of CFOs andaccounting restatements.Accounting Horizons, 19(3), 123-135.

Andres, P D; Azofra, V & Lopez, F (2005). Corporate boards in OECD countries: size, composition, functioningand effectiveness.Corporate Governance, 13(2),196-210.

Bedard, J., Chtourou, S.M. &Courteau, L. (2004).The effect of audit committeeexpertise, independence and activity on aggressive earnings management.Auditing:A Journal of Practice and Theory, 23(2), 13-35.

Bhagat, S &Black B (2002). The non-correlation between board independence and long-term firm performance.Journal of Corporation Law, 27(2), 232-273.

Bhagat, S &Black, B. (2000).Boardindependence and long-term firm performance.Retrieved 10 Mei 2012 from http://leeds-faculty.colorado.edu/Bhagat/bb-022300.pdf.

Blue Ribbon Committee (1999).Report of Committee on Improving the Effectiveness of CorporateAudit Committees.New York Stock Exchange and the National Association of Securities Dealers,New York, NY, Retrieved 24 Mei 2012 from http://www.nasdaq. com/about/Blue_Ribbon_Panel.pdf.

Carcello, J.V., Hermanson, D.R., Neal, T.L. &Riley, R.A. Jr (2002). Board characteristics andaudit fees.Contemporary Accounting Research, 19(3), 365-80.

Carcello, J.V., Hollingsworth, C.W., Klein, A. & Neal, T.L. (2006).Audit committee financial expertise, competing corporate governance mechanisms, and earnings management.Retrieved 31 Mei 2012 from http://papers.ssrn.com/sol3/papers. cfm?abstract_id=887512&download=yes.

Conger, J. A, Finegold, D, & Lawler III, E. E. (1998).Appraising boardroom performance. Harvard Business Review, Jan-Feb, 137-148.

De Zoort, F.T., Hermanson, D.R., Archambeault, D.S. &Reed, S.A. (2002).Audit committeeeffectiveness: a synthesis of the empirical audit committee literature. Journal ofAccounting Literature, 21, 38-75.

DeZoort, F.T. &Salterio, S.E. (2001). The effects of corporate governance experience andfinancial-reporting and audit knowledge on audit committee members' judgments. Auditing: A Journal of Practice & Theory, 20(2), 31-47.

Eisenberg, T; Sundgren, S & Wells, M T (1998).Large board size and decreasing firm value in small firms.Journal of Financial Economics, 48 (1), 35-54.

Fama, E. &M. Jensen, (1983).Separation of ownership and control.Journal of Law and Economics,26,301-325.

Farber, D. (2005). Restoring trust after fraud: does corporate governance matter?The Accounting Review, 80, 539-561.

Fich, E. M & Shivdasani, A. (2004). Are busy boards effective monitors? Retrieve 1 June 2012 from http://papers.ssrn.com/sol3/papers.cfm?abstract_id=607364&download=yes.

Garg, A. K. (2007). Influence of board size and independence on firm performance: a study of Indian companies. Vikalpa, 32(3), 39-60.

Harris, M. & Raviv, A. (2006). A theory of board control and size. The Review of Financial Studies, 21(4), 1797-1832.

Hawawini, G. &Viallet, C. (2011). Chapter 3 - Assessing liquidity and operational liquidity. Finance for Executives: Managing for Value Creation, 4th Edition (pp 63-106). Mason: South-Western Cengage Learning.

Hermalin, B &Weisbach, M (1988). The determinants of board composition.The RAND Journal of Economics, 19(4), 589-606.

Jensen, M., &Meckling, W., (1976). Theory of the firm: managerial behavior,agency costs, and ownership structure. Journal of Financial Economics, 3, 305–360.

Jensen, M., (1993). The Modern industrial revolution, exit, and the failure of internal control systems. Journal of Finance, 48, 831–880.

Klien, A. (2002). Audit committee, board of director characteristics, and earnings management.Journal of Accounting and Economics, 33, 375-400.

Lary, A. M. &Taylor, D.W. (2012). Governance characteristics and role effectiveness of audit committees. Managerial Auditing Journal, 27, 4, 336-354.

Lipton, M.&Lorsch, J. (1992). A modest proposal for improved corporate governance," Business Lawyer, 48(1), 59-77.

Morck, R. & Nakamura, M. (1994). Banks and corporate control in Japan, The Journal of Finance, 54(1), 319-339.

Ng, F (2012a). Alleged irregularities cast doubt on Silver Bird's performance and position, say analysts. Retrieved 29 March 2012 from http://biz.thestar.com.my/news/story. asp?file=/2012/3/5/business/10845179&sec=business.

Ng, F (2012b).Independent auditors find poor record-keeping, unable to verify sales transactions at Silver Bird. Retrieved 29 March 2012 from http://biz.thestar.com.my/news/story.asp?file=/2012/3/2/business/10837501&sec=business.

Oh, E (2012a). Silver Bird directors working to keep operations going and to restore confidence.Retrieved 27 March 2012 from http://biz.thestar.com.my/services/printerfriendly.asp?file=/2012/3/14/business/10908325.asp&sec=business.

Oh, E (2012b).The company needs to explain delay in submission of audited statements. Retrieved 29 March 2012 from http://biz.thestar.com.my/news/story. asp?file=/2012/2/27/business/10811771&sec=business.

Salleh, Z. & Stewart, J. (2012). The impact of expertise on the mediating role of the audit committee. Managerial Auditing Journal, 27(4), 378-402.

Shivdasani, A. &Zenner, M. (2004). Best practices in corporate governance: what two decadesof research reveals. The Bank of American Journal of Applied Corporate Finance, 16 (2/3), 29-37.

Silver Bird. Annual Report (2002–2010). Retrieved on 25 April 2012 from http://www. silverbird.com.my/ .

Silver Bird (2011), Annual Report 2011.Retrieved 10 Mei 2012 from http://www.silverbird. com.my/ .

Sun, F., Wei, X. & Xu, Y. (2012). Audit committee characteristics and loss reserve error. Managerial Auditing Journal, 27(4), 355-377.

Turley, S. & Zaman, M. (2007). Audit committee effectiveness: informal processesand behavioural effects. Accounting, Auditing & Accountability Journal, 20(5),765-788.

Vera-Munoz, S.C. (2005). Corporate governance reforms: redefined expectations of auditcommittee responsibilities and effectiveness. Journal of Business Ethics, 62(2),115-127.

Yermack, D. (1996). Higher market valuation of companies with a small board of directors. Journal of Financial Economics,40(2), 185-212.

Zhang, Y., Zhou, J. &Zhou, N. (2006). Audit committee quality, auditor independence, andinternal control weaknesses. Journal of Accounting & Public Policy, 26(3),

Corporate Governance Issues in Unlisted Companies

*Dinesh Kumar Likhi**

ABSTRACT

Since 1980 companies are increasingly directed and controlled with a new paradigm "Corporate Governance". Governance has become an important and burning issue between corporate leaders, shareholders and stakeholders. In recent years it has become crucial for corporate leaders to establish and accomplish a system that guide and scrutinize their managerial activities. A competent system of governance helps to balance the rights of both managers and owners and induce the management to make investment in the projects and schemes which are beneficial for overall business. The variables such as Ownership Structure, Accountability, Directors' Remunerations, Risk Management, Internal Audit, Dividend Policy and Sustainability, have been reported to affect Corporate Governance/Performance. Both internal and external mechanisms of corporate board of directors play vital role in the area. The objective of the study is to understand effect of these variables in unlisted companies (Public Sector Undertakings), as SEBI guidelines are not applicable to such companies. It will require better insight on internal mechanisms required for effective companies' performance. The issues are understood with a hypothetical case of owner of small medium sized company who is ignorant about the subject of corporate governance.

Keywords: Corporate governance, audit, stakeholders, unlisted companies, sustainability, SEBI.

THE BACKGROUND

It was morning of 12th July'12, Deepak Gulati (DG), an entrepreneur was sitting in his office of private limited company with a Turnover of about Rs 100 Crores. He was going through his daily papers. He came across with an advertisement of a seminar on Corporate Governance, planned on 14th August'12 at Delhi. He reflected for

---

* Dinesh Kumar Likhi is Director (Production and Marketing) Mishra Dhatu Nigam Limited, Hyderabad .
E-mail: dinesh_likhi@hotmail.com

a moment and became inquisitive to know about the subject. Though he never felt the need of such issue in his private limited (un-listed) company, he felt necessary to understand the subject so that he could improve working of his board. He called his Private Secretary and advised her to send his nomination to the seminar.

On 14th August'12 he reached the venu of this seminar, well in time hoping not to miss the very introductory words.

A Professor of one management institute explained that Governance had been derived from Latin word 'gubernare' which meant 'to rule' or 'to steer'. He stressed that Corporate Governance indicated ability, capability and stability of corporate through Corporate Governance practice. These practices imparted balance between 'exercise of power' and 'acceptance of accountability'. Professor further explained that such problems arose in corporations because the agents (top management) were not willing to bear responsibility for their decisions unless they owned a substantial amount of stock in the corporation. He concluded his presentation saying that Corporate Governance was about promoting corporate fairness, transparency and accountability.

Gulati raised his hand after the presentation of seminar and stated that in his company such problem did not exist. He conducted his board meetings, where all Directors either his relatives or friends, participated with clarity of powers and acceptance of accountabilities. Gulati mentioned that, " We all bear responsibility of our decisions. We know if any wrong decision is taken, survival of the company will be in danger". Professor explained that importance of Corporate Governance issues were more relevant for large corporations, where equity participation was widely dispersed amongst small and large number investors. Mr Gulati started feeling uneasy with this answer. He felt that he had come to a wrong seminar. The learning from the seminar might not be of any use to his company. However he decided to continue in the seminar as he hoped that some good points might come up during the seminar, which might be useful for applicability in his organization.

In the session that followed he came across slides of second speaker which stated :

"The corporate governance should ensure the strategic guidance of the company, the effective monitoring of management by the board, and the board's accountability to the company and the shareholders. The board is the main mechanism for monitoring management and providing strategic guidance to the company. Boards are to be concerned with providing a strategic vision for the corporations. The accountability of the board to the company and its shareholders is a basic tenet of sound corporate governance everywhere. The responsibilities of the board include: reviewing corporate strategy and planning; overseeing management (including remuneration); managing potential conflicts of interest; and assuring the integrity of accounting, reporting and communication systems."

Gulati started reflecting on his own board meetings which were either five minute affairs or just on papers (as all directors sign papers, as advised by company Charted Accountant). He thought why he alone should provide vision and strategy to the company; monitor the management, be accountable to profit of the company and responsible for conflict resolution in the company. Soon after this thought, he started reflecting replacing some of members of board, considering their abilities to contribute in these areas. He thought of replacing his wife with one of strategy professors of his management school and his old uncle by a retired Indian Administration Service Officer for better policy inputs.

In the next presentation, he was excited to note that a study investigated the relationships between the internal corporate governance mechanisms and firm performance in Indonesia (Nuryanah and Islam, 2011). The study highlighted relationships between internal corporate governance mechanisms and performance in Indonesia. The findings showed that many internal mechanisms were significant in explaining company performance. It was also explained that the similar results were also highlighted from other countries including Indian industry (Yang, 2011, Chug, Meador and Kumar, 2010). Therefore, Gulati realized that the role of some specific aspects of internal corporate governance mechanisms affecting company performance might be necessary in his company. He started looking for some such internal mechanisms.

He started thinking in terms of timely and accurate disclosure on all material matters regarding the corporation, including the financial situation, performance, ownership, and governance of the company to his fund investors (equity and loan providers). He also considered that transparency would play a significant role in this area. He thought of hiring professionally qualified persons to prepare all documents with high quality standards. He also thought of considering for an annual independent audit so as to impose an external, objective control on the preparation and presentation of financial statements. He also visualized that journey would be helpful when he would bring Initial Public Offer in the market and would get listed in some of exchanges.

His reflections were endorsed in post-tea session, where one of SEBI official highlighted that SEBI guideline on corporate governance need to be followed up by each listed company. These guidelines summarize the structure of corporate governance in India as set forth in Clause 49. Clause 49 was introduced primarily to attract long investments into India. The report/guidelines addressed principally to the reporting and auditing of company results, but its effect had gone far beyond this rather narrow focus. It was intended that code would apply to listed companies-- and strictly speaking it did. But there were many different types of corporate entities, each with boards of directors, including unlisted private companies, subsidiaries of domestic or foreign companies, public sector undertakings, charities and educational institutions. It was worried whether such code needed to be extended to other Board driven organizations. It was also realized that developments in the corporate governance field were not fully controlled with legislation. There had been profound changes in Indian boardrooms as a result of Awareness, Advocacy and Adherence, and public attention in the last few decades. But focus to unlisted companies remained an important issue of corporate governance, to be taken by the regulatory department.

Gulati decided that he would work towards an effective internal audit function, which was supposed to assist management to fulfil its governance responsibilities.

During one of paper presentations, he came across that the amount of research on corporate governance in the United States, Europe and Korea was enormous. However, most of them focused on the individual components of corporate governance, rather than the corporate governance as an organized system (Choi, 2011). He got motivated to work on corporate activities such as governing activities, managing activities and investing activities, as an organized intervention.

He also learnt that most of the executive remuneration research focused on the principal-agent framework and assumed a universal link between executive incentives and performance outcomes. He thought of introducing compensation of his senior executives in terms of its organizational contexts and potential complementarities/ substitution effects between different corporate governance practices at both the firm and national levels (Filatotchev and Allock, 2010).

He also noted in his diary to fund poor and bright children of villages from his retained earnings. It was his desire to serve such population of the country from childhood. He could not do so due to different priorities in the life. He got impetus when anchor of the seminar presented results of a research that CSR highlighted engagement with the community, environment, diversity, and employees played a significantly positive role in enhancing Corporate Financial Performance (Jo and Harjoto, 2012).

One of the officials from Government of India gave a presentation on Corporate Governance issues in Public Sector Undertakings (listed and unlisted). He mentioned that there were about 250 Central Public Sector Enterprises (CPSEs). Majority of these CPSEs, including Maharatnas, Navratnas and Miniratnas, were earning profit and had improved their financial performance over the years. In the context of the policy of the government to grant more autonomy to the CPSEs and encourage them to access the capital markets for their fund requirement, Corporate Governance had become even more important. Under the recently introduced Maharatna Scheme, CPSEs were expected to expand international operations and become global giants, for which effective Corporate Governance was imperative (www.dpe.nic.in/sites/upload_files/ dpe/files/gcgcpse10.pdf).

The guidelines on Corporate Governance for listed and unlisted CPSEs were explained in sequence of Board of Directors, Audit Committee, Remuneration Committee, Subsidiary Companies, Disclosures and Report, Compliance and Schedule of Implementation. Official also provided a format to evaluate extent of implementation of effective governance. Gulati noted all these contents carefully in his diary, including structure and process of good governance at Board Level (Annexure-1).

End of the seminar, Gulati was surprised that there was no one from an unlisted company. With mixed satisfaction, he boarded his car and asked his driver to drive down to club for relaxation. On the way he pondered another issue of decision making process in his board. He had serious concerns about the quality of decision-making by the board of directors. He believed that decisions by the board were often taken on the basis of insufficient information and without due regard for either risk or the environmental, social and governance (ESG) issues involved. He recalled that a recent example of poor decision-making had been a decision by the board to invest a large amount of money in developing a major new product, only to discover later that there were serious concerns about the environmental impact of the product and a very high probability that the product would be banned by the government's Product Standards Agency. The board had therefore cancelled the product development project, with a large write-off of the expenditure already incurred. This was just one example of badly-informed decision-making by the board and he recalled that there had been others. He wanted to improve the work of the board, but was unsure about what needed to be done, and he was not sure lessons from the seminar would help him in this regard.

He was also not able to appreciate differences in guidelines issued for Public Sector undertakings and Listed Companies to draw lessons for his company. He wondered whether he needed a consultant for the same or he himself would be able to draw lessons from the seminar.

REFERENCES

Choi S. (2011), Towards an operational model of corporate governance, International Journal of Technological Management & Sustainable Development, Volume-10 (2), 165-179

Chugh L.C., Meador J.W. and Kumar A.S. (2010), Corporate governance and firm performance: evidence from India, Journal of Finance and Accountancy, Volume-7, 1-10

Filatotchev I. and Allock D. (2010), Corporate Governance and Executive Remuneration: A Contingency Framework, Academy of Management Perspectives, February, 20-29

Guidelines on Corporate GovernancedAccesed on 2nd June'12 at www.dpe.nic.in/sites/upload_files/dpe/files/gcgcpse10.pdf

Jo H. and Harjoto M.A. (2012), The Causal Effect of Corporate Governance on Corporate Social Responsibility, Volume 1006, 53-72

Nuryanah S. and Islam S.M.N. (2011), Corporate Governance And Performance: Evidence From An Emerging Market, Malaysian Accounting Review, Volume-10 (1), 17-42

Wheelen and Hungar (2009), Business Policy and Strategic Management, Pearson

Yang J. (2011), Does Adopting High-Standard Corporate Governance Increase Firm Value? An Empirical Analysis of Canadian Companies, International Business & Economics Research Journal, Volume-10 (9), 17-26

ANNEXURE 1

BOARD STRUCTURES AND PROCESS FOR GOOD GOVERNANCE

Structures	Processes
Limit the size of the board so that each director can contribute and avoid coalitions.	Develop guidelines for the use of committees to ensure that basic tasks are fulfilled and complex topics are explored in sufficient depth.
Separate the roles of CEO and Chairman to avoid potential conflicts of interest	Rotate directors through the various committees to ensure a mix of views.
Avoid inside directors on the committees so that executives do not audit, evaluate, and reward themselves	Ensure that outside directors, as a group, meet alone on a specific number of occasions every year.
Ensure a majority of outside directors so that tough questions are asked.	Choose a lead director to prevent insiders from dominating the agenda.
Require directors to resign upon retirement, or upon change in employment or responsibilities	Ensure unrestricted access for board to management so that information is not filtered.
Limit the number of other boards of directors on which directors can serve	Establish additional models of information-flow to ensure sufficient information.
Place the whole board up for re-election each year to maintain a mix of skills.	Insist on regular attendance at board meetings by all directors
Impose term limits to introduce fresh and potentially critical viewpoints while avoiding groupthink.	Establish an orientation programme so that new directors can contribute quickly
Establish a set of qualifications for directors, and use them to screen new candidates	Develop effective recruitment and evaluation process for the board
Impose a retirement age to maintain a mix of skill, energy, enthusiasm, and commitment	Ensure that the management reports regularly to the board on succession planning

PART VI: Crafting Strategy for Sustainability

Thompson,Stickland and Gamble(Crafting and Executing Strategy, McGraw Hill Irwin 2010) refer that 'a company's strategy consists of the competitive moves and business approaches that managers are employing to grow the business, attract and please customers, conduct operations, and achieve the targeted levels of Organizational performance'. The authors further point out that 'a company achieves sustainable competitive advantage when an attractive number of buyers prefer its products or services over the offerings of competitors and when the basis for this preference is durable'. An organization therefore needs not only a well crafted strategy but also a competitive advantage for a sustainable business for a long time to come. Organizations plan to reach these objectives through several approaches. Management literature refers to many classical approaches as building of a strong brand, cost leadership, cultivating niche customers, creating focused organization as well as out of the box concepts. There have been remarkable successes but also unexplained failures. Market dynamics, fast changing customer preferences, not understanding the moves of the competitors are some factors which contributed to failures of once highly successful business ventures. This provides a strong motivation to researchers to discover fresh strategies for sustainability.

This section is devoted to such thought process. A total of eight case studies are presented. Two of them (Abha et al., and Sahay) bring out the achievement of a high success by entrepreneurs in such a short time. The entrepreneurs happen to be first time businessmen without any exposure to a B-School education. Mark of 'out-of box' thinking is so visible. Jean talks of yet another out of box thinking initiated. Pathak, Nabiha, discuss new challenges of environment, and heritage protection vs economic advantage. Debasree talks of role of women in entrepreneurship. Katja discusses social capital.

Abha Rishi et al. present a case study in Chapter 29 on Emmsons International Limited- a fast growing company, dealing in physical trading of farm and energy commodities. It throws up the eternal dilemma of the entrepreneur- whether to focus on core business or think alternative growth markets.

Since 2004, winegrowers of the Saumur-Champigny appellation d'origine controlee have been committed to biodiversity. For the first time in France, winegrowers have chosen more ecological weed control methods . The aim of this case study in Chapter 30 from Jean-Pierre Noblet et al. is to show how some wine producers, in the quest for quality, have 'looked outside the box'

The Dawei Industrial Estate is principal means by which the newly-opening Myanmarese economy will engage with the world. It is being constructed largely by Ital-Thai Development (ITD), a company which has been involved with various controversies in large-scale infrastructure projects. John Walsh in Chapter 31 refers to major concerns as forcible evictions and environmental concerns.

The automobile has rapidly developed into the de facto standard for passenger transport. The study from Pradip Pathak and Rahul Dayal in Chapter 32 identifies various environmental challenges as faced by the industry.

The importance of women-led enterprises for any country's economic growth, and competitiveness is well known. However, gender gap in business initiatives in India is among the highest in the world. Debasree Das Gupta in Chapter 33 highlights this gap using the cases of progressive Indian states Gujarat and Kerala.

Swiftlet farming in Malaysia has contributed to its agriculture industry since 1980s. A.K.Siti-Nabiha et al. in Chapter 34 discuss swiftlet farming in Georgetown, a city which was conferred a world heritage status by UNESCO in 2008. How to balance the lucrative economic return versus the negative social, health impact arising from swiftlet farming, also posing a threat the heritage status of the city are major issues of concern.

Katja Karintaus and Hanna Lehtimäki in Chapter 35 discuss social embeddedness of strategy implementation. The case study presents an analysis on the values inherent in communicating with colleagues. The authors draw on a network survey conducted in four compenies.

The eist case tracks the story of Mr. Anil Agarwal and his amazing entrepreneurial run to become Chairman of Vedanta Resources Plc, the number two global diversified mining company. Sahay in Chapter 36 presents this teaching case where issues related to entrepreneurship like idea, ambition, risk, financing, technology, growth etc. have been dealt with.

Emmsons International Limited – Winging to New Horizons

Abha Rishi*, Anupam Varma** and Rupali Singh*

ABSTRACT

This case is about Emmsons International Limited- a fast growing company, dealing in physical trading of farm and energy commodities, in India. Emmsons has a global expansion of commodity businesses both from a geographic and product perspective, having seen a fast cycle of growth over the last ten years. It has increased its dealing from basic commodities to energy markets. But, the changing global trends are tossing up challenges for further expansion for Shivaz Monga, the group's ED. It throws up the eternal dilemma of the entrepreneur- whether to focus on core business or think alternative growth markets. The case also discusses the need to set up trading centers in geographical proximity to the top and bottom of the trading chain. The case has learning objectives:1. To understand how commodity traders have to balance global pressures with local demands and regional needs, and 2.To understand the need to diversify when dealing in volatile emerging markets

Keywords: Global expansion, physical trading, changing global trends, farm and energy commodities

THE CASE

As the flight started its descent into the Indira Gandhi International Airport in New Delhi, Mr. Shivaz Monga, ED, Emmsons International Ltd., could see the twinkling lights of the city spread out under him. In the twilight time, the many hued colors of the sunset looked very beautiful, but Shivaz's mind was on the issue which had been troubling him for quite a few days. The Emmsons Group, under his father, Mr. Anil Monga's tutelage had just touched $ 1bn in June 2012, but the commodity markets seemed set for a recession. The backlash of the tremors in the American and Euro markets were being felt in the Indian markets also.

* Abha Rishi and Rupali Singh are faculty with Birla Institute of Management and Technology
**Anupam Varma is Professor and Deputy Director with Birla Institute of Management and Technology
E-mail: abha.rishi@bimtech.ac.in; rupali.singh@bimtech.ac.in, dydir@bimtech.ac.in

During his immigration checkout, Shivaz casually glanced around. To his eyes, it seemed that the immigration lines echoed the world status, with fewer Americans and Europeans. As his chauffeur navigated the car through the streaming night traffic, Shivaz's thoughts flew back to the beginning of Emmsons.

EVOLUTION OF EMMSONS

Shivaz's grandfather, Mr. Madan Lal Monga, had been a highly reputed commission agent of paddy and rice from Punjab. He was known for his knowledge, expertise and honesty and was the face of paddy and rice for Indian exporters' when it came to procurement from India. Even the biggest rice exporters used to depend on him, but for all this efforts, his grandfather used to be paid a paltry commission. Shivaz's father, Mr. Anil Monga, had been vehemently against joining his father's trade as he felt that the exporters did not give Mr. Madan Lal Monga, the respect due to him. Anil Monga had been preparing to appear for the prestigious Civil Services exams in Mumbai, when ill-health forced him to return back to his hometown, Ferozepur, Punjab. It was at this time that the state of Punjab was going through turmoil, due to insurgency. This propelled the family to send Anil to Delhi. He had big dreams and determination, but the route was still hazy. It was with a view to check out the markets that he took a flight to Dubai. Enroute to Dubai, Anil found out that his co-passenger was a top executive of a large business house of Dubai and he in turn introduced Anil to his MD, who would be the reason for naming Emmsons. "EMMSONS," as he said, "represents sons of Excellent Madan Lal Monga – E (Excellent) M (Madan) M (Monga) Sons (Sons of M L Monga)."

That had been the beginning of Emmsons – no registered company, no bank account or knowledge of export/import business, but what had held true was the reputation for fair dealing and honesty. Emmsons started off in 1992 with just one employee and a contract of 5000 metric tons of Sulphur valued around Rs. 35 lakh (around $1, 30,000 in 1992) for import to India. That was 20 years ago and now in May 2012, they had crossed the $ 1 billion mark.

COMPANY OVERVIEW

The EMMSONS GROUP has its headquarters in New Delhi, India. The core business is to trade in physical commodities throughout the globe. It deals with various commodities in agriculture, energy products and industrial raw materials. The core strength of the group lies in its ability to procure commodities from its point of origin and bring it to the end consumer. It has an excellent supply chain management system.

In addition to procurement of various commodities, Emmsons has also made investments in assets that would supplement the trading activity and offer growth in the areas of farming, mining and milling, globally. The flagship company of the

Emmsons Group, Emmsons International Ltd is a listed company on the Bombay Stock Exchange. In India, Emmsons is a well known company in the Agro trading sector.

The group's global operations extend to 22 countries in 5 continents, including places like Switzerland, Ukraine, UAE, Indonesia and Singapore. Emmsons International Limited also follows the corporate governance route with fifty percent independent directors in the Board of Directors. The directors bring in with them proficiency and competency in the areas such as accounting, finance or even business experience with industry knowledge, strategic planning experience and tax expertise. Shivaz, himself, was a certified CPA from Australia.

Besides marketing various energy and agro-commodities, EMMSONS also grows and mines a range of commodities at different points in the food and power supply chain. At present, third party sourcing is also done from millers and mining companies. Some of the commodities that Emmsons trades in originate from the group's own investments in farming and mining. The company also has interests in milling and storage assets. Continuous and constant efforts are made to make the procurement process more proficient and competent. One of the methods that are followed to accomplish this is through increasing the number of suppliers. In the field of commodities trading in an emerging market like India, it is a vital component of a trading company's risk management strategy to have a diversified portfolio. In consonance with this, the group has acquired assets in Ukraine (farms), Indonesia (coal mining) and long term contracts (rice mills). Some of these long term contracts are in the form of tolling contracts. The group is also considering opportunities up and down the commodity value chain, particularly in ports, oilseed crushing and power sector. One of Emmsons strategies has been by staying in close proximity to the markets and regular contact with end-customers. This helps Emmsons in responding more rapidly to the opportunities and challenges that accompany commodity markets globally.

Trading

Emmsons is present in trading of around 20 major commodities, which are organized in 4 segments, i.e.:

- *Agricultural Products:* Rice, Corn, Wheat, Soya meal, Barley, Sorghum
- *Raw Materials:* Energy Coal, Manganese Ore, Cement, Clinker Aggregates, Iron Ore, Chrome Ore
- *Soft Commodities:* Sugar, Cotton & Yarns, Pulses, Rubber
- *Fertilizers: Urea, D.A.P.,MAP, Sulphur, Chemicals, MOP & NPK*

Farming

According to Shivaz, "*After a lot of consideration, Ukraine, which is also known as the bread basket of Europe, was chosen for the Group's foremost venture into commercial farming. Ukraine is geographically a good location. Add on to this the fact that it has a large domestic market which helps when it comes to volumes. Ukraine has a significant potential for the development of commercial farming. Moreover, its location allows Emmsons to control the value chain in terms of quality and delivery for trade-both in exports and domestic. The company has 7500 hectares of land on long term lease, wherein active cultivation of oilseeds, wheat, barley, sorghum and yellow peas are carried out. The easy access to Middle East and South East Asia is also a factor which swung the decision in Ukraine's favor. The Group's Ukrainian land banks are organized in clusters and are located close to the city of Nikolayev and port of Yuzhny. This helps reduce production and logistics costs and also provides access to required infrastructure and personnel.*"

Mining

The entry into the fields of energy commodities was triggered off by Anil Monga, MD, Emmsons group. His belief that energy security is an important driver globally and especially for developing economies to create sustainable and efficient growth platforms, was one of the reasons for the Group entering the coal and energy commodity sector. The Group also wanted to diversify its portfolio from just agro-commodities to newer sectors. Keeping in view the fluctuating trade policies of the Indian government, in relation to commodities, Emmsons decided to enter into the coal trade in 2008. As of today, Emmsons supplies coal across the Asia Pacific region, specifically China and India. It counts among its buyers to the various steel mills, cement producers, chemical plants and power utilities. As Anil Monga, MD of Emmsons, pointed out, "*It was a very lucid and clear strategy to enter into the field of energy commodities. The idea was that the activities in this area would not be limited to trading but would also include acquisitions across the countries. The plan to start the global expansion in coal mining with Indonesia was taken after considering all the alternatives and weighing the factors involved. The company entered into an agreement to mine coal in the East Kalimantan region of Indonesia through a 100% subsidary – Emmsons Gulf DMCC. The agreement is also linked to infrastructure development like creating and developing roads, jetties and integrated loading facilities.*"

Other Activities

Besides trading in energy and agro-commodities, Emmsons also has its own storage and milling operations. It also has its own packaging unit. The group has also set up Emmsons Asia Pte limited in South East Asia to concentrate on supplying to the region's burgeoning needs in food and energy commodities. Besides, Indonesia and Ukraine, the Group has associate offices in Switzerland, Dubai, Singapore and Cyprus.

YEAR-WISE EVENTS

1990-1992   – The foray of Monga family into the trading business as Emmsons International, a partnership firm, with import of sulphur and DAP in India as its first business.

1993   – Incorporation of Emmsons International Limited

1994   – Emmsons International Limited, the company, takes over the business of the firm

1995   – Emmsons expand into export of rice and wheat from India

1996   – Emmsons enters the market with an IPO and is listed on Bombay Stock Exchange (BSE)

1997   – It enters first foray into export of sugar from India

1998   – Company is awarded National Award for Non-basmati Rice exports.

1999   – Company awarded Niryat Shree by FIEO for agricultural sector

2000-2001   – Company awarded APEDA EXPORT AWARD for wheat and rice exports in both years'

2002   – Awarded NIRYAT SHREE GOLD TROPHY by FIEO

2003   – Certification of Merit awarded by APEDA

2004   – Import of Pulses and export of Corn are added to the trading basket

2005   – Awarded CERTIFICATE OF EXCELLENCE by APEDA

2006   – Enters into business of importing coal into India

2007   – Signs a joint venture with ETA STAR group with a view to acquire coal mines in Indonesia

2008   – Opens first overseas office in the name of EMMSONS S.A. in Geneva, Switzerland. Makes foray into corporate farming in Ukraine

2009   – Company establishes EMMSONS GULF DMCC in Dubai to focus on the growing middle-east business and manage the African Business. Awarded the Niryat Shree Certificate of Excellence by FIEO

2010   – Company Consolidates farming business in Ukraine by creation of EMMSONS GRAINS LIMITED in Cyprus. Awarded NIRYAT SHREE by FIEO and APEDA EXPORT AWARD – GOLD by APEDA for CEREALS in the same year for the first time

2011   – EMMSONS DMCC established a subsidiary in Singapore – EMMSONS ASIA PTE LIMITED to focus on South East Asian and Australian markets. Minerals and industrial raw materials are added to the trading portfolio. Ranked 18th in the middle weights segment (INR5000-9999 million) of the top companies in India and overall 349th in the list of India's 'Business World Real 500' in 2011.

INDUSTRY OVERVIEW

As the world slowly limped back from the great depression of the 1980s, the commodities sector saw a sudden boom. The emerging economies like the BRICS were in a large measure the reason behind this spurt in commodity trading. Rising demand in food commodities and other infrastructure related physical commodities went in tandem with the rise in the middle class. In the agricultural basket, domestic prices of commodities such as edible oil, rubber and coffee are driven by international trends. However, prices of other commodities such as wheat, sugar and cotton are largely driven by domestic fundamentals. This boom saw a slowdown in 2008 and 2009 due to the debt crisis, but then the markets recovered by the late 2009. The major slumps and surges have occurred in the oil (petroleum) and agro-commodities. Political, economical and social instability and unrest in many countries across the globe was another reason for the fluctuating commodity prices. Oil had reached a nadir at $101.80 on 30 and 31 January 2011 but the Middle East and North African unrest again led to a surge in the Brent crude.

FOOD STUFF / GRAINS

The food commodity prices increased globally quite significantly in 2007 and throughout half of 2008 creating a catastrophe of worldwide dimension. After peaking in the second quarter of 2008 prices again took a drastic swing down and fell during the recession but then again increased during 2009 and 2010 and reached a pinnacle in early 2011. The trend started reversing from late 2011. Commodity prices have been on the decline since the beginning of 2012 as reflected in the 12% drop in the S&P Commodity Index. Brent crude prices have dipped 19% so far till June 2012, while copper, which is used as a barometer of industrial activity because of its multiple uses, is down 7%. The main reason for the commodities' fall has been the slowdown in demand as a result of slackening industrial activity in China (the largest consumer of commodities) and Europe. In China, GDP growth and industrial production have fallen to 3-year lows. While GDP grew at 8.1% during the January-March 2012 period, industrial production stood at 9.3% in April 2012 and 9.6% in May 2012.

During the 2012 March quarter the rupee was trading at an average 50.3 to the US dollar. Though raw material prices have fallen since the March quarter, the value of the rupee too has declined, falling to levels like INR 58 to the US dollar have been denying Indian companies any significant gains in raw material costs. The rupee's decline has muted the effect of the global drop in commodity prices in the local market. For instance, Brent crude prices have dropped 15.9% since the beginning of the current quarter, but in India, the prices have fallen just 11.6%. Similarly, the 19% global drop in palm oil prices quarter to date has translated into only a 2.3% decline in the domestic market. The rupee's sharp depreciation in the current quarter is denying Indian companies any benefit from the global fall in commodity prices. If the sustained fall in commodity prices continues, it will eventually bring down inflation, giving RBI some reason to bring down interest rates.

COTTON

According to the Economic Times, Investor's Guide, 18th June 2012, "in the past one year 2011-12, average cotton prices) have fallen by over 20%. This decline can be attributed to weak demand not only in India but also overseas, especially in the US and Europe. In the international market cotton prices have fallen 50% over the past one year. With global harvest at near-record levels, the price of cotton is likely to remain under pressure for some time, unless there is a significant rise in demand. Weak demand has prompted companies across the value chain, from producers to garment-manufacturers, to refrain from placing new orders."

SUGAR

White sugar prices have depreciated 26.5% in international markets over the past one year in 2011-12. However, the prices in India have remained flat on account of expected surplus production this season. However, sugar production for the October 2012 - September 2013 season is anticipated to be around 26 million tons as against a projected consumption of 22 million tons. Sugar prices have been rallying over the past quarter, due to delay in the onset of monsoon in key sugar producing areas of the country. A deficient rainfall this season might result in a rally in sugar prices in the coming months. With sugar prices staying flat, many sugar companies have made losses in the past couple of quarters.

WHEAT

Talking about the fluctuations in wheat trading, on 15th June 2012, Dr Anupam Varma, an expert on commodities said, "*Global wheat prices had corrected by 16% in the past one year in 2011-12, but in India, they have changed little - rising a marginal 2%. Good harvest of the crop globally has ensured adequate stockpiles. However, the lifting of the four-year-long export ban has provided support to wheat prices in the domestic market. It means there is not much respite to the Indian food and bakery industry that uses the grain for biscuits, flour, malted foods, etc. However, with global prices remaining weak and inventories at all-time high, wheat prices are likely to be under check. However, the monsoon can play truant and change the outlook for the commodity.*"

Wheat is a staple food in many of the Asian and African countries. Increasing populations in these places combined with low incomes in Latin America and other countries like Nigeria, Kenya, Sudan, Bangladesh and the South-East Asia (Indonesia, Philippines, and Vietnam) have lead to spiraling prices. These places have a very limited production potential and need to import food grains. Another factor which has also contributed to the increase in food grain prices has been the unfavorable weather in major importing nations of Middle East and North Africa.

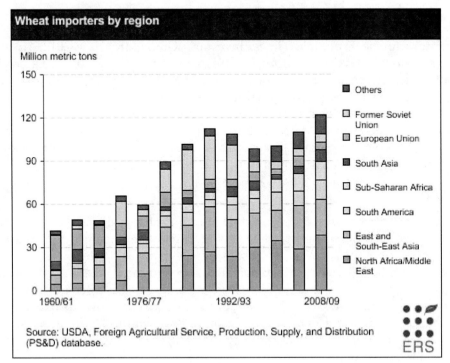

Quoting from the Business Standard, India, dated 28th June 2012, "Around 17 countries, including Japan, the Netherlands and Iraq, have evinced interest in importing wheat from India in end of June 2012, the world's second largest producer. Experts said that India is in a better position to export as the CIF (Cost, Insurance and Freight) of wheat grown in Australia and the US is close to USD 315 per tons. Wheat production is estimated to be bumper 90.75 million tons in the 2011-12 crop year (July-June)."

COAL

Referring to the trade statistics, India's GDP rose 6.1 per cent last quarter 2011 from a year earlier, the slowest pace in more than two years. The country imported 6.75 million tons of steam coal and 2.59 million tons of coking coal, Interocean data showed. Mundra port, on the west coast, received the highest volumes of 1.07 million tons of coal. Paradip, Krishnapatnam, Gangavaram and Ennore on the east coast received 984,543 tons, 796,994 tons, 747,843 tons and 706,041 tons of the fuel, respectively, the data showed.

Global coal prices today are at a 20-30% discount to their year-ago levels. The benchmark Newcastle, Australia thermal coal fell to a two year low of $87 per tons in June 2012 - it was trading at around $142 per tons at the beginning of 2011. Supply of coal outpacing demand has been the major reason for this steady fall. The global coal market has seen US producers increasing exports as cheap domestic natural gas replaced coal to a large extent in power generation. Countries such as Indonesia, South Africa and Australia increased coal exports, while imports slowed in China as inventory levels rose. This over supply is unlikely to correct quickly. But the situation may not worsen either, as high cost of mining in countries like the US may lead to supply cuts. Coal is a critical input for industries like power, steel and cement, and a fall in its prices is a big positive for them.

Falling commodity prices globally have brought some good news for India's policy makers. Due to the fall in crude oil prices and the import duty increase on gold and polished diamonds, India's import bill for the current financial year is expected to come down by about $60 billion or 12.27 per cent. India's import of crude oil and petroleum products in 2011-12 is estimated to have happened at an average price of $112 a barrel. Prices are currently $90-91 a barrel, a fall of about 20 per cent. According to data compiled by ICRA, a rating agency, crude oil imports for 2011-12 were $155.6 billion.

THE ROAD AHEAD

It was getting late by the time Shivaz reached home and he was still mulling about which markets and commodities that Emmsons needed, to gear themselves up to retain their leading position. Moreover, he wanted to make sure that the company had the diversified portfolio required to ride out the storm. It was then that he remembered his father's words, 'Commodity markets follows trade, whereas retail markets follow customers.'

QUESTIONS

1. If you had to advise Mr. Shivaz Monga, which country would you advise him to invest for the next level in international expansion? Give reasons.

2. Why did Mr. Anil Monga say, 'Commodity markets follow trade, whereas retail markets follow customers.'

3. Which products do you think are still unexplored by the international commodities trade?

4. Should Shivaz stay with the current portfolio of commodities or should he expand into other sectors? If yes, which commodities do you think Emmsons should deal in?

5. In the current scenario, what kind of expansion strategy would you suggest Emmsons, for future growth?

ACKNOWLEDGEMENT

The authors wish to express their thanks to Mr. Anil Monga, Managing Director Emmsons International Ltd. for permission to access information and data at Emmsons to develop this case. The authors are grateful to Emmsons management for consent to present and publish this case.

REFERENCES

B. S. Chimni, International Commodity Agreements: A Legal Study. 1987, Published by Routledge

Baretto Crystal & Somvanshi, Kiran K, " A Raw Deal", The Economic Times, Investor's Guide, 18th June 2012

Bhayani, Rajesh, "Commodity import bill to drop by $60 bn", Business Standard dated 28TH June 2012,

India Commodity Trade Statistics Database March 2012

The Guardian (London) dated 25 July 2010.

The Financial Express, October 16, 2008

www.ers.usda.com (United States Department of Agriculture- Economic Research Service, open source data sheet on food grains database)

http://www.emmsons.com

http://www.thinkingfinance.net/commodities.html#ixzz1sUHNmxU1

http://www.financialexpress.com/news/ban-on-maize-export-ends/373952/0

Good Absorptive Capacity for Good Wines: Saumur-Champigny in the Varinelles Domaine

Jean-Pierre Noblet,* Yvon Pesqueux** and Eric Simon***

ABSTRACT

Since 2004, the one hundred and thirty winegrowers of the Saumur-Champigny appellation d'origine controlee have been committed to biodiversity. In a sector sometimes resistant to change, and indeed for the first time in France, winegrowers have chosen more ecological weed control methods and concentrated on creating and maintaining plant hedges within zones écologiques reservoirs (ecological conservation areas)(ZER)[1]. The growers' Syndicate, backed by a powerful regional cooperative, rallied all its members and urged them to commit to the process. Collective awareness has driven the majority of winegrowers to "go organic" and with the ultimate benefit of being awarded an organic label. But going organic is costly in terms of time, labor and finances and inevitably increases production costs. However, despite the less favorable cost equation, their business model is nonetheless effective, and most producers manage to sell their entire product. The aim of this case study is to show how some wine producers, in the quest for quality, have 'looked outside the box' for new information (for example: sustainable agriculture, biodiversity, biodynamics), assimilated that information and applied it to their own operation and production for improved commercial results.

Keywords: Absorptive capacity, innovation, biodiversity, collective strategy, winegrowers, France

INTRODUCTION TO THE AOC

The name Champigny comes from the Roman "Campus Ignis" (or field of fire). Campus Ignis indicates a micro-climate ideal for making good wine. The wine in question is produced in an area where nine communes are dotted around the village

---

[1]   Jarno, S. (2011). *Grains de folie. Télérama, 3220,* 28th September 2001, pp. 27-32
*   Jean-Pierre NOBLET, ESSCA, Lunam, Angers, France
**   Yvon PESQUEUX, CNAM, Paris, France
*** Eric SIMON, ISC Paris, School of Management, Paris, France
E-mail: yvon.pesquex@cnam.fr, esimon@iscparis.com

of Champigny: Saumur, Montsoreau, Parnay, Turquant, Souzay, Dampierre-sur-Loire, Varrains, Chacé and Saint-Cyr-en-Bourg.

When they arrived in the 12th century, the monks at Fontevraud Abbey[2] started developing viticulture throughout the Saumur region. When Henri Plantagenêt, Count of Anjou, came to the English Throne in 1154, strong demand from the English nobility resulted in a wine making boom. Throughout the Middle Ages, despite the Hundred Years War, under the influence of the Dukes of Anjou, and specifically the renowned King René (1434-1480), the wine making sector saw considerable expansion. In the 17thcentury, Richelieu charged the Abbé Breton, officiating priest in Fontevraud, with the mission of planting the region with Cabernet vines. He obtained Cabernet Franc plants from Guyenne which he planted around the Abbey. This golden age continued until the French Revolution when the wars in the Vendée region caused devastation to the vineyards.

In 1886, an extraordinary individual came to live in the region: Antoine Cristal. He was an ambassador for Champigny and a fierce opponent of chaptalization and "anything chemical". He was also an ecologist of his time and slowly but surely discovered the nature of refinement and defined standards of quality for Saumur-Champigny. The prestige created by "Father Cristal" and many other winegrowers in the region brought about a gradual expansion in wine production which, from a few dozen hectares at the start, now covers almost the entire surface area of the *appellation*. Today, 1550 ha owned by 130 producers are shared by 9 communes and produce an average of 80,000 hectoliters.

When he died in 1931, "Father Cristal" had spread the reputation of Champigny far outside the area. His always authentic wine led his friend George Clémenceau to remark: "A country producing this wine is a great country, since there is no great country without history and civilization". Saumur-Champigny is one of the best red wine *appellations* in Anjou and the Loire. It is similar to the tuffeau[3] in the caves on top of which it is grown. Tender when young, it ages gently to gain the softness of its place of origin and acquires a purple color and an elegant and rounded flavor, with subtle elements of violet giving way to tones of raspberry and blackcurrant. The caves cut into the tuffeau[3] keep the wine at a constant temperature (12°C).

Recent history in Saumur-Champigny has seen both highs and lows. There have been euphoric times interspersed with difficult ones. The visit from the Pope in April 1996 and that of President Chirac[4] were both important events. In the early 1980s, Saumur-Champigny wine was much sought after for the tables of Paris, the "cheap

---

[2] Founded in 1101 by Robert d'Arbrissel, a Breton monk.
[3] Tuffeau is a porous limestone rock. It is a soft and porous limestone tufa which hardens when exposed to the air and is used in construction.
[4] http://www.youtube.com/watch?v=fFidRvX9X38

and cheerful drop" which can be enjoyed straight away. At that time and to satisfy demand, wine production increased considerably. For winegrowers, it was a time when it was raining wine (Laurent Daheuiller). The big distributors were buying in quantity, meaning less stock, and winegrowers were generally happy. The nineties saw the arrival of new problems: 1990 was still an exceptional year, 1991 far less so and 1992 was disastrous; overabundant produce harvested in the rain, rotten grapes, lack of color, negligible tannins and flavorless fruit[5]. Prices would plummet for some time to come.

INTERVIEW WITH LAURENT DAHEUILLER, SAUMUR-CHAMPIGNY WINEGROWER

We had arranged an interview by email two weeks previously with Laurent Daheuiller, explaining that we were investigating innovation and in particular dynamic capacities. Our exact words were: "…we are researching knowledge-sharing in organizations…" He responded that he would be happy to speak to us and a meeting was arranged. Upon our arrival in the Varinelles domaine, we were met by Laurent Daheuiller, tired after his return from China the night before. He told us briefly about his business trip, his discoveries, potential sales in China, etc. He was enthusiastic and the interview lasted over an hour, during which he did not avoid a single question, even the more indiscreet ones: "How much do you earn? Are price premiums in China really that high?" He proved to be a passionate man, and he was occasionally interrupted by his son (6th generation!) or employees requesting his approval, needing information or just letting him know a certain operation was underway or a particular vehicle would not be ready for another few days.

We found a cordial, spontaneous working atmosphere brimming with enthusiasm for the business! Today, he explained, "We are in a very good position: wholesalers come to tastings from November onwards in order to pre-empt the good wines and quickly grab the best ones. The quality of Saumur-Champigny wines has improved in leaps and bounds in just a few years".

The biodiversity journey then began in the early 2000s with Thierry Germain (another winegrower synonymous with the *appellation*), the first to discuss it with his colleagues at a meeting. From there, the Syndicate immediately took over. Relationships among the winegrowers were very good; many of them were taking over from their parents; several of them had been at school together and also knew each other socially. At the time, F. Filliatreau, Syndicate President, was a genuine and well-respected man in the *terroir*due to his extensive knowledge. He was able to promote good decision-making which allowed the Syndicate to surround itself with the right people. He then appointed a specialist from the Bordeaux ENITA (Maarten Van Helden) and

---

[5] http://www.lepoint.fr/archives/article.php/72525

encouraged the recruitment of a young woman to manage the project[6] who had proven very dynamic in assisting with the implementation of the procedure. Next, students arrived for the initial study phase and the hedge-planting period. The Chamber of Agriculture also played an advisory role in determining the best places for the hedges to be planted. Next, the funding: both regional and European grants soon arrived. Laurent Daheuiller adds that "the biodiversity concept came at the right time; wine-making was "quality-oriented and sales were good". Soon afterward, the powerful Saint-Cyr-en-Bourg Cooperative joined the project, encouraging its members to sign up to the movement. This is how all the members of the winegrowers' Syndicate came to be associated with the newly implemented Biodiversity Charter.

Laurent Daheuiller explains, "Since our launch into biodiversity, it has been a pleasure to stroll around the vineyards: everything has changed. We have hedges, there are no parasites and there are grassy areas in the vineyards." Indeed, walking in the vineyards of Saumur-Champigny exposes one to all kinds of encounters, from deer to sparrows, passing birds of prey, lizards, spiders and other crawling insects: there's life among the vines, which are in turn producing ever improving wines.[7] The effects of these decisions, he explains, are felt quite rapidly; the brand image of Saumur-Champigny continues to rise, the vineyards have become places to visit and tourist numbers are on the increase. Lastly, insecticides are no longer used (economy and quality improvement). Many winegrowers are now committed to this way of wine-making and are starting the process of obtaining an Organic Label. Today, more than fifteen producers have taken this option and their number is set to increase considerably in the next two to three years.

FROM GROUND COVER BETWEEN THE VINES TO COLLECTIVE RESULTS

For Saumur-Champigny producers, compulsory reduction of production is a reality, dropping from 68 hectoliters per hectare ten years ago to 57 last year (in 1982 it was a steady 77 hectoliters). Some of the best winegrowers never produce more than 50. At the request of the winegrowers' Syndicate, INAO[8] officers carry out "overloading" checks in the vineyards. If there are too many grapes on the vines, they inform the producer. "The producer then has to remove some of the green grapes; otherwise s/he risks another check at *"l'ebourgeonnage"*: the process of pruning opposite buds on the vine. This operation ensures that from the very start of spring the potential number of grapes is reduced. "... even if we had another year like 1992, we would do much better..."

---

[6] There is general consensus about this young woman due to the quality of her work and her many achievements in terms of motivation and administrative and human relations planning.

[7] Télérama, No.3220, pp. 27-32

[8] INAO: Institut National des Appellations d'Origine (National Institute for Appellations d'Origine)

Today, Saumur-Champigny is the first red wine *appellation* in the Loire to be sold by supermarket chains[9], around seven out of ten bottles are sold in supermarkets and hypermarkets (Laurent Daheuiller). Saumur-Champigny has a very positive sales record (+5% in 2011) in a market where sales of Anjou red wines are decreasing in favor of sparkling wines and rosés.

QUESTIONS

1. Who are the stakeholders of the Saumur-Champigny *appellation*? You may group them into primary and secondary stakeholders.

2. Identify the prior knowledge and past history (cultural elements, perceived characteristics of wine, etc.) present in Saumur-Champigny before the arrival of biodiversity.

3. Identify the typical variables (Appendix 3, Col. 3) which constitute the different absorptive capacity dimensions proposed by Zahra and George (2002).

4. In terms of the process exploitation phase, what are the effects of the process for the winegrower? Can one extrapolate these results to the Syndicate members?

5. Complete Todorova and Durisin's model (2007) (Appendix 4).

6. Can one say that a collective strategy has been implemented?

ACKNOWLEDGEMENT

The authors wish to express their thanks to Administrative Sciences Association of Canada for their permission to present and publish this study.

APPENDICES

Appendix 1: Some information about Laurent Daheuiller and his *Domaine*

The Domaine des Varinelles, with its lovely bucolic name reminiscent of lavender fields, is an old property run by the Daheuiller family. The Vineyard currently covers 42 ha planted with Cabernet Franc, Chardonnay and Chenin vines over several hamlets known as "les Petits Clos, les Bonneveaux, le Clos Marconnet and les Poyeux". The vines are very old, on average 35-60 years, with some plants dating from 1900.

The soil is calcareous clay. Grass is planted between the vine rows and the aim is to grow sustainably. This delicate work is carried out by a young, environmentally aware team. Nearby, at the house, the temperature-controlled cellar stores the vats in thermo-regulated *autopigeantes* (automated crushing) stainless steel tanks where the entire harvest will arrive once it has left the sorting table. Maceration takes between 15 and 30 days.

---

[9] Le Point, 10/09/1999 modified 23/10/2007, *www.lepoint.fr* consulted on 15/01/2012

Awarded numerous prestigious distinctions: "Saumur-Champigny 2010"- Silver Medal at the 2011 Independent Winemakers Competition and listed in the 2012 Dussert-Gerber Guide. "Saumur-Champigny Vieilles Vignes 2009"- Silver Medal at the 2011 General Competition in Paris, Silver Medal at the 2011 Independent Winemakers Competition and awarded a star in the 2012 Hachette Guide. "Saumur-Champigny Larivale 2008"- Gold Medal at the 2010 Independent Winemakers Competition. "Crémant de Loire Rosé"- Silver Medal at the 2011 National Sparkling Wine Contest. "Saumur Blanc 2009 L'Ingénue"-listed in the 2012 Dussert-Gerber Guide.And "Saumur-Champigny Laurientale 2010"- awarded a star in the 2012 Hachette Guide, etc., to mention but the most recent.

Source, and to find out more: http://www.daheuiller.com/, consulted on 22/12/2011.

Appendix 2: Thierry Germain, winegrower and founder of the biodiversity concept in Saumur-Champigny

Thierry Germain, a Varrains producer, is the man who persuaded the Saumur-Champigny winegrowers' Syndicate to sign the now famous biodiversity charter. An advocate of biodynamics, motivated by his reading of *The Metamorphosis of Plants* by Johann Wolfgang von Goethe, Thierry Germain views and treats his vines as living beings and equals. "Never harm it in any way when pruning, don't cut the new shoots or brutally constrain it, on the contrary you must let it grow at its own pace, guide it gently. It is not a wine pump; it is another living being which deserves respect. I like to think of the vine as an upside-down person, feet in the air, pointing to the cosmos and head in the nutritious earth". Amongst the vines, the Bordelais, planted in Varrains in 1991, is thriving. "This will be a difficult year, especially for the whites", he says, inspecting his grapes. In 2010, Thierry Germain was voted "Winegrower of the Year" by the very exacting *Revue des vins de France*, a title granted for the first time to a producer of Loire wines.

In discussion with Thierry Germain one sunny Wednesday in December 2011, he confessed that his inspiration had come from Roussillon, specifically the Rousselot *domaine*. Rousillon remains for him a prime example of biodiversity, so great is the improvement of its landscape and wines.

Source: http://prumtiersen.typepad.com/journal/2011/10/au-pays-du-saumur-champigny-adieu-chimie.html (consulted 23/12/2011) and entretien auteurs /Thierry Germain 21/12/2011

Appendix 3: Different absorptive capacity dimensions according to Zahra and George (2002)

- **Acquisition** is defined as the firm's ability to identify, value and acquire external knowledge critical to the firm's operations.

- **Assimilation** is defined as the firm's ability to absorb external knowledge; it refers to the routines and processes that allow it to understand, analyze and interpret information obtained from external sources.
- **Transformation** is the firm's ability to develop routines that facilitate combining existing knowledge and the newly acquired and assimilated knowledge.
- **Exploitation** is the firm's ability to apply the new external knowledge commercially in order to achieve organizational objectives.

Appendix 4: Todorova and Durisin's Absorption Capacity Model (2007)

Todorova and Durisin (2007) suggest a model for the absorptive capacity of knowledge:

- At the input stage, the organization seeks to recognize the value of past knowledge, its own experience and the experience of others.
- The absorptive capacity process takes Zahra and George's categories (Appendix 2) and determines power relationships, regimes of appropriability, social integration mechanisms and activation triggers.
- At the output stage, the authors concentrate on the competitive advantages generated by the previous process.

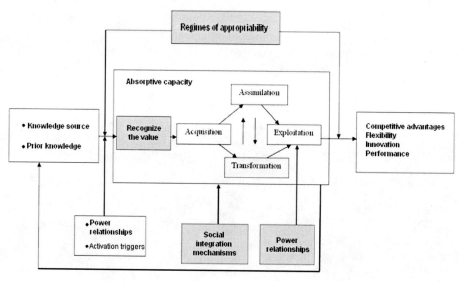

BIBLIOGRAPHY

Astley, W.G. & Fombrun, C.J. (1983). Collective strategy: social ecology of organizational Environments. Academy of Management Review, 8(4), 576-587.

Fourcade, C. (2006). L'internationalisation des PME et ses conséquences sur les stratégies entrepreneuriales. In les Actes du 8ème Congrès CIFEPME, Fribourg, 25-27 octobre 2006.

Gueguen, G., Pellegrin-Boucher, E. et Torrès, O. (2005). Des stratégies collectives aux écosystèmes d'affaires : le secteur des logiciels comme illustration. In S. Yami, F. Le Roy (éds), Les stratégies collectives : rivaliser et coopérer avec ses concurrents, EMS, Caen.

Todorova, G. & Durisin, B. (2007). Absorptive Capacity: Valuing a Reconceptualization. Academy of Management Review, 32(3), 774-786.

Zahra, S.A. & George, G. (2002). Absorptive capacity: A review, reconceptualization and extension. Academy of Management Journal, 27(2), 185-203.

Ital-Thai Development Co. Ltd.

*John Walsh**

ABSTRACT

The Dawei Industrial Estate is one of the principal means by which the newly-opening Burmese [Myanmarese] economy will engage with the world. It is being constructed largely by Ital-Thai Development (ITD), a company which has been involved with various controversies in large-scale infrastructure projects. Dawei faces concerns over forcible evictions and environmental concerns: how does ITD deal with these issues?

Keywords: Infrastructure, environmental concerns, Special Economic Zones, Italian-Thai Development Public Company Limited (ITD).

INTRODUCTION

For several decades, Myanmar* remained locked into oppressive military control and it seemed as if nothing would change. Western countries, led by the USA, maintained a boycott on investment and tourism but this was only partly effective because there were sufficient companies, mostly East Asian, willing to conduct business with the junta to provide sufficient revenue for it to continue in business. Crucially, the Chinese government provided diplomatic and military support, the former to shield the Burmese government from meaningful censure in the United Nations Permanent Security Council by virtue of its veto and the latter to enable the armed forces, the *Tatmadaw*, to continue to prosecute campaigns against a variety of insurgence ethnic minority groups and also to intimidate the population into timid deference.

However, change did eventually come, through a variety of events which may or may not have been directly connected to each other. In 2005, the Burmese government announced that it would be moving the capital from the colonial city of

---

* John Walsh, Shinawatra University, Bangkok, Thailand.
E-mail: jcwalsh100@hotmail.com

Yangon (Rangoon) to Naypyidaw, a small town that had been historically important in the past but of no apparent significance in the present. The move was controversial in that the new capital seemed to offer few if any facilities beyond the newly-built government buildings and both embassy staff and business headquarters preferred to maintain their presence in Yangon. The new site did have the benefit of being located close to a site which had once symbolized legitimization of the Burmese state and it was suggested that this was merely a case of reinventing the long-standing Burmese tradition of moving the capital from time to time. The site was also free of all colonial connotations and appeared to be strategically located within an emerging road network that would permit government forces to be transferred swiftly around the country.[1]

In 2008, the Saffron Revolution of the monks in search of democracy and observance of human rights was brutally suppressed, while the indifference of the junta to the suffering of millions of its people in the wake of the devastation of Cyclone Nargis led to international condemnation. Meanwhile, behind the scenes, Chinese influence was growing as its corporations began to build the infrastructure that would be necessary to move oil and gas by pipeline directly from the coast of Myanmar to the provincial capital of Kunming. Already, small-scale and often informal migration and investment by Chinese individuals in firms in the north of the country around Mandalay had made the area more Chinese than Burmese.[2] Now the Chinese presence was to take on a more formal and permanent aspect.

The Cyclone Nargis period had also been marked by the junta's attempt to pass by referendum a new constitution which would ostensibly lead to a road map to democratization and normality – the democratic system had been placed in abeyance after the 1991 elections had resulted in a crushing victory for the opposition National League for Democracy (NLD). This result was simply ignored by the junta and the NLD leader, Daw Aung San Suu Kyi was placed under lengthy house arrest. Suddenly, it seemed, in 2010, the country was preparing for new elections and a return to some form of democracy. Opinions about what had brought about this change of heart were, in outside observers, mixed. Some assumed it was the result of outside pressure, others that the junta had realised the old way of governing was becoming unsustainable and incommensurate with the complex economic activities and knowledge required in the age of globalisation and, therefore, had created a new model of governance with a patina of democracy; few thought that the generals had had a change of heart and repented of their former actions. Whatever the reason, Aung San Suu Kyi was released, elected to parliament as a member of the opposition and began to travel

---

[1]   Preecharushh, Dulyapak, *Naypyidaw: The New Capital of Burma* (Bangkok: White Lotus, 2009).

[2]   Myint-U, Thant, *Where China Meets India: Burma and the New Crossroads of Asia* (New York: Farrar, Straus and Giroux, 2011), pp.36-44.

the world to receive both the Nobel Peace Prize she had been awarded some years before and the good wishes of numerous international observers.[3] In March, 2011, democratic rule was proclaimed.

DAWEI SEZ

The city of Dawei is located on the south western coast of Myanmar and has the potential to become a deep-water port and, hence, of significant importance for the shipping trade. The potentially large-scale extraction of oil and gas from the Gulf of Martaban, not to mention the expected arrival of freighters full of oil bound for China necessitated such a part of the provision of a suitable area in which hydrocarbon and chemical processing facilities could be conveniently situated. Such a site, presumably an industrial park of some site, would require reliable connections with electricity, water and telecommunications, security and the provision of substantial numbers of properly trained workers, preferably workers who were both docile and cheap. The Chinese model of development, as demonstrated by the building of the Three Gorges and other dams, would require any villagers inconveniently located in the area to be developed simply to be resettled elsewhere, at government expense. The Burmese government, too, had been quite willing to resettle thousands of people, forcibly if required, when building its own dams. Indeed, it had been rumoured that the resettlements had been arranged primarily as a means of dispersing large concentrations of sympathisers of ethnic insurgencies using them as part of the Maoist strategy of the fish living in the water that sustains it.

The city of Dawei itself is part of a generally poor province that offered most of its villagers a decent enough living through fishing or harvesting rice, fruit and cashew nuts. However, education and other public services were scanty and the lack of opportunities available for young people unwilling to be part of the prevailing subsistence agricultural system demonstrated by the fact that so many of them preferred to cross the nearby border to take their chances working in Thailand, irrespective of the often difficult and even abusive workplace and daily conditions most of them who could not manage to become part of the formal, registered sector would face. Millions of workers entered Thailand from neighbouring Burma, Laos and Cambodia, attracted by the thought of relatively well-paid work in the fishing and plantation sectors, where they could work legally or in the construction sites, service stations and homes of rich Thais in Bangkok, where they could hope for the best on a mostly illegal basis.

Being close to the border, citizens of Dawei were familiar with the idea of their family members, friends and neighbours crossing the border on a short-term basis

---

[3] "Burma's Aung San Suu Kyi Set for US Visit," *BBC News Online* (July 18th, 2012), available at: http://www.bbc.co.uk/news/world-asia-18881492.

as well as on lengthier absences as a means of earning additional income, perhaps to meet some family emergency, support someone in education or just generally try to build up some household capital in the event of another disaster. The border crossings were made more problematic because of the border refugee camps, the Tatmadaw patrols and the presence of insurgent Karen National Liberation Army (KNLA) fighters but periods of ceasefire were common enough for people to have confidence to make the journey on a more or less regular basis. The enmity felt by some from Thai employers and officials resulting from a long history of a conflict kept alive by bursts of nationalism on either side of the border was considered simply another part of a price worth paying.

The neighbouring Thai province of Kanchanaburi was part of a much richer and more developed country. Its fertile agricultural lands were boosted by advanced chemical inputs and linked to important markets by good transport links. Its many factories were part of special economic zones (SEZs) and industrial estates (IEs) that had been an important part of both the development of the economy and the modernization of society. They were powerful symbols of the factory age through which most of the rapidly developed countries of East Asia had passed on their route out of poverty. They were also important parts of the means by which China had created its own so-called 'miracle.' They would seem to be an important tool for the Burmese government, democratic or otherwise, to govern its own country using new and valuable streams of income.

SPECIAL ECONOMIC ZONES

The economic benefits of placing commercial firms in close proximity with each other had been established since the work of Alfred Marshall in the C19th.[4] Proximity enabled the exchange of ideas, the development of an extremely specialised workforce and the embedding of technical and managerial competency within a specific location. The particular benefit of using an SEZ for this purpose is that, by manipulating the legal system and taxation schedule within a specific but limited area, it is possible to create conditions attractive to both domestic and international investors to establish their projects there at a place specified by the governing powers. The concept has proved very popular not just with governments and investors but also with international funding partners (e.g. the World Bank and the Asian Development Bank) because SEZs offer apparently tangible measures of progress in development with easily quantifiable metrics of success in terms of numbers of jobs generated, dollars invested and products manufactured and exported.

IEs and SEZs became popular around the world but particularly in Asia, where the thought of putting millions of peasants into more productive employment appealed

---

[4] Marshall, Alfred, *Principles of Economics* (London: Macmillan, 1890).

greatly to authoritarian and democratic governments alike. The former type had the ability more easily to suppress troublemakers in the workplace through criminalizing freedom of speech and association and using deadly force to keep the conveyor belts moving. Similar tactics were employed to prevent inconvenient details of pollution and other negative externalities from appearing in the press. Rates of cancer around the factories of Thailand's Map Tha Put IE, for example, are notoriously difficult to discover, as too are credible statistics about the incidence and severity of workplace accidents within its factories.

Not all SEZs are successful, of course: some are poorly located and unpopular, some attract a mix of investment projects which fail to combine together in any positive way and some seem to be blighted by ill luck or natural disaster which makes them too expensive to operate. However, by carefully selecting the location and spending what is necessary to ensure the right kind of stable connectivity with all necessary inputs and markets, the risks can be minimised, although not eliminated altogether.

In the case of Dawei SEZ, the location was determined by the presence of the port, the need for space for processing facilities and the relative proximity of the Thai market. Although Thailand had been successfully operating its own version of the factory age for some decades, it had started to reach the limit of the economic development that could be achieved by that means. This is known as the Middle Income Trap and it is a trap because powerful incentives exist with many organisations and institutions that, having prospered because of the factory age, wish to keep it in operation for as long as possible. Nevertheless, different means are required if high income status is to be achieved, as the examples of South Korea, Japan and Singapore all attest.

That the limits of the factory age were being reached in Thailand had become evident for some years: not only were wages and standards of living improving, thereby squeezing profits on goods offering competitiveness primarily through low labour costs but some new investment projects aiming to compete on that basis had instead been diverted to Vietnam or China. In 2011, the newly-elected Pheu Thai party promised to signal the beginning of the end of the factory age in Thailand by raising the minimum wage rate in a number of industrially important provinces by more than 40% and to roll out the policy nationwide in due course.[5] This had been an important manifesto pledge and one derided as 'populist' by the pro-establishment Democrat Party, which was swept out of the office it had only won by the intervention of the Royal Thai Army. Clearly, therefore, there was a significant pool of Thai investors and managers who could see the benefit of creating a new factory age across the border and beginning with Dawei SEZ, which, with its projected size of some 250 sq. kms. was projected to be the largest such venture in Southeast Asia.

---

[5] Charoensuthipan, Pernchan, "Entry Wages Backed by Bosses, Workers," *Bangkok Post* (February 9th, 2012), p.2.

THE ITD PROJECT

With all the other elements for a successful SEZ apparently in place, all that remained was for a suitable agency to be commissioned to make sure that all the necessary construction and connectivity was completed as required. Since most western countries continued to operate under the boycott of the country, there was a comparatively shallow pool of potential bidders from which to select a winning bid. ITD was awarded a 75-year concession to build a deep-sea port, steel mills, refineries, petrochemical complex and power plants in the 250 sq. kms area.[6] The total value of the contract is thought to be around some US$50 billion. The principal local partner will be the Myanmarese entrepreneur Zaw Zaw, the owner of the Max Myanmar corporation largely responsible for the building of Naypyidaw and reportedly a favourite of Senior General Than Shwe.[7] Zaw Zaw's close relationship with the former military government has meant that he has been placed on the USA's list of Specially Designated Nationals. Persons on such a list have their assets blocked in international transactions which the USA can influence and US citizens are generally barred from having business with them.[8]

THE COMPANY

Italian-Thai Development Public Company Limited (ITD)[9] is a one-stop construction company that has undertaken many of Thailand's largest construction projects and has also been successful internationally. It was founded in 1958 jointly by Dr Chaijudh Karnasuta and Signor Giorgio Belingieri. From being a construction company, it has grown to become active in nine different areas: buildings (office buildings, condominiums, skyscrapers and hotels); industrial plants; pipelines and utility works (oil, gas and water transmission pipeline, conduit and manhole system and storage tank); highways, railways, bridges and expressways; airports, ports and marine works; dams, tunnels and power plants; steel structures; telecommunications and, finally, mining. The company has been involved in a number of high-profile projects in Thailand, including the Bangkok Mass Transit System and Mass Rapid Transit System (and extensions), bridges across the River Mekong and shopping centres and hospitals throughout the metropolis. ITD is also active in Vietnam, Laos, India and Malaysia. In Bangladesh, it has been awarded a 25-year concession to build the Dhaka

---

6   Mahitthirook, Amornrat, Nareerat Wiriyapong and Thanida Tansubhapol, "Burma Keen to Prove It's Open to Foreign Investors," *Bangkok Post* (January 7th, 2012), p.1.

7   Moe, Wai, "Tycoon Zaw Zaw Reportedly Gets Dawei Port Contract," The Irrawaddy (November 29th, 2010), available at: http://www.irrawaddy.org/article.php?art_id=20211.

8   US Government of the Treasury, "Resource Center: Specially Designated Persons List" (July 24th, 2012), available at: http://www.treasury.gov/resource-center/sanctions/SDN-List/Pages/default.aspx.

9   Information in this section is drawn from the corporate website (http://www.itd.co.th/index.php/en) and annual reports.

Elevated Expressway PPP Project. In 2011 alone, the company completed the SVPI Airport in Ahmadabad in India (1,220 million rupees), Metropark Sathorn Building Phase 3 (1,363 million Baht) and the Central Phra Ram 9 shopping centre (1,534 million Baht), among many others.

ITD was awarded a prestigious gold medal award for civil engineering from the International Federation of Asian and Western Pacific Constructor's Association (IFAWPCA) in 1982 for work on the Khao Laem Dam, which was then the largest and most complex such construction project in Thailand. Later, from 2003-5, the President of ITD Mr Premchai Karnasuta was appointed President of IFAWPCA. More importantly, perhaps, in 1985 the company received the Royal Seal of the Garuda and the concomitant tight to use the term 'By appointment to His Majesty the King.' This is the most prestigious award that can be awarded to a company and the association with the King makes it very difficult to make any negative public comment about the company for fear of being thought of traducing the king, especially since this award was given for exemplary service to the Royal Household, to Thailand and its people. ITD is the only construction company to be

Table 1: Financial Statement of the Company Only

Description	Unit	2011	2010	2009
Total Assets	Million Baht	37,907	35,446	37,993
Capital	Million Baht	4,194	4,194	4,194
Shareholder's Fund	Million Baht	9,338	11,536	10,680
Sales	Million Baht	23,298	20,478	23,359
Net Profit after Tax	Million Baht	(1,362)	633	(1,268)
EPS	Baht	(0.32)	0.15	(0.30)
Book Value	Baht	2.23	2.75	2.55
Par Value	Baht	1	1	1
DPS	Baht	0.00	0.05	0.00
DPS x 100/EPS	%	0.00	33.12	0.00

Source: Annual Report 2010, p.3.

given such an award. The company has also received ISO certification for its various sites and awards for 5,000,000 man hours registered without an accident at the Thai Oil HDS and Rayong Refinery Projects and for 20,000,000 man hours for the Star Refinery Project. The name of the company is physically prominent throughout Bangkok because of being displayed on some of the projects it has completed throughout the city.

Table 2: Consolidated Financial Statement

As of 31st December	Unit	2011	2010	2009
Total Assets	Million Baht	52,404	50,826	53,982
Total Liabilities	Million Baht	43,522	39,174	42,503
Total Shareholder's Equity	Million Baht	8,882	11,651	11,481
Revenues from Construction Work, Sales and Service	Million Baht	44,247	36,076	39,683
Total Revenues	Million Baht	44,945	39,143	41,455
Profit before Taxes and Other Expenses	Million Baht	3,158	2,398	2,149
Net Profit	Million Baht	(1,698)	298	(1,774)

Source: Annual Report 2010, p.3.

ITD is, therefore, a very large, successful and diversified company which is set to increase further in size in the future. The 2010 Annual Report noted that the company's work in hand is projected to rise from 160 billion baht in 2012 to a record high of some 200 billion baht. The company is also likely to benefit from the continued emphasis on physical infrastructure in driving economic and social development in the region. The Asian Development Bank (ADB) has been responsible for creating and organising the Asian Highway Network (AHN) which will link all major population centres across the continent with good quality road or rail links. The purpose of this is to improve social coherence at the national and regional level and, more importantly, help link the places of production and consumption in Asia, thereby helping to increase overall production of goods and the efficiency of transportation and transaction costs generally. The Thai government is also committed to the use of physical infrastructure in promoting development, both with respect to Dawei and elsewhere. A series of four border region IEs is planned which will augment job and income generation in important regional areas (also, they are important electoral areas for the Pheu Thai government) and are also positioned to accommodate more incoming migrant workers and the first of these is likely to be Ban Phu Nam Ron in Kanchanaburi Province, through which a new road will link Bangkok with Dawei.[10] These developments take place in the shadow of 2015, when the ASEAN Economic Community (AEC) is due to be launched and this will provide more opportunities for free cross-border movement by people in a variety of skilled categories.[11] The company will also benefit from the 2011 floods, which in Thailand were responsible for more than 700 deaths and necessitated the building or rebuilding of dykes around existing IEs, since the loss

---

[10] Praiwan, Yutthana, "Four New Industrial Estates Planned for Border," *Bangkok Post* (January 7th, 2012), Business B6.

[11] Wongsamuth, Nanchanok, "More Border Estates to Support AEC," *Bangkok Post* (April 13th, 2012), Business B12.

of production that resulted was a significant brake on the economy overall, as well as other projects aimed at public safety.

Just as in the case of other East Asian states which have passed through periods of rapid economic growth and modernisation, a comparatively small number of important corporations have been instrumental in the state's ability to complete specific developmental goals. However, in the case of ITD, the company's size and scope mean that it is effectively beyond the state's ability to control. The relationship between company and government might be influenced by personal relationships and the national agenda but, fundamentally, it has become one that is dominated by market-based transactions.

DIFFICULTIES

The construction process has begun and some objectives have started to be realised. However, some problems have been encountered. These are described in the following sections.

Capital Requirement

One of the principal issues any company will face when undertaking a project of this size and complexity is the sheer amount of capital required. ITD has been operating in a number of different markets and undertaking numerous projects in which it may be several years before revenue streams begin to come on line. Somewhat paradoxically, the company's success in achieving new projects can work against it because of the demands it places on new sources of capital.

ITD established the Dawei Development Company (DDC) as a means of managing the project and it was understood that Max Myanmar would take a 28% stake in this corporation. Even so, it was estimated that ITD would need to raise an additional US$8 billion to meet the costs of construction of the project. Additional partners in the DDC were being sought from China, Korea and Japan.[12] In April, 2012, it was reported that ITD was seeking to sell some ownership of mining operations in Laos to raise capital, although the company itself has maintained that only accounting issues are involved.[13] Subsequently, in July of 2012, it was further reported that Max Myanmar was negotiating a gradual withdrawal from the project, with no reason made public.[14] Such an event is not unprecedented in projects of this nature, of course, although it does show the need to maintain a flexible posture in financial terms when such large amounts of money are involved.

---

[12] Wiriyapong, Nareerat and Piyaporn Wongruang, "Dawei Developer Seeks More Funding Partners," *Bangkok Post* (January 23rd, 2012), Business, B1.

[13] Wiriyapong, Nareerat, "ITD to Sell Stakes," Bangkok Post (April 28th, 2012), Business B1.

[14] Reuters and Post Reporters, "Key Myanmar Partner Pulling out of Dawei," Bangkok Post (July 5th, 2012), Business B1.

Social and Environmental Issues

The Burmese government had become accustomed to simply moving ahead with construction projects without having to take account of the views of those people who might be inconvenienced as a result. However, as openness and international scrutiny have intensified, the government's willingness and ability simply to ignore anyone else has been seriously constrained. There have, of course, regularly been mostly small-scale protests about development projects which are supported by concerned local people and international non-governmental organisations (NGOs) and others. Routinely, protesters blame both businesses and government as being responsible for any problems caused, irrespective of the actual division of responsibilities. Since the company's personnel and equipment is on site, it is the company that tends to be blamed for any failings by the government. Such protests might focus on the churn below the big picture: that is, on the large scale, projects increase aggregate income, number of jobs and so forth and so can be presented as positive phenomena. However, at the lower level, the stories of individual people, families and communities can be found and these stories are very often those of dispossession, forced relocation and difficulties in adapting to life elsewhere. These protests are evident at Dawei too.[15] Such protests are mostly ineffective because the power of the protestors is much smaller than the developers and, even in the internet age when news can be flashed around the world almost instantaneously, those powerful interests can still be effective in suppressing the spread of information.

Nevertheless, protestors in Burma secured a stunning success when the government announced that it was reversing the decisions to permit the Myitsone Dam to go ahead, which was seen as a great victory for local conservation. This was followed by the suspension of construction on a 4,000 MW coal-fired plant in the Dawei SEZ, to the consternation of partners ITD and Ratchaburi Electricity Generating Holding.[16] Plans are being made for an alternative means of provision of energy through a network of smaller power plants but it is not sure to what extent the Burmese government, having yielded to public pressure once, would do so again in the future.

SECURITY

A third area of concern is in security. Although the central government has signed a series of ceasefire agreements with insurgent ethnic groups, the potential for renewed hostilities remains very high, given that the underlying causes for insurgency have not been addressed, the grievances that have accumulated after bloody fighting over the years and the presence of large numbers of weapons in the country. Incidents

---

[15] See, for example, Szep, Jason, "Betting It All on Dawei," *Bangkok Post* (Feb 6th, 2012), Business B10.

[16] Yuthana Praiwan and Reuters, "Thais in the Dark on Dawei Plant," *Bangkok Post* (January 11th, 2012), p.B1.

could break out at any time and, at the very least, disrupt construction. In July 2011, for example, some 50 ITD workers were evacuated to Kanchanaburi after an attack by KNLA fighters on an army base left an estimated six Burmese soldiers dead.[17] The threat of renewed hostilities cannot be discounted and would have considerable impact upon investor confidence, in addition to the possible human costs involved.

QUESTIONS

1. How should ITD approach the future development of the Dawei SEZ?
2. How should ITD manage its relationship with the Burmese government?
3. What role has the Thai government played in the construction of Dawei SEZ?

REFERENCES

"Burma's Aung San Suu Kyi Set for US Visit," BBC News Online (July 18th, 2012), available at: http://www.bbc.co.uk/news/world-asia-18881492.

"Italian-Thai Company Workers Evacuated from Burma," BNI Online (July 31st, 2011), available at: http://www.bnionline.net/news/kic/11274-italian-thai-company-workers-evacuated-from-burma.html.

Charoensuthipan, Pernchan, "Entry Wages Backed by Bosses, Workers," Bangkok Post (February 9th, 2012), p.2.

Italian-Thai Development Public Company Limited (ITD), Annual Report 2010 (Bangkok: ITD, 2011), available at: http://www.itd.co.th/annual_report/AR_ENG/ar-2010-e. pdf.

Mahitthirook, Amornrat, Nareerat Wiriyapong and Thanida Tansubhapol, "Burma Keen to Prove It's Open to Foreign Investors," Bangkok Post (January 7th, 2012), p.1.

Marshall, Alfred, Principles of Economics (London: MacMillan, 1890).

Moe, Wai, "Tycoon Zaw Zaw Reportedly Gets Dawei Port Contract," The Irrawaddy (November 29th, 2010), available at: http://www.irrawaddy.org/article. php?art_id=20211.

Myint-U, Thant, Where China Meets India: Burma and the New Crossroads of Asia (New York: Farrar, Straus and Giroux, 2011).

Praiwan, Yutthana, "Four New Industrial Estates Planned for Border," Bangkok Post (January 7th, 2012), Business B6.

Praiwan, Yuthana and Reuters, "Thais in the Dark on Dawei Plant," Bangkok Post (January 11th, 2012), p.B1.

Preecharushh, Dulyapak, Naypyidaw: The New Capital of Burma (Bangkok: White Lotus, 2009).

---

[17] "Italian-Thai Company Workers Evacuated from Burma," BNI Online (July 31st, 2011), available at: http://www.bnionline.net/news/kic/11274-italian-thai-company-workers-evacuated-from-burma.html.

Reuters and Post Reporters, "Key Myanmar Partner Pulling out of Dawei," Bangkok Post (July 5th, 2012), Business B1.

Szep, Jason, "Betting It All on Dawei," Bangkok Post (Feb 6th, 2012), Business B10.

US Government of the Treasury, "Resource Center: Specially Designated Persons List" (July 24th, 2012), available at: http://www.treasury.gov/resource-center/sanctions/SDN-List/Pages/default.aspx.

Wiriyapong, Nareerat, "ITD to Sell Stakes," Bangkok Post (April 28th, 2012), Business B1.

Wiriyapong, Nareerat and Piyaporn Wongruang, "Dawei Developer Seeks More Funding Partners," Bangkok Post (January 23rd, 2012), Business, B1.

Wongsamuth, Nanchanok, "More Border Estates to Support AEC," Bangkok Post (April 13th, 2012), Busi ness B12.

Environmental Challenges: A Case Study of Indian Automobile Industry

Pradip Kr Pathak* and Rahul Dayal**

ABSTRACT

Over the course of the 20th century, the automobile rapidly developed from an expensive toy for the rich into the de facto standard for passenger transport in most developed countries. The effects of the automobile on everyday life have been a subject of controversy. This case study focuses on automobile industry and finds out various environmental challenges/ pressures faced by them as well as to establish their adopted measures to counter/ curb these issues with excellence. For this purpose an in- depth study of select company of the industry has been carried out. The methodology includes circulation of a suitable structured questionnaire to the staff at various levels, face to face interaction wherever feasible and other secondary data available through annual reports, media, web etc. A careful analysis and synthesis of the data obtained, yields meaningful inferences and consequent findings & recommendations.

Keywords: Environment, automobile industry, pollution, challenges, corrective measures.

INTRODUCTION

In the dynamics of the corporate world, industries nowadays, are facing multiple challenges in keeping the momentum. The Darwinian theory of "survival of the fittest" has been proved time and again in dealing with the specific issues. The industries resort to various ways and means to be in the race. The major challenges include the global competition, rising customer expectations, cut- throat price and corporate social responsibility being viewed as necessity. Lately a large number of organizations have become environmental conscious and are adopting environmental management as a part of the corporate social responsibility. While the introduction

---

* Pradip Kr Pathak is faculty with Krishna Engineering College, Ghaziabad, India.
**Rahul Dayal is faculty with Krishna Engineering College, Ghaziabad, India.
E-mail: pradippathak27@rediffmail.com, rahuldayal1411@gmail.com

of the mass-produced automobile represented a revolution in mobility and convenience, the modern consequences of heavy automotive use contribute to the use of non-renewable fuels, a dramatic increase in the rate of accidental deaths, social isolation, the disconnection of community, the rise in obesity, the generation of air & noise pollution, urban sprawl, and urban decay. While cost reduction remains very important, the automotive industry's emphasis is on the environment and the demands that it puts on innovation. The environmental issues top the list of challenges facing the automotive industry, outranking cost reduction. A basket of environmental factors such as fuel economy, CAFÉ, and emissions or clean air regulations are the top challenges. This has been endorsed by automotive designers and engineers time and again. Consequently, the environmental considerations include driving system & vehicle design and development. These together have become the key differentiator in the consumer marketplace. Automotive designers and engineers are working to address these issues and to design and develop cost-effective, fuel-efficient vehicles with reduced environmental impact.

ENVIRONMENTAL ISSUES AFFECTING MANAGERIAL STRATEGY

Pressure

An organization resorts to change when subjected to external environmental pressures. According to the three pressure theory, an organization adopts change due to normative pressures (pressures from internal and external stake holders), coercive pressures (pressures from law enforcing agencies, local community and NGO's) or under mimetic pressures (need to follow the successful competitors). Lately a large number of organizations have become environmental conscious and are adopting environmental management as a part of corporate social responsibility CSR.

During a recent study, it was found that the environmental pressures faced by different industrial sectors vary in magnitude. The automobile sector faces high pressures as it is bound by stringent exhaust emission laws (Euro-IV). These laws are well defined and are very strictly enforced, for example every automobile manufacturer has to produce engines conforming to these laws and every customer has to get the pollution certification done once in 3/6 months.

Benefits

An organization is motivated to adopt EMS as this brings in numerous benefits in the form of environmental and economic benefits.

(i) *Environmental benefits.* An organization aims to reduce its risk to business by adhering to the laid down environmental laws. Reduction in air-liquid pollution reduces penalties on the organization. Additionally, the organization can seek grants from various national and international agencies. A green image of the organization reduces irk of some visits from various agencies. Improvement in environmental performance through reduction of solid/liquid waste as well as in air and water pollution results in resource savings indirectly leading to resource generation (Rahul Dayal, Pradip Kr Pathak,2012).

(ii) *Economic benefits.* An organization is motivated to adopt green status as this opens up new markets for it. The present markets being global, an organization needs to design products for all markets. However, non-green products may not be allowed in developed countries. By making the product green, an organization is able to enter all such markets. A green product is sold at a premium and helps an organization to increase its profit margins and market share. Automobile sector has been able to extract high benefits.

Costs

To effect a change in the organization, major modifications in terms of plants, technology, procedures and strategies is required. Change of plant is a costly proposition and requires considerable time. In certain cases new plants and technology may not be readily available or may require high amount of foreign exchange which may deter a management to effect this change. Change of plant and technology is normally accompanied by change in the policies, procedures and the skill level of the workers. This creates a feeling of uncertainty in the minds of employees who resist such changes. The automobile sector incurs moderate costs for adopting the required EMS.

Management Support

High costs of the equipment and technology along with uncertainty and chances of failure may deter a management to adopt required changes. The management also has to dispel the fears in the minds of employees regarding retrenchment; promotions etc. and have to prepare them to meet the challenges of change. This needs strong support from the management to effect this change successfully. Lately, organizations have adopted EMS as a part of their corporate social responsibility (CSR).

STRATEGIC MANAGEMENT AND EMS : AN OVERVIEW

Environmental concerns have affected the managerial strategy at large. The corporate sector which was not much sensitive to the after effects of its activities and also not much concerned about the society in general, has come to realise the significance of these aspects. These can be seen in their approach to the managerial activities and also at the level of strategic formulation. The corresponding decision making process takes into consideration the various associated factors responsible for changing the constituents of the environment. It is therefore, imperative to have a glimpse of the underlying concept of strategic management.

Significance

Strategic management is a level of managerial activity under setting goals and over tactics. Strategic management provides overall direction to the enterprise and is closely related to the field of organization studies. There is a strategic consistency when the actions of an organization are consistent with the expectations of management, and these in turn are with the market and the context. "Strategic management is an ongoing process that evaluates and controls the business and the industries in which the company is involved; assesses its competitors and sets goals and strategies to meet all existing and potential competitors; and then reassesses each strategy regularly to determine how it has been implemented and whether it has succeeded or needs replacement by a new strategy to meet changed circumstances, new technology, new competitors, a new economic environment., or a new social, financial, or political environment.It is that set of managerial decisions and actions that determine the long term performance of a business enterprise. It involves formulating and implementing strategies that will help in aligning the organisation and its environment to achieve organisational goals." (Lamb, Robert, Boyden(1984)

Strategic Formation

Strategic formation is a combination of three main processes which are as follows:

- Performing a situation analysis, self-evaluation and competitor analysis: both internal and external; both micro-environmental and macro-environmental.
- Concurrent with this assessment, objectives are set. These objectives should be parallel to a time-line; some are in the short-term and others on the long-term. This involves crafting vision statements (long term view of a possible future), mission statements (the role that the organization gives itself in society), overall corporate objectives (both financial and strategic), strategic business unit objectives (both financial and strategic), and tactical objectives.

Strategy Evaluation and Choice

An environmental scan will highlight all pertinent aspects that affect an organization, whether external or sector/industry-based. Such an occurrence will also uncover areas to capitalise on, in addition to areas in which expansion may be unwise.

These options, once identified, have to be vetted and screened by an organization. Subsequently, the actual modes of progress have to be determined. These pertain to:

   (i)   *The basis of competition.* The basis of competition is the competitive advantage used or established by the strategy. This advantage may derive from how an organization produces its products, how it acts within a market relative to its competitors, or other aspects of the business.

(ii) *Mode of action.* In corporate strategy there is a model in which strategic options are evaluated against three key success criteria (Johnson and Whittington 2008).

Suitability. Suitability deals with the overall rationale of the strategy. The key point to consider is whether the strategy would address the key issues underlined by the organization's strategic position and whether it will be suitable in terms of environment and capabilities.

Feasibility. Feasibility is concerned with whether the resources required to implement the strategy are available, can be developed or obtained. Resources include funding, people, time, and information. or cash flow in the market Tools that can be used to evaluate feasibility include: cash flow analysis & forecasting, break-even analysis and resource deployment analysis.

Acceptability. Acceptability is concerned with the expectations of the identified stakeholders (mainly shareholders, employees and customers) with the expected performance outcomes, which can be return, risk and stakeholder/stakeholders reactions. Tools that can be used to evaluate acceptability include: what-if analysis and stakeholder mapping.

Strategic Implementation and Control Once a strategy has been identified, it must then be put into practice. The implementation of strategy is of great importance. Conducting a corporate strategy is worthless as long as it is not implemented correctly by each department of the organization This may involve organising, resourcing and utilising change management procedures:

(i) *Organizing* Organizing relates to how an organizational design of a company can fit or align with a chosen strategy. This concerns the nature of reporting relationships, spans of control, and any strategic business units (SBUs) that require to be formed.

(ii) *Resourcing* Resourcing is literally the resources required to put the strategy into practice, ranging from human resources, to capital equipment, and to ICT-based implements.

(iii) *Change management* In the process of implementing strategic plans, an organization must be wary of forces that may legitimately seek to obstruct such changes. It is important then that effectual change management practices are instituted. These encompass:

• The appointment of a change agent, as an individual who would champion the changes and seek to reassure and allay any fears arising.

- Ascertaining the causes of the resistance to organizational change (whether from employees, perceived loss of job security, etc.)
- Via change agency, slowly limiting the negative effects that a change may uncover.

Research Model. On the basis of above discussions, the following model was adopted to assess the factors affecting strategic change management in any organization:-

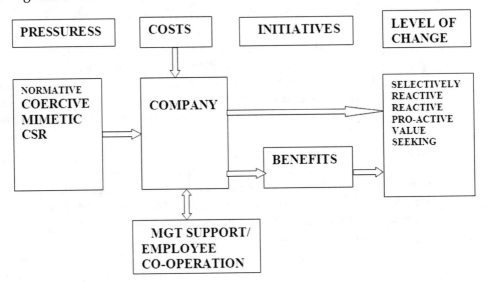

Fig. 1. Research Model

Testing the Strategic Alignment of the organization. Until 2010, Change management was used to implement a strategy. The optimal performance of organizations is highly dependent on the level of Strategic Alignment. The S-ray Alignment Scan is a measure used for effective strategic implementation. The S-ray Alignment Scan is a visual of the Corporate Strategy measured against the level of understanding and implementation of the organizational departments.

ENVIRONMENTAL NORMS (ISO 14000 SERIES) AFFECTING MANAGERIAL DECISIONS

A set of rules and norms for environmental management of industrial production has been incorporated in ISO 14000 series that applies to all businesses including the automobile industry and is designed to reduce environmental damage and industrial waste. The ultimate goal of these guidelines is to promote useful and usable tools to businesses to help them manage their environmental impact.

The numbers of ISO-14001 certified companies in India have increased gradually from 138 in 2001 to approximately 3000 in 2010. ISO-14001 certification requires an organization to plan its activities in such a manner that reduces the adverse effect of its operation on the environment. The organization experiences environmental pressures forcing it to consume minimum natural resources, save energy at every stage as well as cause minimum damage to the environment.

To achieve these objectives, an organization needs to introduce major changes in its plants, technology, processes and procedures. These changes are costly, time and resource consuming and full of un-certainties. An organization would adopt changes depending upon the strength of these pushing forces called pressures. On the other hand, the very philosophy of environmental management system (ISO-14001) is based on reduction of wastages in raw material, energy and resources at every stage of production. Reduction in wastages amounts to generation of resources. Also, adoption of green initiatives reduces penalties as well entitles it to various national and international grants. By creating an image of a green company, an organization can extract environmental as well as economic benefits. Therefore, an organization is tempted to adopt changes under the influence of these motivating forces called benefits.

ENVIRONMENTAL CHALLENGES: A CASE STUDY

ERQ, (name disguised) is an authorized car dealer in New Delhi of Maruti Suzuki dealer in New Delhi. Its well organized showrooms in New Delhi help a customer choose and select his/her Car. The representatives are well equipped with the product knowledge which helps a customer to understand technical aspects also, while making a purchase decision.

Objectives of the Study The objectives of the study are enumerated as follows:
- To take up the environmental issues confronting Indian automobile industry
- To assess the degree of efforts made by the industry in general and by the company under study in particular and its effectiveness in dealing with environmental issues
- To analyse and synthesize the data and information obtained and match the same with common industrial norms
- To find out the key issues to be addressed in order to ensure an effective EMS
- To recommend various measures necessary for effective and efficient implementation of the environmental decisions

Research Methodology The case study has been built around secondary sources of information and information in public domain. The following methods were used to take up an intensive study on the topic and efforts were made to maintain confidentiality by way of allowing the respondents to choose the option of "No Response"

(i) A structured set of questionnaire was framed for select segment of respondents. There were two types of questions. Nearly half of the questions were related to the strategic management patterns of the company in question. The other half portion of the questionnaire was intended to establish the awareness and involvement of the staff in the process of strategic EMS. The target segment of the respondents included personnel conversant with the managerial activities and employees entrusted to ensure the implementation of managerial decisions intended to resolve the environmental issues. In addition, efforts were made to include a number of product consumers for meaningful interaction and making inferences corresponding to the issues raised in the said questionnaire. A total of 27 respondents reverted back with their responses out of a total of 39 individuals approached. The questionnaire was floated through e-mail and personal visits to the HR office of the company. The researcher also had face to face interaction with HR official to discuss few significant aspects associated with automobile industry. Efforts were made to generalize the responses for universal application to an extent. These responses, however, were subjected to certain perceptual differences among the respondents on the basis of profile, awareness and specific understanding of the issues concerned. A summary of the pattern of response in percentile is appended below as Table 1.

Table 1: Questionnaire and corresponding Responses

SI No	Question	Percent SA	Percent A	Percent D	Percent SD	NA
1	There is an urgent need to be environmental conscious for the benefit and survival of the society at large.	44.4	33.3	22.2		
2	Environmental science deals with analysis of the conditions, circumstances and influences affecting life and how life in turn responds to such things.	66.6	11.1	22.2		
3	The corporate world can do its bit by being sensitive to the harmful effects of various emissions and effluents.	66.6	33.3			
4	The different kinds of pollutants should be identified and an approach of backward integration can be adopted to establish their reasons and remedial measures.	22.2	22.2	55.5		
5	Your company has a well established integrated safety, occupational health and environmental policy.	66.6	22.2	11.1		

6	Your company carries out various environmental promotion campaigns and special initiatives at regular intervals.	22.2	22.2	11.1		
7	Your company ensures that its stakeholders including the suppliers are totally engaged with company in this Endeavour through green supply chain management initiative.	44.4	44.4	11.1		
8	The managerial strategy of training and motivating not only its employees but also its suppliers plays a significant role in the successful Environment management system (EMS) .	22.2	77.7			
9	In your company, the management had dominating role in the successful implementations of the Environment management system (EMS)	44.4	33.3	22.2		
10	Adoption of environmental management system (EMS) necessitates changes in the strategy, operations and managerial technique.	88.8		11.1		
11	An organization adopts change management pertaining to EMS due to normative pressures, coercive pressures or mimetic pressures	22.2	22.2	55.5		
12	Usually the companies adopt EMS either to reduce penalties due to non conformity to environmental laws or, to extract environmental and economic benefits.	11.1	22.2	44.4		
13	Off late the concept of corporate social responsibility has necessitated adoption of environmental management by companies.	33.3	33.3	33.3		
14	High costs of the equipment along with uncertainty of success may pose a constraint to the management for adopting the required changes	22.2	55.5	22.2		
15	Green initiatives taken by the automobile industry in accordance with ISO-14001, have resulted in reduction of exhaust emissions matching the international standards		22.2	11.1		66.6
16	Your organization maintains proactive approach while undergoing change process pertaining to EMS.	33.3	55.5	11.1		
17	The cost benefit analysis is the basis for incorporation of any change intended to reduce environmental pollution	22.2	44.4	33.3		
18	The measures e.g. use of solar and wind energy, product recycling and waste handling has been satisfactory post green initiatives	22.2	55.5	22.2		

19	Change in product/technology in the industry e.g. development of fuel efficient 'K' series engine and intelligent gas port injection yielded the expected outcome	11.1	11.1	44.4		33.3
20	The introduction of K- series engine and development of intelligence gas port injection technology as a measure to minimize environmental impacts of its products, have yielded the desired results.	22.2	11.1	55.5		11.1
21	Use of energy efficient motors and pumps in paint shop provide better savings of energy	55.5	33.3	11.1		
22	The companies usually conserve water through rainwater harvesting, ETP and STP waste water treatment, bio filter treatment plant, green belt development and environmental projects, etc	33.3	22.2	33.3		
23	The use of cell deck make system provides for air supply with reduced energy consumption	11.1	11.1	44.4		33.3
24	The use of reciprocating air compressors with efficient screw compressor facilitates for better energy efficiency	22.2	55.5	22.2		
25	Energy conservation(ENCON) measures are being taken by the industry with considerable potential	22.2	77.7			
26	The motor vehicle Act 1938 enacted for the protection and conservation of the environment, has been effectively implemented in India	33.3	22.2	44.4		
27	Is your company aware of its responsibilities towards the impact generated by its corporate activities and the use of its products	33.3	33.3	33.3		
28	Your company sets specific goals in the context of Product life cycle assessment system, which is used to measure, assess and analyze environmental impact	44.4	22.2			33.3
29	In your company, the planning and execution are not delegated to specialists rather associates in all departments, are directly involved	44.4		22.2		33.3
30	All associates are engaged with environmental issues as part of their duties		55.5	22.2		22.2

{**Abbv:** *SA- Strongly agree, A- Agree, D- Disagree, SD- Strongly disagree, NR- No Response*}

(ii) Data and information were also obtained from various business magazines, journals, newspapers, internet and select publications on the subject. Efforts were made to take up wide extensive study across the different kind of media so as to concentrate on the important and relevant facts. The research works done on the subject till date also provided an important source for exploring various aspects and subsequent trend analysis. Finally a selective intensive study formed the basis for findings of the research and consequent recommendations.

Analytical and Critical Thinking

A rigorous analysis of the data was made. It was our endeavour to first gain an overall impression of the case and isolate key information. Subsequently a questioning frame of mind was cultivated and ability to shift information and voluminous data given in the case was developed.

Interpretations

A careful analysis of the processed data and information obtained through various sources reveals the following:

- A majority of the respondents agree to the need of having an effective EMS.
- The respondents fully agree that a proactive role of the corporate world is necessary in order to reduce harmful effects of various emissions and effluents.
- The respondents have reserved comments over the effectiveness of the green initiatives taken in accordance with ISO 14001.
- The implementation of the motor vehicle act 1938 enacted for the protection and conservation of the environment in India is required to be adhered to a higher degree in order to ensure its effectiveness.
- A very high percent of respondents say that fuel-efficient vehicles with reduced environmental impact are important to consumers.
- The corporate world has realised the significance of having a well established integrated safety, occupational health and environmental policy.
- There is a need to enhance the environmental promotion compaigns and special initiatives at regular intervals.
- The concept of corporate social responsibility has gained the momentum in the recent past and the firms adopting the same appear to have an edge over the rival firms operating without adopting this ideology

FINDINGS AND RECOMMENDATIONS

- Alternatively powered vehicles are predicted to have the greatest impact on the industry. The same could be experimented by the industry with a futuristic view.

- Diesel engine technology is a key focus to help achieve 2020 efficiency regulations
- In 10 years from now, vehicles may have to run on bio-based diesel fuel; petroleum-based diesel and E85. Gasoline also can prove to be a major factor in determining the vehicle design.
- The companies need to set specific goals in the context of product life cycle assessment system which is used to measure, and analyze environmental impacts.
- The planning and execution are not to be delegated to specialists rather associates in all departments should be directly involved.
- The companies must focus on the concept of corporate social responsibility and see this as a part of their duty.

CONCLUSIONS

At a global level, the transportation sector is pretty much related to greenhouse gas (GHG) emissions and global warming since the utilization of the vehicle and other activities related to the sector are responsible for a significant amount of carbon dioxide emitted to the atmosphere. More than 16% of human made CO_2 emissions are caused by road transportation in general whereas another 7% to 10% is assigned to passenger cars only . In India, the vehicle population, currently at more than sixty million, is growing at a rate of more that 10% per annum. Of this, 80% are two/three wheelers. Growth rate has been very high for passenger cars and two/three wheelers. The industries resort to various ways and means to be in the race. While cost reduction remains very important, the automotive industry's emphasis is on the environment and the demands that it puts on innovation. The environmental issues top the list of challenges facing the automotive industry, outranking cost reduction. The companies therefore, need to set specific goals in the context of product life cycle assessment system which is used to measure, and analyze environmental impacts. Subsequently an effective and efficient Environmental Management System can be developed. The companies must also focus on the concept of corporate social responsibility and see this as a part of their duty.

REFERENCES

Lamb, Robert, Boyden(1984). *Competitive strategic management*, Englewood Cliffs, NJ: Prentice-Hall.

Johnson, G, Scholes, K, Whittington, R(2008). *Exploring Corporate Strategy*, 8th Edition, FT Prentice Hall, Essex, 2008, ISBN 978-0-273-71192-6

Rahul Dayal, Pradip Kr Pathak(2012). *Environmental challenges affecting the change management.*

Female-owned Small Business: A Case Analysis of Women Enterprises in India

Debasree Das Gupta*

ABSTRACT

The importance of women-led enterprises for any country's economic growth, and competitiveness is well established. According to a 2009 study, in India female-run enterprises in recent years have performed significantly better than other enterprises in terms of productivity and export percentages. However, gender gap in business initiatives in India is among the highest in the world. In this regard prior studies identify "management and business environment" as major barriers limiting female-owned businesses. Although accepted as crucial, the role of public policy towards addressing these barriers is under-researched in the entrepreneurship literature. The aim of this study is to highlight this gap using the cases of Gujarat and Kerala. The analysis presented in this study indicate the need for additional policy focus on developing managerial skills, in addition to technical skills of women entrepreneurs in both formal and informal sectors of the economy.

Keywords: Female-owned businesses, women entrepreneurs, small-scale initiatives, gender-gap, entrepreneurship.

INTRODUCTION

Multiple reports from the Global Entrepreneurship Monitor (GEM) highlight the importance of women-led enterprises in national economic growth, and competitiveness. For example, in the *Global Entrepreneurship Monitor, 2010 Report: Women Entrepreneurs Worldwide*, Kelley, Brush, Greene, and Litovsky (2011) argue: "When a major part of a population does not engage in entrepreneurship, these economies lose the benefits that would otherwise be provided by new products and services, additional revenues, and new jobs. More specifically, when women do not participate equally in entrepreneurship, society loses out on the value that can be created by half its populace (p.5).

* George Mason University, Arlington, Virginia, USA
E-mail: debasree_dasgupta@yahoo.co.in

In India, where small-scale initiatives serve as major drivers of economic growth, female-owned businesses are concentrated in these small-scale initiatives. Small-scale initiatives are classified in to three categories on the basis of their investment on plant and machinery: (i) *micro* enterprises with less than $50,000 in investment; (ii) *small* enterprises with investment between $50,000 and $1,000, 000; and (iii) *medium* enterprises with investment between $1,000,000 and $2,000,000 (MSMED Act 2006).[1] In 2006-2007, majority of the small-scale women-run enterprises fell under the micro category with 50 percent engaged in manufacturing and 40 percent in services (Government of India 2006).

Similar to other developing economies, in India push or necessity factors are more important than pull or opportunity factors in motivating women to become entrepreneurs (Kelley et al. 2011). A larger share of female entrepreneurs exists in the informal sector in developing countries.[2] Compared to their male counterparts, female entrepreneurial and business participation is influenced by unemployment (push factor) and life satisfaction that allows participation in entrepreneurship only after developing social capital through life and work situations (Kobeissi 2010; Verheul et al. 2006).[3]

The potential of female-run small-scale business enterprises to contribute to the Indian economy is profound. Indeed, a 2009 study surveyed women-owned small-sector industrial and service enterprises in India and reported that in recent years these enterprises have performed significantly better than other enterprises in terms of productivity and export percentages (Nagadevara 2009). In this regard, the role of women enterprises in the formal sector has been particularly highlighted in the literature (Ghani et al. 2011). However, gender gap in business initiatives in the formal sector in India is among the highest in the world (Global Entrepreneurship Monitor 2002). Prior studies identify "management and business environment"—such as networks, access to finance and market opportunities—as major barriers limiting the operation and survival of female-owned businesses (Coad and Tamvada 2011). Although accepted as crucial, the role of public policy towards addressing these

---

[1] Conversion rate: $1 = Rs. 50

[2] In India, the informal and formal sectors of the economy are respectively referred to as the "unorganized" and "organized" sectors. Enumeration of the organized sector is covered under the Annual Survey of Industries (ASI) and comprises of units registered under the Factories Act that employs (i) 10 or more workers if using power, or, (ii) 20 or more workers if not using power. Units that are not covered under the ASI constitute the unorganized sector of the economy. The National Commission for Enterprises in the Unorganized Sector was established in September 2004. Under the National Sample Survey Organization (NSSO), a survey of the units in the unorganized sector was conducted for the first time in 1999-2000 (Chakraborti 2009).

[3] Some of the push factors discussed in the literature are economic considerations and necessity that include inadequate family income, job dissatisfaction, flexible work schedule, glass ceiling and gender wage gap. Pull factors, on the other hand, relate to motivations for independence, self-fulfillment, entrepreneurial drive, and desire for wealth, social status, and power.

barriers is under-researched in the entrepreneurship literature. The aim of this study is to underscore this gap in the literature using the cases of Gujarat and Kerala. The motivation behind the choice of these two states as cases are: (i) both states have been successful in pursuing and implementing national- and state-level policies targeting women enterprises; (ii) next, the base of female-run businesses in both states is among the highest in the country; (iii) yet gender gap in small-scale initiatives is high.

The organization in the rest of the paper is as follows. In the first section, state-level trends and factors in women enterprises in India are presented. In the next section, a synopsis of the various policy efforts to foster and develop women's participation in small scale industries and businesses is provided followed by a discussion on state-specific schemes and programs, and institutions and organizations in Gujarat and Kerala in the third Section. The concluding section wraps up this study with policy implications and stresses the need for additional policy focus to develop managerial skills, in addition to technical skills of women entrepreneurs in both formal and informal sectors of the economy.

WOMEN ENTERPRISES: TRENDS AND FACTORS

The Government of India defines "women entrepreneurs" as a Small Scale Industrial Unit/ Industry related service or business enterprise, managed by one or more women entrepreneurs in proprietary concerns, or in which she/ they individually or jointly have a share capital of not less than 51% as Partners/ Shareholders/ Directors of Private Limits Company/ Members of Cooperative Society. This definition is an accepted and widely applied benchmark to identify and distinguish women-led enterprises in India. Based on this definition the most recent national census on micro, small, and medium enterprises in India reports that almost 2 out of every 10 enterprises that were registered and working in 2006-2007, were women-led. The report also found that women's work participation in men- and women-led initiatives working enterprises was about 1.6 million or twenty percent of the total work participation (Government of India 2011). Entrepreneurial and work participation of women in India is much lower than other countries at similar levels of economic development (Das 2001).[4]

In countries with factor-driven economies that include India, the proportion of female entrepreneurs ranged between no more than one-third of the total number of entrepreneurs in the Middle East / North Africa (MENA) region to about half of

---

[4] The Global Entrepreneurship Monitor (GEM) groups countries in to three levels of economic development: factor-drive (stage I), efficiency-driven (stage II) and innovation-drive (stage III). This classification is based on the World Economic Forum's groupings of economies into levels of economic development according to GDP per capita and the share of exports comprising primary goods. In 2011-2012, a total of 37 nations, including India, were categorized as factor-driven economies (Kelley et al. 2011; Schwab 2011).

the total number of entrepreneurs in sub-Saharan Africa. The rate of total early-stage entrepreneurial activity (TEA) in MENA countries is much lower than that in countries in sub-Saharan Africa.[5] For example, TEA among females in 2008 in Angola, and in 2004 in Uganda, respectively were 25.2, 25.5. In Egypt and Iran, TEA rates in 2008 respectively were 5.9 and 4.5. TEA in India which was 7.1 in 2008 was comparable to that in the MENA region countries (Global Entrepreneurship Monitor 2008). Also, historically the rate of female labor participation in India has been much lower than her neighbors in the Indian sub-continent and only higher than that in Pakistan. For example, rates of female labor participation in 2010 in Bangladesh and Bhutan respectively were 57 percent and 66 percent, almost double the rate prevailing in India which was 29 percent (World Bank 2011).

Moreover, wide gender disparity typifies business ventures across all states of India. In 2006-2007, gender gap—measured in terms of women enterprises as a share of men-owned enterprises—in ownership of micro, small and medium enterprises was highest in Daman & Diu and lowest in Meghalaya (see Table 1). In fact, a north-south divide in the gender gap in entrepreneurial and business initiatives exists, a characteristic that has been widely discussed in the literature as a consequence of, among other things, religio-cultural factors (Ghosh and Cheruvalath 2007).[6] This gender gap, however, narrows down for employment generated in the two types of enterprises. While female-run enterprises on average employed about 5 employees in 2006-2007, male-owned enterprises on average engaged about one additional employee more than their female counterparts.

At the state-level, the number of women-led enterprises varied widely and was concentrated in the seven states of Tamil Nadu (25.46), Kerala (17.84), Karnataka (12.43), Gujarat (10.90), and Madhya Pradesh (4.74) accounting for about 70 percent of all such enterprises. Ghosh and Cheruvalath (2007) find that in states, such as Gujarat, Karnataka, and Maharashtra, that record a greater proportion of women entrepreneurs show that these women (i) are from business families, or (ii) have a background in services, or (iii) have a highly educated male member (father or husband) in the

---

[5] The Global Entrepreneurship Monitor defines TEA among female working age population as the percentage of female 18 to 64 population who are either a nascent entrepreneur or owner / manager of a new business. A nascent entrepreneur and a new business are defined respectively as the percentage of 18 to 64 population who are "actively involved in setting up a business they will own or co-own; this business has not paid salaries, wages, or any other payments to the owners for more than three months" and the percentage of 18 to 64 population "owning and managing a running business that has paid salaries, wages, or any other payments to the owners for more than three months, but not more than 42 months" (Global Entrepreneurship Monitor n.d.).

[6] Female business and entrepreneurial activities in India vary across socio-religious groups which subject women to differing gender norms. These gender norms hold across economic stratifications with both affluent and poor women in Hindu upper cast not likely to engage in entrepreneurship and business ventures.

family. However, even in these states the gender gap in small scale initiatives is high and women-run enterprises in 2006-2007 ranged between 1.1 to 3.4 ventures for every 10 male-led enterprises (Government of India 2011).[7]

Table 1: State-wise Entrepreneurship Profile, 2006-2007

State / UT Name	Number of Enterprises Owned by (in thousands)			
	Female	Male	Total	Gender Gap
				(female-owned as a share of male-owned)
Jammu & Kashmir	3.09	11.90	14.99	2.60
Himachal Pradesh	1.31	10.62	11.93	1.23
Punjab	3.01	45.10	48.11	0.67
Chandigarh	0.10	0.90	1.00	1.11
Uttrakhand	2.43	21.34	23.77	1.14
Haryana	1.46	31.69	33.15	0.46
Delhi	0.38	3.38	3.76	1.12
Rajasthan	5.99	48.90	54.89	1.22
Uttar Pradesh	8.39	179.36	187.75	0.47
Bihar	2.57	47.47	50.04	0.54
Sikkim	0.02	0.10	0.12	2.00
Arunachal Pradesh	0.10	0.32	0.42	3.13
Nagaland	0.22	1.12	1.34	1.96
Manipur	1.15	3.35	4.50	3.43
Mizoram	1.29	2.42	3.71	5.33
Tripura	0.16	1.18	1.34	1.36
Meghalaya	1.19	1.83	3.02	6.50
Assam	4.07	15.80	19.87	2.58
West Bengal	4.42	38.84	43.26	1.14
Jharkhand	0.75	17.44	18.19	0.43
Orissa	2.16	17.44	19.60	1.24
Chattisgarh	2.09	20.68	22.77	1.01

[7] Gender gap was also low in the north-eastern states. However, in these states the base, in terms of total number of male-led enterprises is small and much lower than the states of Maharashtra, Gujarat, Karnataka, Kerala and Tamil Nadu.

Madhya Pradesh	10.18	96.82	107.00	1.05
Gujarat	23.40	206.43	229.83	1.13
Daman & Diu	0.01	0.58	0.59	0.17
Dadra & Nagar Haveli	0.04	1.68	1.72	0.24
Maharashtra	8.98	77.61	86.59	1.16
Andhra Pradesh	5.23	40.47	45.70	1.29
Karnataka	26.68	109.51	136.19	2.44
Goa	0.33	2.30	2.63	1.43
Lakshwadweep	0.00	0.00	0.00	0.00
Kerala	38.30	111.89	150.19	3.42
Tamil Nadu	54.65	179.23	233.88	3.05
Pondicherry	0.33	1.12	1.45	2.95
Andaman & Nicobar Islands	0.20	0.55	0.75	3.64
All India	214.68	1349.37	1564.05	1.59

Source: Fourth All India Census, 2006-2007

A sizeable number of micro-level studies use primary data and investigate the barriers and challenges associated with female-run business initiatives in the small-scale enterprises in India.[8] Limited by scarcity of data, a handful of country-level studies that examines small-scale women-led ventures in developing countries including India, add to the micro-level studies and identify aggregate-level factors impacting female enterprises.[9] However, the effect of programs and policies on women entrepreneurs is an area that has not been studied adequately by the entrepreneurship literature (Carter et al. 2001).

Factors identified by prior studies as barriers for female-run businesses fall in to three broad groups: (i) personal characteristics, motivations and experiences, (ii) socio-cultural gender contexts and (iii) gender differences regarding business management, particularly business and personal networks, access to finance and market opportunities.

Women perceive the need for growth of business differently than men and non-profit motivations are more common among women (Ghosh and Cheruvalath 2007). Mitra (2002) examines the growth trajectory of women-run businesses in India and report that women-run businesses are motivated by a need for self-fulfillment instead of profits (economic v. non-economic goals) and often adopt non-organic growth

[8] See for example Field et al. (2010); Pillania et al. (2010); Ghosh and Cheruvalath (2007); Mitra (2002).

[9] See for example Kobeissi (2010); Verheul et al. (2006).

strategies keeping their ventures small despite growth in profit and sales.[10] Moreover, family demands limit their ability to grow and also dictate their choice of activity and / or desire to remain small. Next, with regard to socio-cultural gender contexts, familial responsibilities, traditional restriction on mobility and social interaction add to low status of women in India to severely constrict the number of female-run businesses.

Finally, the literature on women entrepreneur considers the effect of gender on management and performance of small-scale enterprises.[11] Compared to men, women business owners have smaller personal networks and limited geographic mobility. These factors combined with the persistence of the "old-boys network" limit their access to information and opportunities.[12] In addition, women entrepreneurs, more often than not, view the resources—that, among other things, include relational networks, financial and technical resources, contracts in government and other agencies—required to grow quite differently. Gender discrimination introduces market imperfections resulting in women pursuing relational contracts within families, ethnic and gender groups. In other words, women pursue different networking strategies than men and most often seek support from female networks (Mitra 2002). These characteristics impact women's ability to raise capital at start-up and generate finances to keep their businesses running. In this regard, most studies highlight limited supply of credit as a barrier impeding women's access to financial resources. However, Field et al. (2010) instead argue that limited demand instead of supply of credit is the factor qualifying access of women to financial resources. Gender gap in education, training and business network limits women's knowledge on investment opportunities or ability to conduct cost-benefit analysis. These limitations constrain their ability to seek out credits and loans.

In addition to the above factors, existing studies find certain aggregate-level factors as important determinants of women enterprises in a region. These factors are: (i) socio-cultural (female educational attainment, gender norms, etc), (ii) economic (female economic activities such as employment undertaken by women, female earnings, economic development and population base representing market demand),

---

[10] Mitra and Pingali (1999) define organic growth strategy as a strategy that would "involve relatively little start-up capital followed by phase-by-phase growth using internally accumulated capital" (Mitra and Pingali 1999: 64). In contrast non-organic growth strategy is one in which firms grow "through strategic alliances or through networking in clusters...in terms of profit or sales but may choose deliberately not to reinvest these revenues in fixed asset expansion or in employing more people" (Mitra 2002:219).

[11] See for example Chagantiv(1986); Holmquist and Sundin (1988); Brush (1992); Stanford et al (1995); Brush (1997); Gardiner and Tiggemann (1999).

[12] Traditionally women have been excluded from the "old-boys network" in large organizations. As a result, when needed, women seek business support from their female counterparts (Mitra 2002).

(iii) institutional (property rights and rule of law, business licensing, availability of capital, child care and parental leave in wage employment, etc.), and (iv) demographic (fertility, importance of family, marriage, etc.). Estrin, and Mickiewicz (2009) questioned if institutions impact women enterprises more than men-run businesses and found that women are less likely than men to undertake entrepreneurial activity in countries where (i) the rule of law is weaker, (ii) the state sector is larger, and (iii) the informal financial sector is weaker.

INSTITUTIONAL SUPPORT TO WOMEN ENTERPRISES

The Policy Landscape

Historically, the policy environment in India has been especially favorable to its small-scale industrial and business initiatives. Policy tools and institutional support were established since the decade of the 1970s at both the central as well as state levels to develop women enterprises and their economic contribution to the country (Coad and Tamvada 2011). Central and state governments work in consort with non-governmental organizations (NGOs) to foster and facilitate women entrepreneurs. In so doing, the central aim has been the empowerment of women of India through a two-pronged strategy. First, an employment centered policy strategy has prioritized women enterprises to address their low status and limited bargaining power in society. Second, in order to develop self-reliance and autonomy, women entrepreneurs has been treated as a special target group in India's five-year plans as well as other development programs and policies (Deshpande and Sethi 2009).

A majority of these landmark acts and institutions target economically backward and rural women. However, it is beyond the scope of the present study to provide an in-depth chronology of national- and state-level efforts. Instead, the most important of these endeavors are as below.

In 1971, the Government of India established a committee that reviewed the status of women to recommend gainful employment to women in recognition of their services. About decade and a half later in 1986, another standing committee comprising of women entrepreneurs and representatives was created to provide fiscal and financial incentives such as marketing, training and publicity. This committee focused on curriculum development particularly to nurture women in rural areas, in addition to providing incentives to small-scale initiatives employing more than 50 percent of women. Later, in the Seventh Five year Plan that was implemented between the years 1987 and 1992, the empowerment and equality of women through self employment and enterprises were highlighted. The next five-year Plan further built on the same goals in recognition of the fact that women constituted about half of the Indian populace. The National Perspective Plan (NPP) was adopted and the National Commission for Women Entrepreneurs (NCWE) was established in 1992.

Much of the focus through these plans and commissions were (i) the support and development of women entrepreneurs in the informal sector, and (ii) the organization and coordination of research and training through a network of national- and state-level resource centers. Some of the important national- and state level programs, schemes and initiatives that came out of these efforts are listed below.

NATIONAL-LEVEL PROGRAMS AND SCHEMES AND INITIATIVES

- *Support to Training-cum-Employment Program* (STEP) was established in 1987 and aimed to develop skills of women particularly economically weaker ones depending upon local and sectoral needs;
- a number of poverty alleviation and rural development initiatives were launched as sub-components of the *Integrated Rural Development Program* (IRDP), such as the *Development of Women and Children in Rural Areas* (DWCRA), *Council for Advancement of People's Action and Rural Technology* (CAPART), *Training of Rural Youth for Self-Employment* (TRYSEM), etc.;
- *Rashtriya Mahila Kosh* (RMK) was instituted as a dedicated fund in 1993 to fulfill the credit needs of poor women;
- a number of employment generation schemes, such as *Nehru Rozgar Yozna, Prime Minister's Rozgar Yojna,* etc. were set up to generate employment through micro enterprises giving preference to women and backward sections of the society;
- *Assistance to Women Cooperative* was launched as a vehicle of financial assistance in terms of capital and managerial subsidy to cooperatives run by women;
- *Trade Related Entrepreneurship Assistance and Development for Women* (TREAD) was launched in 1995 to improve institutional capacities and other market development activities;
- a host of central government institutions, such as *Small Industries Development Organization* and banks such as, *Industrial Development Bank of India, Small Industries Development Bank of India,* etc. were set up to provide financial assistance that included informal lending at concessional rates and training and extension services to develop and support women entrepreneurs;
- in addition, national-level training Institutions, such as *National Institute for Entrepreneurship and Small Business Development* or NIESBUD, *Entrepreneurship Development Institute of India* or EDII, etc. was founded to develop women's entrepreneurial activities in small businesses and small industries through education, training, and research;
- finally, several national level women entrepreneurs association and organizations, such as *Women Entrepreneur's Wing of National Alliance of Young Entrepreneurs* or NAYE, *Federation of Indian Chambers of Commerce and Industry, Ladies Organization,*

etc., undertake lobbying activity to represent the interests of women entrepreneurs at various levels of government.

STATE-LEVEL PROGRAMS, SCHEMES AND INITIATIVES

- To foster women enterprises, state-level financial packages and schemes were set up through *State Financial Corporation* that extended financial assistance at special rates and terms to help women entrepreneurs start their business in the small-scale sector;

- specialized training institutions, such as *Technical Consultancy Organizations* or TCOs, *Institute of Entrepreneurship Development* or IEDs, etc., have been set up in a number of states that impart training, intervention programs, research and publications to help existing and potential women enterprises;

- state-level women's organizations association, such as *Association of Women Entrepreneurs of Small Scale Industries* in South India, etc., conducts lobbying activities and imparts training.

NON-GOVERNMENTAL INITIATIVES (NGOS)

A bevy of voluntary organizations and non-governmental organizations operate in India that offer financial, technical and training assistance to women enterprises. In addition to training, education and financial assistance, these organizations also provide networking opportunities to women entrepreneurs. Many of these non-governmental organizations, such as Self Employed Women's Association (SEWA) target women enterprises in the informal sector and provide them with grants and loans to start and operate their businesses.

ROLE OF POLICY

To derive an understanding on the effect of policy, the cases of Gujarat and Kerala are discussed in this section. Both states have been successful in developing and implementing state-level organizations and training institutes that help and facilitate women enterprises. In Gujarat the International Center for Entrepreneurship and Career Development (ICECD) has been a successful and experienced institute for inculcating women's self sufficiency in rural and urban areas. It also imparts training and education towards management capability in enterprise establishment. Gujarat also has a number of initiatives that established state-level specialized training institutes that include *Gujarat Industrial Technical Consultancy Organization or GITCO, Gujarat Small Scale Industrial Corporation or GSSIC, Gujarat State Khadi and Village Industries Board or GSKVI, Gujarat Industrial Development Corporation and Gujarat State Financial Corporation or GSFC*. These institutes are involved in advising and assisting women enterprises.

In addition to technical and skill development organizations, Gujarat Chamber of Commerce and Industry (GCCI), Women's Wing has been successful and active in championing the cause of and advises women entrepreneurs. It also organizes seminars and showcases products made by women entrepreneurs that facilitate networking and marketing opportunities for these enterprises. Further, the non-governmental organization called Self Employed Women's Association (SEWA), focuses on advising women-run businesses particularly those in the informal sector.

Similar to Gujarat, the state of Kerala has specialized organizations and institutions that help women enterprises. For example, Kerala State Women's Development Corporation provides (i) self employment loan programs, (ii) educational loan, (iii) single women benefit schemes, (iv) job oriented training programs, and (v) marketing support for women entrepreneurs. In addition to these opportunities, the Kerala Government's Women Industries Program serves as a targeted policy tool to attract women entrepreneurs to the industrial sector. It provides financial incentives that assist in generating start-up capital.

As noted earlier, the effects of policy on women entrepreneurs is a topic that has not received adequate attention in the entrepreneurship literature. Not surprisingly, the abovementioned state-specific policy and programmatic efforts in India have also not been analyzed systematically to assess their effectiveness. Nonetheless, despite these efforts, existing women enterprises continue to face credit shortage and business management related problems in both these states. For example, Das (2001) conducted a survey on women entrepreneurs in Kerala and reported inadequate capital and cashflow, and lack of marketing and managerial experience as two of the major challenges faced by women entrepreneurs. Conversely, marketing and management skills were highlighted as a salient factor behind the success of some of the women enterprises surveyed. Also, the gender gap (as evidenced in Table 1) in small-scale enterprises is high in both states, indicating the need for additional policy tools to assist establishment of women enterprises in the formal sector. These findings are not unique to the two states discussed here. Instead, such trends typify women entrepreneurs uniformly across all states in the country (Nagadevara 2009).

CONCLUSION

Given the importance of women entrepreneurs in developing countries, this study presented state-level trends and factors related to women entrepreneurs and the barriers and challenges faced by these enterprises. Stressing the crucial role of policy, it also reviewed policies and programs, and institutions and organizations geared towards the development of women entrepreneurs. Finally, it discussed the specialized policy tools (institutions and organizations) in Gujarat and Kerala, two states leading the field in women entrepreneurs. Yet marketing and management challenges in women-led small-scale initiatives continue to plague these states, a problem endemic to women enterprises across India. This finding indicates the need for additional policy focus on developing managerial skills in addition to technical skills of women entrepreneurs in both formal and informal sectors of the economy (Jerinabi and Santhiyavalli 2001).

Policymakers in Ministries and Offices at various levels of government as well as NGO groups are urged to consider the following additional factors in developing policy options to address managerial, networking and marketing opportunities for women entrepreneurs.

- Business decisions of each group of women entrepreneurs are not only gender specific but are also influenced by their perception and need to do business (Mitra 2002).
- Lack of infrastructure, more often than not, limits access to training and opportunities (Kobeissi 2010).
- Skill development and training programs (in business management, marketing and networking) should address contexts defining a women entrepreneur in a region such that programs and schemes are (i) region-specific, (ii) opportunity versus necessity female entrepreneurship specific and (iii) entrepreneurial motivation specific.
- Better education does not necessarily translate in to better business management and performance or vice versa. For example, in contrast to the rest of the country, women entrepreneurs in Kerala enter in to self employment with better levels of education. Conversely, women-run micro enterprises with lower levels of education in Andhra Pradesh perform at par with their more educated counterparts in Kerala (Ghosh and Cheruvalath 2007).
- The socio-cultural context that limits women's ability to steer their enterprises adequately should be addressed in conjunction with policy efforts to develop women-led initiatives. Effects of programs designed to develop managerial skills of women entrepreneurs may be limited in the absence of policies to counter social norms and mores in conservative male-dominated states such as Gujarat.
- Finally, to be proactive and not only reactionary, policymakers should advocate for (i) motivational training, particularly early in school, (ii) vocational training geared towards practical application of academic education, and (iii) curricular training to develop social interaction and networking skills among girls and women (Field et al. 2010).

REFERENCES

Brush C (1992). Research on women business owners: Past trends, a new perspective and future directions. *Entrepreneurship Theory and Practice*, 16(4), 5–30.

Brush C (1997). Women-owned businesses: Obstacles and opportunities. *Journal of Developmental Entrepreneurship*, 2(1), 1–25.

Carter, S., S. Anderson, and E. Shaw (2001). Women Business Ownership: A Review of the Academic, Popular and Internet Literature, A Report to the Small Business Service. Department of Marketing, University of Strathclyde, August 2001.

Chaganti R (1986). Management in women-owned enterprises. *Journal of Small Business Management*, 24(4), 18–29.

Chakraborti, S (2009). Gender Dimensions of the Informal Sector and Informal Employment in India. Paper presented at the *Global Forum on Gender Statistics*, 26-28 January 2009 Accra, Ghana.

Coad, A. and J.P. Tamvada (2011). Firm growth and barriers to growth among small firms in India. *Small Business Economics*, 39(2), September 2012, 383–400.

Das, M. (2001). Women Entrepreneurs from India: Problems, Motivations and Success Factors. *Journal of Small Business and Entrepreneurship*, 15(4), Winter 2000-2001, 67–81.

Deshpande, S. AND s. Sethi (2009). Women Entrepreneurship In India. *International Research Journal*, 2(9-10), Oct.-Nov.-2009, 13–17.

Field, E., S. Jayachandran, and R. Pande (2010). Do Traditional Institutions Constrain Female Entrepreneurship? A Field Experiment on Business Training in India. *American Economic Review* 100(2), May 2010, 125–29.

Gardiner M and Tiggemann M (1999). Gender differences in leadership style, job stress and mental health in male- and female-dominated industries. *Journal of Occupational and Organisational Psychology*, 72, 301–315.

Ghani, E., W.R. Kerr, and S. O'Connell (2011). Local Industrial Structures and Female Entrepreneurship in India. Working Paper 12-036, Harvard Business School, November 8, 2011.

Ghosh, Piyali and Cheruvalath, Reena (2007). Indian female entrepreneurs as catalysts for economic growth and development, *The International Journal of Entrepreneurship and Innovation*, 8(2), May 2007 , 139–148.

Global Entrepreneurship Monitor (n.d.). List of Key Indicators and Definitions. Retrieved from http://www.gemconsortium.org/key-indicators.

Government of India (2012). SSI in India: Definitions. Development Commissioner (MSME), Ministry of Micro, Small & Medium Enterprises. Retrieved from http://dcmsme.gov.in/ssiindia/definition.htm.

Government of India (2011). Final Report – Fourth All India Census of Micro, Small and Medium Enterprises, 2006-2007 Registered Sector. New Delhi, India: Development Commissioner, MSME, 1–303.

Government of India (2006). The Micro, Small and Medium Enterprises Development Act, 2006, No. 27 Of 2006. The Gazette of India, Legislative Department, Ministry of Law and Justice, New Delhi. Retrieved from http://www.msme.gov.in/MSME_Development_Gazette.htm.

Holmquist C and Sundin E (1988). Women as entrepreneurs in Sweden – conclusions from a survey. In Kirchoff B, Long W, McMullan W, Vesper K and Wetzel W Jr (eds), *Frontiers of Entrepreneurship Research*. Wellesley, MA: Babson College, 643–653.

Jerinabi, U. and G. Santhiyavalli (2001). "Empowerment of Women through Convergence Technology." *Delhi Business Review*, 2(2), July - December 2001.

Kelley, D.J., C.G. Brush, P.G. Greene, and Y. Litovsky (2011). Global Entrepreneurship Monitor, 2010 Report: Women Entrepreneurs Worldwide, Massachusetts & London: Babson College, and the Global Entrepreneurship Research Association (GERA).

Kobeissi, N (2010). Gender factors and female entrepreneurship: International evidence and policy implications. *Journal of International Entrepreneurship*, 8(1), 1–35.

Mitra, R. (2002). The growth pattern of women-run enterprises: An empirical study in India. *Journal of Developmental Entrepreneurship*, 7(2), 217–237.

Mitra, R. & Pingali, V. (1999). Analysis of Growth Stages In Small Firms: A Case Study Of Auto Ancillaries In India. *Journal of Small Business Management*, 37(3), 62–75.

Nagadevara, V (2009). Impact of Gender in Small-scale Enterprises: A Study of Women Enterprises in India. *International Journal of Business and Economics*, 9(1), 111–117.

Pillania, R.K., M. Lall, and S. Saha (2010). Motives for starting business: Indian women entrepreneurs perspectives, *International Journal of Indian Culture and Business Management*, 3(1), 48–67.

Schwab, K. (2011). The Global Competitiveness Report 2011–2012. Geneva, Switzerland: World Economic Forum.

Stanford J, Oates B and Flores D (1995). Women's leadership styles: a heuristic analysis. *Women in Management Review*, 10(2), 9–16.

Verheul, I., A. van Stel, and R. Thurik (2006). Explaining female and male entrepreneurship at the country level. *Entrepreneurship and Regional Development*, 18, 151–183.

World Bank (2011). World Development Indicators. Retrieved from http://data.worldbank.org/indicator/SL.TLF.CACT.FE.ZS.

Economic Profit vs. Heritage and Social Well-being: Swiftlet Farming in the Heritage City of George Town, Malaysia

A.K Siti-Nabiha*, Dayana Jalaludin** and Hasan Ahmad ***

ABSTRACT

This case is about swiftlet farming in Georgetown, a city which was conferred a world heritage status by UNESCO in 2008. Swiftlet farming is a lucrative industry in Malaysia and is considered one of the key projects under the Malaysian Economic Transformation Program. Thus, the issue that needs to be addressed is on how to balance the lucrative economic return versus the negative social, health impact arising from swiftlet farming which also poses a threat the heritage status of the city.

Keywords: Sunrise Industry, heritage, sustainability , swiftlet farming, Malaysia, economic transformation.

INTRODUCTION

George Town, the capital of the state of Penang in Malaysia, is a historical yet metropolitan city. The city well known for its unique architecture and rich culture has great potential in becoming a tourist hub in the Asian region. George Town together with Melaka, was listed as the UNESCO (United Nations Educational, Scientific and Cultural Organization) World Heritage Site in July 2008 (UNESCO website). Both cities are cited as living multicultural heritage and the historic cities of the straits of Malacca. The listing as a world heritage site means the responsibility of the relevant authorities to conserve and protect the sites. If this is not done, then the site will be listed under UNESCO endangered sites and could lead to its being taken away from

* Graduate School of Business, USM.
** School of Management, Universiti Sains Malaysia.
*** School of Management Studies, University of Khartoum, Sudan.
E-mail: nabiha@usm.my, dayana@usm.my, hassanahmed9336@yahoo.com

the list of world heritage (Eckhardt, 2010). For the cities to maintain their status, there are guidelines and obligations that need to be adhered to and these cover the preservation of heritage buildings from those those pertaining to development of new commercial areas, among others.

However, three years after George Town gained its world heritage status, UNESCO issued a letter dated on January 14, 2011 to Malaysia's permanent delegate in Paris, expressing concern over the reports that it had received over the swiftlet issue in the city of George Town. More importantly, the letter had raised the alarming issue of heritage buildings in George Town being converted into bird houses hence jeopardizing the city's prospect in maintaining its heritage status (Yeoh, 2011). The importance of the shop houses to the heritage character of the city was pointed out in the letter. The Malaysian authorities were then requested to determine the accuracy of the reports and to determine the impact to the city if the allegations were true.

Swiftlet farming is not something new in Malaysia and has been a contributor to its agriculture industry since the 1980s. Nevertheless, the existence of swiftlet farming only gained its momentum in Malaysia after 1998. Similar to the rest of the Asian region, the economic crisis of 1997-1998 hit many businesses in Malaysia, especially those that were small to medium sized, resulting in many shops to be closed down. As a result, many business premises were left vacant with no occupants. One economic alternative for these building owners was to turn these idle properties into swiftlet farms (Marican, 2007). Ten years down the road, swiftlet farming has now prospered into a multi million ringgit industry in Malaysia with sales currently touching about RM1.5 billion per year and annual growth of 20 percent (Bernama, 2011)

The governement authorities especially the state and the local government need to rethink on the future of George Town, particularly with regards to two different but interconnected issues i.e. swiftlet farming and heritage status. A quick and rational solution is needed in response to UNESCO's letter. As one of the oldest cities in south east Asia, George Town, with its multiracial culture has so much to offer as a tourist spot. A lot of effort has been done by many parties so that George Town is internationally recognized as a heritage city. The effort towards obtaining heritage status started during the 1980s and the formal application to UNESCO was made in 1996. It took twelves years before the city was listed as a world heritage site. Hence, the concern raised by UNESCO could be said as a reminder to relevant parties to take action or face the possibility of George Town being delisted as a world heritage site.

At the same time, the swiftlet industry is a source of income for the swiftlet farmers in George Town, contributing substantially to Malaysia's agricultural industry. Nevertheless, the well being of the residents in the densely populated city needs to be considered as well. On overall, it is vital to reach a decision that would ensure a sustainable future for George Town as a city that offers comfort living for its people.

SWIFTLET INDUSTRY IN MALAYSIA

Swiftlets are small size birds equipped with narrow wings, wide gape and small beak with bristles to catch insects. Originally, their homes are the dark caves where they build their nests and breed. Swiftlets are best known for its edible and nutritious bird nest, made from the strands of their gummy saliva which will be hardened when exposed to air. These White-nest and Black-nest rare type of nests are mainly found only in the south east Asian countries. These nests are usually eaten after being simmered with chicken broth or sugar. In the Asian society, swiftlet bird nest is a much sought after food as many still believe that eating them would bring various health and beauty benefits. The swiftlet industry is very lucrative. In Malaysia, the price for unprocessed swiftlet nest is between RM3,000 to RM5,000 per kg while those that have been processed fetch a minimum price of RM7,000 per kg (Wong, 2011)

Swiftlet farming has been done for over 100 years with the first recorded farming done in Niah Caves in Sarawak in 1878 (GHP, 2010). Traditionally, the swiftlet nests are harvested from the dark, high corner of the caves by skillfull nest collector who would climb using bamboo ladder. Due to the high risk nature of farming from the cave and while at the same time realizing the lucrative bird nest market, swifltet farming has moved from the caves to villages and in urban areas (GHP, 2010). Hence, some entrepreneurs have ventured into the modern and simpler method in supplying bird nest via swiftlet farming. Swiftlet farming typically involves the conversion of a building or a level of a building to house the swiftlets. These buildings are renovated with dark interiors in order to mimic the environment of a cave. An audio system is put in place to provide continuous chirps and mating sounds so as to attract the population of the swiftlets in the city to fly, mate and build their nest in the building.

At present, Malaysia is the second biggest producer and exporter of Swiftlet bird nest in the world after Indonesia. Edible bird nest from Malaysia is exported to various countries such as Hong Kong, Taiwan, Macau, and China being its largest market. In addition, the Malaysian government has set a target of obtaining 40% of the world market by 2020. The way to acheive this target is through increasing production and downstream industries (Star, January 16, 2012)

The swiftlet industry is highly profitable due to its low cost but high and quick return. Table 1 summarizes a comparison in terms of returns between Oil Palm Industry (which is a major contributor to Malaysian GDP) and Swiftlet Industry in Malaysia. Although the cultivation period of both industries are almost the same, the ROI from Swiftlet Industry increases exponentially hence giving a larger return within a shorter time frame.

Table 1: Oil Palm Industry versus Swiftlet Farming Industry

	Oil Palm Industry	Swiftlet Farming Industry
Land	1-acre	1500 square feet (22 X 70 feet)
Cultivation/Farming	3 years prior to harvest	Almost the same, 3 years
Harvest after 3 years	1 Metric Tonne (MT)	1 Kilogram
Yield	RM 700 (Peak)	RM 4500
Subsequent yield	Constant	Exponential growth

	Oil Palm Industry	Swiftlet Farming Industry
ROI after Year 3	RM700 x 1 MT x 12-month = RM8,400	RM4500 x 1 KG x 12-month = RM54,000
ROI after Year 4	RM700 x 1 MT x 12-month = RM8,400	RM4500 x 2 KG x 12-month = RM108,000
ROI after Year 5	RM700 x 1 MT x 12-month = RM8,400	RM4500 x 3 KG x 12-month = RM162,000

Source: **Swiftlet Eco Park FAQ (2012)** http://www.swiftletecopark.com/english/faq.asp

The Malaysian government through the Agriculture National Key Economic Area (NKEA) has identified edible bird's nest swiftlet farming as one of its 16 Entry Points Projects (EPP) for year 2011. As such, the national policy is to focus on the sunrise high growth industry as the Agriculture and Agro-based Minister expressed and reported in a newspaper:

"The national agro-food policy would not only focus on food sector, but also on new industries with high growth potential like swiftlet nest and ornamental fish industries". (The Star July 19, 2011).

At present, the Swiftlet farming is the top contributor amongst all the agriculture EPP with gross national income (GNI) of RM4,541 million. Among the improvements targeted for the industry in year 2012 are in terms of total bird nest production, total registered and certified premises and processing plants.

The swiftlet farming industry is under the purview of Ministry of Agriculture and Agro-based Industry through the Department of Veterinary Services. The industry is regulated through the enforcement of Good Animal Husbandry Practices and the Veterinary Health of the Department of Veterinary Services (ETP Annual Report, 2011). The Department of Veterinary Services is also given the responsibility for the growth of the industry. The guidelines and standards for swiflet farmers issued in 2010 regulates the industry. Major guidelines pertaining to location of swiftlet premise are reproduced as under:

"Housing or premise of these birds must be located at least 100 meter radius from any urban settlement. This is the distance approved by the Ministry of Science and Environment for noise and sound pollution travel. Or otherwise the farm house should

be located on agricultural land strata. Housing of these swiftlets within the city infrastructure is forbidden. The use of heritage buildings for these swiftlets ranching is against the law. 'Cost town', area where there is minimum human activity and the buildings are left to rot or exist empty can be considered based on the Local Council approval". (Section 5, GAHP, 2010)

THE HERITAGE AND TOURIST CITY OF GEORGE TOWN

George Town, is the second largest city in Malaysia. It is located on the north-east corner of Pulau Pinang (Penang Island). Originally, Penang was a part of the Malay Sultanate of Kedah, until it was ceded to the British East India Company in exchange for military protection from the attack of Siamese and Burmese armies. In 1826, Penang, together with Melaka and Singapore was declared as British territories known as Straits Settlements (Wikipedia, 2012). Today, George Town is a modern and highly urbanized city yet rich in history. Besides Bandar Melaka, George Town is the only city in Malaysia that has been conferred as the UNESCO World Heritage Site. In their effort to recognize and protect significant heritage sites worldwide, UNESCO had adopted the Convention concerning the Protection of the World Cultural and Natural Heritage 1972. Since 1978, UNESCO had listed various location of special cultural or physical significance on their World Heritage List. A city like George Town may benefit in terms of various aspects via the heritage status such as cultural and economic tourism. Additionally, UNESCO also provides funding and expert advice for conservation projects within their heritage sites. Although George Town remains a part of the legal territory of Pulau Pinang, UNESCO now considers George Town under the responsibility of the international community in terms of the preservation of its heritage sites (Wikipedia, 2012).

The city of George Town is literally a home for both human and swiftlets. At present, there are about 200 to 300 swiftlet farms in George Town, making up about 10 percent to 20 percent of houses in George Town. Majority of these farms are located in shophouses inside the heritage buildings, immediately next or a few metres away. In order to attract the swiftlets, these buildings were sealed and set up with a sprinkler system to continuously moisten the environment. Such conversion is not only detrimental to the building fabric, but is claimed to encourage mosquito breeding. The unattended electrical equipment and appliances in these empty buildings may also cause fire hazard (Emmanuel, 2010).

Furthermore, the existence of swiftlet farms in the residential areas brings various public health concerns such as dengue, H5N1 bird flu and bird mites fever. The human residences which are forced to coexist with the swiftlets would have to endure loud chirping sounds broadcast around the clock as well as the nuisance of bird faeces. Such disturbances have forced many of the disappointed residents to move out while at the same time plunging down the rental price and property value of these buildings since their livable condition is basically questionable.

As early as 2005, swiftlet farmers in George Town had been requested to relocate their businesses to a more suitable agriculture area. Then another declaration was made that by end of 2008 the swiftlet farms would be moved out city, but the ruling was deferred by the state government to end of 2009 (Ducket-Wilkinson, 2009). Again the state government deferred the ruling to move out all swiftlet farms from the city of George Town by 2010 (Eckhardt, 2010). This ruling was again deferred. There are still swiftlet farms in George Town. The Deputy Prime Minister made a statement as reported in the national newspapers (September, 2010) that new swiflet farms were not allowed in heritage areas and the existing farms were given three years grace period; they would be allowed to be in operations for another three years (Bernama, 2010).

The guidelines on swiftlets by the Malaysian government have been criticized that there is no clear definition given on the term "fully residential". The 100 meter radius away from the fully residential building (as required by the Malaysian Standard- Good Animal Husbandry Practice) is viewed as too short of a distance for many George Town residences. The Penang Heritage Trust, a non-governmental organization committed in preserving the history and culture of Penang, have voiced out their worries on the future well-being of George Town if current conditions persist (Duckett-Wilkinson, 2010).

Nevertheless, relocation of the swiftlet farms is a costly and complex task. The migration will be a hassle since it will involve thousands of swiftlets. Swiftlet farming has been in George Town for the past twenty years, providing high income generation for its investors. The Association of Swiftlet Nest Industry (ASNI) argue that Swiftlets are part of Penang heritage and majority of the swiftlet farms are legally operated under the Application of License for Bird's Nest Industry, Penang 2005 (Malaysian Explorer, 2012). The Secretary General of Small and Medium sized Industries Association of Penang argues that the those businesses that were in operations before the city obtained its listing should be allowed to continue to operate:

> "I feel that swiftlet farming should be allowed to continue to exist on the condition that those farms established prior to 2008, before the heritage listing, should be allowed to stay" (The Guardian, 2010).

A SUSTAINABLE SOLUTION?

Thus, what are the solutions for the city, especially for the state and local authorities? The option of closing down all swiftlet farms in George Town would stir resistance from the swiftlet farmers due to its financial impact. However, the existence of swiftlet farms in George Town will lead to the possibility of the city being delisted as a world heritage site. On top of that, urban swiftlet farming poses huge health threat and a big nuisance to the rest of the city's population. A fair and wise decision must be taken for the wellbeing of all parties. A sustainable solution that leverages the quality of life for the people in the city, considering all the three aspects of environmental, social and economic must be reached. The following issues need to be considered and resolved:

1. Who are the parties at stake in this controversial issue? What are their interests? Is there a consistency between these interests and the future of the city?

2. Is swiftlet farming a threat to the city? If yes, are there possible solutions that would not jeopardize the edible bird nest industry?

3. Why was it difficult to enforce the ruling of no swiftlet farming by the local authorities? What can be done by the NGOs to ensure that swiftlet farmers move out from the heritage areas?

ACKNOWLEDGMENT

The author(s) would like to extend their appreciation to the Universiti Sains Malaysia for the Research University Grant entitled 'Tourism Planning' [Grant No. 1001/PTS/8660013] that makes this study and paper possible.

REFERENCES

Abdul Kadir, F (2011) Good Animal Husbandry Practices for Edible-Nest Swiftlets Aerodemus Species Ranching and Its Premis, Department of Veterinary Serices, Ministry of Agriculture Malaysia.

Bernama (2010, September 9) Report: Local government council agrees to gated community guidelines.

Bernama (2011, October 7). Report: Malaysian edible bird nest to capture 40 percent of global market by 2020. 15 July, 2012 from http://www.bernama.com/bernama/v5/newsbudget2012.php?id=618407

Duckett-Wilkinson, R. (2010). Swiftlet guidelines in place. 15 July, 2012 from

http://www.igeorgetownpenang.com/opinion/618-swiftlet-guidelines-in-place

Emmanuel, M. (2010). Penang swiflet industry needs a proper nest. 15 July, 2012 from http://www.btimes.com.my/Current_News/BTIMES/articles/swift8/Article/

Eckhart, R. (2010) A Tale of Two Cities, The Wall Street Journal, June, 24, 2010

ETP Annual Report 2011. Agriculture. 15 July, 2012 from http://etp.pemandu.gov.my/annualreport/upload/ENG_NKEA_Agriculture.pdf

Malaysian Explorer (2012). Penang bird nest heritage. 15 July, 2012 from

http://www.malaysian-explorer.com/penangNews-penangBirdnestHeritage.html

Swiftlet Eco Park FAQ (2012). What is the ROI for swiftlet ranching? 15 July, 2012 from http://www.swiftletecopark.com/english/faq.asp

The Guardian (August 10, 2010). George Town fears losing World Heritage status over birds' nest soup. 15 July 2012 from http://www.guardian.co.uk/world/2010/aug/10/bird-farming-swift-penang-malaysia

The Star Online (2011, July 19). National agro-food policy soon to ensure sufficient supply. 15 July, 2012 from http://thestar.com.my/news/story.asp?file=/2011/7/19/nation/20110719164511&sec=nation

Wikipedia (2012, July). George Town, Penang. 15 July, 2012, from http://en.wikipedia.org/wiki/George_Town,_Penang

UNESCO website (www.unesco.org/en/list/1223)

Wikipedia (2012, July). Swiftlet. 15 July, 2012, from http://en.wikipedia.org/wiki/Swiftlet

Wong, J. (2011). Sarawakians going into swiftlet farming in a big way. The Star, January 17, 2011.

Yeoh, W. (2011). George Town's heritage status may be in jeopardy. The Star, February 24, 2011.

The Relational Dimension of Social Capital: The Social Embeddedness of Strategic Management

Katja Karintaus* and Hanna Lehtimäki**

ABSTRACT

The purpose of this case is to deepen understanding about the social embeddedness of strategy implementation. The study draws on a network survey conducted in four internationally operating companies. Managers in different units were asked to name their network connections within the firm and to describe personal and organizational communication. The study presents analysis on the values inherent in communicating with colleagues. As an outcome, the study provides insight into the relational dimension of social capital and into the ways by which social relations within the firm facilitate strategy implementation.

Keywords: Social capital, strategic management, collaborative advantage, relational view

INTRODUCTION

The purpose of this study is to deepen understanding about the social embeddedness of strategy implementation. Focusing on the relational dimension of social capital we examine social connections in four internationally operating companies. The study is built on the widely established argument that social capital is a source of collaborative advantage and value creation for organizations (Lee, 2009; Nahapiet, 2009). Social capital research addresses the growing importance of cooperation between the members of an organization in accomplishing strategy initiatives and in creating and exploiting collaborative advantage (Nahapiet, 2009) Social capital literature argues that intra-firm relationships provide a source for collaborative advantage through access

* Katja Karintaus is a Doctoral Student and Researcher, School of Management, University of Tampere, Finland
**Hanna Lehtimäki is Professor, Department of Business, Innovation Management, University of Eastern Finland, Kuopio Campus, Kuopio, Finland
E-mail: katja.karintaus@uta.fi, hanna.lehtimaki@uef.fi

to information and resources in the social network within and across organizational boundaries (Nahapiet&Ghoshal, 1998).

Much of social capital research has studied the structure of social relations within and between organizations. Research on multinational enterprises (MNEs) argue that the challenge in building organizational advantage lies in the difficulty of managing social connections and in measuring the efficiency and effectiveness of the connections (Kostova& Roth,2003). Furthermore, there is a broad consent that social capital is built on not only efficient reporting and sharing of explicit knowledge but also on rich variety of social interaction, which allows for sharing tacit and complex knowledge (cf. Gupta &Govindarajan, 2000).

Social capital is most commonly treated as a construct with relationship structure and relationship content (Bartkus& Davis, 2009). In this study, we focus on the content of the individual level relationships. The interest is, in particular, in the values inherent in relational activity. The purpose is to gain insight into the social construction of meaning on intra-firm relationships (Gergen, 2009; Heracleous& Hendry, 2000, p. 1255). The study draws on a network survey conducted in four internationally operating companies. The respondents were asked to name their network connections within the firm and to describe personal and organizational communication.

Drawing on the relational constructionism (Hosking, 1995; Gergen 1994, 2009) the interest in the analysis lies in examining the ways by which the norms and values of relationships and the expectations towards the interacting individuals are discoursively constructed. This approach argues that in order to understand individual reason we must first understand the relationships where the individual is embedded in (Gergen, 2009, p. xxi). Thus, interpersonal communication is studied as a discursive construct. The paper joins the interpretive approaches to discourse and conceptualizes discourse as communicative action that is constructive of social and organizational reality (Heracelous& Hendry, 2000, p. 1252). Respondents' expressions about communication are studied as projecting possibilities for being-in-the-world, focusing on the emergent effects of discourse on actors in relation with each other (Heracleous& Hendry, 2000, p. 1256).

The research question in this study is: How do social relations facilitate the implementation of strategy initiative? In seeking to answer this question, we ask: 1) What kind of social interaction do strategy initiatives call for? and2) What do interacting individuals consider as valuable in interaction?

This paper contributes to the social capital literature, first, by presenting results on an empirical research examining the relational dimension of social capital. Second, qualitative analysis on the meaning making in micro-level interaction deepens our understanding about the ways by which social capital fosters collaborative advantage. As a managerial contribution, this study highlights the importance of understanding the construction of meaning in the everyday practices among the members of an organization. For the top management, it is important to understand the fabric of intra-organizational social relations that facilitates action in the chosen strategic direction. Also, understanding the social relations provides for maintaining social capital and transforming the existing social capital into competitive advantage.

The paper is divided into three sections. We will, first, review the existing research on the role of social capital in creating collaborative advantage. Next, we will present the strategic initiatives of four internationally operating companies and the analysis on the social relations within the firms. Finally, we will discuss the implications of our study for research and practice.

SOCIAL CAPITAL CREATES COLLABORATIVE ADVANTAGE

Social capital research addresses the importance of understanding cooperation between individuals when implementing strategy initiatives and creating and exploiting collaborative advantage (Nahapiet, 2009). The most commonly used framework of social capital in research in management literature is that of Nahapiet and Ghoshal (1998). They identify three dimensions of social capital: structural, relational and cognitive. The structural dimension refers to the actors' network positions and the configuration of the whole network (Bartkus& Davis, 2009, p. 6; Borgatti& Foster, 2003). Measures of centrality and betweenness are used to investigate the individuals' locations in the network, and measures of centralization, connectivity and density are used to evaluate the characteristics of the whole network (Scott, 1991; Borgatti& Foster, 2003).

While the structural dimension describes to whom people have relationships, the concept of relational social capital refers to the contents and quality of these relationships (Bartkus& Davis, 2009). Even though two people could be similarly connected with other individuals within the network structure, the outcomes of the relationships may differ depending on the emotional and personal attachments between the interacting individuals. The relational dimension of social capital comprises trust and trustworthiness, norms and sanctions, obligations and expectations, and identity and identification (Nahapiet & Ghoshal, 1998, p. 244).

The cognitive dimension, in turn, refers to the shared codes and narratives among those in interaction (Nahapiet & Ghoshal, 1998, p. 244). We have chosen not to position our study within this dimension as, when adopting an interpretative approach, it would call for analysis focused on sense-making (Weick, 1979) or narrative analysis on the shared codes and language (Czarniawska, 1998). These assumptions highlight the contribution of social capital to understanding value creation and competitive advantage as a relational rather than market based phenomenon (Nahapiet&Ghoshal, 1998). The construct of social capital allows for studying the connections of members of an organization that are not visible in the organization charts and prescribed processes. Furthermore, it allows for taking into account not only the instrumentality of ties between the interacting individuals but also the other aspects of social connectedness, such as sociability, approval, acceptance, social support and pleasure (Nahapiet, Gratton& Rocha, 2005).

Social capital contributes to the intra-organizational knowledge creation and exchange of information. The relational aspects of relationship create the conditions that facilitate the individual capabilities and motivation to exchange and combine knowledge (Nahapiet & Ghoshal 1998, p. 254). It is not only to whom the individuals are connected but also how they are connected. Thus, in order to understand how competitive advantage is created through relational activity, attention needs to be paid on the content and quality of the relationships.

METHODOLOGY

In this research, the research design, data collection and preliminary analysis of network survey results were conducted in close collaboration with the companies. The research design follows the framework of engaged scholarship, according to which the planning, implementation and the utilization of the results are carried out in close collaboration with the participating companies. Such an approach seeks to ensure the relevance of the research while ensuring its theoretical validity (Van de Ven, 2007). This is an inductive collective case study (Stake, 2000; Eriksson, &Kovalainen, 2008) and the interest is in developing a theoretically informed understanding about the phenomenon (Eriksson &Kovalainen, 2008, p. 119; Stake, 2000). Two researchers were involved in designing the study and collecting and analyzing the data.

The data was collected in four internationally operating companies between 2010-2012. The process of data collection followed a similar pattern in all companies. First, an interview or a workshop with the top management of the company was organized to discuss the company's business situation, the future strategic initiatives and the focusing of the network survey. Notes and recordings were taken during these meetings. The interviews and workshops lasted between one to two hours and they were recorded and transcribed.Second, three to five directors in different locations were individually interviewed to deepen the understanding on the key issues in business development. The main interest was to discuss collaboration practices between the distant sales companies and the headquarters. The interviews were made either face-to-face or over a videoconference depending on the location of the director. The interviews were recorded and transcribed.

Third, a social network questionnaire was sent globally to managers. The respondents to the survey belonged to top-middle and middle management and they were located in units in different countries. The questionnaire comprised both network survey and open ended questions to depict how the managers perceived internal communication. The primary data in this study consists of answers to the open ended question which was stated as follows:

'Think about the colleague or workmate that you prefer to cooperate most with. What makes that collaborative relationship successful?' The total number of responses was 173.

The response rate to the questionnaire varied between 70 to 80 %. The analysis of data was conducted using the methods of content and discourse analysis. Attention was paid to the adjectives describing what makes the collaborative relationship successful with other individuals within the firm. The analysis then proceeded to assessing the meanings and the ways by which they construct the inherent values of acting in relationships.

RESULTS

Strategic Initiatives

All four companies were seeking to increase the sales, strengthen the customer interface and enhance the flow of customer knowledge within the firm. The companies were just recovering from the 2008-2009 recession and were seeking to find ways to transfer the operating mode from savings and streamlining the business into looking forward and building new growth for the business. The strategic initiatives of each company and theirs interests in participating in the study are summarized in Table 1.

Table 1

The Strategic Initiatives of The Case Firms

Company	Strategic initiative	Interest regarding intra-organizational communication
A	To increase the sales orientation of the service and maintenance personnel when visiting the customer's site on maintenance duties. The service and maintenance employees pay regular visits to customers' premises, and easily build the relationships of trust with the customer. They were now expected to convey the sales information from the company to the customers, and to inform the company about sales opportunities and new signals from the market.	The management wanted to gain a better view of the flows of activity within the firm and to better understand how the social connections within the firm support the strategic initiative to foster the proactive sales of maintenance personnel.
B	To increase information flow between headquarters and regional sales units. The recession period had obliged the company to exercise very strict and controlled management which had focused communication on continuous reporting of sales results.	There was a need for understanding the unofficial communication practices and structures both within and between the headquarters and sales companies.

C	To enhance cooperation practices between the sales and projects. In order to survive the recession, the company started to make tailored projects for customers, which required new practices for knowledge sharing within the firm.	The company's interest was, first, to understand, whether the sales support group had achieved the role planned for it, second, to learn about how cooperation takes place between the different teams, and, third, how the practices of cooperation could be further developed.
D	To build an organization model which can grow internationally and form strong network of distributors around the world.	To understand how the communication is structured between different units in different countries, and to understand how the new organization model functions. To learn personnel's thoughts about changes and the capabilities of the new organization.

In company A, the strategic initiative and the interest in learning about interpersonal interaction was related to fostering proactive sales by the maintenance personnel and to increasing the efficiency of sharing customer information within the firm. The strategy language used by the top management emphasizes the role of individuals in information sharing and examines information sharing primarily as an activity of exchange. The focus and desire were on the efficiency of information sharing. The company wanted to utilize the social capital already created in the relationships between customers and the service personnel. The service personnel had access to customers, they had created trustful relationships with customers and they had the same language to discuss the technical details with customers.

In company B, the practice of information sharing in the past had heavily relied on the reporting of financial data from the subsidiaries to the headquarters. The interest of the company was to take another look at the communication and to find out whether there was any ground in supporting a richer communication between the headquarters and the subunits. A need to broaden an understanding of the personal interaction between the individuals was expressed.

In company C, the strategy initiative emphasized collaboration between individuals. The interest in individual level collaboration was to understand how it supported complex knowledge sharing. The goal was not only to support the exchange of information but also to foster learning together. The company provided highly technical projects, which required that very complex knowledge was shared efficiently between the different parts of the organization. The interest of the company was to build strong and dense relationships between the sales, project support and research and development.

In Company D, the strategy initiative was related to the capability of the organization to grow internationally. The company had recently implemented a new organizational structure and the aim was to understand how it supported knowledge sharing and information exchange, and the international growth of the company.

Common to all four strategy initiatives is the goal of gaining business benefits from the exchange of information and sharing knowledge. Inherent in the initiatives is the goal of well-functioning collaboration between individuals in different parts of the organization. The interest regarding intra-organizational communication in all companies relate to the practices of knowledge sharing and to the ways by which access to information is created in the organization.

Content of Social Relations

To depict the relational aspect of social capital, the respondents were asked to describe a colleague with whom the respondent preferred to work with and to illustrate what made collaboration with colleagues within the firm successful. Table 2 summarizes the thematisation of the responses. First, the expressions in the questionnaire were grouped together under similar topics that formed a classification of the expressions. The classifications were then grouped together and they formed five themes that express relational values inherent in communication.

The first two themes express the value of goal and task orientation. The first theme, 'Good corporate citizen', comprises an understanding of the business goals for the whole company, showing commitment to the company and fellow workers and manifesting personal skill and expertise. The second theme, 'Skill in information sharing', consists of professional communication behaviour and timely and reliable communication. Also, it was expressed that maintaining routines in communication were helpful in creating successful knowledge sharing and information exchange. Both themes construct an understanding of social relations as instrumental. What becomes emphasised as valuable is efficiency and reliability in information transfer. Also, expertise and good manners are considered as elements to professional relations. This appears to emphasise the mechanistic feature of social relations in a corporate setting.

The three consequent themes emphasise social connectedness as a value in relationships. The third theme, 'Skill in working together', include approachability, capability to listen, skill in giving feedback and capability to cooperate. The fourth theme 'Capability to provide for a rewarding communication', consists of trustworthy behaviour, showing personal responsibility, and delightfulness. The fifth theme 'Sharing a sense of togetherness', comprises of seeing eye to eye, giving from oneself, personal agility, and frankness. These themes construct an understanding of social relations as valuable in terms of sociability and sense of togetherness. What becomes constructed as valuable is the richness and quality of social interaction. The expressions manifest sociability, connectedness and as inherent values in connecting with others and working together within a firm.

Table 2

Relational Values Inherent in Communication

Theme	Classification	Expressions in the questionnaire
Good corporate citizen	Business goals in mind	Looking into corporate interest instead of own The whole company's perspective Understanding the whole picture Both thinking the best interest of the company See the whole business setting, not only one's own sandbox Shared vision Common goals Serving customer
	Commitment	Find common solutions Team spirit
	Personal capability in the subject matter	Competence Competence in technical issues Competence in customer issues Professional skills Knowledge Expertise Experience Effective Fixing problems Providing solutions Capability to tell so that the information is easy to understand
Skill in information sharing	Communication behavior	Communication skills Correct manners Professional in information exchange Open communication Good communication on personal level Honest communication Direct communication Professionalism in response Fluency
	Speed in communication	Immediate feedback Rapid response Prompt reply Fast reaction Immediate response Work with speed Quick and clear replies to questions Quick response to questions
	Reliability in communication	Respect of deadline Reply on request Confidence that you will get an answer Reliable
	Routine in communication	Daily communication Regular discussion and meetings Using all available media

Skill in working together	Approachability	Easiness to do work Easy to contact Easy to communicate
	Capability to listen	Listening Time to listen Ability to listen Understanding even without saying too much Listens to other's perspective Being available
	Skill in giving feedback	Honest and constructive feedback Gives feedback Gives direct feedback without badwill
	Capability to cooperate	Willingness to cooperate Willingness to go the extra mile Willingness to help Getting help when needed Ability to enjoy a colleagues success Active Problem solving mentality Proactive
Capability to provide for a rewarding communication	Trustworthy behavior	Keeping promises Honesty Integrity Supporting each other Mutual trust and understanding Mutual respect and understanding Meeting expectations Same duties
	Showing personal responsibility	Responsible, Taking responsibility Reliable, Reliability Confidence Sense of duty Capable of making decisions Attention to detail Passion Showing commitment Humbleness
	Delightfulness	Joy Inspiring Capability to challenge in a positive way Nice to work with Positive Feel comfortable with the person Friendly attitude Friendliness Positive attitude towards others Positive attitude

Sharing a sense of togetherness	Seeing eye to eye	Long term relationship Personal relationship Similar experiences Likemindedness Same interests Mutual understanding Feeling of togetherness Personal relationship with trust and support
	Giving from oneself	Fruitful discussions Fruitful dialogue Willingness to dialogue Solving questions together Sharing ideas and developing them together Common sense of humor Good sense of humor
	Personal agility	Open dialogue Open communication in good and bad Open mindedness Flexibility Adopting to new Openness Transparency Sincerity
	Frankness	Goodwill No backstabbing No hidden agendas No secrets

The analysis of the expressions shows that both instrumentality and social connectedness become constructed as the features of social relationships. This finding is supported by a finding by Uzzi (1997), whereby ideally there is a balance between arms-length ties, i.e. ties that emphasise transaction and economic exchange, and embedded ties, i.e. ties of close relationships with trust, fine grained information transfer and joint problem solving arrangements.

CONCLUSIONS

In this study, social embeddedness was chosen as the key construct for understanding the implementation of strategic initiatives. A close examination of the relational dimension of social capital allows for a deepened understanding of fabric of social relations. The results of analysis provide insight into our understanding about the intra-firm relationships as not only instrumental but also comprising a rich variety of values inherent in sociability.

The analysis show, that in the everyday social activity, both task orientation and sociability are values simultaneously present. It can be concluded that for collaboration to be successful, social relations need to manifest the values of both instrumentality and social connectedness. However, the strategic initiatives do not explicitly express goals or challenges that link to the value of social connectedness.

The strategic initiatives recognize access to information, trust and collaboration as the important aspects of social activity and knowledge sharing. When put in contrast to the values expressed by the interacting individuals, this understanding of the social activity appears as abstract and universal. The strategic initiatives do not appreciate the richness of social activity, and thus, it could be argued, the benefits of social capital cannot be fully exploited. By increasing the acknowledgement of the importance of sociability in strategic management, the potential of social connectedness could be better capitalized.

In internationally operating companies the connections tend to be weak because of cultural and geographical distances. To achieve functioning relationships that are capable of handling rich knowledge and solve complex problems, the relationships require intended attention (Kilduff, 1993). This study shows that social connections in internationally operating companies are manifold, but without recognition from the top management, the company is not capable of utilizing social connections in building collaborative advantage.

REFERENCES

Bartkus, V. O., & Davis, J.H. (2009). Introduction: the yet undiscovered value of social capital. In V.O. Bartkus, & J.H. Davis (Eds.),*Social Capital. Reaching Out, Reaching In*(pp. 1–14). Cheltenham, UK: Edward Elgar.

Borgatti, S.P., & Foster, P.C. (2003). The Network Paradigm in Organizational Research: A Review and Typology. *Journal of Management, 29,* 6, 991–1013.

Czarniawska, B. (1998). *A Narrative Approach to Organization Studies.*Qualitative Research Methods Series 43. Thousand Oaks: Sage Publications.

Eriksson, P., &Kovalainen, A. (2008).*Qualitative Methods in Business Research.* Los Angeles: Sage.

Gergen, K. (1994). *Realities and Relationships.Soundings in Social Construction.* Cambridge: Harvard University Press.

Gergen, K. (2009). *Relational Being.Beyond Self and Community.* Oxford: Oxford University Press.

Gupta, A.,&Govindarajan, V. (2000). Knowledge flows within multinational corporations. *Strategic Management Journal, 21,* 473-496.

Hansen, M.T. (1999). The search-transfer problem: The role of weak ties in sharing knowledge across organization subunits. *Administrative Science Quarterly, 44,* 82-111.

Heracleous, L.,& Hendry, J. (2000). Discourse and the study of organization: Toward a structurational perspective. *Human Relations, 53,* 10, 1251–1286.

Hosking, D.-M. (1995). Constructing Powers: Entitative and Relational Approaches.In D.-M. Hosking, P. Dachler, & K. J. Gergen (Eds.),*Management and Organisation: Relational Alternatives to Individualism* (pp. 51–70). Aldershot: Ashgate.

Kilduff, M. (1993).The Reproduction of Inertia in Multinational Corporations.In S. Ghoshal, &E. Westney (Eds.), *Organization Theory and the Multinational Corporation* (pp. 250-274). New York: St. Martin's Press.

Kostova, T.,& Roth, K. (2003).Social capital in multinational corporations and a micro-macro model of its formation.*Academy of Management Review*, 28, 2, 297-317.

Lee, R. (2009). Social capital and business and management: Setting a research agenda. *International Journal of Management Review*, 11, 3, 247–273.

Nahapiet, J. (2009).Capitalizing on Connections: Social Capital and Strategic Management. In V. Bartkus, & J. Davis (Eds.).*Social Capital: Reaching Out, Reaching In*(pp. 205–236). Edward Elgar Publishing Ltd.

Nahapiet, J.,&Ghoshal, S. (1998). Social Capital, Intellectual Capital and the Organizational Advantage.*Academy of Management Review*, 23, 2,242–266.

Nahapiet, J., Gratton, L., & Rocha, H. (2005). Knowledge and relationships: when cooperation is the norm. *European Management Review*, 2, 1, 3–14.

Scott, J. (1991). *Social Network Analysis*. London: Sage.

Stake, R. (2000).Case Studies.In N.K. Denzin& Y.S. Lincoln (Eds.) *Handbook of Qualitative Research*(pp.1–28). 2nd edition. Thousand Oaks: Sage.

Uzzi, B. (1997). Social Structure and Competition in Interfirm Networks: The Paradox of Embeddedness. *Administrative Science Quarterly*, 42, 1, 35–67.

Van de Ven, A. H. (2007). *Engaged Scholarship.A Guide for Organizational and Social Research*. Oxford: Oxford University Press.

Weick, K. (1979). *The Social Psychology of Organizing*.New York: McGraw-Hill.

Vedanta Resources' Entrepreneurial Run

*A. Sahay**

ABSTRACT

This case tracks the story of Mr. Anil Agarwal, Chairman, Vedanta Resources, who was a shy lad studying in a School in Patna, Bihar. His move to Bombay and his amazing entrepreneurial run thereafter to the position of the Chairman of Vedanta Resources Plc, the number 2 global diversified mining company has been captured in this case; emphasis being on his last act, that of growth through the acquisition of Cairn India Ltd. It is a teaching case where issues related to entrepreneurship like idea, ambition, risk, financing, technology, growth etc. have been dealt with. The main objective of this case was to make students learn what corporate entrepreneurship is and how a corporate entrepreneur acts. Though, the case has been mainly written for teaching corporate entrepreneurship, it can also be used for teaching Alliances, Acquisition or Growth strategy.

Keywords: Vedanta Resources, Growth strategy, acquisition, alliances, technology, risk, entrepreneurship.

INTRODUCTION

Anil Agrawal, Chairman of Vedanta Resources (VR) announced on 16th August 2010 a deal for acquiring controlling share (51%) of Cairn India Ltd (CIL) from Cairn Energy Plc (CE) for a consideration of $ 9.6bn (Rs. 44931.84 cr). It had taken a long 18 months to complete the deal. Anil had a long wait; he was keeping his fingers crossed but he never lost hope. He was optimistic about the deal and was patiently taking the steps needed from his side. It was Sir Bill Gammel, Chairman of Cairn Energy Plc., who was in hurry to take some cash out from CIL to invest in his new Greenland Oilfield (Cairn Energy Plc, 2011) project. He had been running pillar to post to make the deal go through. The other partner in Cairn India Limited (CIL) was Oil and Natural Gas Commission (ONGC) Limited which held 30% of the equity of CIL. Initially ONGC muddled the deal with their 'first right to refusal' and 'payment of royalty' issues. First, the see-saw game was going on between the two parent companies of CIL but

* Dean Research, Birla Institute of Management Technology, Greater Noida, India
E-mail: arun.sahay@bimtech.ac.in

finally the ball landed in the court of Govt. of India (GOI). Even British Prime Minister, David Cameron had pursued the matter through a letter to Indian Prime Minister emphasizing the importance of the deal. Despite that, the subject of approval of the deal went back and forth between the concerned ministries and the cabinet committee of economic affairs. The Oil Ministry of GOI had provisionally cleared the deal in June, 2011 putting eleven conditions to be fulfilled. These conditions might have adversely affected Vedanta Resources. Anil, however, was a great negotiator. He mooted the idea, "Why not check the legal position?" The petroleum ministry referred the matter to law ministry. The later opined on the preconditions that "any terms and conditions to be stipulated should be mutually agreed and they cannot be unilaterally imposed." One of the officials, further, said, "The condition that Cairn has to forego its legal right shall be void under Indian Contract Act." The Petroleum Ministry made a hasty retreat and put only five preconditions (Annexure I). Anil was not deterred at all. His determination to get into petroleum sector got further fortified. In compliance with the conditions put by Government of India (GOI), Cairn and Vedanta renegotiated the deal and got approval from their respective boards. The final clearance for the deal came from GOI on January 24, 2012. To consummate the deal, Vedanta Resources were looking at various financial options. However, Anil was confident of pooling resources. Even though burdened with this debt, his main worry was – which target next?

It was January 26, 2012. People in India were celebrating the Republic Day. Anil, sitting in his London office at 16, Berkley Street, was wondering whether his India focused mining strategy was right! He had succeeded in earlier acquisitions and Greenfield (virgin field where no mining/industry existed earlier) projects in India but going was getting tougher due to various social and environmental issues. Though he had lapped up the CIL deal at much lower cost as the "no compete" clause and accordingly, the premium to be paid was removed from the agreement, he was not yet contented. He was wondering about the future of Vedanta Resources in general and CIL in particular. While his mind was working on the expansion scenario of CIL, he recalled his journey from a small trader of copper cable to the CEO of a global company. He looked back at his entrepreneurial moves and the twists and turns he faced. Now, he was number 9 in the pecking order (Revenue and EBITDA) in global mining companies (Annexure II). However, if one adds oil and gas to diversification basket, Vedanta Resources is number 2 global diversified mining company next to BHP Billiton. CIL was a jewel in the crown of Vedanta Resources that catapulted it to the top club of miners. After the acquisition, he was not bothered much about the debt he needed to consummate the deal nor was he bothered about the pending issues in CIL acquisition. He was confident of overcoming them as also integrating CIL in Vedanta's fold. His present challenge was to restructure his companies so that the efficiency of the group could be enhanced and the maximum funds could be extracted out of his own companies to meet the cost of the deal and to minimize the borrowings.

THE START OF ENTREPRENEURIAL JOURNEY

Anil Agarwal was born in 1954 in Patna (Bihar, India). He belonged to a family in the business of electrical conductors. He did his schooling at Miller School, Patna; hardly known even within the country. A vegetarian, Anil enjoyed cycling. He is a devotee of the Hindu God Lord Krishna. In the year 1976, at the age of 15, he left the school and undertook his maiden journey to Mumbai (Bombay) with a fire in the belly. Though his parents could well afford his higher education, he had something else in the mind. He wanted to be his own boss; decide his own destiny. Without losing any time, he started his business as a metal scrap dealer under the banner of Rainbow Investments Ltd. that was created to manufacture and deal in electrical wires and cables of all kinds. In the scrap trading, the investment was low, turnover fast and the returns were high though it needed moving pillar to post. "This business showed him the importance of raw materials in industry", he said in an interview in London on August, 2010 (Kayakiran & Katakey, 2010)

Soon, Anil began to feel that his scrap business, which made him understand the metal business, was trading only – a small part of the value chain. He wanted to become bigger. He started looking at forward and backward integration which was beyond the brief of Rainbow Investments Ltd under whose banner he was operating. With his inputs, on the 19th October, 1976, the name of the company was changed to Sterlite Cables Ltd. with much wider objectives. After this change, his first business move of consequence was in 1979. He acquired copper-cable producer Shamsher Sterling Corp. from the king of Nepal. This transaction required him to take a bank loan. Though the loan amount was small, it made him learn the importance of the cost of money and the value of its repayment. Immediately, he ramped up the production and sales of copper cable to repay the loan faster. On the contrary, he realized that it created the need for more money and thus, more borrowing. The demand far outstripped the production requiring capacity expansion that required even more money. By now, he had learnt that based on the business performance, it was easier to arrange more money but he started feeling the pinch on the front of organizational capability. This made him undertake the strengthening of the organization and creating a new organizational structure, which he did with midas touch without losing any time.

CREATION & GROWTH OF STERLITE INDUSTRIES (INDIA), LTD

On 28th February, 1986, Sterlite Cables Ltd was renamed as Sterlite Industries (India), Ltd (SIIL). This required a fresh Certificate of Incorporation; in the process he got initiated to the essentials of company law. With the incorporation of the new company with a much wider scope of activities, he wanted to expand fast. At that time, In India, a big expansion plan for telephone network was undertaken. He did not lose anytime; his first thought was to grab this opportunity by adding a product line to his portfolio of products. He signed a technical collaboration agreement with M/s. Essex Group Inc, USA which was for a period of five years. It provided for the technical information, know-how and knowledge relating to the manufacture of telephone cables. The agreement needed approval by the Government of India which he ultimately got. In the process, he learnt the working of government systems and how to deal with them. M/s. Essex Group Inc, with whom technical agreement was signed, was a division of United Technologies, U.S.A. Implementation of this agreement made him move to and fro between the strategic business unit (SBU) and parent company which, in turn, made him understand the relationship of SBU and parent company as well as the mechanics of working between them.

The entrepreneur in Anil was not satisfied with acquisition of Shamsher Sterling Corp and technology projects taken up thereafter. He had greater ambition. He decided to set up a continuous cast and rolled non-ferrous rods unit. It was located at Taxwe Khurd near Lonawala in the state of Maharashtra. For this project he got the technical assistance from two companies; M/s. Continuus, SpA, Italy and M/s. La Farga Lacambra Sa, Spain; thus, he learnt to manage two husbands. The unit was commissioned at break-neck speed during 1989-90. Instead of borrowing, he took another route this time; raising the funds through debenture and ultimately through IPO in 1988. As an entrepreneur, he had hawk's eye on technology, market and finance. Though he had no technical qualification, he had a strong penchant for technology. In 1989, he sought the technical assistance of Johan Royle & Sons, U.S.A. for Cross linked polyethylene insulated power (XLPE) Cable Unit and Poly Vinyl Chloride (PVC) insulated power and control cable unit. The Company started manufacturing Jelly-filled telecommunication cables (JFTC) in 1990. It had an installed capacity of 625,000 circuit kilometer (CKM). The overhead power transmission conductor unit's capacity was raised to 6,000 tons per anum (TPA) and that of PVC insulated Jelly filled (PIJF) plant, which started manufacture of foam skin insulated telecables, to 1.2 million CKM (The Economic Times, stocks, 2012). He sensed the opportunity arising out of rising demand and accordingly, in 1992, the company set up an additional plant for manufacture of Jelly filled cables. This plant had an installed capacity of 1.5 million CKM. Thus, total capacity was raised to 3.3 million CKM. In the same year, yet another new plant with an annual capacity of 40,000 fiber kilometers (FKM) to manufacture optical fiber cables was set up at Aurangabad, Maharashtra.

Anil was a great dreamer. As he went on growing, he went on creating new teams. The members of the team had different expertise and aptitude that blended well. His teams, that were opportunity seeking, went on converting corporate dreams into reality. The entrepreneurial culture that he created in SIIL helped him in adding new products and projects in its portfolio. Working backwards for his cable for which the main raw material was copper, he commissioned the first privately developed copper smelter in India at Tuticorin (Tamil Nadu) in 1997. But the smelter needed copper concentrate. His team, like him, started hunting opportunities for getting copper concentrate globally. To grab the opportunity identified, he treaded the path where angels fear to tread. Risk taking and mitigating had become his habit. In 1999, he acquired Mount Lyell copper mine through SIIL. Though the company was located in Tasmania (Australia), it was very low cost copper mine. This ensured long term supply of copper concentrate to his Indian copper smelting Company. After its acquisition, SIIL enhanced its capacity immediately from 2.0 million ton per annum (TPA) to 2.7 million TPA. As availability of copper concentrate increased, SIIL went on increasing smelter capacity at Tuticorin through innovative debottlenecking till it achieved a capacity of 400,000 TPA. Anil had, further, planned to set up a plant to manufacture blister copper and allied materials as well as a desalination plant to purify 4.5 million liters of water per day, needed for the copper smelting plant.

Anil's mind always worked in parallel rather than in series. While SIIL was working on various copper projects, he was busy planning a modern aluminum refinery, smelting and downstream projects. In 1997 itself, he decided to construct a new Greenfield aluminum smelter which was to be associated with a captive power plant in Orissa. For this plant, the technical collaboration and technology license agreement was signed with Aluminum Pechiney (AP), France. AP had agreed to give SIIL the latest AP 30 technology while AP's first partner in India National Aluminum Corporation (NALCO) was still running on AP 18 technology. The Company undertook yet another project to manufacture Aluminum alloy rolling sheets and foils. In 1998, SIIL made an open offer of 20 per cent (SEBI requirement) for acquiring shares in Indian Aluminum Co. Ltd. (INDAL) and agreed to accept all the shares of INDAL that would be received by it in response to its open offer to acquire 52.03 per cent stake in INDAL.

His quest for growth was unending. Technology started occupying bigger portion of his mind. Moving back to copper, he observed that SIIL was having copper ingots in plenty. Therefore, he wanted to expand further in telecom sector where he saw the growing opportunity. He joined hands with telecom multinational Alcatel to provide telecom networking solutions in India. No sooner than he signed the technical collaboration, the company bagged an order of $ 36 million (Rs.1.43 billion). This telecommunication business of the company was demerged into a separate company named SIIL Optical Technologies Limited (SOTL) with effect from July 2001 under the Scheme of Arrangement (Indian Company Act, 1956). The SOTL committed itself for providing connectivity products & solutions for the ever-evolving applications in the global telecom and power industries. Soon, they developed a portfolio of quality products and services. This was achieved through the effective use of six sigma, Information technology and a sustained focus on Intellectual Property.

National Democratic Alliance (NDA) came into power in 1998. It had been looking for opportunities for disinvestment in Public Sector Units (PSUs) to improve its fiscal deficit. Pursuing the policy, in 2001, the cabinet committee on disinvestment of Govt. of India (GOI) had decided to sale 51 per cent of government equity in Bharat Aluminum Company (BALCO). SIIL lost no time in grabbing the opportunity for getting the controlling share for a sum of $ 118.35 million (Rs. 551.5 crore). This deal was approved by GOI in the month of March itself but Anil found it difficult to get the reins of the company. His team was not allowed to enter into the offices and works of BALCO. This was a unique situation that he faced. "The union government had sold 51 per cent of its stake in BALCO to SIIL but he could not get control over the affairs of BALCO even after more than a month after the privatization of the company" (Sridhar, 2001). "The State Govt., along with the workers Unions, had a pitched battle with the union government to reverse the disinvestment. A number of cases were filed in different courts including the Supreme Court". The work had come to a grinding halt. It was an unprecedented situation in Indian corporate history. The sale of BALCO, positioned as the first of a "big ticket" PSU in the country, had been stonewalled by the trade unions representing more than 7,000 workers at Korba in Chattisgarh since March 3, 2001. "Something that was worth $ 1180.26 millionn (Rs 5.500 crore) has been sold for $ 118.26 mn (Rs 550 crore). Nobody was told about this sale; even I, as the Chief Minister of the state where the mines are located, was not consulted. This entire deal was done surreptitiously" stated Ajit Jogi, the Chef Minister of Chattisgarh. Retorted Anil Agrawal, "A controversy is great for a magazine strapped for space. This report on the BALCO sell-off, for instance, can start virtually mid-way, assuming that readers know all about SIIL winning the bid, the ensuing brouhaha, and its eventual triumph in the Parliament a day after the budget. The popular press has covered the event in such detail that everyone is aware that SIIL bid almost twice as much as the Aditya Birla Group's HINDALCO. Why, even the most passive among readers must have been impressed at the knowledge of the science of valuation our politicos suddenly acquired" (Jayakar & Roshni, 2001). Despite all problems and controversies, Anil kept cool; only refuted unfounded allegations. In fact, on a number of occasions, he expressed his willingness to acquire balance share of the GOI in BALCO.

Despite all this melodrama in the case of BALCO, Anil remained unperturbed; doing what was needed of him; eyed at next privatization target in India - Hindustan Zinc Ltd. "It did not take him long to achieve this ambition. Competing against Indo-Gulf of A. V. Birla Group, SIIL signed transaction documents for acquiring 26 per cent stake in Hindustan Zinc (HZL) on April 3, 2002 with a provision that SIIL would make the payment of $90.98 million (Rs 445 crore) on April 11, 2002" (The Times of India, April 4, 2002). Banque Nationale De Paris-Paribas acted as global advisors to the disinvestment process. $ 0.83 (Rs 40.5) per share amounting to $90.98 millionn (Rs 445 crore) that Anil had paid for 26% of the equity along with management control of the company was much higher than the reserve price fixed by GOI at $ 0.66 (Rs 32.15) per share working out to $ 72.19 million (Rs 353.17 crore). The SIIL group accounted for 80 per cent of the country's zinc production with the acquisition of HZL. Earlier, in 1991-

92 and 1992-93, GOI had diluted its equity in HZL by 24.08 per cent. The privatisation of the company now had brought down the government holding to about 49 per cent. HZL, a leading profit-making zinc-lead company, was incorporated in 1966 to meet mining and smelting capabilities. HZL operated five lead-zinc mines, with a total lead-zinc ore production capacity of 3.49 million TPA, four smelters with combined installed capacity of 152,000 TPA of zinc and 65,000 TPA of lead, and a rock phosphate mine. The very next week of the acquisition of HZL, Anil was in tears (of joy) when his team reached HZL on April 11, 2002 (The Times of India, February 20, 2003). He could not believe that his team was welcomed and garlanded by the labour unions. "To me, the reason for this change of heart within a year appears to be that the public as well as private sector labour had realised that in a fast globalising world, production units cannot survive, unless they are competitive and are based on modern technology. This was even said by INTUC (Indian National Trade Union Congress) President Sanjiva Reddy after his visit to China" said he in an interview.

Anil's desire for growth was insatiable. SIIL, under Anil and his entrepreneurial team, went on adding new units, both Brownfield (field where a mining or industrial operation was already going on) and Greenfield, one after another. The primary listing of SIIL, which had a portfolio of business, was done on New York Stock Exchange (NYSE) in June 2007. By that time, it had diversified into energy sector as well setting up the new company SIIL Energy. The restless pace of growth can easily be seen from the chart below.

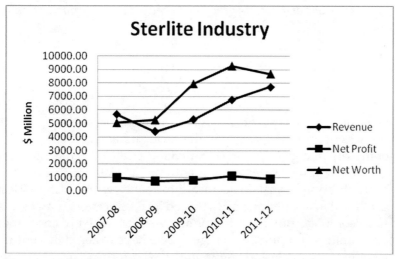

Source: Worked Out from the Annual Reports

"No doubt, it was a rags to riches story. Anil Agarwal, by now, had come a long way from being the starry eyed ambitious lad from Patna to one of the world's richest mining tycoons", stated Gita Piramal, Business Historian. "The real comparison is with Dhirubhai (Business Maharajas, 1997). But while Dhirubhai advertised financial concerns, Anil Agarwal advertises CSR".

VEDANTA RESOURCES

Vedanta Resources plc. was established in 1986. It was, presently (March, 2012) having 31,000 employees in the group. The purpose of creating this holding company (organization structure given in Annexure III) was to bring together a variety of businesses owned by the Anil Agarwal's family including SIIL. Vedanta Resources was first listed on the Bombay Stock Exchange (BSE) in 1988. Later, in 2003, it was listed on the London Stock Exchange (LSE). By doing so, it acquired the distinction of being the first Indian mining and metals company to be listed on the London Stock Exchange. Soon after the listing, it was included in FTSE 100 diversified metals and mining major. The company's vision, mission and values are given below.

VISION

"To be a world class, diversified resources company providing superior returns to our shareholders, with high quality assets, low coast operations and sustainable development".

MISSION

"To be a world-class metals and mining group and generate superior financial returns".

VALUES

Entrepreneurship,Growth,Excellence,Trust and Sustainability.

The company's value of *Entrepreneurship* is at the forefront followed by *growth, excellence, trust and sustainability.* Entrepreneurship as practiced by the company is "to foster an entrepreneurial spirit throughout our businesses and value the ability to foresee business opportunities early in the cycle and act on them swiftly. Whether it be developing organic growth projects, making strategic acquisitions or creating entrepreneurs from within, we ensure an entrepreneurial spirit at the heart of our workplace. Our ability to translate an idea into reality within the shortest possible timeframe is critical to our rapid growth and diversification into new areas and commodities. People are our most important asset we actively encourage them to seek new opportunities and pursue their goals. We have fostered this entrepreneurial spirit amongst the individuals and communities who form a part of our entire value chain" (Annual Report, 2010).

The Annual Report, 2012 brought another aspect of his entrepreneurial thought; the strategy, which stated:

"To deliver growth, long term value and sustainable development through our diversified portfolio of large, long- life, low cost assets".

As per the statement in their Annual Report (March 31, 2012) "Vedanta is a globally diversified natural resources group with wide ranging interests in aluminum, copper, zinc, lead, silver, iron ore, power and oil & gas. We operate in India, Zambia, Namibia, South Africa, Liberia, Ireland and Australia". Vedanta Resources' focus on India is clear from the pattern of their operations which is as under:

India – Aluminium, Copper, Zinc, Iron Ore, Power, Oil &Gas
Australia - Copper
Zambia - Copper
Namibia - Zinc
South Africa – Zinc
Liberia – Iron Ore
Ireland – Zinc

Vedanta Resources, a holding company, had most of its operations through its subsidiary SIIL. However, after its incorporation, it created three other subsidiary; Madras Aluminum Company Ltd. (MALCO), Konkola Copper Mines Plc (KCM) and Vedanta Aluminum Ltd. (VAL).

Vedanta Resources had taken over MALCO in 1995 when the company was declared sick. The operations were suspended for three years from 1992 to 1995. Bureau of Industrial and Financial Reconstruction (BIFR) had sanctioned a rehabilitation scheme which envisaged a change in management. The Vedanta management acted fast; turned around MALCO. As the Company's net worth turned positive, it was delisted from the purview of BIFR in the year 1997. In the year 2008, MALCO changed the business model from that of aluminum manufacture to power generation considering various techno-economic factors and non-availability of key raw materials. MALCO grabbed this opportunity and scaled up generation by commissioning a new unit for wheeling a larger power output for external sales which was more value creator.

With a desire to break the shackles that Vedanta was finding in expansion of BALCO because of the limitations of government partnership, it decided to set up an independent aluminum company. SIIL Transmission Ltd was incorporated on 18th January 2001 for bauxite exploration and mining. It was renamed Vedanta Alumina Ltd. (VAL) on 20th January, 2004 in an effort to align the brand of the firm. Later, they desired to have smelting and downstream products as well. Accordingly, on 25th August, 2007, the name was changed to Vedanta Aluminum Ltd. In the same year, VAL began the progressive commissioning of its 1 million ton per anum (mtpa) state-of-the-art Greenfield alumina refinery project and an associated 75 MW captive power plant at Lanjigarh, Orissa. Subsequently, the firm charted out plans for a Greenfield 0.5 mtpa aluminum smelter and a 1215 MW captive power plant at Jharsuguda, Orissa. The first phase of the aluminum smelter project was commissioned in June 2008.

Vedanta Resources had announced on the 20th August 2004 the acquisition of Konkola Copper Mines Plc (KCM) from Anglo-American for a total cash consideration of $48.2 million (Rs. 222.93 cr) out of which $27.3 million (Rs. 126.26 cr) was payable on completion of the acquisition. While announcing the deal, Anil had stated, "We have been negotiating with KCM shareholders and the Government of Republic of Zambia for a considerable time and I am delighted that we have been able to structure a deal which brings benefit to all parties. The outlook of copper demand remains positive over the medium term and Zambia is one of the great copper areas of the world. Our immediate task will be to stabilize the existing assets and enhance production. The KCM management has done well in running these assets through a difficult period and we look forward to working with them". In an interview after consummation of the deal, Naveen Agarwal, chairman of KCM told, "Along with the production capacity of SIIL, the acquisition of one of the world's largest copper mines makes us the fifth largest producer of refined copper globally," (The Economic Times, Nov 9, 2004). Since then, Vedanta has scaled up its production many fold. "They are mining there in a great hurry so that they consume the ores before the agreement could be revisited (BankTrack, 2012).

By the time KCM deal was consummated, Japanese firm Mitsui Finsider International Ltd. mandated Morgan Stanley to find a buyer for its 51 per cent holding in Sesa Goa. The Japanese firm was selling this stake as part of a global strategy to exit the mining business. The successful bidder was also required to make an open offer to Sesa Goa shareholders, to buy a further 20 per cent share as required by Securities and Exchange Board of India (SEBI). In response to the offer, Vedanta Resources plc acquired 51% controlling stake in Sesa Goa Limited offered by Mitsui Finsider International Limited in 2005, thereby entering into iron mining. The deal was worth $981 million (Rs. 40.7 billion) in cash. In this deal Vedanta had outbid the world top steel producer Arcelor Mittal and the number three Aditya Birla Group. It was speculated that Brazilian miner CVRD and British-Australian giant Rio Tinto pulled out of the race for Mitsui's 51 per cent stake in Sesa Goa after the new tax regime came in India. Sesa Goa's valuations sank after the finance minister levied the duty on iron ore exports. (Bamzai. S, 2012). Later, Chidambaram, the finance minister of India, reduced the export duty on iron ore fines to $ 1.16 (Rs. 50) per ton from $ 6.97 (Rs. 300); he did so only on ore with less than 62 per cent iron content. The duty on ore with over 62 per cent iron content remained unchanged at $ 6.97 (Rs. 300) per ton. The direct beneficiary was Vedanta's Sesa Goa since it exported iron ore with less than 62 per cent iron content. In fact, in 2007 alone, the cut in duty from $ 6.97 (Rs. 300) to $ 1.16 (Rs. 50) saved Sesa Goa $ 54.01 mn (Rs. 232.5 crore) in export levy. Later, Vedanta acquired an iron mine in Liberia. "We are highly delighted with this opportunity to consolidate our iron ore business. The Western Cluster Project presents an excellent opportunity for developing a large integrated mining operation and establish our presence in Liberia and Africa" (The Economic Times, August 6, 2011), Sesa Goa Managing Director, P K Mukherjee, said.

On May 10, 2010, Vedanta acquired the zinc assets of Anglo-American at a valuation (as on January, 1, 2010) of $ 1.338 bn (Rs. 6194.94 cr) despite knowing that Xstrata, its biggest shareholder, Glencore and a Chinese bidder were vying for Anglo American's zinc assets. Lazard & Co had acted as financial adviser to Vedanta. The acquisition was proposed to be done through HZL. This acquisition gave Vedanta the rights as per details below:

- 100% in Lisheen Mines in Ireland
- 100% in Scorpian Mines in Namibia
- 74% in Blackmountain Mines in South Africa which included Gamsberg project having a huge potential (400,000 tons/anum).

"With the announcement of the deal, that was lauded by both parties, Vedanta shares surged more than 11 percent and Anglo American more than 9 percent", reported Reuters, "Vedanta has, thus, become the world's largest integrated zinc-lead producer. It added significant operating expertise with zinc and lead. The zinc assets acquired from Anglo American plc had an excellent operational and strategic fit and were expected to create significant long-term value for the stakeholders." Liberum Capital, in a client note, said, "The deal clearly signals Vedanta's bullish view on the future of the zinc market, calling the deal a good strategic fit (Reuters, May 10, 2010)."

ACQUISITION OF CAIRN INDIA LTD

On 16th August 2010, Anil gave biggest surprise to the corporate world by issuing a press release (Annexure IV) stating that the group intends to acquire 51% to 60% of Cairn India Ltd at $8.5bn (Rs. 39784.25 cr) to 9.6bn (Rs. 44931.84 cr) in cash. "It was the third largest acquisition ever by an Indian enterprise globally. It gave Vedanta control of nation's biggest onshore oilfield in Rajasthan and 9 other properties in India and one in Sri Lanka where a gas discovery was made recently" (PTI, Dec 8, 2011). In this deal, Vedanta's lead financing bank was Standard Chartered. It was also a joint lead financial adviser alongside JPMorgan, Cazenove and Morgan Stanley. Credit Suisse and Goldman Sachs had also provided funding and advice. The announcement, which was a bolt from the blue, opened a Pandora's Box of opinions and comments. The same day, Julie Crust from Reuter reported that "Vedanta has more than quadrupled in value since early 2009, helped by recovering metal demand, and making London resident Anil Agarwal Britain's 10th richest person behind Indian-born steel baron Lakshmi Mittal who tops The Sunday Times Rich List." Alex Mathews of Geojit BNP-Paribas Financial Services in India said, "With this deal, Vedanta is looking to become a company with the scale of something like BHP Billiton. It shows the company wants to be become a major resources player."

In the opening sentences of the Chairman's report, Anil stated, "Vedanta has made considerable progress in executing its strategy this year delivering production growth and increasing reserves and resources across the portfolio, completing two acquisitions, and announcing a consolidation and simplification of the group. Over the years, Vedanta has become a world-class resources group and this year we added oil and gas to our portfolio" (Chairman's Statement, Annual Report, 2012). The addition of CIL in Vedanta's basket resulted in its revenue jumping from $.11.4 bn to $.14.0 bn and net profit from $ 3.6 bn to $ 4.0 bn. The half yearly EBIDTA, pre and post CIL acquisitions were $ 1.7 bn and 2.6 bn respectively (Annexure V). CIL contributed 35% of the profit.

Amidst the rumor of the deal, Business Line (Vidya, Aug 14, 2010) had brought a column with the title "Can Vedanta be the next BHP Billiton?" It further stated that *Cairn deal will make it only 2nd diversified miner with oil, gas assets*. However, there was substantial differences between what BHP achieved and what Anil Agarwal's group was hoping to. BHP made its first foray into energy back in 1960, when the company hired an American geologist to identify potential oil fields in Australia, which ultimately led them to a joint venture with Exxon in the Bass Strait in 1965. BHP had gradually built up its energy assets, through organic growth. By contrast, Vedanta's move would put it in charge of one of India's most significant oil fields, with an estimated capacity, when fully up and running, of 240,000 barrels a day."

"Depending on one's view of where oil prices were heading and the risks involved in the Mangala project (which were not insubstantial, especially given that it is a highly water intensive project) that could either be seen as a bargain or a highly risky gamble. There is no doubt it could be the right move, though it would require a significant amount of debt financing on Vedanta's part," said Mr Knights. "They have also got a very aggressive organic growth plan so their capital expenditure bill for the next few years is fairly sizable (Mishra & Kulkarni, Aug 14, 2010)."

Cairn India was one of the most significant oil and gas exploration and production companies in South Asia with an entrepreneurial spirit (Annual Report, 2011). "Harnessing a combination of innovation and entrepreneurship" Rahul Dhir, the entrepreneurial CEO of Cairn India, in a conference call said "Mangala, Bhagyam and Aishwariya oilfields, the largest of the 18 discoveries the company has made in the Rajasthan block, can produce 240,000 barrels per day (bpd) by 2012. Mangala, the largest field, is currently producing at 125,000 bpd has potential to go up to 150,000 bpd. Bhagyam, the second largest field, is ready for production and can pump up to 40,000 bpd. Aishwariya can produce 10,000 bpd" (IBN.live, Dec 8, 2011). Anil Agarwal, Vedanta Chairman was more optimistic. He said, "Cairn India possesses an enviable talent pool and we welcome them to the Vedanta family. We firmly believe that Cairn India has the potential to double its current capacity and we will work together to achieve it" (Business Line, December 8, 2011).

His insatiable hunger for growth, be it through inorganic or organic route, was exemplary. The CIL deal was still to be consummated but Vedanta, on 6th August, 2011, through its subsidiary, Sesa Goa had announced to acquire 51% stake in Western Cluster Ltd, Liberia for a cash consideration of $90 million (Rs. 402.75 cr) (www. livemint.com, Aug 6 2011.)". The Goa-based iron ore miner made a filing to this effect in Bombay Stock Exchange (BSE). "The acquisition, which is subject to ratification by the Liberia Legislature, is expected to help the Anil Agarwal-led Vedanta Resources' subsidiary to become a significant player in the West African iron ore hub" (Ram, Vidya and Mishra, Richa, July 03, 2011). The ph enomenalgrowth of Vedanta Resources can be observed from the chart below.

VEDANTA RESOURCES

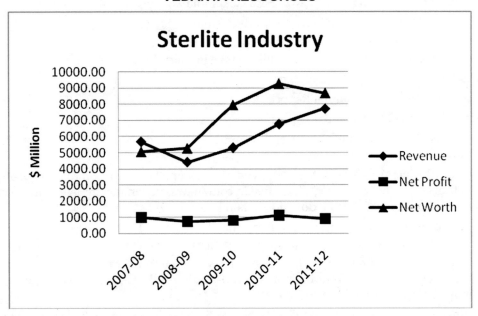

Source: Worked out from the Annual Reports

THE LATEST THOUGHT IN ANIL'S ENTREPRENEURIAL MIND

Anil's latest thought on entrepreneurship and business could be best captured from his address he gave at Shailesh J Mehta School of Manangement, IIT Bombay on 17th December, 2011. While sharing his experiences on what made him the person that he is today as also on the hot business topic – *Vedanta-Cairn deal,* he said, "You have got to be hungry to be successful. The young generation needed to be humble and hungry for success all the time. The limitation came from our minds while the heart would tell one to move on and keep exploring".

Right through his talk, reported SJSOM (Blog, January 12, 2012), "he depicted the unquenchable zeal for leadership and entrepreneurship, and opined that entrepreneurship does not mean owning a company but, owning an idea and leading a team. Also, local people should have a sense of ownership for the business of a successful venture and it is important that an ecosystem is built by the entrepreneur. He concluded with an inspiring one-liner; "The only thing required to succeed is courage and zeal". On his way back from IIT, he was wondering, what should be his next idea and how to enhance courage and zeal in his own team?

REFERENCES

Bamzai, Sandeep (2012, January 14), Benefit of Clout: Chidambaram's 2007 flip-flop let Anil Agarwal's Vedanta take over Sesa Goa, India Today.

BankTrack (2012, May 3), Retrieved on July 4 from http://www.banktrack.org/show/companyprofiles/vedanta_resources on June 27, 2012

Business Line, (2011, Dec. 8), Sesa Goa hikes stake in Cairn India via block deal.

Cairn Energy Plc., (2011), Annual Report.

Cairn India Ltd., (2011). Annual Report.

Cairn India Ltd., (2012). Annual Report.

Gita Piramal,(1997), Business Maharajas, Penguin Books Ltd., New Delhi, London, New York.

IBN.live (Business), (2011, Dec 08). Vedanta completes Cairn India acquisition, Retrieved from http://ibnlive.in.com/news/vedanta-completes-cairn-india-acquisition/210066-5.html, downloaded on June 25, 2012

Jayakar Roshni, (2001, March 21), A Suitable Match. Business Today (Corporates).

Kayakiran Fatim and Katakey, Rakteem (2010, Sept 21). Vedanta Billionaire Agarwal Risks 30% Returns by Mimicking BHP. Bloomberg. Retrieved from http://www.bloomberg.com/news/2010-09-20/india-s-only-scrap-trading-billionaire-risks-30-returns-by-mimicking-bhp.html, June 30,2012

livemint.com, (2011, Aug 6). Sesa Goa to buy 51% stake in Western Cluster for $90 mn. Retrieved from http://www.livemint.com/2011/08/06180728/Sesa-Goa-to-buy-51-stake-in-W.html

Mishra, Richa and Kulkarni, Vishwanath, (2010, Aug 14), Vedanta set for 'smart entry' into petroleum sector, Business Line.

PTI. (2011, Dec 8), Vedanta completes Cairn India acquisition, Retrieved from http://ibnlive.in.com/news/vedanta-completes-cairn-india-acquisition/210066-37.html

Ram, Vidya and Mishra Richa. (2011, July 03). Vedanta seals the deal; acquires 58.5% in Cairn India for $8.67 bn., Business Line.

Ram, Vidya (2010, August 14), Can Vedanta be the next BHP Billiton? Business Line.

Reuters (May 10, 2010), UPDATE 2-Vedanta buys Anglo zinc assets for $1.34 billion, Retrieved on July 12, 2012 from http://www.reuters.com/article/2010/05/10/vedanta-angloamerican-idUSLDE6490BL20100510

Sridhar V, (2001). The Balco Struggle. Frontline. Volume 18 - Issue 08, Apr. 28- May 11.

SJMSOM, (Blog, 2012, January 12). Anil Agarwal, Chairman, Vedanta Resources plc. visits SJMSOM. Retrieved on July 15, 2012 from http://blog.sjmsom.in/2012/01/anil-agarwal-chairman-vedanta-resources.html

Sharma, Rakesh (2011), Cairn India Accepts Government Conditions on Royalties, The Wall Street Journal (Business), September 14 EDT.

The Economic Times. (2011, August 6), Sesa Goa to buy Western Cluster for $90 million. Retrieved on July 14, 2012 from http://articles.economictimes.indiatimes.com/2011-08-06/news/29858819_1_iron-ore-sesa-goa-western-cluster-project

The Economic Times, (2004, Nov 9), Vedanta acquires Zambia's Konkola, Retrieved from http://articles.economictimes.indiatimes.com/2004-11-09/news/27406729_1_zambia-copper-investments-kcm-konkola-copper-mines

The Economic Times (stocks), (2012), Sterlite Industries (India) Limited, Retrived on July 6 from http://economictimes.indiatimes.com/sterlite-industries-(india)-ltd/prices/companyid-12977.cms.

The Hindu (2001, Aug, 23), Accept all Govt Conditions: Cairn Energy to Cairn India.

The Times of India, (2002, April 4), Sterlite Signs Transaction Documents for HZL Stake, Retrieved on July 7, 2012. http://timesofindia.indiatimes.com/business/india-business/Sterlite-signs-transaction-documents-for-HZL-stake/articleshow/5865716.cms?

The Times of India, (2003, February 20), Winners and losers of HZL Privatization, Retrieved from http://articles.timesofindia.indiatimes.com/2003-02-20/india-business/27263364_1_public-sector-privatisation-labour-unions

Vedanta Resources Plc., (2010), Annual Report.

Vedanta Resources Plc., (2011), Annual Report.

Vedanta Resources Plc., (2012), Annual Report.

Vedanta Resources Plc., Presentation (2011, December 8). Completion of Acquisition of a Controlling Stake in Cairn India Ltd.

ANNEXURE I

The five preconditions:

1. Royalty being made cost recoverable,

2. Cairn India withdrawing arbitration cases

3. Cairn India accepting its liability to pay cess,

4. Cairn India obtaining partner ONGC's no-objection and

5. Vedanta providing performance and financial guarantees

Source: (Jayakar, Roshni, 2001)

ANNEXURE II

Top 10 Global Mining Company
(Annual Report -2011)

Sl. No	Name	Country	Portfolio	Turnover $ (billion)	Profit $ (billion)
1	BHP Billiton	Australia	Diversified	71.739b	21.684b
2	Rio Tinto	UK	Diversified	60.537b	13.214b
3	CVRD	Brazil	Iron ore,Copper	58.990b	22.652b
4	Anglo American	UK	Diversified	36.548b	11.1b
5	Freeport McMoran	USA	Copper, Gold	20.880b	4.560b
6	Codelco	Chile	Copper	17.515b	5.253b
7	Barrick Gold	Canada	Gold	14.312b	4.7b
8	Norilsk Nickel	Russia	Nickel	14.122b	5.646b
9	Vedanta Resources*	UK	Diversified	!4.10	4.02
10	Newmont Mining	USA	Gold	10.358b	2.170b

*Post CIL acquisition

Source: Annual Reports of the Company

ANNEXURE III

Vedanta Group Structure

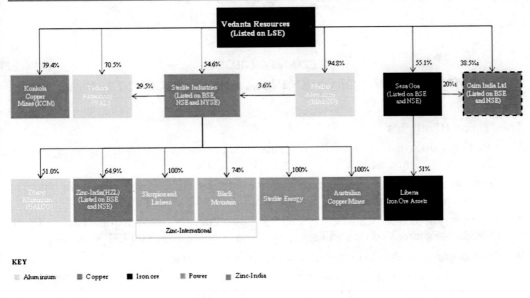

KEY

Aluminium   Copper   Iron ore   Power   Zinc-India

Notes: 1   On a fully diluted basis
Structure as at 30 September 2011 updated for Completion of Acquisition of a Controlling Stake in Cairn India Ltd.

ACQUISITION OF A CONTROLLING STAKE IN CAIRN INDIA LTD. (8 DEC 2011)   18

Source: Vedanta Resources' Presentation, December 8, 2011

ANNEXURE IV

16 August 2010

VEDANTA GROUP

TO ACQUIRE 51% TO 60% OF CAIRN INDIA (THE "PROPOSED TRANSACTION")

Transaction Highlights

Vedanta Group to acquire 51% to 60% of Cairn India Limited (Cairn India) for an aggregate consideration of approximately US$8.5-9.6 billion in cash

- Post completion it is expected that Vedanta Resources PLC ("Vedanta") will hold 31-40% of Cairn India directly and Sesa Goa Ltd ("Sesa Goa") will hold 20%
- Shares acquired from Cairn Energy PLC ("Cairn Energy") to be acquired at a price of INR355 per share; Vedanta will also pay a non-compete fee of INR50 per share
- Transaction to be funded through debt and cash resources
- A unique investment to create the Indian natural resources champion meeting the needs of a growing economy
- Acquisition of a world class asset and management team
- Enhances and diversifies Vedanta's strong growth pipeline
- Leverages Vedanta's core skills and track record of value creation
- Immediately EPS accretive

ANIL AGARWAL, EXECUTIVE CHAIRMAN OF VEDANTA SAID

"The proposed acquisition significantly enhances Vedanta's position as a natural resources champion in India. Cairn India's Rajasthan asset is world class in terms of scale and cost, delivering strong and growing cash flow. The company has a proven management team and very significant further resource potential. Cairn India will benefit from Vedanta's track record of acquiring and growing world class companies, especially in India."

Source: **Vedanta Resources' Press Release**

ANNEXURE V

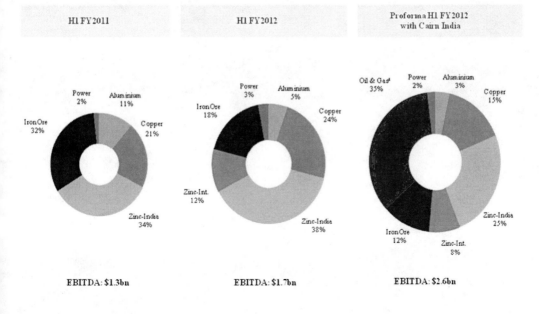

Source: Vedanta Resources' Presentation, December 8, 2011

Author Index

The Editors

DR. G.D. SARDANA, a chartered Mechanical Engineer, Ph.D. (IIT Delhi) and is presently Professor of Operations Management and Chairperson, Center for Development of Management Cases at the Birla Institute of Management Technology, Greater Noida (India).

He has corporate experience of over 40 years having worked in organizations of repute such as BHEL, ABB and Singer at senior positions. In academics, he has earlier worked with Institute of Management Technology, Ghaziabad for four years as Professor Operations Management, Dean-Academics, Editor Paradigm, and later for two years with the Institute of Management Education, Ghaziabad as its Professor Emeritus and Director.

He has to his credit over 80 papers. Three of his papers have won Best Paper awards from the Indian Institution of Industrial Engineering. He has published two books: Productivity Management (Narosa, 1998) and Measurement for Business Excellence (Narosa, 2009). The first book bagged Best Book awards from the Delhi Management Association, and Indian Society for Training and Development. He has co-edited six books on management cases.

DR. TOJO THATCHENKERY (Ph.D. Weatherhead School of Management, Case Western Reserve University) is Professor and Director of the Organization Development and Knowledge Management program at the School of Public Policy, George Mason University, Arlington, Virginia, USA. He is also a member of the NTL Institute of Applied Behavioral Science and the Taos Institute. Thatchenkery's recent books include Making the Invisible Visible: Understanding the Leadership Contributions of Asian Minorities in the Workplace (2011), Positive Design and Appreciative Construction: From Sustainable Development to Sustainable Value (2010), Appreciative Inquiry and Knowledge Management, and Appreciative Intelligence: Seeing the Mighty Oak in the Acorn. Thatchenkery has extensive consulting experience in organization development and knowledge management. Past and current clients include the United Nations, IBM, Fannie Mae, Booz Allen, PNC Bank, Lucent Technologies, General Mills, 3M, British Petroleum, the International Monetary Fund, the World Bank, United States Department of Agriculture, Pension Benefit Guaranty Corporation, United States Environmental Protection Agency, and Akbank (Turkey).